CULTURING MODERNITY

Culturing Modernity

The Nantong Model, 1890–1930

QIN SHAO

STANFORD UNIVERSITY PRESS

STANFORD, CALIFORNIA

2004

Stanford University Press
Stanford, California

Publication of this book was partially underwritten by a grant from the Chiang
Ching-kuo Foundation for International Scholarly Exchange (USA).

Library of Congress Cataloging-in-Publication Data

Shao, Qin.
   Culturing modernity : the Nantong Model, 1890–1930 / Qin Shao.
     p. cm.   Includes bibliographical references and index.
   ISBN 0-8047-4689-3 (alk. paper)
     1. Nantong Shi (China)—History—19th century. 2. Nantong Shi (China)—
History—20th century. 3. Zhang, Jian, 1853–1926. I. Title: Nantong Model,
1890–1930. II. Title.
DS797.56.N365 S43 2004
951'.136—dc22   2003019105

Original printing 2004

Last figure below indicates year of this printing:
13 12 11 10 09 08 07 06 05 04

Designed and typeset at Stanford University Press in 10/12.5 Palatino.

To Ayi

Contents

Illustrations

Preface

A NUMBER OF individuals and institutions on either side of the Pacific have contributed to this study. Some did so indirectly, but not insignificantly.

Gao Chunmei was my first-grade Chinese teacher. Her face radiated when she read to the class. A five-year-old thought there was magic in the written word; she still does. Literature, not history, was my first passion. But I was assigned to major in history at Anhui Normal University as one of the mandatory 1 percent of "educable children" from "antirevolutionary" families. My plans to skip all the history classes to read novels would certainly not have gone over well. Zhang Haipeng, then associate chairman of the department and later president of the university, came to the rescue. He taught me to appreciate the aesthetics and power of historical writing and thinking. Education was devalued in those years; much of what I learned about history was over tea, dinner, and informal conversations at his campus home on weekends. Professor Zhang converted me to history, and I never looked back. In contrast to Zhang's fatherly warmth, Xie Tianyou, my M.A. adviser at East China Normal University in Shanghai, was a strict mentor. He sat facing the wall in his study with his eyes closed while listening to my reports, mostly in silence, and remained so if I had nothing new to add to the subject I was studying. He compelled me to think critically and refused to accept anything less. Occasionally, when I came up with a new idea, he would ask, "Tea?" Years later, John Nicholson of Northern Arizona University took a chance on me, accepting someone who could barely speak any English as his last doctoral student. I did not complete the program with him, but his faith in me was a lasting inspiration in my scholarly journey. In a span of a decade, all three of these professors have passed away. Sadness still overcomes me every time I think of them. I wish they could read this book, and I wish Professor Xie would occasionally stop to offer me tea.

Trained in the field of traditional China, I knew little about modern Chinese history. I must confess that I had never even heard of the Nantong model before my arrival at Michigan State University to study with Stephen Averill. Professor Averill introduced me to the topic of Nantong and guided me through my dissertation with his characteristic professionalism and perfectionism. He has continued to read and comment on my work, including drafts of this book, from which I benefited tremendously. Most kindly of all, Professor Averill helped prepare the maps and most of the photographs for this book. As always, his help came when it mattered the most.

Several scholars have taken a consistent interest in my work. William Rowe believed in the book long before it existed. His unfailing support has helped shape not only my scholarship, but also much of my postdoctoral career. Mary Rankin has improved practically every piece of my publications in English, especially this one, with her expert opinion and unreserved kindness, as evidenced in the countless pages of comments she has sent me. The trust and friendship formed between an author and editor sometimes prove lasting. I was a stranger to Richard Gunde in 1996, when he copyedited my article for *Modern China*. Since then Richard has generously offered his invaluable expertise, thoughtfulness, and time to my work. All three of them—Richard Gunde, Mary Rankin, and William Rowe—read the entire manuscript closely and provided constructive suggestions. Much to my embarrassment and admiration, Stephen Averill, Richard Gunde, and Mary Rankin also corrected my pinyin spelling, invariably correctly. Susan Naquin was always available to help with my inquiries about source materials and fine points of writing. Marianne Bastid-Brugière, an expert on Nantong, has taught me much about the county through her reading of my work over the years. Likewise, I learned something new every time I consulted Samuel Chu's pioneering work on Zhang Jian.

Special thanks go to David Strand. David's own work on the "showman" side of modern Chinese politicians has clearly influenced my thinking on the Nantong story. Reviewing this book for the Stanford Press, David asked thought-provoking questions and pointed to directions that I would never have thought to look at. Henrietta Harrison also kindly read the book for the press during her sabbatical year. She shared with me her insights and saved me from some embarrassing mistakes. I am acutely aware that I did not write this book alone; my gratitude toward all the scholars mentioned above is beyond words. It is indeed a joy to work in the field of late imperial and early Republican China, not only because that time period provides fascinating topics for study, but also because contemporary China scholars unconditionally nurture each other's work. The booming literature in the field is a testimony to the collective devotion and strength of that scholarly community, of which I am privileged to be a part.

I am also fortunate to work among my friends—my colleagues in the history department at The College of New Jersey (TCNJ, formerly Trenton State College) are my friends. They have been wonderfully supportive of my work since I joined the faculty in 1994. I especially wish to thank Tom Allsen. A talented and acclaimed scholar of almost encyclopedic breadth, Tom advised me on topics ranging from taxonomy to numismatics. He carefully read early drafts of my manuscript during his own intense writing of a book project, making detailed, essential suggestions. Dan Crofts, chair of the department, also read the manuscript and shared his opinions. My ongoing exchange with Jo-Ann Gross on interdisciplinary studies often provided me with food for thought. Stuart McCook patiently helped me manage the final preparation of the manuscript. The constant support of Joann Manto, the able and dependable secretary of the department, and her staff was indispensable. I am deeply grateful to all of them.

A fellowship from the National Endowment for the Humanities in the spring of 2001 enabled me to take a full year's leave to complete this project. A research grant from the Pacific Cultural Foundation financed my fieldwork in Nantong in the summer of 1996. TCNJ's Faculty Institutional Research and Sabbatical Leave Committee has consistently assisted me with reduced teaching loads, mini-grants, and a sabbatical leave in 2000. Rick Kamber, the former dean of the School of Arts and Sciences, cheerfully supported my work from the very beginning. The devoted staff at the Office of Access Services/Document Delivery at the TCNJ library supplied me with all the interlibrary loan materials I requested in a timely fashion. They overcame the difficulty caused by different languages, as well as the various Chinese romanization systems, to successfully fulfill my requests. I greatly appreciate their effort.

Parts of the book were published earlier as journal articles. I wish to thank *Modern China* and *Chinoperl Papers* for allowing me to reprint them here. Some parts were also presented at annual meetings of the Association for Asian Studies, the American Historical Association, and the Asian Studies Conference in Japan and at Nanjing University, the Modern China Seminar at Columbia University, and the East Asian Seminar at the Institute for Advanced Studies. I thank the organizers of these events for arranging my presentations, and the participants for their comments. I am grateful to Muriel Bell of the Stanford University Press for enthusiastically assisting me as the manuscript passed through various stages. Tony Hicks, my production editor, was most patient and accommodating. Barbara Mnookin expertly copyedited my book and told me to "just yell" if I needed her help. Their kindness was a source of comfort to this first-time book author.

During my decade-long research on Nantong, I have accumulated the greatest debt to the people there. I wrote about some of them in the last chapter because of their relevance to this work, but I must thank them here as my friends. Zhang Kaiyuan, a longtime researcher and author on Zhang Jian, first introduced me to Mu Xuan, the former director of the Nantong Museum. Mu Xuan has done more than anyone else to help me in numerous ways; without him, this book would simply not have existed. Zhang Xuwu, grandson of Zhang Jian, answered many of my questions about his family by letter and in interviews. He also kept me informed of new publications touching on my research interests in China. The staffs of the Nantong Library, the Nantong Museum, and the Nantong Textile Museum, especially Zhao Peng, Ji Guang, Jiang Ping, Zhang Guolin, and Liang Zhan, became so familiar with my work that sometimes they decided for me what I needed to read or ask about; they were never wrong. Every year, Ji Pei, the editor of the *Selected Materials on the Culture and History of Nantong*, put aside a set of local publications for me to examine and collect in the summer. Shen Jun, the doorman at the Nantong Museum, prepared Chinese medicine for me in his tiny room in the heat of the summer of 1992, when I became ill. I also enjoyed doing other things with some of these friends in Nantong—browsing night markets, sharing a meal at a neighborhood restaurant, or just chatting the night away.

I wish to thank my sister Shao Yi and her family in Shanghai, where I enjoyed many memorable stops on my way to Nantong. Sylvia and Peter Golden and Lucille and Tom Allsen are most generous in offering their friendship, along with many delicious meals. My friends Gao Wenjuan, Tan Jufang, Wang Shihua, Sara Schneider, Tina Wang, and James and Ruby Wick remind me constantly of the boundless capacity of the human heart to love and to care. Years ago in East Lansing, Michigan, Jack helped me keep my sanity as I was trying to complete a dissertation in a matter of months. All of them have helped sustain my work in their own unique ways.

My son Songsong, who learned at an early age to negotiate his play-time with me while I was at my desk, endured with me the emotional stress of years of separation after I came to study in the United States. But neither my desk nor the Pacific has eroded the bond between us. One advantage of taking a leave to write this book at home is that every afternoon I heard Songsong back from school, "Mom, I'm home." His voice is life-affirming, and his smiles sunshine. At this writing, Song-song is a thriving high school junior, looking forward to embarking on his own college career.

And Shao Juhong, my Ayi, my aunt, who raised me as her own daughter with abundant love in a tumultuous era when a political storm deprived my own parents of the power to do so. A fatal illness took Ayi away from me all too long ago, but not her love. Some day, I wish to write about Ayi; till then, this is to her.

Q.S.

Newtown, Pennsylvania

MAY 2002

CULTURING MODERNITY

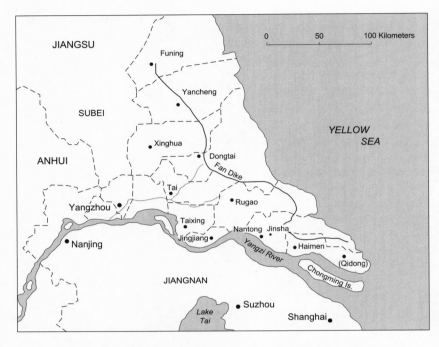

MAP 1. Nantong and the lower Yangzi region in the early Republican period. Source: Kathy Le Mons Walker, *Chinese Modernity and the Peasant Path: Semi-colonialism in the Northern Yangzi Delta* (Stanford, Calif.: Stanford University Press., 1999), p. 115.

Introduction

PLACES HAVE biographies. But the biographic story of a city does not spill into its streets to innocent eyes. In the summer of 1992, when I took my first research trip to the small city of Nantong, north of the Yangzi River in Jiangsu province, I vaguely wanted to write something about local self-government institutions in the late Qing dynasty.[1] In a single-minded pursuit of the written records, I initially paid little attention to the appearance of the city itself.

But as I spent my days in the library and my evenings chatting with people on the street to recover from history and heat overload, the city began to come alive for me. The multistoried Youfei Hotel on the south bank of the Hao River where I stayed was first built in the late 1910s; so was the paved road in front of it, the then-named Model Road, where intellectual and cultural icons such as John Dewey, Liang Qichao, and Mei Lanfang had once trodden. In fact, before 1900, the entire area on the south shore of the Hao River had been a haunt of the homeless. All of the institutions and buildings, including a number of Western-style professional schools, the first library and museum of the region, and a modern publishing house, were products of the first two decades of the twentieth century. As I wandered the streets and viewed the still distinctive Western-style villas and halls where the most prominent local elites once lived, I was overwhelmed by a force from the past that I could not quite identify. Surely the elites and their institutions were long gone. But then what?

Struggling with this quandary, I gradually came to realize that what I had felt was the force of the culture of those long-gone elites as vested in the cornerstones and roof tiles of the city streets. That culture has penetrated the historical deposits of more than half a century to speak silently yet powerfully of its own existence. I began to think about, among other things, what kind of impact this spatial reconfiguration had on the community of the time. What were the intended narratives behind this change? Did the new landmarks also remap the human mind in this provincial town? The present study, though with a somewhat different focus, was inspired by this initial dialogue between the site and the author.

Tongzhou, Tong prefecture, was a rural backwater until the 1890s, when it experienced so rapid a transformation that by the late 1910s it appeared to be phenomenally modern, with, among other things, film companies and English-speaking traffic policemen. It began to attract famous Chinese and foreign visitors alike and came to be touted as a model of modernity and self-government.

The agents directly responsible for what came to be known as the Nantong model were the local elites, of whom Zhang Jian, who held the highest degree, *jinshi*, in the imperial civil service examination, was the leader. Taking advantage of the late Qing New Policies reform, the elites developed dozens of factories, hundreds of schools from primary to college levels, and other well-executed public and social service projects. In 1914, to preserve and expand the fruits of the late Qing reform against the Republican president Yuan Shikai's dissolution of all local self-government institutions, the elites began to shape the image of Nantong as a "model" for modernity and local initiative as a means to both legitimatize their continued dominance and attract outside support.

The model campaign was accompanied by a visionary plan to transform the county seat (after 1911 Tong prefecture became Nantong county) into a cosmopolitan city by opening its ancient city walls and reconfiguring the space with paved roads, imported mechanical clocks, electric street lights, and Western-style buildings. At the same time, Zhang Jian and his associates institutionalized charity for the underprivileged to create an ideal community. Paralleling this spatial and institutional makeover within, strategies were developed to attract attention from without. A Zhang Jian–controlled shipping company offered discounted fares to visitors; famous opera stars like Mei Lanfang were invited to perform in Nantong; national and regional conferences were held there; tour guides and other material containing statistics, photos, blueprints, and maps were published to advertise the county; film companies were created to record local events and to entertain visitors.

The campaign soon paid off. By the late 1910s, Nantong was recognized by the press in and outside the area as an outstanding model of modernity under local leadership. In 1918, Frederick R. Sites, a writer for *Asia*, published an extensive article whose title referred to Nantong as a "model city." The article was based on his visit to Nantong and interviews with Zhang Jian and his associates. Sites spoke of Nantong as a "practical example of modern achievement" in China and described his trip as a "pilgrimage to this Mecca of Chinese progress."[2] The leading intellectual Liang Qichao was equally impressed, pronouncing Nantong "the most progressive city" in China.[3] The Chinese press began to extend the description countywide, and the term "model county" (*mofan xian*) was soon widely employed in newspaper reports and public speeches, and incorporated into school textbooks. Local businesses also discovered the commercial value of this label and used it in their advertisements.

To educated Chinese and also to some foreigners, Nantong's success was an inspiration for an alternative path to China's urban-centered, foreign-dominated modernization. Sites, for instance, especially marveled that "features commonplace in occidental life" were found in this "purely oriental setting," and that "all the changes have been wrought . . . entirely under Chinese leadership."[4] With this model identity, Nantong became a tourist attraction. Among its visitors in this period were major Chinese opinion makers such as Liang Qichao and Cai Yuanpei. John Dewey made a stop there during his much publicized South China lecture tour of 1920. Japanese came to Nantong as investigators, investors, and spectators. Nantong's reputation reached its height between 1919 and 1921. Local traffic policemen were required to study English, to better assist the growing number of foreign visitors. A grand celebration, intended as an international fair of local self-government, was planned to display Nantong's success to a worldwide audience. Preparations for the expected influx of tourists included the construction of large conference and exhibition halls, sports stadiums, and foreign guest houses.

The Nantong model was a product of specific circumstances at both the national and the local level. The long-term decline of the central government after the Taiping Uprising of the 1850s provided a vacuum into which regional and local powers could expand. A national longing for leadership, stability, and development, heightened by the political uncertainty of the warlord Yuan Shikai's government, was conducive to experiments such as the one found in Nantong. Strong and resourceful local leaders like Zhang Jian were able to take full advantage of the time to build a new reality and a new image for their communities.

But these experiments were also vulnerable to external and internal changes. The reputation of Nantong began to decline shortly after 1921 because of the transforming political, economic, social, and cultural environment. Contributing factors included the end of World War I, the emergence of political parties, a renewed nationalistic struggle for a unified China with a centralized state, and the arrival of a new generation of intellectuals influenced by May Fourth iconoclasm. All these constituted new challenges, which coincided with violent floods in 1921 that destroyed many of the projects symbolic of the new Nantong. An aged Zhang Jian struggled to rescue his vision of Nantong, but with his death in 1926 and the subsequent national reunification under the Guomindang (GMD—the Chinese Nationalist Party), local documents began to refer to the Nantong model in the past tense, and its contemporary relevance faded rapidly.

Pioneered by Samuel Chu and Marianne Bastid, Western scholarship on the Nantong of this period has centered on Zhang Jian as a modern reformer or on his political career, and on Nantong's institutional and material transformation.[5] In addition, Zhang Jian and Nantong have been frequently mentioned in scholarly works on the late Qing and early Republic in general and on the Jiangbei region (that part of Jiangsu province north of the Yangzi River) in particular. In this regard, most scholars consider Nantong an exception to an otherwise bleak picture of Jiangbei largely because of its industrial development.[6] Japanese scholars have shown a sustained interest in Zhang Jian's political activities and Nantong's modern history.[7] As one would expect, Zhang Jian has also attracted attention on both sides of the Taiwan strait. Materials produced in Taiwan and Hong Kong by Zhang's students and colleagues present a consistently positive view of him.[8] On the mainland, he was sharply criticized during much of the post-1949 era. The post-Mao reform has brought back his memory and produced several biographies and hundreds of articles and books, and recent works have uniformly praised his achievements.

The story of Zhang Jian and Nantong has thus generated many studies that have greatly enriched our understanding of the subject. None, however, has addressed the question of why and how Nantong attained such an outstanding reputation. Granted that Nantong had an impressive record of modernization projects, but that by itself did not automatically transform the county into a model. Other places in China followed a similar path, yet most failed to attract such attention.[9] A fuller understanding of the Nantong story requires a careful examination of the various mediums that translated reality into image.

The current study focuses on these mediums and explores the making of the model. The model, we will see, was a socially engineered *simulation* of modernity, the work of politically conservative Chinese elites who were disappointed in the ineffective warlord government and in the moral decay of the treaty ports, and searched for an "authentic" Chinese alternative of modernization based on local initiative. The local elites and outside political and cultural brokers consciously promoted Nantong. Of the mediums they used for this purpose, some were newly imported and others, traditionally available, were given new functions. Their most innovative tactics in this direction were what we would today call public relations.[10]

This study thus addresses a host of issues on late Qing and early Republican China. The continuous interest in China's early modernization effort and the creative work produced in other disciplines and fields have led China scholars in recent years to depict social change through a series of new cultural prisms—changes in the concept of time and space, theater and performance, print culture, photography, tourism, and sports.[11] Although these topics have been individually explored within different temporal and social contexts, the Nantong case presents a full menu for study. Encountering an explosion of new forms and artifacts of Western culture, the Nantong elites eagerly introduced things new and foreign. Compared with the generation of the Self-strengthening movement of the 1860s, they expressed a greater desire to be part of what they thought to be the modern cultural world. As a result, their reform programs covered a much broader spectrum, from factories to museums, and they comfortably slotted new institutions and novel ideas into their existing social and cultural framework. The Nantong case illustrates the dynamic of various representations at play, the hybrid characteristics of elite behavior, and, above all, the Chinese concept and practice of modernity—how modernity was understood, played out, and acted upon by a group of largely rural elites beyond China's treaty ports.

In this regard, the one thing that stands out in the Nantong story is what we may call "exhibitory modernity." Modernity is not so much, or merely, about adopting Western institutions and values; it is also about presentation. After all, modernity is a fashion that requires validation— to be modern is to be seen, judged, consumed, and thus legitimized as modern by the public. This dimension of modernity is yet to be extensively treated in the scholarly literature. In fact, in history and reality, all great powers or movements have had an exhibitory dimension to shape and reinforce their greatness. Spectacle entertainments, such as triumphal processions and gladiatorial combats, were tangible expressions of the ideology and power of imperial Rome.[12] Victorian London, the imperial metropolis, was defined not only by its cityscape, but also by its museums and zoos, where objects and wild beasts from the four corners of the globe were on exhibit to represent the vast "imperialized territories" of the British empire.[13] The very name of the Forbidden City and its shape display the once mysterious, untouchable power of the central kingdom of China.

In contrast to these political powers that came and went, modernity is an ongoing process without a "fixed paradise,"[14] a process that holds seemingly infinite promise and universal appeal and thus is a much greater and lasting force. Exhibiting the modern has been an integral component of the modern world. In the West, expositions, often hosted by big cities, have been a regular occurrence since the mid-nineteenth century. These fairs are primarily intended to present, and thus define and promote, the latest achievements in human progress. Through commodities and images, they display and celebrate the modern time and the modern man, and thus modernity itself.[15] Showing the modern also became a measure of social status as expressed in everyday life. The late Victorians' obsession with things, for instance, was not only intellectual—to pursue knowledge in objects—but also exhibitory—to confer or improve their social standing with things that were recognized as trendy.[16]

When the West supposedly set the standard of modernity, the pressure was on the newcomers to imitate. Beginning in the late nineteenth century and throughout the twentieth, advanced scientific institutions, avant-garde cultural technologies, and costly modern facilities were initiated in African, Latin American, and Asian countries. In those cases, their presentational value often overshadowed their practical utility, sometimes producing what E. Bradford Burns described as "the poverty of progress."[17] These countries, however, had to showcase their success in order to be recognized as modern nations by the outside world, mainly by the Westerners who supposedly had the license to judge.

The hierarchy in this license to judge—advanced nations for underdeveloped countries and major urban centers for provincial towns—compels the disadvantaged to perform and prove themselves. As a result, exhibitory modernity prevails in less-developed areas once the consciousness of the modern begins to take hold. This consciousness can and often does stimulate a tremendous desire among groups in the periphery to imitate the center, even if on a miniature scale and in utopian formulas.[18] Nantong fits this case well, not the least because initially the county was backward and little known. The local elites were greatly interested in exhibitory modern cultural institutions, such as museums, and in performative events, such as sports meets. They made extraordinary efforts to ensure an appropriate presentation of the symbols of the new Nantong to visitors. Indeed, to be modern is to appropriate, exhibit, and consume what is perceived as modern; it is a mentality.

Related to this is the rise of a commercial culture, which has become an important issue for understanding the transformation of early twentieth-century China. If, in the 1980s, the modern China field was consumed by state-society relationships, the 1990s witnessed a growing scholarly focus on the emergence and impact of a commercial society, mostly in the economic and cultural domains.[19] This project extends the study of commercialization from economy and culture to politics, and illustrates its interactive impact on those different areas. The production of the Nantong model was first based on the commercialization of the local economy and an advanced transportation and communication system that facilitated the travel of goods, news, and people at an unprecedented speed. Commercial means were also involved in the design of the model and the spread of the image, which were consumer-driven through a series of active marketing strategies, such as public exhibitions and cosmetic changes in the appearance of the city. In all of this, the Nantong elites had in mind their audience and the city's visual appeal—the model image was packaged as a commodity for public consumption. The commodifying of Nantong's reputation justified the local elites' dominance and reinforced their political authority. Furthermore, the use of money for political purposes by buying government positions and influence also provided a linkage between commerce and politics. By examining the manifestation of a commercial culture in the political realm and the crucial role of that culture in the model-making process, this study permits a detailed look at the initial stage in which certain segments of Chinese society operated at a critical juncture of commerce, culture, and politics.

The diffusion of commercial culture into the political domain inevitably affected the way politics was practiced, especially at the local level. Consequently, it had a significant impact on state-society relations, a theme that continues to underline recent studies of China.[20] The growth of a commercial culture devalued the ideology of old China, eroded top-down bureaucratic control, and opened new channels for pursuing local autonomy and interest. Against this background, localism in Nantong was used as an antidote to the central government in times of chaos, but also as a bargaining chip in negotiations with the state for resources and recognition. Whether the strategy was productive disengagement or compromise, local leaders demonstrated a new-found confidence in dealing with the state pragmatically, which led to a more flexible and nuanced relationship between the two.

A study of a provincial town and small county seat like Nantong fills a vacuum left by the current polarization in modern China studies. Scholars have been fascinated, for justifiable reasons, by major urban centers such as Shanghai, on the one hand, and by rural China, the place where peasant revolution in the 1930s contributed to the "red triumph" in 1949, on the other. The effort to go "beyond Shanghai" has expanded Chinese urban studies from treaty ports to hinterland cities.[21] However, what lies between the city and the countryside, namely, the numerous rural market towns and small cities where a significant proportion of the Chinese population lived, has been largely overlooked. Investigating this intermediate zone will certainly increase our understanding of both rural and urban societies, as well as rural-urban relationships. These small towns were a training ground and departure point for peasant migrants to the city, who in turn helped shape city life by recreating their own "villages" there.[22] Conversely, small towns played a crucial role in connecting the city people with their country roots and in transmitting new ideas and culture from the city to the countryside. Because of the small towns' impact on the construction and reconstruction of both the rural and the urban communities, the degree of their development is a more telling yardstick for measuring social change than is transformation in the metropolises. In investigating the specifics of political, social, and cultural transformation in a rural county seat, this study explores the dynamics of the many intersections between the urban and rural communities.

Furthermore, this study examines how, during a period of major social upheaval, strong local leaders directed small-town ambition into modern aspiration, so that the community refashioned itself in reality and in reputation. Indeed, the Nantong story as we know it was shaped to a remarkable extent in Zhang Jian's image. His life interacted with broader historical forces, which both defined his vision and provided opportunities for him to realize it. Zhang Jian's experience underscores the power as well as the vulnerability of the individual. Although he contributed mightily to the rise of the Nantong model, he also played a part in its fall. In this connection, the current work provides a compelling case to compare and test James Scott's elaborate study on some of the planning disasters of the twentieth century. Scott defines a "high-modernist ideology" that blindly believes in the rational design of social order. Under this ideal vision of modernity, he argues, state-planned and -imposed grand schemes to transform society and community are doomed to fail because of the lack of local practical knowledge.[23] This might be true in many cases, including, for instance, the failure of the Great Leap Forward and of many so-called model units in Mao's China. But the Nantong model, though also socially engineered, was not imposed by the center, and local practical knowledge was clearly involved. Why, then, did it fail too?

The ensuing text investigates the rise and fall of the Nantong model. In observing and articulating the past, historians inevitably change it. This, therefore, is my Nantong. As this book goes to press, I am excited by the thought that readers will form their own versions of the story, however different they may be from my own.

CHAPTER 1

The Model in Myth and Reality

The attempt at modernity proved to be what modernity consisted of.

Mauricio Tenorio-Trillo, *Mexico at the World's Fairs*

THE EVOLUTION of the Nantong model can be roughly divided into
three phases. The period from 1895 to 1903 served as a prelude. During
this period, events such as the Sino-Japanese War, the Hundred Days
Reform, and the Boxer Uprising compelled the Qing court to recognize
the necessity of change. But it lacked a systematic plan. Moreover, it
was not at all certain that it wanted to permit reform initiative at the local level. Nantong was one of the places in the mood for reform, but a
strong and well-defined local elite leadership was yet to emerge. As a
result, Nantong witnessed no more than a few random, isolated innovations in this period.

The year 1903 was a turning point in the last decade of the Qing dynasty. The call for a constitutional monarchy had moved from background noise to frontline agenda, and even the Qing court realized that
institutional change was no longer a luxurious option but a painful
must. With the constitutional reform, or the New Policies, taking off in
1904, the local self-government movement, which the court expected to
provide a solid base for a constitutional monarchy, blossomed.

In the second stage of Nantong's development, from 1903 to 1914,
the previously piecemeal changes were replaced by a systematic material and institutional transformation under the single rubric of local
self-government. These years saw the creation of local self-government
associations, the introduction of "Village-ism," and the implementation
of many projects in industry, education, transportation, communication, and banking. In the process, a new power structure emerged, with
Zhang Jian and his brother, Zhang Cha, at the center. Although they

and other like-minded elites began to flirt with the idea that certain initiatives in Nantong could serve as an example for other regions, a conscious effort to present the community as an overall model was not yet detectable. They were preoccupied with implementing a reformist local self-government structure and promoting modernizing policies in their own community.

The 1911 Revolution was not a breaking point in terms of local self-government. To be sure, the collapse of the Qing dynasty demanded the reorientation of local self-government from being a base for a constitutional monarchy to being one for a Republican government, but it did not invalidate the practice itself. If anything, local power was strengthened during this political transition. The challenge came in 1914, when the Republican president Yuan Shikai dissolved all the local self-government institutions nationwide. Once the higher purpose that connected those institutions with the building of a new state no longer existed, the established Nantong elites turned inward, to focus on their own community, and also reached outward for support for their local initiatives.

The period from 1914 to 1921 was thus marked by a campaign to establish and advertise Nantong as a model county through tourism and other means. Village-ism was redefined to emphasize "pure" local autonomy, advocating localism and even separatism to protect Nantong from the crisis of the warlord government. A great many public, social, and cultural projects were initiated to make the community self-sufficient. The construction of a new downtown began to transform the county seat into a modern city. All this was largely successful. From 1915 on, Nantong became a regular stop for many officially organized investigative and learning tours. In the early Republic, this political tourism was a key instrument for various regions and institutions to exchange information on their modernization effort. Naturally, it helped spread Nantong's name. By 1918 local elites had to develop regulations to handle the large volume of visitors.

Clearly, the Nantong story was not a pure invention of fairy-tale proportions; it had a substantial institutional and material basis. But it did have its fictional side. The elites undoubtedly created myths to interpret the path of local development—to justify and give meaning to their undertakings and to empower themselves. Myths express cultural values, imbue political ideology, and shape power in all societies.[1] The Nantong elites used myth and rhetorical symbols to reinvent their history and to portray themselves as heroes. In the process, the image of a model Nantong gradually emerged as a centerpiece. Their myths also created the representation of a new type of leader, whose vision for the future and commitment to public interest turned a rural backwater into a progressive county. Such myths deeply tapped into the national longing under the warlord government for a consistent, moral, and strong leadership to provide direction, stability, and development to China, and thus was appealing to many educated Chinese who in turn helped promote Nantong's reputation.

The History and Geography of Nantong

Tong prefecture (Tongzhou, Nantong county after 1911) was located on the north bank of the Yangzi, near the river's mouth. "Tong" literally means "open" or "through," a term that suggests the geography of the region. On its northeastern side, Nantong faces Liaodong, Korea, and Japan across the Yellow Sea. The Yangzi River on the southwest provides access to the Yangzi region, and the Grand Canal linked Nantong with Shandong, Hebei, and China's central plains. Before steamships were introduced, travel was difficult, and the region was rather isolated because its principal outlets were waterways. Nantong's landscape also features five hills on the riverbank named Jun (Army), Jian (Sword), Ma'an (Saddle), Huangni (Yellow Mud), and Lang (Wolf). The last, Langshan, was a famous religious and scenic site, whose temples attracted thousands of pilgrims each year in imperial times.

The Tongzhou area was developed on a sandbar in approximately the fifth century, when it was named Hudouzhou. During the Tang dynasty (618–907), Hudouzhou was the home of exiled criminals sent to work the salt fields. In the late Tang, Hudouzhou merged with the land on the north bank of the river and was named Jinghai. An administrative unit called the Jinghai Military Commission (Jinghai duzhenshi) was set up, and the position of commissioner was passed on within a family named Yao for the next half-century. Salt production and agriculture developed during this period, and the city wall of Jinghai was built.

In 958 the Latter Zhou dynasty's army from the north occupied Jinghai and set up a formal administrative division, Tongzhou (Tong prefecture), with Jinghai and Haimen as two subordinate counties. Jinghai as the prefectural capital was expanded. Tongzhou was under the command of the Huainan Route (Lu) during the Song dynasty (960–1279), belonged to the Yangzhou Route in the Yuan dynasty (1271–1368), and was part of Yangzhou prefecture in the Ming dynasty (1368–1644). The warfare during the Yuan–Ming transition pushed many people out of their homes in Jiangnan, the region to the south of the Yangzi River. With the Yangzi as a natural protection, those people resettled in the plain north of the river, bringing along with them the sophisticated culture of Jiangnan.

In 1725, Tongzhou was raised to the administrative level of a *zhili* prefecture—directly under the command of the Jiangsu Provincial Commission (Jiangsu buzheng shisi)—with two subordinate counties, Rugao and Taixing. After the 1911 Revolution, when the prefecture structure was abolished, Tongzhou became Nantong county, and it remained so into the 1930s.[2] This study includes relevant information on Rugao, Haimen, and Taixing counties, since historically they often belonged to the same administrative unit. Together, these counties are referred to as the Nantong region.

Nantong county reported a population of 1,286,321 in the early 1910s.[3] Historically, the people in the region were classified into three groups based on the geographical conditions of their place of residence. Those who lived south of the Huai River were called "sand people" (*shamin*), those living by the sea "coastal people" (*haimin*), and those living along the Yangzi River "old bank people" (*laoanmin*), who were mainly peasants. All three types of people were said to lack entrepreneurship.[4] Remote from political and cultural centers and isolated by the Yangzi, Nantong was culturally backward compared with the Jiangnan region and remained so until the late nineteenth century.

Although the Jiangbei region as a whole became increasingly flood-prone and poverty-stricken in the nineteenth century,[5] economic conditions varied from place to place. The area along the north bank of the Yangzi was generally more advanced than the area closer to the Huai River. Cotton was the most important local product, contributing to the development of the household production of cloth, a major traditional product in the region. Of all these areas, Nantong was best known for its cotton production from the early Qing, and certainly more so after the 1890s.[6]

Tongzhou was the first place in Jiangbei to import cotton seeds and planting techniques from Jiangnan, where cotton planting started in the Song dynasty.[7] The soil there, especially the areas near the sea and river, was sandy and rich in humus, both favorable conditions for cotton growth. From the Ming dynasty onward, Tongzhou's cotton enjoyed nationwide fame for its great fiber length and high-quality texture. It contributed to the region's traditional handicraft weaving industry for centuries.[8] With the commercialization of cotton and cotton products at the turn of the Ming dynasty, if not earlier, Tongzhou cotton played a significant role in regional, interregional, and later international trade.

As the only area in Jiangbei to grow cotton in the late Ming, Tongzhou found markets for its cotton products in Xuzhou, Huai'an, and other areas in Jiangbei. It also exported them via the Xu and Huai region to Shandong. Because Shandong people frequently migrated to the northeast in the Qing, the three provinces of the northeast also opened up to Tongzhou cotton. Up to the early twentieth century, Tongzhou cotton steadily dominated the market within the Jiangbei region and was exported through long-distance trade as far away as to northeastern China.[9] The strong, durable cotton products were as popular among the northeast peasants as Levi's jeans were among the gold miners in the American West.

After the Opium War (1840–42), Tongzhou cotton became an important commodity in foreign trade as well. The American Civil War (1861–65) created scarcities in the North and in Europe, and boosted the demand for, and the prices of, cotton significantly. The Japanese textile industry also began importing raw cotton from China at about this time and continued to do so in increasingly large quantities during the booming Meiji period (1868–1912). With the end of World War I, Japan changed its strategy from importing raw material to exporting capital to China, and many Japanese companies built textile mills in the Yangzi region. They set up stations in different towns in Tongzhou to purchase cotton for those factories.[10]

Despite this exposure to national and world trade, Tongzhou was still by and large a traditional Chinese prefecture in its economic and social structure in 1894. The prefectural seat, known as Tongzhou *cheng* (city; the future Nantong city), was a small provincial town, not much different from numerous others of its kind in China. Like other areas in Jiangbei, Tongzhou suffered from frequent flooding. Entire towns were sometimes washed away and the local map often had to be redrawn.[11] The people of Tongzhou participated in what Emily Honig has documented as the infamous emigration of Jiangbei people.[12] The region had no modern enterprises, and education was below the standards of most of Jiangsu province.[13] All of this was about to change in the coming decades.

FIGURE 1. Zhang Jian, ca. 1912. Source: *Nantong shiye jiaoyu cishan fengjing fu canguan zhinan*, p. 1.

Prelude: 1894–1903

Tongzhou's modern history, inaugurated by the construction of the Dasheng Cotton Mill in 1895, was closely linked to Zhang Jian (1853–1926; Fig. 1). Born to a well-to-do peasant family in Changle, Haimen county, Zhang Jian spent years climbing the civil service examination ladder and failed many times. Finally, in 1894, at forty-one years of age, he gained the highest degree, *jinshi*, and was appointed to the prestigious Hanlin Academy.[14] Being a peasant's son and struggling for decades in the examination system had a profound impact on Zhang's character and career. Zhang Pengnian, Zhang Jian's father, was hard-working and pragmatic, but also ambitious enough to push his son to pursue an often-elusive dream of getting the highest academic degree of the land. Zhang Jian suffered physically and mentally from the pro-longed hours of study and repeated failure; he became ill, frustrated, and even depressed, when his hope and, more importantly perhaps, his family's hope was dashed time and again. He almost gave up on the system, as some of his friends were doing. But perhaps the guilt Zhang Jian felt for his father's lifetime sacrifice and the lure of the dream were a greater force. In 1894, his seventy-six-year-old father pled with him to try once more; he did and won. At this triumphant moment, he wept uncontrollably, mostly for the long-accumulated sorrow.[15]

The experience of those years taught Zhang Jian the virtue of perse-verance and gave him a sense of mission; he was no doubt a high achiever. It also highlighted at least two ironies in his life that played out later. One is that he strived to succeed in a system that he had grown increasingly averse to, which eventually led to his departure from his hard-earned post at the Hanlin Academy. The other is that even while he was taking the examinations repeatedly, he was more concerned with practical matters, which explains his focus on building factories and schools later in Nantong. But what he perhaps resented most of all about those years of study was being a prisoner of circum-stances: the examination system and the will of his father, each had a life of its own from which he could not escape. In the next decades, Zhang Jian strove to control his own fate, along with that of Nantong, down to every detail he could possibly think of. Indeed, both his strengths and his weaknesses—he was tenacious and visionary but also overly confident and ambitious—were clearly visible in the evolution of the Nantong story; he achieved remarkable success but also flew on imaginary wings that led to his inevitable fall.

Those years also provided Zhang Jian with opportunities for career development and social contacts. While preparing for the examina-tions, he worked for several politicians outside Tongzhou and partici-pated in some important events of the time, including the Korean crisis of 1882. In the process, he became acquainted with several major fig-ures on the national political stage, including Emperor Guangxu's men-tor Weng Tonghe, the Liangjiang governor-generals Zhang Zhidong and Liu Kunyi, all of whom became Zhang Jian's patrons, and Yuan Shikai, the future president of Republican China. By the time he re-

turned to Tongzhou, Zhang Jian had established himself as an important scholar and an experienced politician.[16]

In 1894, China's poor performance in the Sino-Japanese War (1894–
95), along with the open factional conflict between Empress Dowager
Cixi and Emperor Guangxu, was disappointing to Zhang Jian. These
events coincided with the death of his father, leading to Zhang's resignation from the Hanlin Academy and return to Tongzhou for the required three years of mourning. It was under these circumstances that
he became involved in the creation of the Dasheng Cotton Mill (hereafter referred to as the No. 1 mill because some Dasheng branch mills
were developed later).[17]

The project was commissioned by Zhang Zhidong, the High Commissioner for Military and Foreign Affairs in South China (Nanyang
dachen) and perhaps the most influential figure in the Self-strengthening
movement, a response to the Qing court's permitting foreigners to
build factories in China in the wake of the Sino-Japanese War. After
countless difficulties and setbacks, the No. 1 mill was built in 1898 in
Tangzha, a village five miles northwest of Tongzhou city. Using local
cotton and cheap labor, especially female workers who were skilled at
cotton handicraft production, the factory proved to be a success and began to make a profit soon after it began production.[18] In the meantime,
Zhang Jian and his associates created other factories to process, for instance, flour and oil.[19]

These factories, especially the No. 1 mill, stimulated innovations in
other areas. Because local demand for cotton increased, Zhang Jian in
1901 initiated the Nantong-Haimen Land Reclamation Company (Tong-
Hai kenmu gongsi) to undertake the largest land conversion project in
the region. Its purpose was to develop salt land along the seacoast of
Nantong and Haimen, a total of 120,000 *mu*, into cotton fields that
would serve as a basis for a self-reliant system in cotton production,
from planting to manufacturing.[20] (A mu equaled 1/6 of an acre, so this
project involved approximately 18,000 acres.)

Zhang Jian also started to use profits from the mill to finance other
projects, such as new schools. China's often-failed attempt to deal with
foreigners proved that the traditional civil examination system was inadequate to train government officials. Concerned and open-minded
Chinese began to advocate educational reform to strengthen China;
Zhang Jian was among them. He realized that training qualified teachers for the new schools was the first logical step in that direction. Promoted by Zhang and other elites, the Nantong Normal School was built

in 1902; it was among the first locally sponsored normal schools in China. In the next two years, the Tongzhou Higher Primary School and the Public Middle School were also brought into being. These were the earliest modern schools in Tongzhou.[21]

All of these endeavors not only brought elements of a modern economy and culture to a rural county for the first time, but also made Zhang Jian a rising star on the local political horizon. As a member of the Dasheng board of directors and the principal of several local schools, Zhang soon came to be viewed as a force representing change and progress. The process was filled with struggle, though. In 1894, when Zhang returned to Tongzhou, the local powers tried to deny him a role as a key player. Although culturally the line between national and local elites might have been blurred because all members of the elite shared a common Confucian background,[22] the political division between them could be sharp and clear. A national reputation did not automatically translate into local power; as the Chinese saying goes, *Qianglong yabuguo ditoushe* ("The mighty dragon cannot beat a snake in its old haunts"). Despite Zhang Jian's prestigious degree, the fact that his family was not of the Tongzhou elite and that he had served outside politicians for twenty years hindered his local acceptance. Zhang Jian's brother Zhang Cha, once a county magistrate in Jiangxi province with a purchased degree, was not of much help either. On top of all this, the Zhang family was financially weak. Zhang Jian owed a debt of 6,000 *yuan* after his father's funeral in 1894, and in 1895 he had to pawn twenty-four boxes of his own books in order to start a local militia.[23] Thus, when Zhang Jian became involved in the Dasheng project, the local merchants, skeptical about his ability to succeed, withheld their support, which almost broke the deal. The deep-rooted Tongzhou elites did not respect Zhang Jian either. Zhang also had problems with the prefect, Wang Shutang, who considered Zhang a potential threat and refused to support his industrial activities.[24]

Zhang Jian's eventual rise in the local power arena was due to many factors. With the profits from Dasheng, the Zhang family's financial circumstances improved rapidly and significantly. When the Zhang brothers divided their family property in 1903, they split a total landholding of 3,800 mu, a sufficient indication of the family's wealth without counting in their shares in the No. 1 mill.[25] Socially, the downfall of the Qing dynasty produced a group of potential reformers in Nantong from whom Zhang Jian was able to rally support. These reform-minded local people were not necessarily at the core of the local power elite, but they had a certain influence and reputation in the community by virtue of their gentry family background and social contacts, their own literary talent, or their wealth.

Among them was Shen Xiejun, one of the six original promoters of the No. 1 mill, who started as a *shengyuan* degree-holder and former schoolteacher in rural Haimen. He established a reputation as fair and sincere in helping solve civil disputes. In the 1880s, Shen was outspoken in his opposition to the heavy levy the Qing government imposed on the cotton trade, which not only hurt the cotton business but also adversely affected peasants and their handicraft industry. Allied with other merchants and supported by Zhang Jian, Shen launched a ten-year-long battle with the government, which eventually backed down enough to reduce the levy. In the process, Shen became a cotton merchant himself and enjoyed high regard in the local merchant community. When Zhang Jian started the Dasheng project, he invited Shen to be his partner. Though other merchants doubted Zhang's entrepreneurship, they trusted Shen and gradually came to join Zhang.[26]

Another man Zhang Jian befriended was Liu Yishan. Born into a rich cotton merchant family, Liu was an influential figure in the cotton trade. His family was illustrious for a variety of other reasons. Liu's eldest son joined the Alliance League (Tongmenghui) in Paris with Sun Zhongshan's sponsorship while studying law there. He later served as a diplomat for the Republican government. Another son was a graduate of Peking and Columbia universities and associated with the most celebrated Chinese writers of the day.[27] Not surprisingly, Liu Yishan was a more forward-looking merchant than most of his county fellows, and he too became one of the original promoters of the Dasheng venture.

Although support from local wealthy men like Shen Xiejun and Liu Yishan was crucial for Zhang Jian to break into the elite merchant community and advance his business interests, another group, the young, ambitious, yet disenchanted nonofficial Tongzhou scholars, helped Zhang Jian undertake educational and other reforms. Through them, Zhang was gradually accepted by the local scholarly community.[28] These young men were victims of the late Qing examination system and belonged to the pool of frustrated "surplus," a group that had no hope of ever gaining an official appointment in a system where there were many more degree-holders than government posts, but often refused to adjust to the situation and pursue a different career. Disillusioned with and critical of the examination system and the Qing court, they were motivated and resourceful in taking the initiative in social reform.

Zhou Jialu, a renowned Tongzhou scholar whose writings filled thirteen books, took provincial examinations seven times with no success because he fell ill each time during the examinations.[29] Whenever Zhang Jian failed his examination, Zhou would write to comfort him. In the end, Zhou simply gave up. He searched instead for ways to change the system. In 1892, Zhou Jialu and Liu Yishan created the first Western-style primary school in Tongzhou and supported Zhang Jian's educational reforms.[30]

Fan Dangshi, a *juren* degree-holder, was born into a family known for its "ten generations of poets."[31] He lived in a world of literary talent and prestige, and his credentials included serving as the representative of a well-known literary group, the Tongcheng Literary School, and as a family tutor for the most powerful late Qing official, Li Hongzhang. Fan too was a victim of the civil examination system, having failed the jinshi examination nine times. At the age of thirty-five, he swore not to try again but to work instead to change the system itself. Fan Dangshi became Zhang Jian's main ally in the creation of the first few new schools. He wrote extensively to criticize the traditional system and promote the new one. Because of his own experience and reputation, his works were widely read.[32] All this helped mobilize the community in supporting the reform.

While Zhang the "mighty dragon" was working to gain the support of the local "snakes," the momentum for reform was growing at the national level. Zhang and his associates were now able to have some measure of success as representatives of that trend. Although most of them were traditional scholars and merchants, they began to obtain new identities and to expand their social resources. Shen Xiejun, for instance, transformed himself from a popular village schoolteacher into a major stockholder of the No. 1 mill and served, with Liu Yishan, on its board of directors. In 1902, when the General Chamber of Commerce—Tongchonghai (from Tong[zhou]-Chong[ming]-Hai[men]) zong shanghui—was established, both Liu Yishan and Shen Xiejun played an active leadership role in it, and Zhang Cha became its director. They not only belonged to China's new capitalist class, but were also prominent powerbrokers in local civic affairs. Since the No. 1 mill served as a financial source for local development, its majority stockholders and board members decided what projects should be undertaken. Such decision-making power gave them a more dominant position in the community than that of the appointed prefectural and county officials.[33] Scholars gained status too, thanks to their involvement in new projects and institutions. Fan Dangshi and other elites served on the boards of the new schools. Among their many administrative responsibilities was the control of personnel and financial resources.[34] But for all these early efforts in the 1894–1903 period, modern projects were still at that stage random and few in number, and Zhang Jian was yet to dominate the community.

Transformation: 1903–1914

The events that marked the opening of the twentieth century brought both chaos and hope to China. In the wake of the Boxer crisis (1900), the very court that had suppressed the Hundred Days Reform two years earlier was forced to initiate some major changes itself. It issued an edict on 29 January 1901 calling for the discussion of a broad range of issues and promising changes in policy in due course. With reform proposals from high-ranking officials pouring in, the court issued what is known as the New Policies over the decade, a series of laws that covered everything from education, the economy, and military and police forces, to constitutional reform and local self-government, and aimed at strengthening the central government and bringing wealth and power to China.[35] In the meantime, Zhang Jian took an extended trip to Japan that provided a rare opportunity for him to see concretely how a constitutional monarchy and self-governed local communities worked. Upon his return, he became a prominent promoter of the constitutional reform and a practitioner of the idea of local self-government. As a result, Tongzhou entered a new stage of development.

Zhang's Trip to Japan

In April 1903, Zhang Jian was invited by the Japanese consul in Shanghai to pay a private visit to the Fifth Industrial and Agricultural Exposition in Osaka. Aside from a mission in Korea, this was the only overseas trip in his lifetime. The seventy-day visit was an eye-opening experience for him, profoundly affecting his vision of China's future. By then, Zhang already had some knowledge of Japan and had had personal contacts with Japanese. In the "age of the Japanese teacher" (to use the term referred to by Douglas Reynolds), the Nantong Normal

School had hired Japanese from the outset to chair departments and teach various subjects.[36] Obviously, Japan's advancement was familiar to Zhang, but nothing was more powerful than first-hand experience and persuasive visual evidence in convincing him that China had much to learn from Japan.

Zhang Jian spent whatever free time he had in Japan investigating schools, kindergartens, factories, companies, farms, agricultural experimental fields, banks, printing houses, libraries, and museums. He visited thirty-five educational institutions and thirty agricultural, industrial, and commercial units in different regions, and had conversations with numerous teachers, school administrators, farmers, bankers, journalists, merchants, industrialists, and Chinese overseas students. Zhang considered this visit a rare learning experience, and even the Japanese press was impressed with his careful examination.[37] In his *Diary of Travels East* (*Dongyou riji*), published shortly after his return, Zhang Jian recorded in meticulous detail what he had seen in his visits to schools— budgets, classrooms, dormitories, bathrooms, school uniforms, even the games students played—along with the information he had gained about land reclamation activities, shipping companies, and other technologies.[38] Zhang Jian's attention to details of Japanese society can only be matched with the leading Japanese educator Fukuzawa Yukichi's hunger for all things Western during his 1862 trip to Europe.[39]

Japan to Zhang Jian was not flawless; he criticized some aspects of Japanese society.[40] His overall impression of Japan, however, was completely positive. He was especially impressed by the Japanese school system. Zhang attended the celebration of the Osaka City Elementary School's thirtieth anniversary. There he saw how disciplined the students were and how highly regarded the school was. Even the Japanese prince came to honor the event.[41] Zhang requested a set of the most recent Japanese school textbooks to take home. What he saw in Japan was not only an efficient central government, but also many functional local units, serving as the foundation of the nation. He praised Japan as a "learned nation" (*xueguo*) and attributed all its achievements, especially those in industry and education, to the Meiji Restoration and the constitutional system.[42]

Constitutional Waves

This trip committed Zhang Jian to constitutional reform, on the one hand, and to local self-government, on the other. In respect to the first, his most notable activities were in the domains of organization and propaganda, thanks in good part to his close ties with upper-level elites and officials, especially those from the lower Yangzi region. Controlling the richest and most-developed part of China, the officials, elites, merchants, industrialists, and returned students there were so powerful that they had the potential to form a separate political center, as was evidenced by the Southeastern Mutual Defense movement during the Boxer Uprising.[43]

Zhang Jian was one of the leading figures in this group. Aside from his prestigious academic degree, he carried much weight in regional and national affairs as a well-established elite and creator of successful modern institutions. The Qing court recognized the influence he exerted and tried, through him, to draw the upper elites of the lower Yangzi over to its side. In early 1904, the court appointed Zhang Jian to be the head adviser in the Ministry of Commerce, which further heightened his prestige and reinforced his illusions about the Qing court as an agent for change.[44]

Zhang Jian's industrial undertakings connected him with a large number of Shanghai-based bankers, investors, merchants, and industrialists, many of whom were also active politicians. One of them was Tang Shouqian, a jinshi degree-holder from Zhejiang province, who in 1905 was the chief administrator of the Zhejiang Railway Company. Zhang also frequently visited Zheng Xiaoxu, a diplomat to Japan who returned to work for Zhang Zhidong and became involved in several enterprises in Shanghai, including the Commercial Press and the Shanghai Savings Bank. The Jiangsu governor Cheng Dequan was allied with Zhang Jian. Zhao Fengchang, a Jiangsu native and Zhang Zhidong's private secretary, was one of Zhang's closest associates in this period. Zhao Fengchang had broad personal and political contacts in the lower Yangzi region and beyond. All of these men were among the most vigorous promoters of constitutional reform. In 1904 Zhang Jian, invited by Zhang Zhidong, stayed in Nanjing for two weeks to help draft a petition titled "Request for Constitutional Reform," which was sent to the court in the name of the lower Yangzi officials and elites.[45]

These reformers worked out many ideas and programs that contributed to the Qing court's eventual capitulation.[46] In 1906, the heyday of the constitutional movement, the court was finally forced to set up a nine-year period for the "preparation for constitutional reform." Encouraged by that move, Zhang Jian, Zheng Xiaoxu, and Tang Shouqian immediately created the Constitutional Preparation Association

(Yubei lixian gonghui) in Shanghai; Zhang became one of the two vice-presidents. This instant response, in November of that same year, sent a constitutionalist wave to other parts of the country, where similar associations were soon established. In 1907, the Qing court set up the National Consultative Council (Zizheng yuan) as a step toward the establishment of a formal parliament. Such a council was established in each province as well; the one Zhang Jian headed in Nanjing was considered a model by other regions. In 1909, Zhang Jian and leaders of consultative councils from other provinces organized the Association of Combined Provincial Consultative Councils (Gesheng ziyiju lianhehui) to urge the central government to reduce the nine-year preparatory period and to convene a formal parliament immediately. To that end, meetings were held and petitions submitted. Under pressure, the court in 1910 finally agreed to reduce the preparatory period to six years.[47]

Zhang's influence was also visible in the media. He was fully aware of the importance of public opinion in pressuring the court and pushing the movement forward. To spread his observations on the Japanese constitutional system, he sent copies of his *Diary of Travels East* as soon as it was published to his influential colleagues. In 1904, he managed to have books on Japanese constitutional history translated into Chinese and printed. Those books too were sent to the key figures of the movement, and Zhang arranged to have twelve of them secretly carried into the palace.[48] In 1908, Zhang Jian, Tang Shouqian, and Zheng Xiaoxu together created an organ for the association they had founded two years earlier. Published in Shanghai, the *Newspaper of the Constitutional Preparation Association* (*Yubei lixian gonghui gongbao*) represented the voice of the most powerful constitutionalists. Zhang Jian also had close relationships with Shanghai's *Shenbao, Shibao,* and *Dongfang zazhi* (*Eastern Miscellany*), the chief journalistic voices for constitutional reform. *Shenbao* frequently printed articles by Zhang Jian and other constitutionalists; *Shibao's* three main journalists were members of the Jiangsu Consultative Council; and *Dongfang zazhi* ran a special column on "constitutional government" written by Meng Sen, one of Zhang Jian's protégés and a member of the Constitutional Preparation Association.[49]

Village-ism

For Zhang Jian, local self-government was a fundamental part of constitutional reform, and he consequently devoted considerable attention

to the local self-government movement in Tongzhou. Zhang understood the mutual impact of national and local interests and wanted to
combine the energy at both levels to make the reform a success. He
used the term "Village-ism" (Cunluo zhuyi) to characterize his idea of
local self-government.[50]

In the statecraft of an agrarian society such as traditional China, the
importance of the village was both elusive and tangible. In terms of political hierarchy, the village was the farthest away from the central government, and thus appeared to be remote and insignificant. Yet the village was the most immediate community beyond the family. Whereas
the family was a private entity, the village was the smallest collective
unit. As such, it represented the basic and broad foundation of the empire, holding unique weight in its social stability and economic produc-
tivity. Politicians and reformers from Wang Anshi of the Northern Song
dynasty (960–1127) to James Yen of the 1930s and Mao Zedong of the
Communist Party all paid particular attention to the village. It has also
intrigued Chinese ancient literati and modern intellectuals alike, who
have tended to construct a romantic image of the village and peasant
life as the "other"—where the supposed simplicity of life was said to be
ideal alternatively for aesthetic contemplation, political escape, and intellectual enlightenment. Such sentiments are clearly reflected, for instance, in the well-known poetry of Tao Yuanming of the fifth century
and in James Yen's concept of a new China as a "village Republic."[51]
Liang Shuming, the so-called modern-day Confucian sage, also considered rural reconstruction to be a key to China's modernization.[52] In a
sense, educated Chinese have always been obsessed with the village.

Unlike James Yen and Liang Shuming, Zhang Jian had not focused
on the village when he began working in Nantong. His Village-ism
emerged only at the outset of the constitutional reform movement and
was closely intertwined with it. Building on the idea that the village
represented the foundation of the society, Zhang Jian initially meant to
create a broad and solid local basis for a constitutional monarchy. That
purpose changed in the last days of the Qing dynasty as hopes for the
reform were slipping away. Village-ism had to find a new direction. Its
essence, however, was self-governing, or *zizhi*—local people managing
local affairs. This concept thus inevitably dealt with the local-central relationship.

One of the main sources for Zhang's view of the village was the
Japanese model of self-government (*jichi* in Japanese). In fact, it was after his trip to Japan that Zhang Jian gradually developed the idea of Village-ism.[53] The concept of local self-government had become popular in

Japan between 1888 and 1890 as an apolitical means of national integration: through the self-governing organizations of each local unit, the foundation of the state would be strengthened. The Japanese also believed that so long as localities remained stable, political turmoil in the center could not shake the nation.[54] In reality, though, the "apolitical" nature of the jichi model was questionable, and the practice of local autonomy inevitably caused conflict with the central authorities, even in some seemingly quiescent regions.[55]

The ideal Japanese jichi model started at the village level. Each village as a self-governed unit worked to advance its own interests through its institutions, which oversaw social, economic, and cultural programs. There were also designated "model villages" in Japan to promote the jichi movement.[56] The expectation was that local self-government would at once advance local interests and serve the nation. This view fitted Zhang Jian's own beliefs well. If each family, each village, each town, and each county in China were reformed, China would assuredly be strong.[57]

Another source for Zhang Jian's Village-ism was the age-old debate on the merits of the feudal (*fengjian*) and bureaucratic (*junxian*) governmental systems in China, which can be traced to even before the collapse of the first bureaucratic government, the Qin dynasty (221–207 B.C.).[58] The bureaucratic system came under increasing attack in the Ming and Qing periods because of the intensification of central control and the influence of Japan and the West. Many scholars, including Gu Yanwu (1613–82), Huang Zunxian (1848–1905), and Liang Qichao (1873–1929), vigorously argued the necessity of political reform and advocated absorbing some of the feudal system's advantages of self-government into the prevailing system—encouraging gentry participation in governing local affairs. Their writings and activities had a major impact on the events of the 1900s. Although all of these scholars hoped to improve the existing system by expanding gentry involvement, they put a different emphasis on the self-government idea. Huang Zunxian, for example, argued for using local autonomy to limit and balance imperial power. Unlike Huang and the others, Kang Youwei (1858–1927) did not promote local autonomy as such. He conceived of local self-government as a channel for the gentry to help state power efficiently penetrate local society.[59] Kang's view was reflected in the official local self-government program embodied in the New Policies.

Zhang Jian's Village-ism revealed a position between Huang's and Kang's. His moderate reform approach and his position in the constitutional movement did not allow him completely or openly to accept Huang Zunxian's view in the early 1900s. Yet neither could he fully subscribe to the Kang–New Policies view. Zhang Jian's experience as a sophisticated politician and his local involvement enabled him to recognize the conflicting interests between the state and local society, as well as the significance of local autonomy to elites like himself, whose power was locally based. Political developments in the 1910s also affected his attitude. He leaned toward Kang's position more in the beginning but gradually shifted to Huang's. Initially, Zhang Jian had many illusions about the Qing court and believed that the interests of society and government were merged in one, especially after the court set a fixed date of nine years for the turn to a constitutional monarchy.[60] But he grew less patient and more critical of the court for its lack of sincerity in carrying out its promises as time passed without perceptible results.

Zhang Jian advocated a local self-government model that involved a self-sufficient system with a certain degree of autonomy. That system would be a basis for a strong nation and a central government, but should the central government collapse and the nation fall into turmoil, the local self-government system could sustain itself as an independent entity capable of preserving local order and elite power. This model was designed to have the flexibility both to advance local and national interests together and to pursue local development independently. To that end, Zhang Jian emphasized the development of basic social units, from family to village to county, by implementing industrial, educational, and charitable programs.[61] These principles of Village-ism were gradually realized in Nantong, thanks to the restructuring of the local government after 1904.

Local Self-government Reform

Under Zhang Jian's leadership, new institutions and initiatives mushroomed in Nantong as the constitutional reform movement took hold. More important, local elites gradually incorporated all the institutions and initiatives into a local self-government system, providing coherence in direction on the one hand and legitimating elite power on the other. After the election of a council in Tianjin in 1907 as part of a local administrative reform program, Yuan Shikai recommended to the Qing court that the Tianjin model be adopted throughout China.[62] In October 1907, an imperial edict endorsed the recommendation, and in 1908 the

Ministry of Civil Administration drafted local self-government regulations to formalize the reform. The main feature of the regulations was
to set up elected councils of local elites at the municipal and subprefec-
tural levels to help the state reach local communities and, in turn, to
channel their concerns to the central authorities. The regulations, however, limited elite participation mainly to public service under the supervision of government-appointed officials.[63]

Immediately after the Tianjin election, the reformist Tongzhou elites,
who by then already controlled the General Chamber of Commerce and
the educational association, sent a proposal to the prefectural administration, requesting permission to follow the Tianjin model in experimenting with local self-government.[64] The proposal suggested that local self-government consist of two types of administrative bodies made
up of members elected from and by the county elites, councils (*yishihui*)
to make decisions and directorates (*dongshihui*) as a check and balance
on the councils' actions. These bodies would be set up first in the city,
and then gradually in towns and rural districts. Their responsibility
was broadly defined as covering everything that was related to the
public interest (*gongyi*), which meant that all existing local institutions,
such as the chamber of commerce and the educational association,
would come under their purview as subordinate units. The writers emphasized that Tongzhou was ready for local self-government because
the elites had engaged in educational and industrial innovation for
years. Furthermore, they said, development in Tongzhou, though it had
achieved some results, lacked an overall plan (*tongchou*). Without a co-
hesive leadership in local self-government, "the current situation can
hardly be maintained," and "the future is uncertain and no further
progress can be expected." They went on to express their determination
to carry out this change: "We will endure all hardship to make local
self-government a success, so that we will not disappoint the court's intention in preparing a constitutional government." In proposing that
the new institutions be given broad administrative authority for local
affairs, their blueprint for reform departed significantly from the official
policy, which gave local elites only limited power.

Nevertheless, the proposal was approved, and the Tongzhou Local
Self-government Council and Directorate were established in 1908.
Zhang Jian headed the council, and the prefect, Qi Shan, led the directorate, with Zhang Cha as his assistant. The members of the council and
directorate consisted mainly of local scholars, merchants, and professionals, including Liu Yishan and Shen Xiejun.[65] The two elective bod-

ies together were generally referred to as the Local Self-government Association (Zizhi hui).[66]

The association moved quickly to establish several agencies to help carry out the various programs, including implementing elections in rural districts. Three of the units in this category were the Local Self-government Research Bureau (Difang zizhi yanjiu suo), the Law and Administration Lecture Bureau (Fazheng jiangxi suo), and the Speech Practice Bureau (Xuanjiang lianxi suo). Other organizations, such as the Survey Bureau (Cehui ju), the Agricultural Society (Nong hui), and the Erosion Protection Society (Baota hui), were mainly to provide public services.[67]

Hitherto the elites had exercised their influence chiefly through educational and other public organs; Zhang Jian signed his name to the 1907 proposal, for instance, in his capacity as the head of the educational association.[68] Now the elites not only had an administrative center to work with, but one whose reach expanded well beyond the limits set by the Qing court. This consolidation and expansion of elite force finally shifted the balance of power from officially appointed officials and the old gentry to the new merchant-industrial elites. Zhang Jian and Zhang Cha became the most powerful men in the new structure. Since Zhang Jian often had to attend to regional and national affairs, Zhang Cha wielded the family's local control. He was the active manager of the Dasheng enterprises and held many other positions in public service institutions, such as the Erosion Protection Society, the agricultural society, and the Tongzhou militia, in addition to taking charge of the powerful General Chamber of Commerce.[69]

The restructured government apparatus also produced a new group of professionals and activists. They consisted of managers of public institutions, heads of various self-government organizations, industrialists and merchants, Dasheng stockholders, school administrators, teachers, graduates of modern schools, returned students, journalists, lawyers, and reform-minded landlords. Most of them did not have prominent family backgrounds, but they invested and participated in the reform projects and emerged as leaders in the public domain. These people represented a new segment in the elite society on which the Zhang brothers depended to carry out their reform agenda.[70]

The 1911 Revolution broke the linkage between local self-government and a constitutional monarchy. However, the collapse of the Qing dynasty and the chaotic beginning of the Republic continued to favor the advancement of local elites. In the reorganization of the local administration after 1911, Nantong became a county. During the transition, Zhang Cha was the county military general commander and later took over the post of civil administration officer as well. Other members of the county administration were active participants in the reform; most of them were the Zhang family's trusted followers.[71] The local self-government councils and directorates at the county level and below continued to hold elections and to complete the institutional establishment as earlier planned.[72] The Zhang brothers controlled the Nantong County Local Self-government Association. Zhang Jian often used his home as a yamen to deal with local affairs, and it is said that other county officials had to take their cue from the Zhang brothers.[73] Operating from their social and political base in Nantong, the Zhang brothers had become the dominant force on the local scene.

New Initiatives

The new elite leadership systematically implemented a series of economic, educational, and philanthropic projects to give effect to Zhang Jian's Village-ism. Following the Dasheng lead, at least nine new factories were built from 1903 to 1911, including the No. 2 Dasheng mill. Most of the factories (six of the nine) were directly controlled by the Zhang brothers and thus had close ties to the No. 1 mill. In fact, the No. 1 mill served as the core of local industry in terms of capital investment and management training. Under the Zhangs' leadership, more land reclamation companies were created to ensure the mills' cotton supply. Together, these factories and companies began to take control of the region's economic activities.[74]

The impact of these initiatives cannot be overstated. They represented an emergent modern sector that began not only to challenge the traditional economic structure, but also to change the existing urban-rural configuration by speeding up the urbanization process. Before 1894, Tongzhou had nine towns of considerable importance besides the prefectural seat and the county seats of Taixing and Rugao.[75] In addition, there were nineteen smaller towns and thirty-eight ordinary markets. On average, there had been a market within every ten to fifteen li, a pattern similar to that in other parts of China. These towns and markets were primarily spurred by cotton and salt production, distribution, and transportation.[76]

Urban growth proceeded apace after 1894. By 1909, Tongzhou had thirty-five cities and towns of considerable size.[77] Many towns owed their inception directly to the growth of industrial and land reclamation projects. For instance, Sanyu, originally a marsh outside a dike, did not appear on the map until after 1912, when the Zhang brothers started a land reclamation company there. In three years, while converting this salt marsh into cotton fields, the company brought a town into being, complete with streets, office buildings, residential houses, markets, and shops. Merchants moved their businesses to Sanyu to serve the thriving town and its thousands of laborers. In 1916, a small power station was set up to light the company offices and its cotton rolling mill. In 1918, the company established a primary school. Within less than ten years, the salt marsh became a full-scale town. Many other towns shared Sanyu's experience.[78]

Industrialization and urbanization required new modes of transportation and communication. The Zhang brothers created the Dada Inner River Small Steamship Company in 1903 and then the Dada Outer River Steamship Company in 1908 to provide service on the Yangzi River.[79] The introduction of steamships significantly improved waterway transportation and shortened the travel time from Tongzhou to Shanghai, Nanjing, and neighboring counties by more than half, not to mention saving the troublesome frequent land-water transfers of the past. In the meantime, a land transportation system was budgeted. In 1912, the Nantong Roadwork Bureau was established to plan and construct a county-wide highway system. By the time it was completed, more than twenty bus companies, both private and public, were in operation, providing services for long distance as well as local travel.[80] Official initiative also brought postal service, the telegraph, and long-distance telephone companies to towns and rural markets.[81] The development of a modern communication and transportation infrastructure broke geographical barriers and promoted population growth and commercial activities. With goods, news, and people traveling at an unsurpassed speed and scale, the region opened up to the outside world as never before.

Unprecedented change also took place in education. In 1875, Tongzhou had seven academies (*shuyuan*), twenty-one village schools (*shexue*), and five charitable schools (*yixue*), the bulk of which were located in Nantong district. Most of these institutions were officially supervised and funded by wealthy gentry and by land taxes and other public resources. In addition, there were quite a few family-oriented private schools (*sishu*).[82] Adding all the public and private schools and academies together, Tongzhou before the twentieth century was by no means notable for its educational achievement.[83] In 1898 or thereabouts, some scholars began to sponsor Western-style schools, but they were few in number, and all of them were at the elementary level, with the exception of the normal school.

Changes in the educational domain began soon after Zhang Jian's return from Japan. In 1904, the local elites created the Tong-Hai Educational Bureau (Xuewu gongsuo) to design a universal school system from primary to higher education. Zhang Jian and Sha Yuanbing, a prominent member of the Rugao county elite, were in charge of the bureau. By 1906, thirty-nine lower primary schools were in operation under its supervision. Higher level schools soon followed, encouraged in particular by the abolition of the civil examination system in 1905. In 1907, the bureau, now renamed the Educational Association (Jiaoyu hui), built a women's normal school and initiated a middle school, which was completed in 1909. The year 1907 also saw the addition of two bureaus to promote the new school system, the Exhortation Bureau and the Educational Research Bureau. From 1908 to 1910, sixty-seven lower primary schools were completed. In 1911, Zhang Jian launched an ambitious plan that foresaw a lower primary school every sixteen li, which came to a total of 332 schools. This massive project was expected to be accomplished within five years, and each town and rural district local self-government association was held responsible for seeing it through. In the first year alone, twenty-five lower primary schools were created. All these schools were locally supported through both private donations of land and money by the elites and public tax levies. In 1912, with the establishment of county administrations, the Nantong County Educational Association was formed. Thereafter, each town and rural district set up its own educational association to administer local school projects. The normal school was instrumental in carrying out these ambitious plans by supplying local schools with trained teachers.[84] As a result of these efforts, modern schools in Nantong were rapidly institutionalized and widespread.

In the meantime, the elites also created three professional schools, a textile school, an agricultural school, and a medical school; career training centers and vocational schools, such as the Commercial School; a special education institution, the School for the Blind and Dumb; and two important social and public educational institutions, the Nantong Museum and the Nantong Library. In 1904, Zhang Jian and his associates built the Hanmolin Publishing House, the first modern printing factory, to supply textbooks for the rapidly growing number of local schools.[85]

The elites set up many social and public institutions to serve the needy. Like other local communities in China, Tongzhou traditionally had charitable organizations, but Nantong now developed a more organized and productive welfare system managed by local elites. A new orphanage, a vagrant workshop, an old people's home, and other charitable institutions were all created before 1913. The Zhang brothers alone sponsored several of these institutions. Plans were made to take care of the aged, to train the disabled, and to help the poor with the expectation that everyone could lead a self-sufficient and productive life.[86]

The decade between 1904 and 1914 thus witnessed a profound change in Nantong. With the institutional and material transformation came a new elite leadership and a series of innovations in the economic, educational, social, and public arenas. Nantong was well on its way to becoming a self-sufficient unit, not far from what Zhang Jian envisioned in his Village-ism. In 1911, Zhang expected that these developments would fulfill his ambition to create a "blueprint for a new world" (*xinshijie de chuxing*). This new world for him was by no means a complete departure from the past, but it would have the institutions, public works, and functions that the Japanese jichi model had offered, so that "[we can] wash away the shame that local society in China cannot practice local self-government."[87]

The collapse of the Qing dynasty further diminished state restrictions on local society, providing a golden opportunity for the elites to expand their power. However, local self-government now had to be redirected to support the new Republic. After the 1911 Revolution, many constitutionalists, including Zhang Jian and Tang Shouqian, became Republicans. Tang in fact became the first Republican governor of Zhejiang province. Zhang Jian soon accepted Sun Zhongshan's invitation to become the Minister of Industry and the Liang-Huai Salt Commissioner, in which capacity he helped the new government deal with its daunting financial problems. Later, in 1913, at Yuan Shikai's request, Zhang Jian joined the Xiong Xiling cabinet as the director general of the National Water Conservancy and the Minister of Agriculture and Commerce.[88]

Clearly, Zhang Jian pinned his hopes of restoring a central government on Yuan Shikai and wanted to contribute to that cause. Yuan Shikai, however, proved to be a disappointment. He not only dismissed the provincial and national parliaments, but also, against the will of his cabinet, closed down local self-government institutions nationwide in 1914. Instead, Yuan now intended to make himself an emperor. As a result of these and other developments, the Xiong Xiling cabinet was dissolved, and Zhang Jian, for the second time in his political career, re-signed from his post in the central government and left for Nantong—before Yuan Shikai even had a chance to approve his resignation.[89] It was this turn of events that finally provoked a conscious effort among the Nantong elites to promote the county as a model.

Model Campaign: 1914–1921

Chinese culture, characterized by Confucianism with collectivism at the core, is prone to model production. The basic political ideas of Confucianism rest on role models that reflect social hierarchy—Emperor to subjects, father to son, teacher to student, and so on. The assumption is that if each plays his role appropriately, this hierarchic model system ensures social stability. The late Qing–early Republican period proved to be an especially fertile ground for the growth of this culture. In that era of rapid social change and uncertainty, models helped political leaders to explore new paths to move China forward. Although foreign success in modernization served as a useful reference, China's own experience was especially invaluable. Throughout this period, both the central and the regional governments constantly searched for examples and experiences in pioneering new policies and projects. A great deal of effort was devoted to investigative tours and information exchange; people traveled or otherwise contacted one another to explore the many new areas that were opening up for experimentation.

The use of the term *model* was common. In the beginning of the educational reform, officially sponsored schools were simply called "model schools," because they were supposed to represent the "official system decreed by the Minister of Culture."[90] Yuan Shikai's 1907 Tianjin election was used as an example by other regions in the local self-government reform. Long before the arrival of James Yen in the mid-1920s, Ding county of Hebei province was known as a model because of its magistrate's reform programs. The magistrate then went on to Shanxi with the ambition to build a model province there.[91] The rise of the Nantong model occurred in a period when model building was commonplace. What was unique about Nantong, though, was that where other regions earned fame for certain specific projects, Nantong emerged as an overall model for modernity and local self-government and did so amid much fanfare. This process, however, was a gradual one that began with a few modest steps.

Turning Point

Zhang Jian started promoting Nantong before 1914, but in a subtle way based on individual projects. As a policy maker at both the local and the central level, he was mindful of the connection between local and national politics and well positioned to use it to serve the interests of both. After 1913, Zhang's post in Beijing allowed him access to privileged information. He often used such information to help Nantong stay ahead of national trends. In 1914, on learning that his ministry was going to order all the provinces to follow the lead of the people of Qingdao in Shandong province, who had planted trees to commemorate National Day, he immediately wrote to his brother, instructing him to have Nantong's schools start planting trees to observe their school anniversary days.[92] At the same time, Zhang Jian used his influence to recommend certain local practices to the central government. During the early stage of the local self-government reform, when the Interior Ministry was considering a nationwide land survey, Zhang immediately sent the regulations and results of the Nantong Survey Bureau to Beijing as a model. The Interior Ministry's ultimate adoption of that model allowed Zhang to credit Nantong with initiating land surveying in the nation.[93] In 1912, when Zhang was being considered for a cabinet position in Yuan's government, he wrote to Yuan to suggest that he was most suited for posts related to salt production and trade, water conservation, and the textile industry because of his local experience. He added that in all these areas Nantong could serve as an example for other provinces.[94]

Zhang Jian's very visibility and promotion of Nantong at the highest levels led to an ironic event in 1914 that, perhaps more than anything else, started the model campaign. In mid-June 1914, Yuan Shikai asked the State Council to investigate the functions of local self-government institutions.[95] Yuan's intention was to find reasons to dismiss those institutions as part of his attempt to consolidate central power. Although Zhang Jian at the time seems to have naively regarded Yuan's request as a sign of his interest in local self-government, both Zhang and Xiong Xiling recognized the importance of providing the kind of material that would convince Yuan to value the practice. Not surprisingly, the State Council selected Nantong as an ideal site to make such a case. It instructed the Jiangsu governor to collect information on Nantong's achievements for Yuan's consideration and for distribution to every county in China.

Zhang Jian immediately took control of the project. The result was *Achievements of Nantong Local Self-government in the Last Nineteen Years* (*Nantong difang zizhi shijiunian zhi chengji*), a book produced under Zhang's close supervision by the Hanmolin Publishing House. Unfortunately, by the time it was printed, in late 1915, Yuan had dismissed local self-government institutions, Xiong's cabinet had collapsed, and Zhang Jian had returned to Nantong. As a consequence, the more than one thousand copies of the book that had been destined for all the counties in China sat unsold in Hanmolin's warehouse.

This book not only failed in its immediate mission to rescue local self-government nationwide, but also fell victim to its own cause. It did, however, mark a turning point in the construction of the Nantong model. To be sure, there is not a clear-cut date or a single event that marks the starting point of the model campaign. The Nantong elites neither controlled the political situation outside the county nor were always conscious of where their actions were leading. Just as the elites' actions were shaped by the unfolding events, so was the process of the model making. Some events, however, did affect the process more than others. The writing of the *Achievements*, the causes behind its production, and its fate of collecting dust say much about the unpredictable political atmosphere at the time the Nantong model began to emerge.

If 1903 was a turning point in Zhang Jian's political life, 1914 was no less so. Seeing his ambition as a statesman, his hopes for a centralized state under Yuan Shikai, and his desires for the further growth of local self-government evaporating into thin air, Zhang was consumed by disillusionment and frustration. His writings during this period revealed his gray mood, in which he saw the world full of travails and human affairs like bubbles vanishing without a trace.[96] His despair, however, was only temporary; Zhang's perseverance did not allow him to surrender to adversity. More important, Nantong had much to offer, as the *Achievements* illustrated. The unsold copies of the book testified to one closed door—the officially sanctioned local self-government—but opened another by providing incentives for local elites to move forward. The book was produced because the State Council had singled out Nantong as an example. It represented an outside, official recognition of Nantong. Moreover, that recognition was not based upon any single individual project but on the county's entire practice. Indeed, the writing of this project gave the local elites an opportunity to review and present an overall picture of their effort. I will have more to say about the contents of the book in Chapter Three, but for now what needs to be emphasized is that the book for the first time established a conceptual framework to view and define Nantong's success. It took 1895 as the starting point of local development and covered the subsequent years under four sections: industry, education, philanthropy, and local self-government. In the following decade, this became a standard narrative of the new Nantong.

Thus by 1914 Nantong had simply come too far in terms of elite power building, project initiatives, and the community's self-perception to give up self-government. Although central support for local self-government was no longer available, Zhang Jian decided not only to continue but to accelerate the practice. This time, local self-government was presented as a means and end in itself—solely to meet local needs instead of serving the higher purpose of strengthening the central government. Village-ism was reinterpreted to mark this shift as Zhang Jian came to consider local self-government the only cause left that was worth pursuing. "I should now concentrate on Village-ism and make progress [in accomplishing it]," he confided to one of his close friends in 1916.[97] Zhang put greater emphasis on initiative, resources, and interests at the local level and claimed that "all of the programs in Nantong are carried out by initiative instead of the local elites assuming a passive position."[98] He criticized both government and society—"Government is so stubborn and society is so corrupt"—and stressed that Village-ism was "the fundamental solution."[99] In the following years, Zhang would push these points further, to state that the true spirit of Village-ism did not even need outside help; he called this "pure self-government" (*chuncui zhi zizhi*),[100] a term that revealed in Zhang Jian a growing disengagement with the central government and an expanding commitment to local interests.

Investigative Tourism

Not by coincidence it was around 1914 that Zhang Jian began to consider how Nantong could be a leading force in national development.[101] Accordingly, he and the other new elites, for the first time thinking in terms of building a "model city" (*mofanshi*), started a series of projects geared to polishing up the city's appearance and providing entertainment facilities to attract visitors.[102] These projects turned an emerging trend into a full-fledged campaign. The trend was a tourism phenomenon called *canguan*, meaning visit, and *kaocha*, meaning on-the-spot investigation. These investigative tours were responsible for introducing

Nantong to outsiders. Though the casual word canguan was commonly used for domestic and regular tours and the more serious term kaocha for overseas or official visits and inspection, the domestic visits referred to here were more of the kaocha kind—investigative and learning tours. Such tours were not limited to Nantong. As mentioned above, a rapid growth of things new and a demand for information and experience characterized the late Qing and early Republican period. As a result, canguan became an institutionalized instrument widely employed for information exchange, since personal face-to-face communication and on-the-spot investigation were still considered most effective. The overall improvement in transportation made all this feasible.

Take education as an example. According to a 1916 report of the Jiangsu Provincial Educational Bureau, both kaocha and canguan were mandatory tasks of the bureau and its subordinate county offices. In the section on provincial education, kaocha was listed as one of the eight agendas. Evidently, the report deemed domestic canguan too common and thus too well known a matter in the provincial educational bureau to be even worth documenting, because it spoke only of overseas kaocha. The bureau sponsored three such trips in 1913 alone.[103]

County education was a different matter. In this section of the report, canguan was one of the six tasks. Understandably, county educational bureaus lacked the resources to organize trips abroad and had to settle for domestic tours. Canguan was thus quite popular at this level. According to the report, the first order of business for canguan was to explore a standard educational reform program for all the scattered and arbitrarily administered primary schools in Jiangsu. Such investigations started before 1911 among village schools and gradually expanded to the county level and beyond. The report indicated that in 1912 the provincial educational bureau organized a province-wide tour for a group of school principals from an area where schools were in crisis. The tour was said to have significantly helped the area improve its educational record. As a result, "Visitors are now dispatched one after another and there is no sign [that they are] slowing down."[104] Regulations were set up for such canguan, one of which was that visitors must embark on the mission as an organized delegation (*canguan tuan*).[105] Conditions such as this were probably intended to ensure the host organization of the legitimacy of visitors and to make the touring a controlled process.

What happened in Nantong confirmed that canguan were a commonly used means of information exchange and learning. It was not limited to administrators and experts either. Some of the professional schools in Nantong required their seniors to take investigative tours of factories, companies, schools, and districts that were relevant to their majors.[106] Nor were canguan limited to the field of education. Nantong sent people as far away as Shandong to learn certain industrial and craft skills.[107] All this visiting demonstrated the increasing traffic in investigative and learning tours in general.

Nantong's reputation, however, was built by visits to the city, not by the visits of its representatives to other places. From about 1914 on, if not earlier, Nantong gradually became a popular site for such investigative tours, mainly because of its success in industry and education. Even overseas Chinese came to visit Nantong's factories.[108] The attraction of Nantong's schools is even better documented. In the 1916 report of the Jiangsu Provincial Educational Bureau, the Nantong Museum was listed as the only such institution in the province in the social education category, and the city was designated as a must-see for visitors because of its "convenient transportation and advanced educational system."[109]

The schools in Jiangsu responded, and the visitors came. In 1916, for instance, a normal school in the Suzhou area sent a graduate class of twenty-three on a week-long canguan mission to Nantong and Shanghai. Led by two faculty members, the group spent four days in Nantong, visiting more than a dozen institutions. The report on the mission concluded that Nantong's schools were the best in Jiangsu: "No wonder all the counties [in Jiangsu] came to visit Nantong for educational affairs!"[110] The increasing fame of Nantong's educational system seems to have overshadowed even that of Shanghai. Though the Suzhou group passed through Shanghai twice on their round-trip to Nantong, and the schools there were clearly of interest to at least some members, in the end it was able to find the time and money to visit only one Shanghai school.[111]

Outside attention, of course, was duly noticed by the local elites. In one of his speeches at the Normal School Alumni Association in 1916, Zhang Jian pointed out that visitors from provinces far and near were all impressed by Nantong's school system, and that the Jiangsu provincial inspector had said that Nantong could be the model for the whole nation in education. Evidently, they all attributed this achievement to the normal school. "Upon hearing their praise," Zhang Jian said, "how could I not be overjoyed?"[112] This speech reveals several points relating to the model-making process. First, Jiangsu provincial officials were among the promoters of Nantong. This official endorsement was evident in the 1916 report of the provincial educational bureau and in the response of other schools mentioned above. Second, education in Nantong, together with industry, was one of the first things to catch outside attention, and the normal school was perceived as representative of local schools. Moreover, Nantong's reputation began to go beyond Jiangsu. Finally, whereas Zhang Jian would later take the model label for granted, at this early stage of Nantong's prominence, he was by his own admission a bit overwhelmed by outside recognition.

Growing Fame

Nantong's reputation, still young and tenuous, had nevertheless begun to enter the national dialogue as something that held great promise. From this point on, the interactive dynamic of supply and demand between visitors and hosts helped shape Nantong's growing fame and gave the story a life of its own. On the one hand, the elites strove to build upon Nantong's appeal and present the place as a rare example of progress. On the other hand, the visitors' need for novelty and their search for a better China stimulated the hosts to take the canguan business seriously—to refine their tour-guide skills and to show off. Moreover, in addition to official tours, which were routinely reported, some of the visitors were professional journalists and writers who recorded and spread their experiences in Nantong. The full-fledged model that was so celebrated later resulted from this interaction between the hosts and visitors.

The local elites' effort was evident in the presentation of Nantong in both rhetoric and practice. One notable rhetorical change after 1915 was that the word model was more and more frequently applied to individual projects. As a result, "model" became the hallmark for all that happened in Nantong. In his introduction to a 1916 report on the newly built meteorological observatory in the Langshan area, Zhang Jian marveled at yet another accomplishment under his leadership. In a teasing tone, he wrote that though his Village-ism might be laughable, the experiment of a model was nevertheless satisfying.[113] Here the term model referred not only to the observatory itself, but also to the broad practice in Nantong, as indicated by the mention of Village-ism. Indeed, "model" crept in everywhere. After the prefectural jail in the old downtown of the city underwent a reform to include workshops for criminals, it was renamed Model Jail.[114] The main street of the new downtown was named Model Road (Mofan Lu). When, in 1915, Zhang Jian started to develop the traditional pilgrimage site of Langshan as part of a large plan to re-landscape Nantong, he sought to renovate the temples in a way that would make them a model for temples elsewhere.[115] All these projects termed or intended as models were located in the centers of local traffic.

From presenting these individual projects as models to spreading the notion of the whole county as a model was only a short leap. Thus the application of the term model to the whole of Nantong represented another shift in the model-making process. What it conveyed was no longer the process of implementing a reform program, but rather the image of an already successfully reformed and distinctly advanced community; it highlighted the anticipated results instead of the ongoing process. Also during this period, in his writings for local and Shanghai newspapers, Zhang Jian increasingly made a point of mentioning how domestic and foreign visitors had all praised Nantong as an advanced example for local self-government in China.[116]

But the process was in fact still ongoing. Zhang Jian later recalled the road Nantong had traveled during those years, and said that once Nantong began to gain a reputation, substance had to follow.[117] In other words, it was the perception of Nantong that was acted upon. Paralleling the model rhetoric and the increased outside attention, local elites accelerated programs of change by shifting the emphasis of the previous decade. If education and industry were the main themes of the past, concerns over Nantong's visual and scenic appeal, entertainment, and recreational facilities now moved to the front. Charitable and other projects targeted at social reform and welfare also became more important. Institutions such as the prostitute reform bureau, the beggars' home, the old people's home, and the dumb and blind school were established to clean up the streets, to help those in need, and to create the picture of a healthy, caring, and ideal community. By 1917, the ambitious project initiated only a couple of years before to turn the county seat into a "model city" had brought five parks equipped with a tennis court and a swimming pool and a new downtown complete with electric street lights. The next year, plans were made to establish a magnificent modern theater and a local acting school. Side by side with this effort to give Nantong's appearance a fresh makeover, new activities of a performative nature, such as sports meets, conferences, and public speeches, were employed to display, and thus magnify, Nantong's success. Other innovations, like experimental crop fields, were also introduced with visitors in mind. In 1915, Zhang Jian started a cotton-planting experiment. After giving much thought to the location of the test field, he eventually chose the Langshan area because the observatory and the temples, not to say the scenery, attracted thousands of visitors annually.[118]

Indeed, attracting visitors and effectively impressing them had become a serious matter for local elites. Zhang Jian personally invited and encouraged his friends and acquaintances to tour Nantong.[119] Because of his broad social contacts, politicians, officials, warlords, intellectuals, educators, and other friends and colleagues in high places were the first to be aware of Nantong's achievements. Those people in turn sent their subordinates or introduced their associates to Nantong.[120] Word of Nantong's progress thus spread, bringing still more admirers to the county. Some of them were kin to the "professionally curious" or "curiosity seekers" Charles Hayford describes, people who in the early 1930s crowded the dusty roads of Ding county to see the results of James Yen's rural educational movement.[121] In fact, the visitors of Ding county were the successors of those who flocked to Nantong more than a decade earlier. In both cases, they came to see the modern transformation of those particular places in rural China precisely because the local people made a concerted effort to advertise their successes.[122] As in Ding county, for instance, institutional promotion of tourism was available in Nantong. The Dada Shipping Company offered 50-percent discount fares to visiting educational delegations; later the discount was extended to the visitors' other travel-related expenses.[123] Zhang Jian, a celebrity of national stature, often met visitors in person and gave welcoming speeches, which many considered an honor.[124]

The Model at Its Height

With visitors rolling in, Nantong was constantly in the spotlight. Sources indicate that by 1918, the image of Nantong as a model county had entered the public domain, and the term was comfortably employed by various media. The Chinese press played an important role in publicizing Nantong. Celebrities' visits to Nantong, for instance, were often reported in the Shanghai newspapers.[125] Foreigners also joined in promoting Nantong, above all Frederick Sites, whose 1918 article was quoted earlier. That article perhaps had an impact on the foreign press and readers. For example, it may well have inspired the Shanghai-based English-language newspaper *Millard's Review* to include Zhang Jian in its "Who's Who in China" the following year as the "greatest industrial leader" in China, who had succeeded in "transforming his wretched birthplace into a modern industrial town."[126] The recognition of both the foreign and the Chinese press gave the Nantong story powerful exposure and legitimated Zhang Jian's claim that "investigators from the central state and provinces and Chinese and foreign visitors have all considered Nantong a model county."[127] The model had arrived.

No longer do we find the Zhang Jian of 1916 who was a bit uneasy about public praise; the rhetorical image of Nantong the model was now transformed into and comfortably accepted as reality. Around 1918, Nantong's reputation entered its heyday. Several trends emerged or intensified. One was the broad use and rapid diffusion of Nantong's reputation in the public domain through political, educational, journalistic, commercial, and other channels. It was summoned up, for instance, at celebratory occasions, in welcoming visitors, in persuading outside investors, and in applying for government funding.[128] Sometimes the model label did not directly appear, but the basic idea did.[129] The term model county frequently appeared in Nantong's newspapers and other publications, often in connection with the activities of tourists.[130] Stories about "model Nantong" were also written in locally produced school textbooks.[131] The business community cashed in as well. Merchants capitalized on Nantong's reputation and made a special point of their addresses on Mofan Road in advertising their trades, giving the impression that doing business with them assured quality and profits.[132]

This broad publicity intensified an existing trend: the increase of tourists. Though statistics are not available, there is no doubt that Nantong was gaining more admirers. A group of about forty elite scientists and educators that came in 1922 for the Seventh Annual Conference of the Science Society of China drew the most attention. More women were now joining the crowds of visitors, mainly professional educators who were attracted by women's education in Nantong. In 1920, proposals were made to build a women's guest house near the women's normal school as part of the preparation for a major convention in 1922.[133] The number of visitors from Japan, America, Germany, and other countries also grew. They became aware of Nantong through personal contacts, the press, and word of mouth. At the time, a number of experts of various nationalities worked in Nantong as teachers and engineers, and the local schools also sent their top students to study overseas. Those foreigners and Chinese formed a bridge between Nantong and the outside world. After meeting with Zhang Jian in 1918, for example, a visiting Japanese aristocrat was said not only to have been convinced that Japan's China policy should be more friendly, but also to have promised to send more of his countrymen to visit Nantong.[134] The high point came in 1920, when John Dewey made a stop in Nantong on his lecture tour. Anticipating more tourists from abroad, the local elites immediately made plans to build a hotel exclusively to serve them.[135]

With the increase of visitors, especially celebrity visitors, tourism itself became a matter of status. Although all tourists were certainly welcome, not all of them were treated in the same way. Some came on their own simply because they wanted to learn something; others were invited VIPs who had something to offer. Some came with references from Zhang Jian's friends and colleagues, and others *were* his friends and colleagues. The different attention accorded to visitors was of social significance. Zhang Jian and other prominent local elites selectively accompanied certain guests on their tours and held poetry parties and banquets for them, thereby establishing a clear hierarchy. To be linked with Nantong and Zhang Jian had become a political resource for many, a symbol that one belonged to China's progressive, successful, and powerful elite. As a result, some people came to the city merely to satisfy their own ego and vanity. This situation was especially evident after 1919, when the opera master Mei Lanfang performed in Nantong and received a high-profile welcome. That brought other performers to Nantong, not a few of whom sought fame offstage as well. They used Mei Lanfang's treatment as a precedent and tried to obtain Zhang Jian's poems and calligraphy.[136] They came to be seen; the visitors became the visited.

Show Time

Zhang Jian did not mind others' pursuit of fame, so long as Nantong was the stage and he was at the center. Indeed, he encouraged such pursuits because they satisfied his own growing vanity and heightened Nantong's reputation.[137] Zhang also understood that unless Nantong continued to reinvent itself, outsiders would stop paying attention to it. As early as 1918, the beginning of Nantong's heyday, he already planned to hold a large convention in 1922. Evidently, he first "leaked" this news in the interview with Sites, who said as much in the conclusion of his article:

Three years hence it is just possible that an invitation may reach you from . . . Chang Chien [Zhang Jian], requesting your presence at a Convention in Nantung Chow [Tongzhou]. At that time he hopes to bring together the real leaders of China from all parts of the Republic, as well as visitors from other parts of the world. He hopes to show his fellow countrymen what can be accomplished by any sincere and able leader in his own community, when he is actuated constantly and consistently by humanitarian and patriotic motives.[138]

In other words, the event was meant to showcase the Nantong model for a national and international audience. Nearly seventy years old, Zhang Jian planned to conclude his lifetime contribution with this grand event and then turn the torch over to his son, Zhang Xiaoruo.[139]

Political developments in the next three years were to highlight the significance of the intended convention. With the renewed conflict between military factions and the outbreak of war in 1920, a national wave to promote the idea of local people governing local affairs, which some called "feudalism," was on the rise.[140] This trend was reflected in such popular slogans as "Jiangsu people governing Jiangsu" ("*Suren zhisu*") and "Zhejiang people governing Zhejiang" ("*Zheren zhizhe*"). Local self-government once again became a central public focus. In 1920, Zhang Jian and other prominent Jiangsu elites formed the Jiangsu Society (Sushe) to put into practice the idea of "Jiangsu people governing Jiangsu." The society, with 145 delegates from all sixty-four counties, held its inaugural meeting in Nantong and elected Zhang Jian as its president. The delegates believed that the local self-government movement needed the united force of all counties in Jiangsu to strengthen it, and that the Jiangsu Society would serve this purpose. Its more specific goals were to protect regional stability and development. In a sense, Zhang Jian wanted to extend what Nantong had accomplished to the entire province through the Jiangsu Society. In the meantime, local self-government associations were reestablished in various counties; the one in Nantong was headed by Zhang Jian's son, Xiaoruo.[141]

This new wave of local self-government not only reaffirmed the Nantong model, but also provided Zhang Jian with a timely framework for the anticipated convention: the celebration of the twenty-fifth anniversary of the local self-government movement in Nantong. In 1921, in a letter to the Beijing government regarding the plans for the convention, Zhang Jian stated that the 1922 event would last "only" three months because of limited funds. He invited the government to send its officials to "give instructions."[142] Invitations were to be extended to various provinces, counties, and companies in China, and also to at least six foreign countries. Zhang Jian intended to use this opportunity to "report" to both the "government" and "society" what he had accomplished in terms of local self-government, and to have the national and international community evaluate the Nantong model so that a public judgment could be made "whether it is truly excellent."[143] In the meantime, other provinces and countries were invited to bring their own products to exhibit. In a sense, Zhang considered the convention an international fair of local self-government, but thought that making such a claim would risk his being criticized as arrogant.[144]

The convention had another, and probably even more important, purpose: to attract potential investors for the various enterprises in Nantong, a task that had grown more urgent during the planning process. A shortage of capital was an outstanding and ongoing problem in China's early industrial effort. Zhang Jian's own experience testified to that. Looking for investors and creditors and managing debts marked much of his career. The model campaign was in essence a drive to bring capital to Nantong to promote economic growth on which both elite power and Nantong's name were based. Unlike the treaty port cities, where the seemingly endless business possibilities naturally lured investors, a traditionally isolated rural area like Nantong needed an extra push to win their confidence.

The early attempts at development laid a certain financial foundation for Nantong. But the broad range of projects initiated, not all sound investments, thinned the accumulation of capital, and Zhang Jian drained off most of the profits of the No. 1 mill to finance other projects. He often did so without obtaining the consent of the majority stockholders. By 1908, he had invested the No. 1 mill's profits in eighteen other enterprises, most of which were losing money.[145] The stockholders, deeply concerned, had already moved by then to put a stop to the practice. In 1907, they decided to separate the No. 1 mill from all the other enterprises by forming the Tonghai Industrial Company (Tonghai shiye gongsi) to take charge of them, including their debts, and to release the No. 1 mill from being their life support. The move was meant to limit Zhang Jian's power in appropriating Dasheng's funds and to protect the mill, and therefore the interest of its stockholders. But political power, once formed, is not so easily overcome. Zhang Jian and his brother became the top officials of the Tonghai Industrial Company and at the same time they continued to control the No. 1 mill. Dasheng's majority stockholders finally yielded, apparently reassured by the promise that they would get their dividends and that the Zhang brothers would keep things under control. In the end, nothing changed; a boundary between the company and the mill was never truly established.[146] The various enterprises in Nantong were later collectively referred to as the Dasheng System Enterprises (Dasheng xitong qiye),[147] but the name is deceptive in suggesting that there was some centralized institution in charge of their operation. There was not; the decision-making power rested in the hands of a few individuals. Therefore, the Zhang brothers continued through the years to take money from where it was available, which meant the No. 1 mill, and to spend it on whatever projects they deemed important, which were often too many.[148]

The demand for funds rose considerably in the 1910s as wartime prosperity encouraged overgrowth. Zhang's reputation and that of Nantong did appeal to outside investors, which helped raise some funds.[149] But new projects were inaugurated faster than the growth of capital, something that Zhang himself recognized.[150] In 1921, the No. 1 mill, after functioning for two decades as the "cash cow" that the Zhang brothers and some of their associates milked for public projects and private use, started to decline. Financial pressures had become so overwhelming in the midst of the preparation for the convention that many programs were beginning to die because of underbudgeting. Although Zhang Jian in 1919 still boasted that Nantong's enterprises involved no foreign capital,[151] this tattered national pride faded quickly in the cruel reality when he actively pursued foreign loans in the next two years. The planned convention thus became a perfect opportunity for the elites to attract outside capital.

A series of steps were taken, and taken seriously, to ensure that the convention would be a great success. Some steps were to meet practical needs, and others were purely for public relations purposes. Students were exhorted to demonstrate their competitive spirit in the athletic games that were going to be performed for the conference participants.[152] A souvenir book, with more than one hundred pictures and captions in both English and Chinese, was published.[153] Scenic appeal became all the more important. Zhang Jian in 1920 instructed the county magistrate to initiate a wide tree-planting project in the hill and river areas to benefit agriculture and enhance the scenery; he personally pledged to cover all the cost for labor and saplings.[154] Plans were put in

train for new hotels, auditoriums, exhibition halls, a large sports stadium, additional roads, and other conference facilities. Items such as
the products of the Dasheng mills and students' work were to be put on
display. On-site inspection tours of highways and waterworks were to
be arranged. To coordinate and oversee all the conference-related activities, a county-wide planning committee headed by Zhang Xiaoruo was
set up in 1921, consisting of several subcommittees in charge of industry, education, and other sectors.[155]

Tourism was also to be closely supervised. Though visitors contributed importantly to Nantong's reputation, they could also cause
problems, coming as they did from mixed backgrounds and with various motives. In 1919, several interns from two companies outside
Jiangsu who were studying at the textile college, and so had access to
the No. 1 mill, were rumored to be secretly recruiting managers and
workers for their own companies from the experienced Dasheng employees, luring them with promises of higher pay and better treatment.
Zhang Jian, infuriated, expelled the interns and wrote an open letter to
condemn such conduct.[156] This incident probably raised a red flag. To
avoid a repetition and to ensure success for the convention, Zhang Jian
notified the county magistrate and the regional military commander in
1920 that he had laid down some rules to manage tourism and requested the two officials to see that they were carried out. He emphasized the importance of having a special bureau in charge of visitors to
ensure a uniform policy. That bureau would distribute passes to legitimate visitors—those who came with acceptable references—allowing
them to enter any areas open to them. Rules for visitors were printed on
the passes. Private or official references made no difference; anyone
without a pass would be turned away.[157] In short, touring—who could
come, what they would see, and how they were going to perceive Nantong—was to be tightly managed.

The creation of a traffic police training center in 1919 was another
part of the preparations for the convention. It was rare for a provincial
town like Nantong to have a specialized traffic police force, let alone
one whose members were required to study the English language. To
be sure, since many of the foreigners were likely to have at least a smat-
tering of this, the most popular foreign language, English speakers
were needed in Nantong.[158] But the main reason for requiring the policemen to learn English was to boost Nantong's reputation among the
visitors. In his speech at the opening ceremony of the police training
center, Zhang Jian said: "If foreign visitors have questions and our po-

licemen do not understand them, it will shame the Nantong local self-government movement." He also made an interesting point about why the Japanese language was not required, though Japanese were prominent among the tourists: "You [the policemen] can speak to the Japanese in English as well, because they will know English; if they do not, that is their shame, not ours."[159] What Zhang expressed here is both his expectations of Japan as a modern nation and his subtle resentment of Japan as a competitor.

Behind all these public relations tactics was a heightened sense of "model consciousness" among the local elites. Zhang Jian had become extremely sensitive to any publicity the town might receive and considered impressing the visitors a priority. In addition to institutional mechanisms such as the visitor passes that were meant to ensure Nantong a friendly audience and positive exposure, Zhang Jian personally instructed his staff to consider dealing with visitors an essential part of their job. Once when he saw some trees at a land reclamation project and asked the company manager their age and number, the man did not have an answer. Zhang lectured the manager on the importance of learning seemingly insignificant pieces of information, because when visitors asked these questions, he had to give them appropriate answers. On another occasion, on finding out that one of the office managers of a land reclamation company had no idea of the size of his office building, Zhang scolded: "Visitors will ask questions like these and you need to be prepared."[160] In 1920, Zhang wrote to several ministries in Beijing regarding funding for Nantong's prison and hinted that a backward prison system would tarnish the county's reputation in the eyes of the public.[161] By the same token, when negative information about Nantong came out, Zhang often acted quickly to control the damage. In 1921, when visitors criticized some aspects of Nantong, he immediately wrote an open apology addressed to the "Nantong visitors," in which he promised that their complaints would be attended to.[162]

Unfortunately for Zhang, because of a combination of factors, the intended celebration, budgeted at 300,000 yuan, never took place. In fact, Nantong's heyday was short-lived, from about 1918 to 1921. Thereafter, the Dasheng cotton mills were heavily in debt, and local development steadily declined. The extensive preparations for the celebration turned out to be a swan song.

Myth Making

Each of the three phases in Nantong's development, the prelude to change (1894–1903), the systematic transformation (1903–1914), and the model campaign (1914–1921), was accompanied by the creation of an image of Zhang Jian as a hero with an uncanny sense of planning for the future and an iron will to carry his plans through. Zhang's life provided ready material for myth making. As soon as he obtained the jinshi degree, stories about his unusual early talent began to surface; some believed that he was a literary star falling from heaven (*wenqu xing*).[163] Perhaps the fact that a peasant's son was able to gain the most prestigious degree of the land demanded such a myth to help comprehend it. Although it is not clear who was behind the creation of stories about his scholarly success, Zhang Jian himself invented the myths about his experience in local affairs. Those myths portrayed Zhang as a man with a consistent vision and unwavering commitment to local self-government from the very beginning of his return to Nantong. To be sure, Zhang Jian did not come up with those stories in a day; they evolved together with the transformation of the community. Zhang used them to help interpret the transformation from one phase to another. They were an integral part of the Nantong experience.

The change from the piecemeal improvement before 1903 to systematic planning afterward represented a major shift in local development that required a new vision. To shape this change, Zhang Jian created two myths to reinterpret the past, giving the impression that he had an overall plan in mind as early as 1895, so that the current shift would be viewed as a natural growth from the previous effort.

First, Zhang Jian reinvented the reason for his resignation from the Hanlin Academy. According to his explanation after 1903, he was simply discouraged by government affairs and uninterested in officialdom, so he decided to "engage in village affairs [*cunluo shi*] instead."[164] To be sure, Zhang Jian's disappointment with the Qing government did contribute to his departure from Beijing, but it was also because of his father's death in 1895, which obligated him to take a customary mourning leave. Upon his return to Nantong, he bounced around different projects. One involved six months of work in erosion control, and another—building the Tongzhou militia at Zhang Zhidong's request—took several more months.[165] His Village-ism was hardly detectable at that time.

To emphasize the importance of both industry and education for

self-government, Zhang Jian later employed a rhetorical device to interpret the origins of the No. 1 mill. As noted earlier, he was commissioned by Zhang Zhidong to build the factory to compete with Japan,
but Zhang later stated that he did so to finance the normal school. He
started this myth in his speech at the school's opening ceremony in
1903. There he claimed to have long wanted to set up a normal school to
promote education, but "with no hope [of getting funding] . . . , I had
the idea of starting industry [the No. 1 mill]."[166] The students were
about to become very familiar with the story, because Zhang Jian tire-
lessly reiterated it. On another occasion, he stated that ever since the
Sino-Japanese War of 1894, he had been determined to create a normal
school to strengthen China from the base, but, "being a poor scholar,
where could I get [the] money?" "Industrial undertakings were the only
way to make profits," he continued, "that was why I built factories."[167]
To be sure, the No. 1 mill did lay a financial foundation for the development of schools and many other projects in later years, but it was not
at all clear in the 1890s what the new enterprise would lead to. Zhang
Jian almost gave up on it during the most difficult years of building the
factory, and it was not part of a large local agenda at the time.

These two myths—the reason for his resignation and the origins of
the No. 1 mill—were repeated in many of the public speeches Zhang
delivered, to local as well as to outside audiences. What messages did
he intend to convey? One point Zhang stressed was that much as he
valued industry, he valued education even more. Several factors contributed to this presentation. One was Zhang Jian's trip to Japan, which
highlighted for him the importance of modern education. Another was
the impetus for educational reform around 1905, when the civil examination system was abolished. In criticizing the traditional system, the
functions of the new schools in strengthening the country and in training a good citizenry were greatly emphasized. Still another was
Zhang's personal beliefs and proclivities. A traditional scholar at heart,
he was often compelled by his own ideological conviction to justify his
industrial ventures with scholarly motives and thus give them a noble
touch. He had little regard for traditional Chinese merchants and considered merchants and industrialists with scholarly origins somehow
morally superior to those without such a background.[168] Most important of all, however, is that Zhang Jian wanted to convince people that
he had a plan for Nantong's development as early as 1895.[169]

If Zhang Jian did not have a consistent reform agenda before 1903,
he worked hard at developing one thereafter. Emphasizing past success

heightened his reputation and made it easier to mobilize people to implement his plans. To prove himself was a constant concern for Zhang, perhaps because of his non-elite family background and outsider status. This sense of inferiority was not altered by his advanced academic degree and prominent career; rather, it was reinforced by the difficulties he encountered in building the No. 1 mill. Zhang Jian was gravely humiliated by the distrust of the community.[170] He never forgot that experience, nor did he forgive those who disdained him.[171] He later turned the humiliation into an inexhaustible source of political capital by presenting an image of personal sacrifices and costly struggle for the well-being of the community—a familiar Confucian moral stance he claimed to have been behind all of his accomplishments. Even when his position in Nantong was considerably improved after 1898, he never stopped promoting himself and proclaiming his honesty and devotion to the interests of the community. In 1920, when he tried to encourage people to invest in local bonds, he said that such investment would make everyone rich: "You can trust me since I have never lied to you."[172] If "myth is an articulation of symbols,"[173] the myths Zhang Jian created about the causes of his resignation and the Dasheng project portrayed him as a moral, successful leader who symbolized a better Nantong in the past, and, therefore, in the future as well.

Myth is also an instrument to build a consensus for community reconstruction.[174] In the case of Nantong, the invention of the past and the rhetoric employed were part of the creation of a new reality for which Zhang Jian needed justification and support. One of the eminent features of political propaganda is looking backward to serve new objectives; in doing so, the past becomes raw material that can be shaped in ways useful to the present. The stories Zhang Jian created helped transform the history of piecemeal improvement into the history of a structurally developing Nantong. The rhetorical device blurred the distinction between past and present, and provided the community with a new purpose.

This myth creation continued with the rise of Nantong's reputation. In 1918, at a luncheon with Sites, Zhang Jian confided another of his "secrets of success"—that he "had pledged himself twenty years ago to initiate each year two new construction projects." Sites was fully convinced that this was indeed the case, and concluded that Zhang Jian "has kept his promise and has done even more during certain years."[175] However, "twenty years ago" in 1898, the No. 1 mill had just started production, and such ambitious construction plans were nowhere to be found. Considering the trouble Zhang Jian encountered at the time, we have reason to doubt the existence of such a pledge, but in 1918 this myth helped to highlight the model experience as a result of a consistent practice under the leadership of one man, who was not only remarkably farsighted but also extremely capable.

The preparations for the 1922 observation of the twenty-fifth anniversary of the local self-government were another occasion for myth making. Among other things, they provided an opportunity for Zhang Jian to invent a formal birthday for the local self-government movement. Unlike specific projects such as the No. 1 mill or the normal school, which had a definite opening date, the local self-government movement developed in a process, and its exact starting date is hard, if not impossible, to pinpoint. If one must, the year 1908, when the local self-government councils and directorates were established, is the most plausible starting point, but that would contradict Zhang Jian's portrayal of Nantong's success from as early as 1895. Thus, an earlier beginning date was needed. In the speeches he delivered over the years at the anniversary celebrations of the No. 1 mill and the normal school, Zhang Jian often mentioned the two establishments as the core of the local self-government movement, thus implying that the celebrations of the former were also meaningful for the latter. However, a line must be drawn. For one thing, the factory and the school did not start in the same year. Evidently, this presented no problem for Zhang. He simply chose the earlier date of the two undertakings, the beginning of Dasheng, to represent something that was yet to rise—local self-government in Nantong. In doing so, he fashioned a longer and more substantial new chapter for the Nantong story.

In each of these myths, Zhang Jian employed a "retrospective logic" to reflect upon his career.[176] One theme that ran through this mythic narrative was that Zhang Jian, motivated by a single, moral principle—to serve the interests of the people—was a master planner and expert practitioner of modern development. In reality, he suffered setbacks, hesitated at crossroads, and rode waves set in motion by others. When he did form his own visions, they often took a while to crystallize. But the reiteration of a consistent theme was important precisely because of the fragmentary beginning of the Nantong story. The political uncertainty of the era desperately called for clear direction and strong leadership. Zhang Jian created an image of a leader of a totally different stripe from any that China had ever seen before. Combining action and contemplation, he seemed to hold the key to modernizing China and catching up with the more advanced nations. The Nantong story thus became a moral statement, deeply tapping into the intense national longing for a farsighted and strong leader who could confidently steer China into the open sea as an equal to the early arrivals there. Because the narrative resonated with the hopes of the people, it was more readily accepted than questioned.

The production of the Nantong model was based on both formal and informal channels within and without the community. Official sponsorship, media propaganda, visitors' comments, business advertisements, and, most of all, the local elites' self-promotion all played a part in shaping that image. But the single most important contributing factor was perhaps the fragmentation of the Republican government, which not only failed to keep talented and ambitious politicians like Zhang Jian at the center but also created a power vacuum to allow a small rural town like Nantong to emerge as a political model. In this sense, the Nantong story was a strictly historical one—it could only appear at that specific moment in China's history.

From the historical point of view, consequently, the Nantong experience in turn tells us much about that era. Though central political authority was dissolving, social integration seemed to be rising. The combination of geographical mobility and the flow of information, reflected in tourism and the press and facilitated by new transportation and communication modes, increased the effectiveness of propaganda, making it possible for what was local to become national, and viceversa. Without this integration of the local and national political markets for products such as the Nantong model, the local elites could not have defined and advertised their county in the way they did, and what happened there would have gone unremarked and eventually faded from memory altogether.

CHAPTER 2

The Model in Space and Time

From prefecture to county; in the end of the river and the mouth of the sea.

Zhang Jian, *Complete Works*

SPACE AND TIME are both "raw material" that can be manipulated to construct political power and create an image.[1] In terms of space, visual persuasion is perhaps the most powerful of all relevant devices. Not surprisingly, the model campaign in Nantong began with a plan to transform the county seat into a "model city," where a new downtown with an array of modern institutions, Western architecture, paved roads, and public parks would serve as a window on Nantong's progress. However, spatial change in Nantong was not limited to the city; it took place on a broad scale as a result of industrialization and a deliberate effort to re-map the county according to elites' visions. The concept of time, by contrast, is rather abstract, but its transformation in Nantong was no less visible, and its effect on people's minds was equally profound. During the period under consideration, factory time and the clock began to challenge nature's rhythms, a familiar story of the early industrial age that played out in a rural surrounding where the workers were at the same time peasants. Along with the instilling of the modern concept of time, new chronological markers of significance, such as anniversaries of the No. 1 mill and the normal school, were celebrated to mark the unprecedented achievements after the late 1890s. In doing so, the linear connection between this period and the past was denied and the present was accented as a temporal representation of model Nantong.

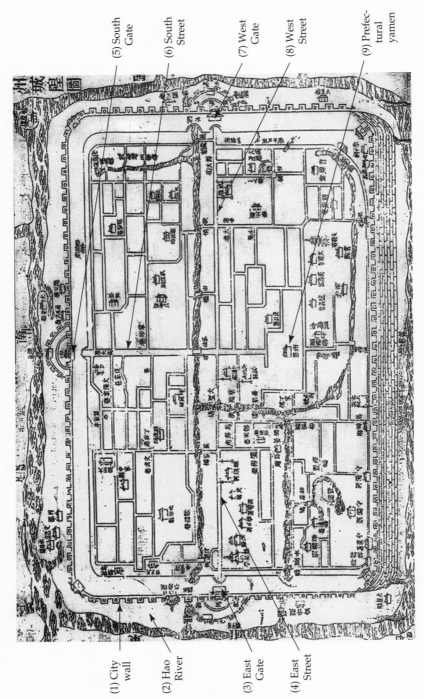

(5) South Gate

(6) South Street

(7) West Gate

(8) West Street

(9) Prefectural yamen

(1) City wall

(2) Hao River

(3) East Gate

(4) East Street

MAP 2. The city of Tongzhou before 1870 showing the city wall (1), the Hao River (2), the three gates and the main streets, and the prefectural yamen (9). Note that the map is oriented south–north. (Courtesy of the Nantong Museum)

The Reconfiguration of Space

From 1895 to 1926, the time of Zhang Jian's death, important construction projects were undertaken every year, and the county seat and its suburbs witnessed a great deal of redesign and expansion. This transformation was uncoordinated, if not haphazard, in the beginning but gradually became carefully planned, with different themes emphasized at each stage.

Before 1914, local initiatives focused on industry and education. The emphasis was on providing a foundation for further development, not on decorating a particular place for show. Projects were sited by practical considerations of convenience and feasibility. For instance, the No. 1 mill was located in Tangzha, five miles northwest of the city near the Tong-Yang Canal, a spot chosen for its easy access to both waterways and roads. The port of Tiansheng, between the city and Tangzha, was built thereafter, and roads were constructed to connect Tangzha and the port. All these were necessary for the initial industrial takeoff. The normal school, like many new schools in the late Qing, was built on a ruined temple outside the city wall, just to the southeast of the city, for no other reason than that the temple happened to be there. The open space outside the South Gate made it an ideal area of development. The Hanmolin Publishing House and the museum were built there to support the rapidly growing number of schools.[2]

But at this point there was no master plan. It was only around 1914, when outsiders began to notice Nantong, that Zhang Jian initiated a plan to build a model city.[3] The emphasis was now shifted to entertainment facilities and scenery. The plan had two main goals. One was to revamp the old county seat and to define a new downtown; the other was to expand the county seat by developing its suburbs. This plan represented the first conscious effort by elites at spatial reconfiguration on a large scale, a process that went on for more than a decade.

The New Downtown

The centerpiece of Zhang Jian's ambitious city renewal plan was the county seat, known as Nantong Cheng (city; hereafter referred to as the county seat, Nantong city, or the city). Before 1894, the county seat, about two square kilometers near the Yangzi River, was typical of many provincial towns in China (Map 2).[4] It was surrounded by a wall, which in turn was encircled by the Hao River. There were three gates, each with a drawbridge. A popular folk rhyme revealed the social contours of the city: "Rich West Gate; poor East Gate; begging South Gate."[5] The West Gate had the advantage of being near the Tong-Yang Canal and ports along the Yangzi River, where the homes of officials and wealthy merchants and their stores and shops were located; around the East Gate were stands selling handicrafts and farm products; outside the South Gate were temples, cemeteries, and fields, the haunt of the homeless. The prefectural yamen was located in the northern center of the city, at the intersection of South Street, which led to the South Gate, and the street that stretched between the East and West gates. Next to the yamen stood a few big buildings, a Confucian temple, and some shops, which together constituted the downtown area. One of the three big buildings was the office of the Langshan General Commander, the highest military officer in Nantong. Lower-ranking officials had to get out of their sedan chairs and walk when passing before the yamen of the general commander.[6] The city temple (*chenghuang miao*) on East Street and a square in front of the Confucian temple were among the public spaces where festivities on Chinese New Year and other holidays took place.[7]

Zhang Jian's plans to recast this typical provincial town emphasized scenic and entertainment facilities to accommodate the growing number of visitors, ceremonies, and other social and public activities, and to project an image of a progressive community where culture and commerce complemented each other. The old downtown, with its many cotton fabric shops and commercial contacts, remained important for the distributing of Dasheng products. Zhang Jian and other elites thus made some attempt to revitalize it, including building a clock and fire tower and two new schools there.[8] At the same time, they also renovated the city jail there.[9] Though all these were eye-catching innovations for this ancient city, the crowded conditions in the old downtown made significant new construction problematic. The main street was so narrow that salesclerks in shops on opposite sides could carry on conversations with each other.[10] Since widening the street would have meant razing many residential houses and age-old shops, a large scale makeover was impossible.

The focus was thus shifted to building a new downtown. At the time, the most promising area for the purpose was a large, open, and desolate tract outside the South Gate, which could be obtained at a low cost. Also, part of that area had already been developed with significant landmarks, such as the normal school, the museum, and the Hanmolin

Publishing House, all completed before 1910. These made a fine core for the systematic development of an educational and cultural center. A start was made in 1910, when the Zhang brothers opened a commercial school to train new businessmen to meet the growing demands of local commerce. They created a medical school in 1912 and then the Nantong Hospital the next year.[11] In 1913, Nantong's first public sports stadium was constructed; sports games at once became novel public spectacles.[12] That same year, at the initiative of Zhang Jian, another declining temple, next to the museum, was renovated and made into a multistoried library, with dozens of rooms for books and offices. In 1917, when Zhang Xiaoruo returned from his American tour and reported to his father how wealthy Westerners donated their money to building magnificent public libraries, Zhang Jian embraced the idea. As a result, the library was expanded considerably with a new building and other additions.[13] In the meantime, charitable institutions such as the first of three old people's homes and an office to assist the needy were also built in the area.[14]

Though most of these projects were located either right outside the South Gate, such as the library, or stretched out toward the east, such as the normal school, new construction works initiated after 1914, most of which were culturally and commercially oriented, began to fill in the space west of the Hao River. Outstanding among these was the construction of five public parks, which were to become the heart of the new downtown. As in other provincial Chinese towns, the county seat had only private elite gardens. Zhang Jian decided to change that. According to him, after twenty years of promoting industry and seventeen years of engaging in education, his success would be incomplete without providing parks for the community, for factories and schools all demanded hard work that should be balanced by recreation.[15] Zhang also thought about the park project in a larger context: "All the other countries have parks, and some major metropolises in America have as many as twenty splendid parks." Why, though, did Nantong, an inland town, have to be comparable to Western urban centers? Because, Zhang Jian explained, "The local self-government in our county is the model for the whole nation, and the city is a leader in the twenty-one districts of the county. It is a flaw that [the city] does not have beautiful and well-equipped parks."[16] In other words, if Nantong was to fully qualify as a model, it must have Western urban staples such as parks to accompany the new schools and factories.

And beautiful and well-equipped the new parks were.[17] On the

FIGURE 2. Children's playground in Nantong city's East Park. Source: *Nantong shiye jiaoyu cishan fengjing fu canguan zhinan*, p. 79.

Moon Festival day of 1917, the five parks, located on either side of the Hao River just to the west of the library and museum, were unveiled. Each was named according to its position relative to the river—west, east, north, south, and central—and four bridges were built to connect them. Though they shared certain landscaping features—rockeries, lawns, trees, flower gardens, halls, pavilions, and multistoried buildings—each had its own unique characteristics. The East Park was designed as a children's playground, with swings, slides, and other similar facilities; certain areas in the park were exclusively for women and children (Fig. 2). The North Park was built on eight mu of lawn that included a tennis court. In addition, there were rooms for pool tables and exercise equipment. Within the West Park were a zoo, a public exercise ground, a swimming pool complete with life jackets, and a dock where people could go boating on the river. The Central Park probably had more of a traditional and cultural flavor. It was centered around a hall originally built in the Ming dynasty that later became a site for local literary activities. In time the hall declined, and a Taoist priest occupied it to eke out a living. After much renovation and expansion, the Central Park was known for its spacious halls and exquisite pavilions, with their finely inscripted couplets. The South Park had a lily pond, and as of 1920, a new prestigious gathering-point for the elite, with the construction of the Longevity Hall (Qianling guan) in honor of Zhang Cha's seventieth birthday.

From funding and land to furnishings, Zhang Jian enlisted others' help in building the parks. While the construction was still under way, he wrote an open letter to all the districts for donations, listing trees, wall hangings, mirrors, flower vases, and curtains as ideal items for the interior decoration of the parks. At the same time, he managed to present the parks as a gift from him and his brother to the community. Needless to say, he was immensely proud of this accomplishment. To many of the spectators, the opening ceremony, purposely scheduled on the Moon Festival day and coinciding with the introduction of electric street lights, seemed almost surreal and a truly masterly intertwining of tradition and innovation. In a commemorative essay, Zhang Jian dwelt on the importance of the parks and described in full detail their landscaping, facilities, and functions. He concluded by saying that the parks would benefit everyone, and that those who worked for the comfort and happiness of the majority of the people were "men of Heaven" (*tianzhiren*). The same year, 1917, Zhang Jian composed the "Nantong Park Song" to tout the highlights—the tennis court, swimming pool, and children's playground. He could hardly contain his pride as he ended the song with a cry: "Nantong is truly superior!" In the following fall, when the debt for the park construction was paid off, and the remaining work finished, Zhang Jian announced an anniversary celebration. He invited the people from all the twenty-one districts to come and observe whether he had lived up to his promises. "I am awaiting your arrival!"

His excitement was justified. These were the first public parks in Nantong. Many of the facilities, such as the tennis courts and swimming pools, were representative of all that was Western, cosmopolitan, and progressive. For a small town to have these novelties was a sensation indeed. The parks, however, meant more; they were expected to be pedagogic tools. For Zhang Jian, a beautiful, cultured environment helped mold people's character and was thus instrumental in education. These ideas of his were reflected in some of the local campuses, where tree and flower planting was considered part of education. The parks were expected to have the same function of public instruction and were decorated accordingly. A hall in the East Park near the playground, for instance, was adorned with pictures of "female teaching" (*nüjiao*)—depictions of how to be proper women and mothers. In addition, Zhang Jian mentioned that toys such as popguns would encourage a military spirit, an idea current in the late 1910s, when military education was promoted as a way to energize China. He also pointed out that the popular exercise ground and the boating and swimming facilities would help strengthen the body and stretch the mind of the local people. At the same time, Zhang Jian used the parks to promote public service. In the South Park, a chamber called Sharing with the People (Yuzhong) was devoted to displaying the names of contributors to local education, charities, and other public projects.

The parks invoked a distinct feeling of cultural progress. Decades later, former students still recalled how the parks and other cultural establishments in the city created an atmosphere that was conducive to learning.[18] In fact, with the normal school in the east, the parks in the west, and the museum and the library in the center, the southern area along the Hao River came to be identified as a "cultural district," and the road in front of the South Gate along the Hao River was paved and named Mofan (Model) Road. The park area was further enhanced when the Nantong Club Hotel was built next to the West Park as a gathering-place for local elites and their distinguished guests. The hotel held its grand opening in 1922 and was the site of a major conference of the Chinese Science Society.[19] Zhang Jian used the hotel to host foreign visitors as well.[20]

The development of the new downtown continued to focus on commercial attractions as well as entertainment into the early 1920s. The city boundary was pushed farther west beyond the parks, where the Hao River turned to the southwest. Once used for paupers' graves, the area was now designated for the development of a business district. A new road called Taowu (Peach Terrace) formed the center, along which many new buildings were erected. In 1919, the magnificent Gengsu (Change Customs) Theater, modeled on the China Theater in Shanghai, was constructed on Taowu Road; it had 1,200 seats and a spacious parking lot. Many small shops immediately sprang up around it.[21]

Major commercial enterprises were also on the rise in the area. Three multistoried hotels, two on Mofan Road and the other across the river to the north, were built in the late 1910s. The two on Mofan Road were named Youfei (Literary Grace) and Taozhihua (Peach Flower).[22] Their advertisements indicated that their business was booming because of Nantong's growing fame, and that most of their guests were merchants, industrialists, new professionals, and admirers of Nantong. Both hotels advertised their modern buildings, rooms, and furniture, and their perfect locations, where visitors could easily reach the new landmarks and thus experience the Nantong model first-hand. Indeed, the picturesque parks and the Hao River could be viewed from their rooms. In dealing with the increased volume of visitors, these hotels became rather sophisticated. Youfei, for instance, worked with shipping companies to provide coordinated land-and-water transportation services that automatically delivered luggage to the hotel without burdening travelers. In addition, it started a chain of hotels and inns outside the city. Every possible way to attract and serve visitors seems to have been thought out. The Youfei staff, for instance, met guests at the port when they arrived and returned them when they departed.[23]

Other, mostly new, businesses were also surging along the Hao River. There were at least two photography studios, both of which claimed to have the most up-to-date Western equipment, a car rental company with Ford automobiles, a bus station, an office of Socony Oil, and a branch of a Shanghai insurance company. Bookstores, drugstores, and electrical supply shops were in evidence as well. Financial institutions also became a familiar part of the scene. The prestigious Shanghai Commercial Savings, commonly known as the Bank of Shanghai, with branches in London, New York, and Paris, as well as in major cities in China, had an office in Nantong; so did the Bank of Jiangsu. In 1920, the Zhang-controlled Huai Hai Industrial Bank was erected across the Hao River from Mofan Road. The new downtown also housed *Nantong bao* (*Nantong Times*) and other news media to record its ever-changing face. *Nantongbao*, managed by Zhang Xiaoruo, claimed to be the official voice of the new Nantong and the Zhang family. It urged those who wanted to learn the "true story" of Nantong and to enjoy Zhang Jian's writings to subscribe.[24]

With the completion of a city highway in 1920, many merchants from outside moved to Nantong and located their businesses along Taowu Road. The county construction bureau anticipated a shortage of residential and office space. As a result, multistoried apartments were constructed, and plans were made to build markets and shops there. Taowu Road was fast becoming the new business district of the city. Appropriately, in 1920, on a forty-mu plot of land at the very center of Taowu, the Nantong Chamber of Commerce, headed by Zhang Cha, erected an imposing office building. It imitated the style of its Shanghai counterpart but was grander still. Inside there were more than a hundred rooms and a lecture hall with 1,000 seats. In 1921, the short-lived Nantong Stock Market operated from the building, making Taowu

Road the most crowded spot in the city. It remained the most stately building in Nantong well into the 1950s.[25]

During this period, Zhang Jian started to construct villas and summer houses for his private use and amusement. Before 1914, he had no settled residence in the city and often lodged in the museum and other places. His first villa, named Haonan (South of the Hao River), was built next to the museum in 1914; two more villas were completed in 1915, another two were added in 1919, and yet two more were under construction in 1921. These villas, and those of Zhang Cha, were scattered throughout the city near the South Gate and in the Langshan area.[26] The ones located around the South Gate added appeal to the new downtown. Zhang Jian's first villa was equipped with more than a hundred electric lights, supplied by a small generator that exclusively served the Zhang family. In a city where the rest of the homes were lighted by candles and oil lamps, his villa quite literally lit up the night.[27] The Zhangs' villas not only provided accommodations for their dignitary guests, but also became instant tourist attractions.

With elite villas, educational and cultural institutions, entertainment and leisure facilities, and modern businesses, the new downtown expanded rapidly, while the old downtown, save for a few new buildings, remained old—it retained its traditional shops and consistently lost modern trades. Between 1919 and 1921, at least four banks moved out of the inner city to set up operations in the burgeoning southern area.[28] Other business and shops, especially those with the trappings of the new era, were all eager to be part of the new downtown, and real estate on Mofan Road became extremely valuable. In 1920, the Xincun (New Village) Photo Studio moved from a room next to the Gengsu Theater, not a bad location, to Mofan Road. It immediately used its new address in its advertisements, boasting of its new spacious studio, advanced Western equipment, and skilled technicians—as befitted a business whose address epitomized progress.[29] The women's normal school, first built in the old downtown, also relocated in the south to join the other campuses there.[30] The young downtown so boomed that two of the three hotels mentioned above underwent significant expansion only a year after their opening; Taozhihua added an entire new building, and Youfei dozens of rooms.[31] Through twenty years of unplanned and later of deliberate effort, the southern area of the city was completely transformed.

Much attention was given to providing the requisite infrastructure to make the new downtown fully functional. New roads and bridges were built, and some of the existing streets were paved and made wide enough to allow two cars to pass comfortably, a far cry from the cramped streets in the old downtown. Unlike the old city streets, mere footpaths really, the new ones had sidewalks, and from 1917 on, street-lights every thirty-three meters and traffic policemen every sixty. In 1915, the construction of a highway system began, including a highway that encircled the city, and local people soon witnessed automobiles in regular use. In 1920, a highway was built to serve the area outside the South Gate, where many of the new institutions were located, which benefited both the local people and visitors. To better connect this new center with the old business quarter, Zhang Cha in 1920 used 17,000 sil-ver yuan given him on the occasion of his seventieth birthday to build a thirteen-span, 260-foot concrete bridge, Yuelong (Leaping Dragon) Bridge, said to be the longest in the region. In 1922, the old city wall was demolished, but the three city gates were kept as historic sites. A new market was built near the South Gate as part of a larger plan to es-tablish markets at all three gates (Maps 3, 4).[32]

With changes such as these, the city began to shake off its provincial character. The spatial transformation of the downtown signified a shift of cultural values, as well as of political power. Gone was not only the prefectural yamen, but also the vision of Nantong as a provincial town confined within its ancient walls. In its place was what was thought to be a cosmopolitan community, an idea expressed as much, if less visi-bly than the new buildings and roads, by the two professionals, one lo-cal and the other foreign, who were hired to construct them.

Sun Zhixia, a native son and the main architect, was one of the finest products of the new local school system. At a time when only those who had traditional academic degrees such as *xiucai* and *jiansheng* were qualified for admittance to the normal school, Zhang Jian broke the rules for Sun because of his knowledge of mathematics and surveying, which he had acquired at a private school and from a Japanese teacher. In 1906, Sun Zhixia was among the first group to study in the newly es-tablished surveying and civil engineering department of the normal school. Upon his graduation in 1909 and on the recommendation of Zhang Jian, Sun went to Nanjing to participate in the design and con-struction of the office of the provincial consultative bureau. In the course of that work, he was sent to Japan to examine the architecture of the Japanese Diet building, after which the office building for the con-sultative bureau was supposedly modeled. In late 1909, at the age of twenty-seven, Sun completed the Nanjing project. Because the provin-

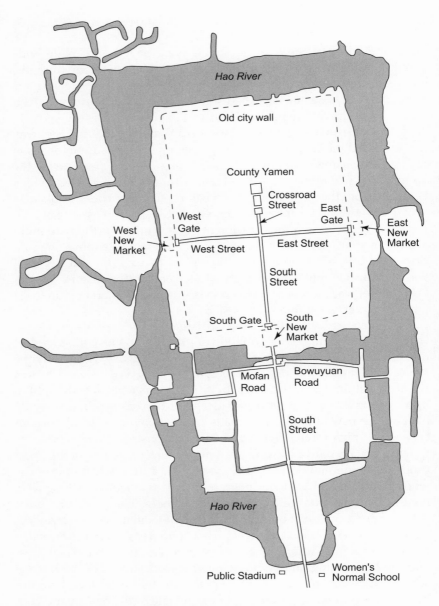

MAP 3. Nantong city in 1925. (Courtesy of the Nantong Museum)

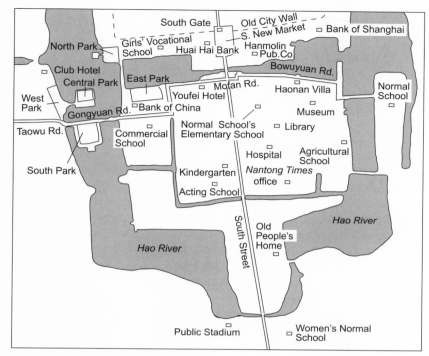

MAP 4. Southern Nantong in 1925. (Courtesy of the Nantong Museum)

cial consultative bureau, headed by Zhang Jian, was extremely influential during the constitutional movement, the success of this project brought Sun fame. He was a major player in Nantong's spatial rearrangement, credited with all the landmark works mentioned above. He also designed all of Zhang Jian's private villas.[33]

The other person noted for his contribution to the city renewal was the Dutch engineer Hendrik C. de Reike, who in 1908 came to China to join his father in fashioning an irrigation system in the lower Yangzi region.[34] Hendrik de Reike was experienced in city planning. Before his arrival in Nantong in 1916, he worked for the construction bureau of the public concession area in Shanghai for five years. Though Zhang Jian invited de Reike to Nantong primarily to deal with waterworks, he consulted him on matters of city renewal. In 1917, after months of on-the-spot investigation, de Reike wrote "Suggestions for Nantong City Reform," which, true to his European background, took sanitation and public hygiene as a central concern. He provided details for the design of a sewer system, running water, and city streets. Zhang Jian's first priority, however, was not exactly to thoroughly update the city's utility system; instead, it was to make the city *look* modern and functional. As a result, de Reike was asked to turn his talents mainly to highways and bridges, including the bridge in the Central Park. He contracted cholera in 1919 and died on that very bridge while on the way to the hospital.[35]

Suburbs

The construction of a new downtown, the face of a forward-looking Nantong, satisfied one goal in the plans for the spatial reconfiguration. The other goal, enlarging the city, was met by developing its suburbs, consisting mainly of three towns, Tangzha, Tiansheng Port, and Langshan. Aside from the logistical connection between the city and its industrial base, the port, and the scenic spots, the particular importance of these three towns lay in the concern to have visitors gain a broader view of the area's accomplishments. They would see industry, the foundation of Nantong's development, in Tangzha, a transport hub in Tiansheng, and natural beauty in Langshan. These three towns thus complemented the city in presenting the rich variety of the new community.

Tangzha started to grow in the late Qing as industrialization began. The building of the No. 1 mill was the first step in transforming this village of a few families into the most important industrial center in the region. The giant imported clock tower standing above the factory front gate declared the arrival of a new era (Fig. 3). In the following decade, more than a dozen factories were built in Tangzha. At the same time, Tangzha also became an important commercial center, especially known for its grain market. With Dasheng's demand for raw material, more and more local peasants switched from growing grain to growing cotton. In turn, their need for grain was met by imports. A mill was built to process rice shipped in from southern Jiangsu and Anhui. Many grain shops were located in Tangzha to make purchases and distribute the goods to local markets and residents. There were often days when thousands of boats loaded with grain were moored on the river.[36]

These intense industrial and commercial activities inevitably brought other changes to further the growth of this young, bustling town. Factory dormitories, apartments, inns, shops, warehouses, restaurants, and teahouses came to dot the local landscape and to stretch the town's boundaries. With wealth generated from manufacturing and commercial activities came the improvement of education and cultural life as

FIGURE 3. The pier of the Dasheng No. 1 textile mill. Source: *Nantong shiye jiaoyu cishan fengjing fu canguan zhinan*, p. 19.

well. Zhang Jingru, son of Zhang Cha, started the first middle school, named after himself, and the first industrial elementary school, in Tangzha. Li Yunliang, a graduate of Jingru Middle School, went on to attend Fudan University in Shanghai. Upon his return, he occupied some important positions in a local shipping company, as well as at the No. 1 mill. In those capacities, Li helped enrich the cultural life of Tangzha by creating the first public library, a small park, and more schools. He is properly remembered as a famous local figure.[37]

The most important educational establishment in Tangzha was the Nantong Textile School, created in 1912. It was intended to prepare experts for the principal industry in Nantong, but as China's first school specializing in textiles, it attracted students from all over the country and overseas. By 1927, the school had turned out three hundred graduates, a first generation of Chinese experts who would serve as the backbone of the nation's textile industry for years to come. Most moved on to major Chinese cities and overseas to carry the legacy of the school far beyond Tangzha.[38]

The new institutions and developments brought floods of newcomers to Tangzha. There were so many merchants from Ningbo in Zhejiang province, for instance, that they established their native place associations, as did merchants from elsewhere.[39] The visual appeal of the town also changed considerably. It was said that one saw in Tangzha factories, schools, and shops standing in great numbers, a forest of masts rising on the river, merchants and visitors crowding the streets, and traffic flowing in an incessant stream.[40] A town with boundless energy fueled by manufacturing had emerged in this once largely rural community.

The rising fame of Nantong was another source of the energy. Since industry was a prominent component of the new Nantong, Tangzha was a must-see for visitors. The No. 1 mill and the textile school were among the main attractions. In the early 1910s, a highway was constructed between Tangzha and the city to accommodate the increasing flow of traffic. John Dewey came to Tangzha twice during his four-day stay in Nantong. In addition to visiting several factories and schools, he made a speech at Tangzha park.[41] His visit and those of other prominent people were closely followed by the press, which put the town in the spotlight. In the early 1920s, when the plans for a model city were well under way, Zhang Jian intended to fill the sides of the highway from the city to Tangzha with factories, shops, apartments, and homes, so that the bare road between the two locations would be replaced by a prosperous compound of industry, commerce, and residential quarters. This was perhaps among the earliest attempts at suburbanization in China. Zhang Jian imagined that it would serve as an ideal model for local self-government, though his financial difficulties after 1921 prevented him from realizing his dream.[42]

The development of Tiansheng, the closest port to Tangzha, was induced by the need to transport fuel, raw materials, machines, and other products for the factories in Tangzha. In 1901, when Zhang Jian and his associates created the Dasheng Shipping Company to provide service between Shanghai and Nantong, ships could only anchor in the middle of the river because Tiansheng Port was not deep enough. Smaller boats had to bring passengers and cargo to shore, a procedure that was neither efficient nor safe. In 1904, two docks were built that greatly improved the port's usefulness. In 1903, a canal was dug between Tangzha and Tiansheng to improve the water route between the two points; and two years later, they were connected by road. All this facilitated not only transportation between the port and local factories, but also between Nantong and the outside. In time, Tiansheng, along with Shanghai, Zhenjiang, and Nanjing, became an important stop on the lower Yangzi River, serving both business and travelers.[43]

With the steady increase of port traffic in those years, Tiansheng gradually expanded into a town in its own right, with warehouses, transfer stations, inns, restaurants, teahouses, shops, and other necessary facilities. In 1913, a paved road was constructed to connect the port with the city.[44] In the meantime, fishing, a traditional occupation in the area, continued to develop, keeping the port even busier in the high seasons of spring and summer. Zhang Jian and other Nantong elites recognized that Tiansheng would make an ideal industrial site as well. In 1917, the Zhang brothers opened a match factory there. By 1920, it was producing matches of eighteen different trademarks, distributed to twenty provinces and cities in China. In that same year, Zhang Jian drew up plans to build a power plant in Tiansheng to meet regional needs for electricity. Though the plant had not materialized by the time of his death, the port as a transportation hub continued to grow. Like Tangzha, Tiansheng had a clock tower on its customhouse to signal its new identity. It was the first object that visitors saw before landing in Nantong.[45]

As a gateway to Tangzha and the city, the importance of Tiansheng to the presentation of Nantong was self-evident. Zhang Xiaoruo prominently featured it in the 1920 souvenir book he produced to promote Nantong.[46] The town was in turn shaped by the model. Guoyuan (Orchard) Road in Tiansheng, for instance, was brought into being as a direct response to outsiders' comments. One of the most frequent complaints that was heard from otherwise admiring visitors concerned the lack of fresh fruit, which Nantong did not produce. Accordingly, the elites opened up more than ten mu of wasteland in Tiansheng for an orchard and transplanted many types of fruit trees from Jiangnan. Hence a new road named Guoyuan was born.[47]

The growth of Langshan was a different story. The Buddhist monastery Guangjiao (Broad Teaching) for which Langshan was noted can be traced back to the Tang dynasty, when the hill it now stands on was still an island in the Yangzi, and a ferry was used for pilgrimages. Langshan subsequently became one of the earliest small towns in Nantong, for the thousands of visitors who were attracted by the monastery and the vistas of the river demanded restaurants, inns, snack shops, joss stick and candle shops, and other services.[48]

In the Song dynasty, pilgrims began to come to Langshan to worship Seng Jia, an eminent Tang monk whose reputation seemed to increase after his death. In time, the popular creation and re-creation of myths made Seng Jia the founder of Guangjiao, and he came to be known as the Great Holy Buddha of Langshan. In 1866, the Qing court awarded an inscribed horizontal board to the Great Buddha. In part because of this official recognition, Langshan gradually became an exclusive site for worshiping the Tang Buddha in the Jiangbei region, attracting pilgrims from all over Jiangbei, as well as from Shanghai and Guangdong province. As was true of religious sites on other noted mountains, Langshan was also known for stelae and carved inscriptions of poetry and essays left by both famed and anonymous literati from the past. A further stimulus to the growth of Langshan was its strategic position as a pass from the river to the northern plain of Tongzhou, in consequence of which it was a fortified military outpost during the Ming and Qing dynasties. The main street used to be called Paotaijie (Cannon Street). In the early Republic, with a change in defense concerns, the military installations were either converted into homes and shops or demolished.[49]

In the early 1910s, Zhang Jian tried to bring Langshan's traditional strengths—a strategic location, a religious center, a scenic spot, and a tourist attraction—up to date with several large-scale projects that were in line with the progressive image of Nantong. First, he proposed an ambitious plan to reforest the hill area with 50,000 trees and made tree planting a responsibility of the Langshan monastery. People and animals were officially banned from entering those areas to protect the seedlings. Encouraged by Zhang Jian, one of the monks donated a piece of temple land to start a tree nursery. A forest bureau was established to oversee the project. The years of effort more than paid off. By 1917, 60,000 new trees were said to have been planted, and plans for various orchards were also on the agenda. One of the local newspapers pronounced Langshan a "model district" for the country in tree planting.[50]

New buildings began to dot the hill area as well, the most prominent of which were the private villas that Zhang Jian constructed near each of the five hills.[51] All these structures were built as showcases, beautifully landscaped with gardens, pavilions, streams, and rocks. The one on Langshan proper was a summer house that Zhang proudly compared to Beidaihe, a renowned summer resort near Beijing.[52]

Zhang Jian also chose to locate the school for the blind and dumb, the home for the disabled, and other charitable institutions at Langshan because they were appropriate to the Buddhist spirit of the site. Though Zhang personally covered their operating cost, he also used Buddhist rituals to raise funds, and in time the students at the dumb and blind school themselves performed in public—singing and dancing—to help with the budget.[53] What motivated Zhang Jian to create these institutions was his belief that everyone could be trained to at least a degree of self-sufficiency. But he had other concerns as well. He was troubled by the crowds of beggars in the Langshan area, who in numbers of a thousand or more during pilgrimage seasons harassed visitors and abused anyone who refused them.[54] Zhang considered these beggars a "stain on the reputation" of local self-government.[55] Moreover, this unemployed or unemployable "floating population" was perceived as a disruptive force in society and a threat to local security. After some investigation, Zhang found out that there were some disabled among the beggars. The school for the blind and the dumb and the home for the disabled were meant to take the beggars off the street and teach them practical skills.[56] In 1916, there were 123 people, both men and women, in the home for the disabled. Between 1917 and 1923, 200 students graduated from the dumb and blind school, and some of the mutes found jobs at publishing houses as typists.[57] While helping these people, these institutions were also a boon for public relations. They not only removed the "stain" from the local scene, as Zhang Jian intended, but also won Nantong much praise. Chinese and foreign visitors, especially philanthropists, were immensely impressed with the success of Nantong's special education, something that was considered to lend unique substance to the model claim.[58] Decades later, some people still remembered Nantong as a model because for a period of time beggars, almost an institution in rural Jiangbei, had vanished from its streets.[59]

Again, when Zhang Jian began to erect new temples and remodel existing ones, it was not merely to enhance Langshan as a tourist site. Troubled by the increasing influence of radical ideas articulated during the May Fourth movement, Zhang Jian saw Buddhism as a useful tool for preserving social stability. Enhancing Langshan as a Buddhist center was more of a social than a religious act. Zhang Jian's plans included a series of temples arranged on the five hills to mirror the story of Buddhism coming from the west.[60] Like the landscape in the city, what appeared in Langshan was carefully designed. As with the planning in the city and elsewhere, Zhang Jian meant for the new temples to become models.[61]

The renovation of some of the old temples served the same purposes. A case in point was the Guanyin temple, located on the northern side of Langshan. Zhang Jian was particularly fond of it, for the birth of his only son was said to have resulted from several visits he and his wife paid to the temple. The renovation of the Guanyin temple, started

FIGURE 4. The temple of Guanyin at Langshan. Source: *Nantong shiye jiaoyu cishan fengjing fu canguan zhinan*, p. 89.

in 1914 and completed the next year with a three-story addition, was funded by the Zhang brothers and some of the monks (Fig. 4). Around this time, a monk from Mount Putuo, in Zhejiang province, obtained 150 precious Guanyin portraits that dated back to the Tang dynasty. Concerned for the safety and preservation of those treasures, he decided to turn all of them over to the Nantong Museum for safekeeping, a measure of Nantong's reputation and the public trust placed in the museum. Zhang Jian, however, did not think the museum was a proper place for the sacred artifacts. He instead built a special hall at the Guanyin temple for them. Because the portraits made the temple even more appealing to worshipers, Zhang sponsored a lecture hall as an adjunct to the temple. All the work on the Guanyin complex was completed during the high tide of the May Fourth movement.[62] To prepare for the opening, Zhang Jian issued detailed regulations concerning the responsibilities of the monks in caring for the temple and in handling visitors. The regulations differentiated special and famous guests from ordinary visitors and showed Zhang's keen concern over the presentation of the temple. The only two sets of keys to the rooms where the Guanyin portraits were stored were kept in the temple and Zhang Jian's home.[63] Zhang Jian practically treated this temple as an extension of his personal property and responsibility.

The new temples and building additions were only part of Zhang

Jian's plans to promote Langshan. Now he needed new men—reputable monks—to be the chief residents for Guanyin and other temples. "Famous mountains deserve famous monks to give them solemnity," he held.[64] Learned as he was in Buddhism, he did not have a high opinion of the local monks, whom he considered poorly educated and vulgar.[65] With the development of schools in Nantong, things began to change. Two of the monks from Langshan actually attended the normal school, and some of them also became involved in public affairs such as building schools.[66] But these were only small departures from the past. Nantong did not have any well-known master monks. Zhang Jian did two things to rectify that. As soon as the Guanyin temple was completed, he invited Master Taixu of national fame to Nantong for a three-day lecture tour; Zhang himself was among the audience of several hundred.[67] At the same time, he was looking for a well-educated monk to be the head of the Guanyin temple; at one point, the name of Master Hongyi came up. Taixu and Hongyi were no ordinary monks. Taixu was interested in Western social science theories such as socialism and used modern sciences in his interpretation of Buddhism.[68] Hongyi, born Li Shutong, was a college professor and renaissance man, admirably accomplished in literature, the arts, music, drama, and calligraphy. He studied in Japan, where he became acquainted with the theater reformer and actor Ouyang Yuqian.[69] Zhang Jian tried to contact Hongyi through Ouyang and others. When that effort failed, he settled on Master Jingyuan from the Jinshan (Golden Mountain) temple in Zhenjiang, Jiangsu province.[70] It is telling that Zhang Jian wanted the temples to be associated with monks who were not only high-minded and eminent, but also well informed about current trends. Such qualifications would at once give the temple the kind of respect and forward-looking image that were appropriate to Nantong's status and appeal to the young generation who were increasingly attracted to new ideas.

Tangzha, Tiansheng, and Langshan were of course not the only fast-growing towns in the area. With the rapid commercialization and urbanization of the time, many towns and markets were expanding, each with its new schools, factories, and roads. The large-scale land reclamations especially created many new towns in the region, as earlier discussed. But from the 1910s, this expansion of Nantong city, with Tangzha, Tiansheng, and Langshan standing like the three legs of a tripod surrounding and supporting it, was highlighted as a unique spatial characteristic of the county.[71] More than geographical expansion, this so-called "one city and three towns" structure represented a deliberate effort to define Nantong's progress from different, tangible angles. The city made a cosmopolitan statement, Tangzha and Tiansheng an industrial statement, and Langshan a cultural and artistic statement. Though the landscape in Langshan, with villas, trees, and temples, was much different from the grand theater, high chimneys, and docks in the city and the other two towns, it was intended for, and in turn served, the same purposes.

Architecture and Landscape

Architecture and landscape speak silently yet explicitly of the social change they manifest and help shape. The variety of architectural styles that emerged in Nantong during this period undermined its old homogeneity of building forms. Before 1895, most of the buildings had black-tiled roofs and were low and single-storied to withstand the violent typhoons that often batter the region in autumn. The houses of the rich were usually outwardly distinguished not so much by their height as by their decoration, elaborate gardens, and spacious surroundings. Today in Nantong, when a new wave of modernization has put these old houses in the shadow of skyscrapers, preserving them has become a public concern. But in the early twentieth century, it was the newly arrived Western-style architecture that captured the imagination of the city.

Western-style buildings started in Nantong (as they perhaps did elsewhere in China) with a Roman Catholic church. Built outside the East Gate before the Taiping Uprising, its strange shape often invoked a mixed feeling of curiosity, fear, and resentment in the rural population.[72] The perception of Western-style architecture changed with the birth of the No. 1 mill, designed by British engineers and constructed by a Shanghai contractor. The brick-and-wooden workshops resembled many factories in England. As the first factory in Nantong, it was imitated by all others thereafter. Western-style architecture thus became fashionable in Tangzha and quickly spread to the county seat. From factories to schools, British style dominated, though Chinese features were often retained. The normal school, built in 1903, for example, was a mixture of Chinese and Western styles (and also Japanese, to the extent that its classrooms were configured in Japanese fashion, a reflection of Japan's influence on Chinese education). However, in the first decade of the twentieth century, foreign-style houses in Nantong were confined to

FIGURE 5. Zhang Jian's Haonan Villa in Nantong. (Courtesy of the Nantong Museum)

the church area, where Western missionaries, doctors, and nurses who worked for the church and its hospital had their homes.[73]

This began to change in the 1910s, and the rich and powerful led the fashion. Haonan, built in 1914 as Zhang Jian's first villa and the family's main residence, was among the first Western-style private dwellings in the city. Designed in the mode of a villa that Empress Dowager Cixi had built in Beijing, Haonan was in an eclectically English style (Fig. 5).[74] The roof, chimneys, and gables, all in Pompeian red, were reminiscent of the eighteenth-century English Georgian style, but the overhanging roof and the porches were typical of Anglo-Indian colonial architecture. It had Corinthian and Ionic columns on the front and Chinese columns supporting the side balcony. Also typically English were the arched brick lintels over the windows, the moldings, and the grand staircase. The fireplaces, five in all, were decorated with neoclassical details.

Zhang Jian's favoring of this style perhaps had more to do with its Western origins than its association with Cixi. Western-style buildings soon became a dominant feature in the southern part of the city and together formed a distinct architectural group. The Nantong Club Hotel, for instance, had a rather Romanesque hexagonal steeple, which lent it a typical North European flavor (Fig. 6). The hotel's other European features included a classical porch, eighteenth-century-style gables, and

FIGURE 6. The Nantong Club Hotel. (Courtesy of the Nantong Museum)

a porte-cochere to the right of the steeple, with a neoclassical balustrade above it. The building's strong geometry was realized by a decorative facade to the left of the steeple. The three-story Huai Hai Industrial Bank was another example of classical European architecture. Based on English Renaissance models dating from the middle of the eighteenth century, it was an adaptation from early nineteenth-century English adaptations of the earlier style.[75] This grand, elegant building, with its eclectic mix of foreign features, projected the social superiority and financial authority of the Zhang family. Although not quite as ostentatious as the building group that was known as a Western architectural museum on the waterfront of downtown Shanghai, the club, the bank, and other Western-style buildings in Nantong, perhaps more than anything else, spoke of the rejection of the traditional provincial pattern and gave the city space a modern, metropolitan tone.

Zhang Jian also promoted what might be called the social attraction of the new landscape of Nantong by mixing Western and Chinese styles. The five parks, for instance, resembled traditional Chinese gardens with pavilions and lily ponds and without much of the open space characteristic of Western parks. But they also featured multistoried buildings and imported leisure facilities. Frederick Sites was deeply impressed by the artistic design of various public projects. The library, as he described it, was housed in a "charming group of buildings, well lighted, and set amid gardens which are fragrant with roses and bright with the red glow of the berries of the 'Heavenly Bamboo.'"[76] Other visitors were reportedly equally impressed, and even shocked, by the novel features of the city.[77]

Finding appropriate names for the new streets and buildings was an integral part of the spatial reorganization. A name is not just a means of identification, but also a statement that gives a certain meaning to a place. Street and building names are expected to last for generations to come. Therefore, naming is very much a matter of image- and history-making. During the period under consideration, even some of the existing streets and buildings were renamed. On the whole, the question of names was treated quite seriously. When the No. 1 mill was constructing a new apartment building for its workers, a written report was sent to Zhang Jian asking him to select a name. He dubbed it Zheng, after one of his concubines, a name that remained in use until the 1980s.[78]

If naming relatively insignificant projects required care, we can only imagine how serious a matter it was to name major landmarks. Zhang Jian carefully selected the names of the No. 1 mill and many other local factories and institutions. The term Dasheng was from a sentence in the *Book of Changes* (*Yi jing*): "*tiandi zhi dade yue sheng*" ("the great virtue of Heaven and earth is called creation"). That choice reflected Zhang's hope that the factory would "create" a livelihood for the people. Embedded in such concerns was the highly valued concept of *minben* in Confucian statecraft.[79] The names of some factories were extended to streets; there was a Dasheng Lane and a Dada Street, for example. Such street names were especially common in Tangzha and Tiansheng. Also, as the map of southern Nantong indicates, the names of Gongyuan (park) Road between the Central and South parks, Bowuyuan (museum) Road, in front of the Nantong Museum, and Mofan Road were examples that new projects not only demanded new roads and streets, but also provided new names for them. Since naming streets after important buildings and institutions was quite typical in Chinese towns in traditional times, these new names were not in themselves the least exotic. But inasmuch as they were names of factories and other modern projects, they symbolized a new era in local history. Today, the people of Nantong still tell stories about how these names came into being.[80]

Around this same time, foreign characters and lettering began to appear on buildings, such as Roman numerals on the face of clocks and the English name Hui Hai Industrial Bank inscribed above the bank's front gate. Though these strange signs might have alienated ordinary people, they also invoked a sense of curiosity and awe, since things foreign meant progress. For visitors, especially those from abroad, they were a token of what Nantong had become and where it intended to be.

Inscripted poems and other writings in the hand of Zhang Jian and other elites also adorned the new edifices of Nantong. Chinese culture places tremendous value on the literary embellishment of a building. Like a painting without a poem and calligraphy, a building without inscriptions was considered incomplete and was depreciated. In China, architectural literature, like travel writing, constitutes a distinct literary genre. Many ancient landmarks were treasured because of certain writings on them. Some of the sayings in fact outlasted the landmarks that inspired them.

This union of landmarks and literary marks was evident everywhere in Nantong. Virtually every doorway and every wall of the many new buildings was a blank sheet on which the local elites could give free flow to their literary and political imagination. Zhang Jian himself relied on the couplet, the most popular form of literary decoration for buildings, alone composing one or more for 135 buildings and landmarks in the region,[81] including such favored projects as the No. 1 mill, the normal school, the Nantong Museum, and the Gengsu Theater. The first two institutions were especially full of Zhang's creations. One of the most memorable couplets he wrote for Dasheng expressed his excitement and high expectation for the factory: "The operation of the machines will shake the earth and Heaven; the cloth [made here] will spread to cover the southeastern region." That this couplet was in the calligraphy of Weng Tonghe, mentor of Emperor Guangxu, lent additional prestige to it.[82] For the normal school, he composed a motto, "Hardworking, self-sufficient, loyal, and truthful," which was prominently inscribed over the entrance to the auditorium (Fig. 7). Zhang Jian provided mottoes for at least eleven other schools, which, mostly in his own calligraphy, were inscribed on their buildings to give each campus its own identitiy.[83]

The five parks likewise inspired and invited literary enhancement. The poems, inscribed boards, and couplets there reflected collective elite talent across the region and through time. Some were selected from renowned works of ancient writers; others were produced at elite gatherings Zhang Jian hosted, where conversations were often accompanied by wine and poetry composition well into night, and the cool moonlight seemed to always fire up more creative energy. The Zhang brothers and Zhang Xiaoruo all contributed their work to the parks. The Central Park even had a pair of couplets authored by Wu Chang-shuo, one of the greatest artists of modern China.[84] Also in the Central

FIGURE 7. Zhang Jian's inscriptions at the Nantong Normal School. (Courtesy of the Nantong Museum)

Park, the presence of the Zhang family was especially felt, with the portraits of both Zhang Jian and Zhang Cha on display.[85]

Literary decoration and activities tended to give each park a distinct identity. The South Park's Longevity Hall, built in honor of Zhang Cha's seventieth birthday, was not extraordinary in its architecture, but it was associated with memorable social and literary events and visiting celebrities. Among the selected guests at Zhang Cha's birthday banquet was a special envoy sent by the then-president of the Republic, Cao Kun. The gift he brought from Cao, a red horizontal board with an inscription, was hung above the gate to the hall. Zhang Jian composed many couplets that adorned its rooms and hallways. He also wrote a special essay in its honor. Soon after, Hanmolin Publishing House printed the essay as a copybook for calligraphy and spread it further.[86] Contemplating mortality in a built form, Zhang Jian's essay tried to distinguish the Longevity Hall from the private homes of rich men by indicating that the hall would prosper along with the park, like it, supposedly a public space.[87] But the hall's origin, its distinctive gate, and Zhang Jian's essay helped define it as a special place linked to the power of the Zhangs. It retained its prestige long after they were gone.[88]

The area around Langshan had long been associated with literary works of historical significance. Emperor Kangxi of the Qing dynasty authored two poems inscribed on one of its pavilions, a gift to a court official who served in Tongzhou. A poem by Zhu Xi, the great Confucian scholar of the Song dynasty, carved on a stone tablet, had been composed in honor of one of the Tongzhou prefects. The Zhang brothers lent their work to Langshan as well. Zhang Jian wrote a number of boards and couplets for the temples and other landmarks there, some at the monks' request.[89] His couplets for the main temple, Guangjiao, highlighted the connection between the Great Buddha Seng Jia and Langshan, while also expressing his equal respect for Buddhism and Confucianism.[90] Zhang's writings were meant to furnish the hill with a cultural refinement that he felt it seriously lacked, for as earlier noted, Zhang perceived the monks as a culturally impoverished group.[91] Zhang's villas in the area were also decorated with abundant literary and art works.[92] All this helped Langshan gain high cultural marks befitting of Nantong's image. Indeed, Zhang Jian elected to use the renovated hill area for many of his social and political functions. In 1920, for instance, he arranged for the Jiangsu Society to hold its first standing committee meeting in the Guanyin temple.[93]

Clearly, Zhang Jian's inscriptions were in great demand, not merely or perhaps even principally because of the beauty of his compositions and calligraphy, but also because of who he was. Together with the landmarks of Nantong, they reinforced his influence and the perception of a new Nantong throughout the community. The impact of his inscriptions was by no means limited to the scholarly classes. Literary marks, especially couplets, on buildings cross the boundaries between elite and popular cultures and between written and oral literature. To begin with, the form of couplets was a familiar and important one to ordinary people. Most took couplets on their own doors seriously, putting them up at a designated time on New Year's eve. Seen as a good omen, couplets reflected the family's values, hopes, and identity. There were plenty of stories about how the older generation used couplets to teach their children virtues such as diligence and frugality. Couplets were one of the few links ordinary people had to the literary world; in fact, they were often the weapon of the poor. Folk tales tell how clever peasants composed pointed couplets to annoy the powerful. Unlike long essays and poetry that were often written in classical style, couplets tend to be short, ranging from two to ten words, for whether on the doors of houses or on structures in scenic spots, they were supposed to catch the attention of passersby and tourists and be easily remembered. Many famous couplets, as well as stories about them, are passed along from one generation to another, even among the peasants, and brevity helps the memory.[94]

Thus couplets are an accessible and effective way to reach the people, something that elites all over China no doubt recognized. Though many of the peasants in Nantong did not know what Zhang Jian's model county was all about, they did learn about Zhang's "great name" (*daming*) and admired him in part because of his well-written couplets.[95] Even today, the authors and meanings of historical inscriptions and couplets remain a vital source of local fascination, inspiring endless reminiscences and interpretations.[96]

Visitors' Impressions

All these changes in building style, road types, place-names, and literary decorations constituted "an objectified symbolic world,"[97] where the model of modernity became something tangible. They greatly influenced the way in which people understood the city. The overall impression visitors took away with them, confirmed in their individual accounts, was that Nantong's city planning was the best in China. Sites's first impression of Nantong, for instance, had to do with its physical presence. While taking a carriage ride into the city, he felt that a New China was at once visible in the "wide, well graded roads, lined with young trees," which to him were "the first indication of a guiding hand and the new spirit" in the community.[98] *Millard's Review* reported that Zhang Jian had transformed his birthplace into a "modern industrial town" where "everyone [was] prosperous."[99] Of course, Nantong city was not Zhang Jian's birthplace, and poverty did exist there. The reporter probably did not look very hard, if he looked at all. More than likely, he was captivated, like others, by what was most apparent: the new look of the city.

Sources do not disclose whether these particular observers saw the old business district, but for visitors who did, the new downtown appeared all the more impressive in comparison. Because of the stark contrast, they instantly recognized the extent of change. In 1922, when Tsurumi Yusuke from the Japanese Ministry of Railroads visited Nantong, he was amazed at the fresh character of the city.[100] From the road between the port of Tiansheng to the city, Tsurumi recognized "Zhang Jian's unique talent in city planning and management." Among all the things he was invited to see, he seemed to be most impressed by the Club Hotel, which he considered to be superior to any of its counterparts in Tokyo. To his own surprise, what Tsurumi saw in Nantong, together with what he witnessed at Beijing National University and Yan Xishan's enterprises in Shanxi, changed his pessimistic view of China. In the early 1920s, his reports on Nantong and those of several other Japanese generated in Japan considerable interest in Zhang Jian's success.

Though steeples, columns, and cornerstones in themselves communicate with people, the stunning effect Nantong's appearance had on visitors was more the result of the masterly presentations of Zhang Jian, whose "guiding hand" arranged such matters as who would collect and guide the guests, what they would see, and how their questions would be handled. In the end, visitors' impressions could not but be framed by both what was presented and how it was presented.

A case in point is the Seventh Annual Conference of the Science Society of China in 1922. The society, established in 1914 by a group of Chinese students in the United States, relocated to Nanjing, Jiangsu province, a few years later, in 1918. Zhang Jian had been its patron ever since, lobbying for its causes and supporting it financially.[101] In return, the science society elected Zhang to be its only honorary member in China (the others included the American inventor Thomas Edison). The society originally planned to hold its convention in Guangzhou, but the political situation there was unstable. Zhang invited the society to come to Nantong instead. He gave considerable thought to the event. Two months prior to the conference, a special committee headed by Zhang Xiaoruo was formed to prepare for it. On 19 August 1922, all the delegates of the science society arrived in Nantong.[102]

That China's leading scientists and intellectuals gathered in Nantong instead of a major city was itself a national sensation, but Zhang Jian made use of this highly marketable event for even more publicity, mainly by exploiting the new downtown. He carefully arranged for all of the conference activities, except for on-site investigations, to be held there. The delegates stayed in the newly completed Nantong Club Hotel and used both the hotel and the office of the chamber of commerce as meeting places. Gengsu Theater served as an entertainment center, where the delegates enjoyed performances by students of the local acting school and locally made movies. They also visited the museum, library, and other cultural and educational institutions, all of which could be reached only by passing the parks and Mofan Road along the Hao River.

Locked in this showcase for five days, with occasional inspection tours of factories and land reclamation sites, the delegates, especially those who were first-time visitors, were simply overwhelmed. In their speeches at the meeting, they marveled at the new institutions and buildings in Nantong, and praised Zhang Jian's application of "scientific knowledge" (*kexue zhishi*) in creating the "great enterprises" (*weida shiye*). Above all else, they identified a "spirit [*jingshen*] of Nantong" at work. For some of them, Nantong even eclipsed Shanghai, where, so they said, the spirit of Chinese culture had been lost because of Western influence. They considered the Nantong model to be genuinely Chinese, with all the right ingredients for strengthening the nation. Liang Qichao, one of the few delegates who had the power to sway public opinion, probably best expressed the group's impression when he proclaimed that "Nantong was the publicly recognized [*gongren*] number one progressive city in China." The press, in reporting on the conference, was responsible for widely disseminating comments such as these. An enlarged photo of Zhang Jian and the delegates was printed in the society's house journal, *The Science*, and other media outlets. At the meeting, Zhang Jian was elected to the society's board of directors, together with Cai Yuanpei, Liang Qichao, and five other renowned intellectuals and scientists. The conference of course cost Zhang Jian a fortune, but he gained another kind of capital beyond measure. It boosted Nantong's prestige tremendously. Ever mindful of outside recognition, Zhang acknowledged that the conference had "added luster" to Nantong.[103]

The man who painstakingly built a reputation for Nantong made sure that future generations would remember his Nantong his way. In 1921, Zhang Jian sponsored the writing of a gazetteer focusing on the county's recent history. Unlike local gazetteers of the past, this one was to contain numerous maps—nearly one hundred of them—including specialized maps of all the major landmarks of the time. The work was appropriately titled *Illustrated Gazetteer of Nantong County*.[104]

The Changing Concept of Time

Time, like space, can be fashioned to serve political interests. We need only mention the complicated rituals to redefine the calendar at the beginning of each new dynasty and the countless reign names in imperial China. The remaking of the concept of time often takes place after new groups come to power and involves new calendrical systems, new units of time, and new official festivals and holidays. The dominant political force often manipulates the remaking of the calendar to serve its interests and promote its values, as was the case in the French and Russian revolutions.[105] The ruled also often try to use time as a weapon of resistance. We can see this today in northwestern China, where the Muslims set their watches two hours behind the officially defined "Beijing time" in defiance and protest of the central government and as an affirmation of their own identity.[106] The struggle with time reveals much about the political and cultural landscape in any given era. In Nantong, time changed both officially, with the introduction of a Republican calendar, and unofficially, with the arrival of factories and modern schools. The local application of the new calendar to confirm national unity, the imposition of an industrial concept of time, and the choices of local festivals and significant events were instrumental in undermining the traditional concept of time and in projecting a changing community.

National Time

Traditionally, people in Nantong, like Chinese elsewhere, lived by the lunar calendar, which was based on the agricultural cycle and included numerous annual festivals, both religious and secular, that helped reinforce family and community solidarity.[107] The establishment of the Republican calendar (*minguo lifa*) and the adoption of the Western calendar after the 1911 Revolution brought an additional, sometimes competing, focus—the nation and national unity. Nantong had nothing directly to do with these changes, but their local application was a tension-charged process. In fact, the county did not immediately adopt the Republican calendar, nor did some members of the local elite like

Zhang Cha openly break the tie with the fallen empire by cutting off their queues—a symbol of the Qing dynasty—right away.[108] Rather, in the public announcement declaring the region's independence from the Qing court, the local elite proclaimed the year to be 4609, based on the calendar of the Yellow Emperor. This adoption of the Yellow Emperor's calendar was a politically correct move, though the people in attendance felt it to be a bit strange.[109] The sensitivity toward the question of which calendar to use and the decision to retain the queue reflected the cautious attitude shared by many at this uncertain time.

But it was not long before the dust settled. The Republican calendar was adopted, and the 1911 Revolution was observed as marking the "first year of the Republic" (*minguo yuan nian*). The day when Nantong declared independence from the Qing court (8 November 1911) was also celebrated. On 10 October 1912, the first anniversary of the revolution, representatives of all Nantong's institutions and occupations gathered to hold a large lantern festival in a school hall. Thereafter, celebrating the National Day became a newly invented tradition, often with a day off for people to organize and participate in various activities. The main event was often marked by a gathering of delegates from all local institutions and occupations, especially government offices and schools, at which they raised flags, hung lanterns, sang songs, and marched in the streets.[110]

An event related to the National Day was also observed in Nantong. A major meeting was held on 12 May 1913 to applaud the diplomatic recognition of the Republic of China by various foreign governments. The meeting was announced beforehand in local newspapers and was well organized. It took place in a military camp, which was colorfully decorated with lanterns and equipped with offices, banquet halls, and reception areas. Three thousand people, including some foreigners, attended. The formalities of announcing the foreign governments' acknowledgments and reading President Yuan Shikai's response were followed by congratulatory speeches, student singing, and much photo-taking all around. The next day, another gathering took place to specifically celebrate the U.S. government's recognition of the Republic; an American missionary stationed in Nantong made a speech praising Sino-American friendship.[111]

In time, such celebrations became a civic ritual that was meant to reinforce the integration of the National Day, national time, and national unity. This process, however, was not free of conflict. These celebrations were a mixture of both tradition and novelty. Though raising the national flag and taking photographs were something new, other forms were not. But for the most part, traditional forms were invested with new meanings that went beyond the family and the local community. Lantern hanging, for example, an essential activity of the traditional Lantern Festival, was now used to celebrate China as a nation. Processions, a common component of temple fairs, now largely took on the air of celebratory parades for the same purpose.

To the peasant majority outside the urban areas, in fact, the concept of the National Day was elusive, and its supposed solemnity was beyond comprehension. The common folk attended formalities such as flag raisings, but few had any grasp of what those rituals symbolized and why they demanded respect. To them, the National Day was little different from a holiday like New Year, a time simply to be playful, to have fun and good food. That attitude toward the National Day was a sore point that was slow to heal. To some reform-minded new intellectuals, it became a touchstone in distinguishing progress and backwardness. They were openly critical of those who were judged to show insufficient interest in the holiday. As late as 1918, for example, *Tonghai xinbao*, a reform-oriented local newspaper, found the celebration of 10 October in Haimen county unacceptable. Only the students saluted the national flag, and then even they went on to join a street parade that was led by people in clown-like clothes, which the reporter deemed totally inappropriate for the occasion. He saw the whole thing as a fiasco: for the educated among the onlookers, the parade was not grand enough, and the plainly stupid lower classes were just laughing and making noise. So far as he was concerned, such an undignified handling of the National Day illustrated that the people in Haimen were ignorant, the place was backward, and China had no hope.[112] Yet to the "lower classes," this occasion was probably not much different from a temple fair, and they simply acted as they always had.

Factory Time and the Clock

Where the National Day was a matter of politics and patriotism, factory, or industrial, time was identified directly with Western progress. With the development of modern schools and factories, the age-old Chinese concept of time had to change. Now time had to be precise. To this end, the mechanical clock was introduced. To be sure, clocks and other kinds of instruments for measuring time, invented domestically or brought in from abroad, were not entirely new to the Chinese of the time. However, in a society where calendar dates mattered more than precise daily time, those timepieces became objects of suspicion or were belittled and forgotten. At best, the response to Western-made clocks was to treat them as toys.[113] This began to change in the late nineteenth century. Mechanical clocks were now imported not as an isolated marvel, but as a necessary accessory for that new institution, the factory.

Not surprisingly, the first clock towers in Nantong were built at the No. 1 mill, the industrial town of Tangzha, and the port of Tiansheng. The one at the mill was installed in 1899 above the front gate of the factory, at a height of twenty-five meters. The intimate connection between factories and clocks, and between clocks and the industrialized West, is evident in the origin of that clock: it was a gift of the British manufacturing company, J. Hetherington & Sons of Manchester, from which Dasheng purchased its textile machines. It was installed by the British engineers who were building the Dasheng workshops.[114] To the British industrialists, the clock and factory machines were natural partners. Just as the introduction of the clock changed the lives of middle-class urbanites in Republican Shanghai,[115] so that innovation profoundly affected the lives of the ordinary people of Nantong. But there were two fundamental differences between the treaty port cities and Nantong in this regard. First, in Nantong, but not in Shanghai and other metropolises, many factory workers were at the same time peasants who lived in rural suburbs and continued to pursue agriculture. Such peasants cum workers were torn between two worlds, and it was extremely difficult for them to adjust to factory time. Second, whereas many urbanites were likely to have a watch or clock and thus to have some control, or a sense of control, over their time, most of their rural counterparts were too poor to own such a luxury. Thus the workers of Nantong were especially vulnerable to the change in the concept of time.

Indeed, the recollections of Dasheng workers are filled with stories of their struggle with rigorously imposed time discipline in the factories. Peasants for thousands of years had lived free of the inflexible rule of the clock; now workers were required to regulate their lives literally to the very minute. In 1917, a female Dasheng worker lost her job because she was one minute late for work. She cried and fell to her knees to beg for forgiveness, but was dismissed nevertheless.[116] Workers on the early morning shift would run madly to the factory as soon as they heard the first sound of the whistle. Fearing to be late, but having no clock at home, women on the graveyard shift had to leave home early, cradling their children with one arm and carrying their meal basket in the other, and wait for their shift to start at midnight. They depended on ancient indicators of time: the morning star and the cockcrow.[117]

Under tremendous pressure to arrive in time, some women gave birth en route to the factory. Not a few of the children of Dasheng female workers were named for the roads and bridges where they were born. The factory life was so horrifying that peasant women often changed their names after they entered Dasheng, because a folk tale had it that those who retained their original names would still be workers even in death as "yarn ghosts" (*shagui*—a new term arising from factory work), a thought too appalling to contemplate. Somehow they believed that a different name would fool the authorities in the next world and spare them from a factory life,[118] a powerful fantasy by the powerless to control their own fate, if not in this life, at least in the next. In the past, as household weavers, these peasant women had certain joyful moments of release during traditional time markers such as the annual meeting between the Cowherd and the Girl Weaver, a folk tale about love and separation. Now the indifferent factory clock brought them the unrelenting stress of time. Their experience reflected what E. P. Thompson has described as a cultural conflict between nature's rhythms and industry's imperatives, where time had become a precious commodity.[119]

Much as the railroad was a driving force behind the establishment of standard time throughout America in the nineteenth century,[120] so the factories helped set the time for many in Nantong. They served not only as the "nerve center" that regulated workers' lives,[121] but also as a guide for the quotidian activities of the people in the surrounding areas. The factory whistle that blew according to the Dasheng schedule came to represent *the* time. People within earshot simply arranged their daily activities according to the whistle. The terms people used to refer to time also changed. Traditionally, the Langshan General Military Office beat a drum three times a day, the so-called *da geng* (literally, beating the watches). In the early Qing, the drums were replaced by guns, and the terms *toupao* (first firing) and *erpao* (second firing) were used. This practice stopped soon after the 1911 Revolution, with the availability of clocks and watches. Whereas many city residents began to apply *shi* or *dian* (o'clock) to the time of day, workers and peasants near Tangzha used *qi*, the whistle from the factory.[122]

After some delay, clocks gained a public presence in the city, introducing the new time to its inhabitants, in ways similar to what American cities experienced in the second half of the nineteenth century.[123] In

1914, Zhang Jian suggested building a clock tower in the old downtown, next to the old watchtower in front of the prefectural yamen that served as a fire alarm. At the cost of 6,000 silver yuan, donated by a local merchant, a four-story tower was completed in five months. It was said to be patterned after the famous clock tower of the Houses of Parliament in London (Fig. 8). A large mechanical clock purchased from Shanghai was installed on the third story, and on the second was inscribed a couplet Zhang Jian composed, which played on the change in Nantong's nomenclature from *zhou* (prefecture) to *xian* (county) to symbolize the region's tremendous progress.[124] Perhaps not as much of a wonder as some famous counterparts in the West, this clock tower was nevertheless the highest structure in downtown Nantong city, a phenomenal undertaking that generated much curiosity and excitement. People traveled miles just to get a look at it.[125]

The introduction of the telegraph, radio, and telephone also helped shape the new concept of time. The instantaneous transmission of time to distant places (or the illusion of it)[126] reinforced the importance of a uniform time. From 1895, a telegraph line had connected Nantong to Yangzhou, a major city in Jiangbei, and thence to Shanghai, Nanjing, and all the other important cities in China.[127] The Nantong elites were quick to take advantage of the new form of communication to further their political interests and business opportunities. The intense use of the telegraph by the Chinese elites played a dual role in tightening political control and facilitating subversion, as demonstrated in the upheaval of the late Qing and early Republican transition. In a period when timing meant everything for the success of concerted actions at the national and regional levels, the telegraph was an indispensable tool.[128]

In subsequent years, radio played a similar role. In 1917, after years of preparation orchestrated by Zhang Jian, a meteorological observatory was established on the top of Junshan. Its staff was sent to Shanghai to study meteorology and radio techniques, and the observatory was fitted with necessary equipment, including a radio station.[129] The institution was naturally time sensitive, for it recorded weather changes hourly. Appropriately, the observatory was used to report not only weather but also time, which it received by wireless twice daily from Xujiahui Observatory in Shanghai. This "Shanghai time" was treated as standard time and phoned to the Tangzha, Tiansheng, and city clock towers each day at noon so they could calibrate their clocks. "Shanghai time" was also the standard against which the observatory

FIGURE 8. The Nantong city fire and clock tower.
Source: *Nantong shiye jiaoyu cishan fengjing fu canguan
zhinan*, p. 67.

measured weather patterns and made its local forecasts. Within a year of its founding, local newspapers began to print its daily weather forecasts.[130]

In defining the modern concept of time, the telegraph, telephone, radio, clocks, and other new instruments helped create or otherwise reinforce social hierarchy and control. Unequally distributed as they were, concentrated on the whole in the major urban centers, they augmented the cities' control of provincial towns in ways that were not only invisible but also perceived as progressive and universal.[131] In general, those who had access to these instruments dominated those who did not, which was best expressed in the use of clocks in factories and elsewhere. Clocks as such had a mysterious yet strong hold on people's minds because they told people when to do what. Moreover, they represented the emergence of a new set of cultural values that were supposed to be superior to the traditional ones. It would be wrong to think that the exchange of the watchtower for the clock tower was simply a matter of one instrument giving way to another. With their imposing height, the magical rhythm of the bells tolling the hour, and the strange Roman numerals, the new clock towers declared the arrival of a powerful yet invisible control mechanism in human affairs that strengthened the existing authority. They also expressed a rejection of the old order and a determination to update the provincial town with the modern artifacts and values that had become prevalent in the metropolises.

To put the new "time is valuable" concept into practice,[132] however, generated conflict and required compromises. On the one hand, the need for precise times was increasing. In addition to factories and schools, there were civic, business, and other professional institutions that were time-sensitive. The Nantong county administration established after the 1911 Revolution, for instance, used the clock to regularize its office hours, usually dividing the workday with a set two-hour lunch break.[133] Meetings and appointments were scheduled strictly by the clock as well. By the early 1910s, most of the politicians and businessmen, as well as the new professionals, probably had personal watches to keep them on time, for some number of them began to keep their diaries in hourly detail.[134] Slowly, as elsewhere in China, punctuality came to be considered a virtue among those groups in Nantong. The Western calendar, including terms such as *xingqi* (week), was also coming into increasing use, especially in schools.[135] The new system of time governed by the state and the market had begun to take hold in the daily life of the city with its own structure and routine.

On the other hand, these innovations were applied in a limited sphere, mainly within the public life of the city and in new institutions such as schools; the Chinese lunar calendar remained essential in many aspects of life. Indeed, Zhang Jian himself often used both the Republican and the lunar calendar in his diary.[136] In this, he was merely following what proved to be a popular accommodation. Local newspapers, for example, were typically dated by both systems. The weight of tradition, and perhaps its resilience, can be seen in the fact that by the late 1920s, almost two decades after the Western calendar had been introduced to Nantong, it was still used only by government offices, schools, and other institutions. Ordinary people, especially peasants, still preferred the lunar calendar. Conflict rose in 1928, when the provincial government mandated the use of the Western calendar in all business transactions. The Nantong Pawnbrokers' Union was particularly vigorous in its protest, because the different dates the brokers were required to use in calculating interest and fixing the deadlines for redemption caused much confusion among their mostly peasant customers.[137]

The Control of Time

Historically, control over time was closely associated with power. In medieval Europe, punctuality became an important concern first in Catholic monasteries and convents, where daily prayer at set intervals was mandatory. But it was the local church, with its bell hung high, that gradually came to be perceived as the temporal authority in regulating community life, a notion that was not inconsistent with the divine power of God the church represented. The appearance of clock towers in places other than cathedrals, such as in town squares, was a sign of the arrival of a new class and of a new era. The bourgeoisie of the high Middle Ages (11th–14th centuries) built mechanical clocks in public spaces to signal its position as a rising secular force in society generally and in municipal government particularly;[138] God's time now faced a competitor. Nowadays, when wristwatches are widely available not only as timekeepers but also as decorations or jewelry, the public clock has lost its symbolic significance, but the linkage between time and political power remains. In China, for instance, all clocks are set to Beijing time (or are supposed to be) to reinforce the idea of the capital city as the undisputed political center of the nation.[139]

In Nantong, as mentioned, the Langshan General Military Office, the highest military office in Tongzhou, used to control time by beating a drum, and later changed to firing a gun. The opening and closing of the city gates and shops, as well as people's daily life, were scheduled according to the sound of the gun. For instance, the second firing was called the "quieting the market firing" (*jingshi pao*), for after this stores and the city gates were closed. The third firing, in early morning, was known as the "wake-up call" (*xinggeng pao*) that started the day.[140] This system was officially abandoned, together with many other changes in formalities, after the 1911 Revolution, but it was modern development in Nantong that effectively replaced it as a temporal authority. Zhang Jian not only initiated the factories and promoted Western-style schools that demanded precision in time, but also consciously presented himself as the representative of the new concept of time. In 1914, in elaborating on the significance of building a clock tower in downtown Nantong, Zhang Jian attacked tardiness as an ugly old habit and stressed that every local undertaking should begin with "understanding and making sure of the time."[141]

The political ramifications of Zhang's teaching regarding time discipline were clear. In 1905, when the normal school held an athletic contest, a major event in the community, some invited elites did not show up at the scheduled opening time. Conventionally, in a case like this, things would just be put off till the dignitaries arrived. But Zhang Jian, who came to preside over the event, started the opening ceremony on time. When some of the elites finally arrived in their sedan chairs, the gatekeepers denied them entrance.[142] Zhang Jian decisively won the "game"—he not only underscored the value of punctuality but also demonstrated that he commanded time in the community. Indeed, Zhang could not have found a better occasion to make these points. Athletic contests, a modern public spectacle, are frequently tied to time—in their opening and closing ceremonies and in using time as an absolute measure of scores in games where the fastest are judged the best.

Zhang Jian's effort to promote the new concept of time significantly contributed to Nantong's reputation. In 1918, a Japanese visitor reported that as soon as he saw the clock tower of the No. 1 mill "thrusting into the clouds," he became aware of the vigorous energy and prosperity of the place; "everything is flowing, and modern," he gushed.[143] Ouyang Yuqian, manager of the local acting school from 1919 to 1922 and a man whose experience in Nantong was not all pleasant, complained about the countless celebrity gatherings he was compelled to attend. However, he admitted that though most Chinese banquets hardly ever started on time, the gatherings and parties in Nantong were at least always punctual. "This," he said, "is an example of why Nantong was a model county."[144]

Zhang Jian's power to control time manifested itself in other ways. He instituted new festival events and celebrations such as the openings and anniversaries of local projects. Somehow these events came to outweigh the significance of traditional festivals and holidays, especially for the younger generation and new professionals. When the five parks were opened on the Moon Festival of 1917, people crowded into the jam-packed green spaces. They came with their families to *duoyue* (walk with the moon), as they traditionally did on this day. But that year the Moon Festival was meant to be different. Recalling the spectacular scenery of the parks, the new halls and pavilions, the novel facilities, the glowing electric street lights and their reflections in the river, and the festive crowd, Chang Shou, then a student, remembered the day years later as "the most exciting and unforgettable Moon Festival" in his life.[145] A year later, Zhang Jian organized another special event to commemorate the first anniversary of the park opening,[146] thereby initiating what would become a new civic holiday. In this case, the new and old were intertwined: though the Moon Festival remained an important traditional holiday in its own right, it now assumed new significance and generated new excitement.

The Zhang brothers also turned a number of their birthday celebrations into civic events and made them worth commemorating for years to come. In May 1912, a large gift-giving party was expected for Zhang Jian's sixtieth birthday. In an open letter to the community, Zhang announced his intention to found an old people's home and urged those who wished to honor his birthday with gifts of money to contribute to the proposed institution instead. "One person's enjoyment has no comparison to the peace of the people; one day's extravagance means nothing in the light of centuries-long benefit," Zhang Jian wrote. "I wish to share the virtue of being kind to others with you, which I know you gentlemen also think highly of," he cajoled.[147] And so they clearly did, judging by the many donors' names inscribed on the stone tablet next to the old people's home.[148] In 1921, contemplating his grand seventieth birthday to come next year, Zhang once again asked the community to forgo personal gifts for donations to a cause, in this case the anticipated celebration of the twenty-fifth anniversary of the local self-government in 1922.[149] Likewise, as mentioned above, in 1920, Zhang Cha used the money he received as gifts from his friends to build the Yuelong Bridge.

Though these events were not exactly like the celebrations of the parks, their opening ceremonies and annual remembrances nevertheless involved civic rituals and attracted press coverage. In this connection, Zhang Jian had a rather enlightened view on life and death. In 1922, speaking at the opening day of a new home for the old, Zhang Jian said that longevity was not measured by the years one lived, but rather by the contribution one made to the community.[150] Indeed, by associating their birthdays with undertakings and institutions that would engage and benefit the public in the long term, the Zhang brothers successfully enmeshed and extended their lives in the community calendar.

Perhaps no local event or even his own birthday was quite as significant to Zhang Jian as the openings of the No. 1 mill and the normal school. They marked the beginnings of modern development in Nantong and fundamentally contributed to the community's well-being. The profits of the mill became a source—at one point a seemingly inexhaustible source—of finance for many local projects. The normal school trained a veritable army of teachers, which enabled Nantong to virtually universalize primary education. To the outside world, those two institutions were the hallmark of Nantong's advancement.

Celebrating the two achievements and their anniversaries therefore not only reminded people of Zhang Jian's contribution, but also reinforced the new status of Nantong. Zhang later tried to emphasize that education was more important to him than industry, so though the anniversaries of the No. 1 mill continued to be celebrated, the real showcase was the normal school. Its opening ceremony on 18 September 1903 was a major community event. First, the incoming students paid homage to a Confucian monument and showed respect to their teachers, and then they went to their respective classrooms to meet one another. Important officials and local elites were presented. Zhang Jian and several others made speeches. The speech Zhang delivered here was one of his most important ones, for it marked the beginning of the myth making that had him sacrificing for years to start the factory so he could build schools.[151] (His speech was posted, and the students were required to read it before dinner that very evening.)[152] In the following two decades, Zhang Jian tried to appear and speak at every special occasion of the school. The school's anniversary was observed every year, and major anniversaries were accorded grand ceremonies, such as athletic contests. Zhang Jian often involved himself in every detail of their preparation, and these events became community fairs.[153]

The selection of 1922 as the twenty-fifth anniversary of Nantong's local self-government reform was, as discussed in Chapter One, an invented tradition. Zhang Jian designated 1897, the year when the construction of the No 1. mill was nearly completed, as the starting point of the reform, though in fact the local self-government institutions were not established until 1908. By conveniently using the date of the No. 1 mill's birth as the beginning of local self-government, Zhang gave the local self-government movement a much earlier start and thus a priority, another way to distinguish Nantong from other counties in China. The celebrations promoted by Zhang Jian were like traditional festivals in the sense that they mobilized and affected the community as a whole and generated excitement and opportunities for employment. But they also contained meanings absent from traditional festivals. The old festivals had performed such civic functions as reinforcing religious beliefs and a common cultural heritage and raising funds for community projects. Their focus was either on the family or on the local community. Such celebrations continued to be appealing to the local people, especially to peasants and the older generation. But they increasingly had to compete with, and often lost out to, the new holidays celebrating the modern advances that had come to Nantong. In general, those holidays found an enthusiastic reception among the professionals and the young generation, as demonstrated by the young Chang Shou's reaction to the 1917 park opening.

Implicit in these new events, at least for those who were excited by what they meant, was the requirement that people adjust their lives to make them fit into the model image. In fact, Zhang Jian made the point explicit when, in preparation for the 1922 celebration, he wrote an open letter to the community emphasizing the importance of reforming customs and habits.[154] Like looking at the clock towers and participating in the sports contests, celebrating the modernity of Nantong connected one, no matter how humble, with sophisticated metropolitan culture such as that found in Shanghai. To distinguish the new Nantong from the old and from innumerable other provincial towns, and to make it acceptable at a higher level, it was crucial to endow it with events, personalities, and artifacts of cosmopolitan significance. Zhang Jian did just that, with considerable success.

Furthermore, the commemoration of anniversaries and other significant events helped Zhang Jian mark this period off as one of unprecedented achievement in Nantong's history. He singled out this particular slice of time in two ways. One was to deny the connection between the pre-1894 Nantong and the Nantong of the years after. Though

Zhang Jian did not declare the past a "zero time," he did by and large underplay the progress made in the decades before the No. 1 mill was founded. In the *Illustrated Gazetteer of Nantong County* sponsored by Zhang Jian, historical Tongzhou was described generally as geographically isolated and culturally backward, a place where people were close-minded and travelers few. Against this background, what Nantong had become since 1894—an industrial and educational center, a model city, and a tourist attraction—was a sharp break from the past. In reality, however, the past did serve the present. For instance, the skilled female cotton handcraft peasants were a great asset for the Dasheng mills, and the many surplus degree-holders were the first group that attended the normal school to speed the process of teacher training. Such connections were often lost when the anniversary and other celebrations emphasized the starting dates of factories and schools as the beginning of a new era.

The other way that helped to isolate this period as unique was to underline its linear, coherent nature. Zhang Jian consciously and frequently employed the temporal framework to count the years of his effort and present local development with an inner logic. For instance, in 1917, writing about the five parks, Zhang Jian said that he had promoted industry for more than twenty years and education for seventeen years, and that the time had now come to consider leisure facilities.[155] Furthermore, the 1915 *Achievements* was brought out to mark the first nineteen years of the local self-government, and the 1922 convention was to celebrate its grand twenty-fifth year. Such reference points reiterated the consistent path in this supposedly distinct time period. They also portrayed Zhang Jian as having a perfect sense of timing in anticipating and initiating new trends, and making the right decisions at every strategic moment; he was a master of time.

Helga Nowotny points out that "time represents a central dimension of power which manifests itself in the systems of time that dictate priorities and speeds, beginning and end, content and form of the activities to be performed in time."[156] This is precisely how time was manipulated in Nantong. In promoting the modern concept of time and in defining anniversaries, festivals, and other chronological events, Zhang Jian distinguished the model county in a temporal structure with his own personal mark.

Zhang Jian and his like had new and more effective instruments at their disposal to express and promote themselves than the gentry that controlled old China. Material culture confers social position, but what is considered prestigious changes over time. In the early twentieth century, things associated with the West, to which the elite had direct access, symbolized the privileged classes. Hence the acquisition of political power and social status became closely linked to the practice of modern culture. In the spatial and temporal reconfiguration of Nantong, Zhang Jian tried to bring in what he thought to be the best of new fashions that represented modernity and progress. The fact that clocks, Western-style buildings, and anything else connected with the West could be just symbols of modernity was often concealed. They greatly influenced the way in which Nantong was perceived. Nantong was by and large Zhang Jian's personal dominion. He attained this remarkable level of local power through a vigorous pursuit of cultural cosmopolitanism and a skillful manipulation of the symbols of modernity.

With the change in the notion of what constituted prestigious material came new trends in the way they were used. Though the traditional gentry often marveled at their personal collections of valuable antiques within their own circles, Zhang Jian put modern staples on public display. What is most striking about Zhang Jian's effort to rearrange space and time is his constant and consistent concern with image and publicity. Whether it was a park or an orchard, Zhang Jian had in mind its audience and its visual appeal. This consciousness about audience is at the core of exhibitory modernity.

CHAPTER 3

The Model in Print

The power to define the nature of the past and establish priorities in the creation of a monumental record of a civilization,
and to propound canons of taste, are among the most significant instrumentalities of rulership.

Bernard S. Cohn, *Colonialism and Its Forms of Knowledge*

THE NANTONG STORY perpetuated itself not only in the spatial and
temporal order of the community life, but also in the printed words and
images of the modern press. Representing a "definite communication
shift,"[1] the printing press has long been considered both a distinct hallmark of the modern era and a primary force that helped shape it.[2] By
the early twentieth century, the modern press had become an integral
part of China's metropolitan life, playing a significant role in shaping
political development and in defining social and cultural trends. However, to the majority of Chinese who lived in small towns and in the
countryside, daily newspapers and the periodical press remained
largely a novelty. Thus the rise of an active press and other varieties of
modern media in Nantong made it conspicuously different from the
rest of the nation's rural counties.

The Hanmolin Publishing House (Hanmolin shuju) marked the beginning of the modern press in Nantong. Created in 1903, six years after the establishment of the well-known Shanghai Commercial Press
(Shangwu yinshuguan) and nine years before the famous China Bookstore (Zhonghua shuju), Hanmolin was one of the earliest modern publishing houses in China, and perhaps the first at the local level. In the
ensuing quarter century, it and other printing outlets in Nantong produced numerous books and other materials on local affairs. In addition,
they published more than ten newspapers and magazines and produced rafts of photographs, maps, postcards, and other sorts of popular materials that had the capacity of carrying messages to ordinary
people. A rarity for a rural county, Nantong had its own motion picture

production companies, which recorded local happenings on film. All this made Nantong a regional media center outside the treaty ports. Moreover, the various media forms intersected. Public speeches, for instance, were not only delivered to live audiences, but also printed in newspapers and books. Such intersections reinforced and amplified the message in circulation.

Print material does not merely record a happening; it is, as Robert Darnton holds, an "ingredient in the happening," and thus an "active force" in history.[3] The Nantong publishing industry played an indispensable role in shaping local history. At every critical juncture of development, Nantong elites used the press as a great resource to meet their needs and to champion their causes. In the process, numerous documents were compiled that directly contributed to the rise of the new elites and Nantong's fame, including some that, like the report on a large-scale land survey, contained vast amounts of numbers. A number, as Bernard Cohn insightfully points out, is a particular form of knowledge, appearing to be certain and objective; whoever possesses such knowledge will also assume the authority to interpret and use it.[4] Indeed, through publishing, the Nantong elites exploited such knowledge to situate themselves as political and fiscal masters. These documents, together with the others that helped create an authoritative record of Nantong's recent journey, became the bible of modern Nantong, for they standardized a narrative that authenticated this period as the beginning of a new era and cemented Zhang Jian as its founding father.

The Rise of the Press

Zhang Jiluan, one of the founders and the longtime chief editor of the influential newspaper *Dagongbao*, once pointed out that the main difference between Western and Chinese newspapers was that the former were for profit making and the latter for intellectuals (*wenren*) to discuss politics.[5] Indeed, from the very start, the Chinese press was intimately connected with politics. The first high tide of newspaper and magazine publishing came during the Hundred Days Reform. That movement, with Liang Qichao as its chief spokesman, played a key role in popularizing the modern press.[6] The circulation of Liang Qichao's *Shiwubao*, for instance, increased from some four thousand to twelve thousand within its first year of publication.[7] A flood of new print media began to appear in 1900 with the intensification of revolutionary activities aimed at overthrowing the Manchus and the rise of the constitutional move-ment. The politically charged atmosphere of those days propelled ur-ban China into, to borrow Peter Clark's term, an "associational world"—the mushrooming growth of new political and professional societies and associations that were to redefine the nation's social land-scape.[8] To establish their identity and voice their concerns, many of those groups started their own publications.[9] Though not all of them survived, they popularized the notion that an organization ought to have its own organ in order to be legitimate and influential. As a result, various publications, distinctly political in nature, proliferated.[10]

Educated Chinese generally held that newspaper publishing in the Western mode differed from traditional Chinese publishing in three im-portant respects. The modern press would print anything and every-thing without restriction; it reflected popular sentiments and public opinion; and it had a broad readership, ranging from scholars to work-ers. In contrast, traditional Chinese gazettes focused exclusively on court affairs and the emperor's edicts, and their readers were limited to the elite.[11] The modern press was thus valued as a free forum with the power to reach ordinary people and the potential of becoming a great political instrument. A glance at the inaugural issues of the many news-papers that emerged at this time reinforces this view. All of them, from Liang Qichao's immensely popular *Shiwubao* to the longest-lasting magazine, *Dongfang zazhi*, stated their mission in terms of a dual re-sponsibility: to enlighten the people and to represent their will.[12] Their articles and editorials, they believed, would help end China's isolation from the world and improve the connection between the throne and its subjects, the two primary causes of China's backwardness, as they saw it.[13] The press, as the self-proclaimed backbone of the public, thus came to play a far greater and more legitimate role in China than any other institution. Journalists were known as "kings without a crown" (*wu-mian zhi wang*), and newspapers were perceived as the closest thing to an embodiment of the Mandate of Heaven.

It was in this context that Zhang Jian became vigorously involved in modern publishing. As briefly mentioned in Chapter One, Zhang first experienced the power of the press during the constitutional move-ment. He was keenly aware of the press's indispensable role in the re-form. In a 1904 letter to Zhao Fengchang, he asked for "good ideas" on how to add "fire" to "warm up" the reform.[14] Zhang soon found the "fire" himself: books on Japanese constitutional history. His correspon-dence with Zhao Fengchang in the early summer of 1904 illustrates just how much Zhang depended on those publications. He frequently wrote to Zhao in Shanghai to ask how the translating and printing process was going and to press him to speed things up. For example, after asking Zhao to mail 100 copies of the *Explanation of Constitutions* to Beijing as soon as they came off the press, he hardly let two weeks pass before instructing Zhao to ship all the available copies, though the order was still being run.[15] Zhang personally managed to have those books sent to high-ranking officials in Beijing to influence the constitutional reform.[16]

Zhang Jian also well understood how newspapers could be used to rally public opinion in support of the reform and other political goals.[17] He was closely involved in the publication of other leading newspapers and magazines in Shanghai, notably *Shenbao*, *Shibao*, and *Dongfang zazhi*. He co-owned *Shenbao* with Shi Liangcai and Zhao Fengchang in 1912, but withdrew from it in 1914 because of an internal conflict.[18] He nevertheless remained close to the newspaper; many of his announcements and official correspondence were made public through *Shenbao*.[19] Zhang was a close friend of Wang Kangnian, his *tongnian* ("the same year"; both Wang and Zhang gained the jinshi degree in 1894), who published five newspapers in Shanghai and Beijing from 1896 to 1910.[20] In the 1900s, Zhang frequently wrote to Wang with criticisms of the press and suggestions about how it could best serve the constitutional cause.[21] Zhang also served as a longtime board member for some of the most powerful publishing houses in China, including the Shanghai Commercial Press.[22] In the early 1920s, when fighting among the warlords provoked a new nationwide wave of provincialism and localism, *Shenbao* became the communications headquarters of the elites in the lower Yangzi who sought to protect regional stability. Zhang Jian joined them in that effort, writing extensively on national and regional affairs.[23]

Zhang Jian's involvement in the local press was as overtly political as it was in the national press, but also more diverse and influential. Zhang effectively controlled the press and other channels that disseminated information in Nantong, where the media, local politics, and the Zhang family interests were intimately wedded.

Landmark Publications

Soon after Zhang Jian established the normal school in 1902, in the expectation that a new school system would rather quickly follow, he realized that the demand for textbooks was unlikely to be met by existing local traditional printing shops or by outside suppliers.[24] Built with his own funds and those of his associates, the Hanmolin Publishing House was completed in 1903 in the beautiful West Garden situated on the northern bank of the Hao River, traditionally a gathering-point of local men of letters. Zhang Jian drew the name Hanmolin (luxuriant writing) from a Tang term with a connotation of cultural refinement.[25]

At the outset, the publishing house was too poorly equipped to meet the high demand that came with the rapid growth of local schools. In 1904, the No. 1 mill made a major investment that allowed Hanmolin to purchase additional printing presses and to build workshops. By 1909, it owned seven presses and employed fifty people. Growing steadily, the staff reached almost a hundred by 1930.[26] Zhang Cha was its director and Zhu Zongyuan, a renowned scholar who had broad contacts with the media in Shanghai, Nanjing, and other cities, was the first editor-in-chief. The publishing house had marketing offices in both Shanghai and Nantong, each of which also operated a bookstore and a stationery shop.[27] Hanmolin initially depended on the No. 1 mill for funding and was considered one of its enterprises. Though profit making was never a priority, as explicitly stated in its regulations, the publishing house was eventually able to support itself and to become financially independent of Dasheng.[28]

Hanmolin occupied a special place in the history of modern Nantong. It provided unique and indispensable services to local education, industry, politics, and public relations. It printed most of the textbooks for Nantong schools until they became a state concern in 1949. It also met the printing needs of local enterprises, from minutes of meetings to accounting records. Needless to say, most of the materials celebrating the achievements of Nantong were also published by Hanmolin.[29]

According to an incomplete count of its publications, Hanmolin printed sixty-nine books from 1903 to 1930.[30] About two dozen of these were personal writings, mostly family histories and poetry, including ten of Zhang Jian's own works. Most of the others, a total of thirty books, were written or edited by the county Local Self-government Association and its various subordinate organizations. Zhang Jian actively participated in the production of many of these books. In some cases, it is unclear whether a certain document was authored by Zhang Jian or one of the organizations.[31]

The thirty official books were of roughly five types: reports on projects in progress, such as local park construction; annual reports of government administration and schools; histories of specific projects over a relatively long period of time; collections of documents of local political institutions and industrial enterprises; and records of milestone events, such as the establishment of the Erosion Protection Society. Three of these publications, two of which were touched on earlier, are especially important: *Documents of Industrial Development in Tongzhou* (1905), *Achievements of Nantong Local Self-government in the Last Nineteen Years* (1915), and the *Illustrated Gazetteer of Nantong County* (1922). Together with a picture book published in Shanghai in 1920, they were the four landmark publications on Nantong.

Documents of Industrial Development in Tongzhou

Documents of Industrial Development in Tongzhou (*Tongzhou xingban shiye zhangcheng*) was a collection of regulations, accounts, and reports about the creation and operation of the factories, shipping companies, land reclamation companies, and other modern enterprises in Nantong since 1896. A supplemental edition with a slightly different title, *History of Industrial Development in Tongzhou* (*Tongzhou xingban shiye zhi lishi*), was published in 1910. It covered about twenty companies and factories, compared with just thirteen in the original edition, as good an indication as any of the rapid growth of industry in the span of five years.[32] As one would expect, the No. 1 mill was the primary focus of both editions, receiving five times as much coverage as all the other local companies put together.

The publication of the 1905 *Documents* was important, not only because it was the first record of local industries, but also because it contained detailed information on the background and process of their formation, the people involved, and their goals and impact on the community. In the case of the No. 1 mill, for instance, it included correspondence between provincial government officials and the Qing court, between provincial officials and local gentry and merchants, and among those local people. It also recorded negotiations and agreements between the government and the initial stockholders and among the stockholders themselves on investment plans and the management of the factory.

The book is important in its own right because of the light it sheds on China's early industrialization and on the transformation of this rural area in particular. But it is more important still because of its great symbolic significance. Reflecting the difficulties, struggles, and setbacks of the period, the book reads like a monument to the local gentry and merchants who, against all odds, brought Nantong's first modern factory into existence. It emphasized their determination, resourcefulness, and hard work. As a leader of this group, Zhang Jian's role was highlighted, and he came across as the father of Nantong's industrialization. Moreover, insofar as factories were viewed as the hallmark of the modern era, the No. 1 mill and other factories symbolized to many the beginning of a new chapter in local history. In the ensuing years, profits from the mill fueled the material and cultural transformation of the community. Through it all, the book served as a perennial reference point for the new Nantong. Indeed, it became the bible of Nantong's industrial age.

The timing of this publication was also significant. By 1905, Zhang Jian had become increasingly visible in the constitutional movement. The publication of the *Documents* further affirmed his leadership role and strengthened his argument in favor of a constitutional monarchy. For if, as the prevailing notion held, a constitutional government must be supported by a self-governing local society, then the success in Nantong well illustrated the potential of local initiative. Though data on the circulation of the book are not available, we know that a second edition was in print only a few months after the first one came out.[33] Zhang Jian's rising fame and the book promoted each other—Hanmolin's publication of the *Documents of Industrial Development* strengthened Zhang Jian's position as a spokesman for the constitutional reform and also heralded the coming of the local self-government movement in Nantong.

Achievements of Nantong Local Self-government in the Last Nineteen Years

The post-1911 period required adjustments. The Nantong community, like China as a whole, was searching for new directions. The establishment of the Republic first brought confusion mixed with excitement and hope, and then disillusionment and intensified confusion. Nantong elites struggled to come to terms with the Republican government. When, in about 1914, the hope for a new China under a strong, central government faded, Nantong's elites redefined their priorities and strategy. Local self-government was no longer framed as a means to strengthen the political center in Beijing, but rather as an end itself, to better the locality. The history of Hanmolin in the post-1911 era reflected this struggle and redefinition.

By far the most important Hanmolin publication in this period was *Achievements of Nantong Local Self-government in the Last Nineteen Years (Nantong difang zizhi shijiunian zhi chengji)*. As mentioned in Chapter One, this publication was compiled at the instance of the State Council in its struggle to keep Yuan Shikai from shutting down the institutions of local self-government. Since Yuan won the battle, the book failed to accomplish its immediate mission in rescuing the nationwide local self-government movement. But it played a significant role in launching Nantong on the model campaign and, in both its birth and its content, it is a classic example of the degree to which the print media helped to shape that model.

When, in 1914, the State Council instructed Nantong to compile material on its local organizations, Zhang Jian, then still holding down a post in the central government, immediately contacted the Nantong county magistrate, Chu Nanqiang, to solicit his support for the project.[34] Jiang Qian, a former president of both the normal school and the Jiangsu Provincial Educational Association, was selected to handle the writing project.[35] Various local scholars, some of whom held responsible positions in different departments of the county Local Self-government Association, were gathered and assigned certain topics to work on. The project was treated as a priority, and the participants were constantly urged to speed their essays up. Correspondence between Zhang Jian and his brother, county officials, and his associates and friends during this time indicate the importance Zhang attached to the production of this document.[36] On 26 June 1914, he wrote to Zhang Cha, instructing him to organize the book into sections on industry, education, public service, and philanthropy. He emphasized the importance of presenting everything in a logical manner—for example, how factory profits financed schools, how the normal school led to the development of primary and secondary schools, and how the need for a land survey resulted in the establishment of a surveying major at the normal school. Zhang also suggested that the book include not only projects completed, but also those in progress and in the planning stage. In July, the impatient Zhang sent his confidant Meng Sen from Shanghai to Nantong to assist Jiang Qian, for "the writing and editing have to be done quickly; hopefully within a couple of months copies of the book will be sent to Beijing."

Concerned about how to produce a quality book in a matter of months that would give a full picture of Nantong's achievements, Zhang Jian instructed that the chapters had to be "clearly written but not too tedious, brief but leaving nothing out." He suggested the use of chronological tables and lists so that the connections among the projects would be plainly illustrated. Various drafts were sent to Beijing for Zhang's review. He responded to each with detailed instructions about the use of specific terms, the manner of presentation, the content, and technical matters, and he corrected mistakes. To Zhang Jian, this opportunity to thoroughly document Nantong's success was "very important."

Despite the best efforts of Zhang Jian and the other participants, because of Hanmolin's limited production capacity, the book was not printed until 1915, too late to influence Yuan Shikai's decision. With more than one thousand copies in its warehouse, this publishing event was a financial loss to Hanmolin. The book nevertheless gained a certain degree of prestige as a major publication of the local establishment; in time, it became an invaluable source in the image making of Nantong.

Written by more than a dozen people under great time pressure, the book was bound to suffer editorially, to lack, for instance, a unity of style and balance.[37] Aware of its flaws, Zhang Jian added the phrase "in the past nineteen years" to the original title *Achievements of Local Self-government in Nantong* to emphasize that the book reflected only the primary stage of Nantong's development.[38] Whatever its shortcomings, they did not undermine its significance as the first publication to systematically document Nantong's recent history. In contrast to *Documents of Industrial Development*, and in keeping with its primary purpose, the book downplayed the link between the No. 1 mill and the other Nantong enterprises. Instead, it attributed everything to the Local Self-government Association. In doing so, it reinterpreted the piecemeal improvements before 1903 as part of an overall self-governance plan.

Under each of the sections—industry, education, philanthropy, and self-government—relevant projects were described. For each specific project, there was a brief account of its history, initiators, operational system, budget, and other details. Tables and columns, which Zhang Jian considered to be much more effective than words,[39] were used to help locate pertinent information at a glance. For instance, there were tables and columns itemizing the budget and cost of the old people's home, as well as personal information about those who had lived there, including gender, age, and native place.[40] The book thus provided detailed and convincing evidence of Nantong's success in transforming the community and improving ordinary people's lives.

Using graphics to buttress the text descriptions was a notable feature of the book. It contained dozens of maps, blueprints, and floor plans of the projects it documented. Its cover was graced with a map of Nantong city and the surrounding towns, against which the brush characters of the title were printed. In contrast to the text descriptions, which were typically dry and impersonal, those maps, blueprints, and floor plans not only brought the projects alive in concrete spatial configurations, but also compelled the reader to recognize their importance to the everyday life of the community. At a time when Western medicine was rare in the countryside, the county hospital, built in 1914, had modern equipment and three departments—internal medicine, surgery, and gynecology and obstetrics. The *Achievements* indicated the layout of the hospital, spread over sixteen mu of land on the southeastern side of the medical school (Fig. 9). Glancing at the floor plan, the reader might question the division of patient rooms into separate first- and second-class sections, and raise an eyebrow at the proximity of the three female patient rooms to the morgue and infectious diseases wing.[41] Nevertheless, one must appreciate the scope of the hospital and the effort behind its construction. Like many of the other projects, the hospital, as the *Achievements* stated, was initiated by Zhang Cha and funded with the Zhang brothers' private savings.[42]

The book's visual presentations were undoubtedly selected to highlight the achievements of the local elites. Under the section titled "Local Self-government" were maps of the entire county and its riverbank along the Yangzi, with symbols for bridges, roads, docks, dikes, and other newly built waterworks. Erosion protection was so prominently featured in this section that it gave the impression that local self-government in Nantong was mainly about flood control,[43] which was not too far from reality. Dealing with landslides along the northern bank of the Yangzi was a life-and-death issue in this region. Without any protection for the shore, high tides and floods annually washed away lives and property during the typhoon season of June to August. Land was eroding at an annual rate of 5,400 mu, at a cost of 162,000 yuan. Though local communities traditionally took care of small-scale water control projects and irrigation works, they expected the government to come up with plans and funds to deal with the mighty Yangzi. But despite repeated appeals from this devastated community for more than two decades, the Qing government did nothing to help.[44] In 1907, the newly established Erosion Protection Society headed by Zhang Cha began constructing an elaborate water control system. Funded with lo-

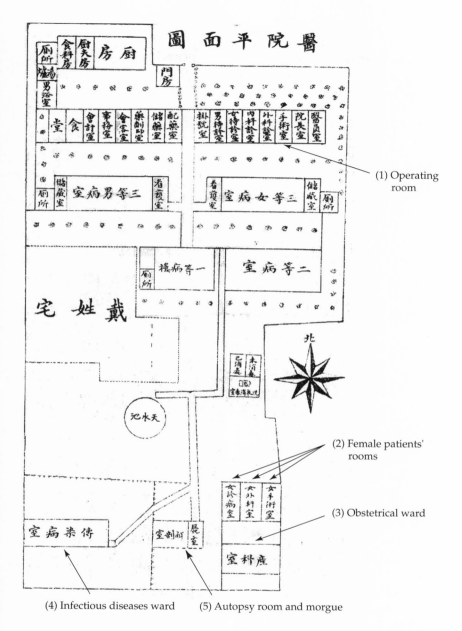

FIGURE 9. Floor plan of the Nantong Hospital. Though the hospital was modern for its time, no hospital today would put some of the patients' rooms (2) and the obstetrical ward (3) so close to the infectious diseases ward (4) and the autopsy room and morgue (5). (Courtesy of the Nantong Library)

cal resources, the project drew on the collective wisdom of Dutch, Swedish, British, and local engineers.[45] The map of Nantong's shore-line, filled with newly built water control symbols, was thus a powerful testament to the capacity of local elites to succeed in a domain that tra-ditionally fell to the state.[46] As in other agricultural economies, the con-trol of water was intertwined with politics.[47]

In this connection, the Nantong Survey Bureau was prominently presented in the *Achievements*. Zhang Jian recognized early on the unique importance of land surveys to local development.[48] Keenly aware of the need for professional surveyors, Zhang soon added a ma-jor in surveying to the normal school. Staffed by its graduates, the sur-vey bureau, budgeted at 14,636 yuan for equipment and staff and headed by Zhang Jian himself, was among the first institutions set up by the Local Self-government Association.[49] It was probably also the most efficient office of all. In 1909, within a year of its founding, the of-fice had produced a general map of the county and was nearing com-pletion of maps of all the twenty-one districts.[50] In 1914, the bureau re-ported that its staff had reached every corner of the county and made hundreds of survey maps.[51] In addition, it had surveyed and classified the county's land into ten categories (farm field, sand land, waste land, cemeteries, and so forth) and had charted all the land routes and wa-terways.[52]

All of this—the establishment of geographical boundaries, the clas-sification of soil and other natural resources, and the investigation of transportation infrastructure, among other things—was crucial for many of the new projects Nantong was undertaking. The significance of surveying, however, went beyond its practical functions. Indeed, surveying and mapping were distinct imperial functions in ancient times and in colonial conquest that always defined and projected au-thority over subjects and resources. In Nantong, surveying was instru-mental in establishing the new local elites' political authority. It helped gather a great deal of information that allowed the elites to control the use of the land and other natural resources and to become—quite liter-ally—"masters of all they surveyed." On one occasion, Zhang Jian is-sued an edict in his own name banning local people from taking rocks from the five hills of Nantong.[53] At another time, he instructed the au-thorities in Haimen, Rugao, and Nantong counties to stop exporting certain natural resources so that the local supply was protected.[54] Zhang Jian expertly employed the statistical data the surveyors gath-ered to justify all sorts of projects, from land reclamation to highway construction. In one of his essays, he mustered an array of facts and figures to show why a new road leading to the meteorological observatory on top of Junshan was needed and why the three existing roads were no good.[55] Such knowledge also allowed him to select quite a few spots in Langshan with good *fengshui* upon which to build his private villas.[56]

Detailed survey data also helped local elites to make tax policy and gain fiscal power. In some cases, the Erosion Protection Society successfully claimed several thousand mu of land as public property to finance water control.[57] In time, the society's financial capabilities grew substantially, to the point where it was able to co-sponsor one of its members for an extensive investigative tour of water control in the United States and Europe.[58] In these and many other instances, local elites manipulated survey data, a particular and supposedly objective form of knowledge, to strengthen their financial and political authority in the local self-government reform. That the *Achievements* accorded a prominent position to the survey bureau was a proper footnote to the unique role played by that institution.

In short, the compilation of *Achievements of Local Self-government* provided local elites with an opportunity to chronicle Nantong's development to date and to define its narrative. The book for the first time presented Nantong's progress in an organized fashion under the rubric of self-government. It thus contributed to the myth that what had gradually emerged over a period of two decades was a result of master planning from the start of the No. 1 mill. The book's dense use of graphic images, tables, and statistics added to its effectiveness and appeal. Such exhibitory quality fitted the initial purpose of its production—to demonstrate Nantong's success to a broad audience.

More important, perhaps, the book was not merely a record of past glory; it helped shift Nantong into the mode of self-promotion that was to become something of a fixation over the next decade. It illustrated to local elites how Nantong could market itself to outsiders through the printed page. The model campaign started precisely during the period when the *Achievements* was being prepared. Furthermore, the *Achievements*, for the first time, established a conceptual and organizational framework for representing the Nantong story—in industry, education, philanthropy, and local self-government. In the following decade, that presentation became a standard narrative of the new Nantong.

Illustrated Gazetteer of Nantong County

The publication of both the *Documents of Industrial Development* and *Achievements of Nantong Local Self-government* served to define the recent history of Nantong, albeit an ongoing and thus incomplete one. Perhaps aware of the historic moment at which they lived, and of the significance of their pioneering work, Nantong's elites displayed a deliberate and consistent—indeed obsessive—effort to preserve history in print; and the existence of a local modern printing house provided the means. Local government offices and bureaus published their histories and documents, and the various schools edited and published their reports, yearbooks, graduation memories, anniversary celebrations, alumni records, and other materials.[59] These publications became part of the collective history of Nantong.

But the grandest undertaking in local history writing was the *Illustrated Gazetteer of Nantong County* (*Nantongxian tuzhi*). Commissioned by Zhang Jian, the book was meant to be a general history of Nantong written in the time-honored Chinese tradition of gazetteer compilation.[60] A classical scholar, Zhang was an ardent reader of Chinese history and also a historian himself. In the 1880s, he helped produce at least two gazetteers outside Tongzhou.[61] Gazetteer writing had in most cases been an official undertaking, but this one was privately financed by Zhang Jian. The project got off to a rocky start, however, because he and his chosen author—Fan Kai, brother of Fan Dangshi, whose family was known for its literary talent—had a falling out. Zhang fired Fan in 1914, when he was only two years along in the work. Fan turned the unfinished manuscript over to Zhang before he left Nantong for good.[62]

The reason for the split was never clearly spelled out by either Zhang or Fan, and it remains a matter of speculation today. Some claim that Zhang faulted Fan for abusing his position as author by placing too much emphasis on his own family history.[63] Others hold that the source of tension was Fan's omission of the details of some of Zhang's initiatives as a subtle way of criticizing them as too ambitious.[64] Though we may never learn the truth of the matter, Fan obviously put himself at risk in agreeing to write a history that was less a record of the past than an evaluation of current affairs, with the main player still alive; worse yet, the main player had personally commissioned the project. The breakup between Zhang and Fan seems to reflect a struggle over the power to interpret Nantong's most recent history. In the end, as in most such cases, the one who possessed the most resources won.

Work on the gazetteer did not resume until 1920. Things were far different at that point from what they were when Fan started the work. Nantong's reputation was at its peak, and its position as a model well established. Many of the projects started in the early 1910s had proved successful, and new ones had been developing steadily since. With grand ceremonies in store to further validate the new Nantong, the need to capture this new identity in print became urgent. Coincidentally, Jiangsu was collecting county gazetteers to prepare for a provincial history project; Zhang thus decided it was time to return to the gazetteer project. This time he invited a non–Nantong native, his friend Meng Sen, to be the author, a man who would bring no family baggage to the project.[65] Zhang himself assumed the duty of chief editor. Based on Fan's work, Meng Sen completed the gazetteer in 1921, and *Nantongbao* printed it chapter by chapter as Meng was finishing it.[66] In 1922, Hanmolin published the gazetteer with two conclusions, written by Fan Kai and Zhang Jian, respectively.[67]

The gazetteer took 1876, the year where the previous prefectural gazetteer left off, as the starting point, but the major portion was devoted to the period between 1894 and 1921. In terms of writing style, the work remained classical, without punctuation, but that style was inevitably compromised by the introduction of new terms such as "high primary schools" (*gaodeng xiaoxue*) and "normal schools" (*shifan xuexiao*) and by descriptions of new activities such as "physical examinations" (*jiancha shenti*) and "elections" (*xuanju*). In terms of presentation, it partially followed that of traditional gazetteers, starting with an account of the county's geographical features and including a collection of biographies.

But the changes that took place in Nantong after 1894 were too extensive to be adequately expressed in the old gazetteer form. As a result, whereas biographies were a substantial component of traditional history writing, the new gazetteer was oriented more toward projects and institutions.[68] Fully half of the twenty-four volumes focused on new developments in the areas of industry, land reclamation, education, water control, philanthropy, and politics. Volume Sixteen, for instance, covered the entirely new matter of the elections of county local self-government institutions. Even the volumes that centered on more traditional topics dwelt on new developments. For instance, nine of the fifteen pages in Volume Three, "Local Products"—a standard subject in traditional gazetteers—were devoted to the experimental products turned out by the agricultural society and the agricultural school, both of which were under the control of the Zhang brothers. Here American strains of cotton and Russian and French varieties of wheat were described in some detail, together with the quality of soil, temperature, and other conditions under which they were cultivated. In this respect, the *Gazetteer* demonstrates another characteristic unknown in traditional history writing. Like *Achievements of Nantong Local Self-government*, it was filled with data on agriculture products, land, schools, and factories, generated through modern methods such as surveying. All this gave the gazetteer a distinctly scientific aura.

Moreover, to the degree that it listed all achievements under the rubric of local self-government, it was in essence a history of that movement, and its publication was timely. In 1922, many localities were operating more or less autonomously because of renewed warlord conflicts. In Nantong, Zhang Xiaoruo had just revived the county Local Self-government Association. Zhang Jian was no doubt aware of the connection between the past and the present. In the last sentence of his conclusion, he pointedly wrote: "Is this book useful to today's advocates of local self-government? I do not dare to know. I do not dare to know."[69] The publication of the gazetteer reaffirmed the Nantong model and thereby gave support to a new wave of the local self-government movement.

In its emphasis on local development since 1894, the gazetteer was an extension of the *Achievements*. However, the gazetteer form has unique advantages. It lends historical perspective to the contemplation of current affairs. In the new gazetteer, Nantong's past often served as a foil to its present. Most of the chapters started with a review of the history of a particular aspect, which was often said to be bleak. For instance, one chapter began by pointing out that negligence over the past two hundred years had caused the infrastructure of the city to collapse. The Hao River was silted up, and human and animal waste polluted the environment, causing disease; worse yet, over time such conditions had come to be accepted as a matter of fact. The chapter went on to note that around 1914, local elites had initiated an urban planning program to reform the city, with markedly successful results.[70] It thus credited elites with bringing fundamental change to the city in less than a decade—a far cry from the perceived stagnation of the previous two centuries. The "Industry and Commerce" volume opened with the statement, "Nantong's various companies of industry, commerce, land reclamation, and shipping all started with Zhang Jian,"[71] which of course implied that such undertakings never existed before.

It then went on to detail the process by which those companies were established, and the obstacles Zhang Jian and his associates had overcome.

When it came to local development under Zhang Jian's leadership, the *Gazetteer* recounted much of the material in the other two works. Stories about the beginning of the No. 1 mill, the normal school, and many other institutions were almost identical in all three publications— hardly a surprise since they were all produced under the same watchful eye. The repetition of such stories was useful in establishing a consistent presentation of Nantong's recent experience. This consistency was reinforced by the fact that no one else in Nantong possessed sufficient power to compete with Zhang's narrative. The publication of the gazetteer, however, bore special importance. As a traditional and formal practice of historical writing, it, perhaps more than Hanmolin's two previous publications, helped legitimate Zhang Jian's version of the community and secured his pioneering role in its modern history.

Nantong Industry, Education, Philanthropy, Scenery, with a Tour Guide Appendix

One of the most important of all the books published about Nantong during this period was the 1920 *Nantong Industry, Education, Philanthropy, Scenery with a Tour Guide Appendix* (*Nantong shiye, jiaoyu, cishan, fengjing, fu canguan zhinan*; *SJCF* for short).[72] It was printed by the Shanghai Commercial Press but edited and issued by the Nantong Friendship Club (Youyi julebu). The book provided no information about its author(s) and editor(s). In fact, few Nantong residents knew much about that organization. Perhaps because of its association with the *SJCF*, which was mainly for visitors, some local people believe the Friendship Club was a travel agency run by Zhang Xiaoruo and his friends.[73] But the club was more than that; it was a group of mostly young, ambitious politicians and professionals gathered around Xiaoruo, then trying to build his own power base in anticipation of replacing his aged father in local and provincial politics. They included, for instance, Xue Bingchu, stage manager of the Gengsu Theater, who was a trusted follower of the Zhang family. Most were apparently not so much friends of Xiaoruo's as sycophants who were intent on capitalizing on his rise to power for their own gain.[74] Some of them joined him in forming the Jinling Club in Nanjing in 1921 to promote his campaign for speaker of the provincial assembly (a subject we will return to in

Chapter Five). The young and fashion-conscious Zhang Xiaoruo named both these groups "clubs," a distinctly English term,[75] instead of using one of the two popular Chinese terms, "society" (*she*) or "association" (*hui*).

The Friendship Club represented the arrival of the prince faction in Nantong. Xiaoruo's study in his father's Haonan Villa and some of the halls in the museum served as offices for the club.[76] Though the club was Xiaoruo's personal toy, not a formal institution of great importance, it came to play a unique role at a particular time for the Zhang family and Nantong. Its sponsorship of the *SJCF* was part of the preparation for the 1922 convention. Zhang Xiaoruo's campaign for speaker in 1921 turned out to be a scandalous failure, a disappointment that alerted Zhang Jian to keep a close eye on his son thereafter, supposedly to protect him from being used by others. The Friendship Club probably ended during those trying years without further legacy. Its activity most notable to outsiders was the publication of the *SJCF*.

The *SJCF* follows the organizational and conceptual framework first set in the *Achievements*, as the title suggests, but it is unique in a number of ways. First, the book was a collection of 125 photographs, and the captions accompanying the pictures were in both Chinese and English. Also, though it was not called a tour guide, it was intended as a tour book—a "souvenir" (*jinian*) for those who came to visit and for those who wanted to take a "spiritual tour" (*shenyou*) of Nantong.[77] The *SJCF* belongs to the pictorial genre of "view books" that originated in the West and the kind of "bilingual souvenir books" that, as Susan Naquin has pointed out, began to appear in China in the early twentieth century.[78] Like most such books of the time, the *SJCF* had no maps of any kind. A more practical tour guide was printed to go with the book.[79] Reflecting its nature and its intended readers, the *SJCF* was sold at four of the best hotels in Nantong, including the exclusive Nantong Club, as well as at the Hanmolin bookstore. The hand of its publisher, the Commercial Press in Shanghai, is evident. The book was clearly packaged as a metropolitan, commercial product. It included thirteen pages of advertisements in the front and the back, featuring a total of nineteen companies or products, such as Socony Oil, the *Nantongbao*, rental car companies, and several hotels and banks. Some of the advertisers had their general offices in major Chinese cities or sold products from there. These new types of businesses accentuated the claim of a modern Nantong and its connection with the outside commercial world.

Immediately following the front advertisements and preceding the formal content of the book was a photograph of Zhang Jian in tuxedo with five medals pinned across his chest (Fig. 1), a positioning that gives the impression that Zhang's photograph was part of the advertising section. Perhaps that impression was intended—the *SJCF* treated Zhang Jian and his achievements as a commodity fashioned for marketing and exhibition. Zhang and his career were the obvious focus of the book. It began with individual photographs of "His Excellency Chang Chien" (Zhang Jian),[80] "The Hon. Chang Cha" (Zhang Cha), and "Chang Chien, Junior" (Xiaoruo), accompanied by introductions to their careers, achievements, and institutional titles. These were followed by photographs of their families and their villas. The introduction to Zhang Jian first recounted his scholarly success and his service to the government, presenting him as a driving force in the many reform movements of the late Qing, and then moved on to establish him as the "mainstay" of the local self-government movement. After listing a number of new projects and institutions in Nantong, it concluded: "All these institutions are the fruit of Mr. Chang Chien's energy and are either entirely supported from his private resources or are considerably assisted by him financially." According to the book, Zhang Jian single-handedly created the system of industry, education, and philanthropy that was the trademark of the new Nantong.

The description of Zhang Cha was brief and to the point: he was Zhang Jian's "right-hand man" in all his activities, and as the local emergency general during the 1911 Revolution, he was responsible for pacifying the region at a time of turmoil.[81] As for Zhang Xiaoruo, next to his picture in a Western suit was a list of his positions as the president, chairman, and executive committee member of eight modern financial, educational, industrial, and commercial institutions in and outside the Nantong region.[82] After the initial sixteen pages describing the male members of the Zhang family, what followed seems more like an account of the Zhangs' private enterprises than a guide to Nantong.

The book contains probably the most complete visual record of the Nantong establishment since 1894, with the exception of a few historic sites. It was organized into three sections. The first section, twenty-six pages long, was mainly on industry and land reclamation. It started with a picture of the Dada Wharf at Tiansheng Port to emphasize not only the understanding in Nantong that "industry cannot be properly developed unless transportation facilities were sufficiently improved," but also the very fact that "modern conveniences" had already been built in Nantong.[83] The rest of the pictures in this section consisted of a bird's-eye view of Tangzha, the customhouse and clock tower at Tian-sheng Port, and various factories.[84]

The second section, fifty-two pages, was mainly on education. Two photographs of the normal school understandably led off the section, but its real focus was on projects and institutions with a more modern and scientific outlook. For instance, the Nantong County Hospital occupied four pages. One picture showed a patient lying under an x-ray machine, and the caption stated that with this "novel invention," the operator was able to "send rays through the human body and to treat efficiently all internal disease."[85] Such inflated statements were characteristic of the book. The photograph of the operating room on the next page showed Dr. Scheidemann, director of the hospital, performing a laparotomy, and the caption stated that the whole hospital, like the operating room, "was fitted with all modern instruments and appliances."[86] The Nantong Museum claimed a full nine pages, the most space given to a single institution in the book.[87] The museum, according to the *SJCF*, housed two thousand "educational, historical, and art specimens," as well as "living specimens of plants and animals, wild and domestic." To illustrate this, the album presented a photograph of one of its most prominent exhibits, a giant fish skeleton discovered locally.[88] The last section of the book focused on scenic and entertainment facilities; it included pictures of the parks, the Nantong Club Hotel, swimming pools, and well-known temples in the Langshan area.

The philanthropic institutions were not grouped together; rather, they were scattered across the three sections. For instance, a home for the old was featured in the section on education, which also included the Model Jail.[89] The *SJCF* also contained things and persons that in one way or another related to the new developments. For instance, it included pictures of the Dutch engineer Hendrik C. de Reike and a giant gingko tree in front of Zhang Cha's agricultural society.[90] The last was probably meant to show the mightiness of the organization.

The *SJCF* was highly selective and exclusive in dealing with objects that were perceived as nonmodern or independent from the Zhang's enterprise, and so what was missing is also revealing. In the section on entertainment and scenery, the book featured a few temples, but none of the pictures showed any other traditional public places. For instance, teahouses and storytelling halls, which had probably been the most important venues of popular entertainment since the Song dynasty, were booming in Nantong, in part because of the rapid commercialization and urbanization. They typically attracted a dozen to forty customers, mostly city dwellers, which meant that a significant proportion of local people participated in these leisure activities. Tour books ordinarily recommended local teahouses and storytelling halls as sites where visitors could relax and observe local culture. But the *SJCF* completely and pointedly ignored the existence of this vital slice of community life. The reason for that had much to do with the cultural atmosphere of the time. Under the influence of the May Fourth movement, a group of young radical intellectuals in Nantong used the local newspapers to attack everything old, including teahouses, as the root of all social ills, from prostitution to gambling.[91] Sources do not indicate whether the Zhangs joined the crusade against the teahouses, but the *SJCF*, as a showcase of the new Nantong, naturally had to exclude institutions that were considered traditional and decadent.

The *SJCF* carried a distinct aura of self-congratulation and self-promotion. The brief caption for each photograph never fails to mention the subject's unique significance. Some projects were claimed to be the first of their kind in China.[92] To accent the advancement of transportation facilities, which were especially important because Nantong was known in the past for its geographical isolation, the caption for the Dada Wharf stated that "Nantong is now regarded by all the passengers as the second important port along the mighty river";[93] the port ranked number one along the Yangzi was of course Shanghai. Words like "famous" and "model" were generously used. The Dada Wharf was said to be one of the conveniences on landing at the "famous city," that is, Nantong city, where there was a "model jail" and a "model market."[94] The *SJCF* also displayed a prized mark of Nantong's achievements, the certificate of the Grand Prize awarded to Zhang Jian at the 1915 Panama-Pacific International Exposition in San Francisco for his role as the originator of land reclamation and his exhibit on his reclamation companies at the exposition.[95]

In order to avoid the impression that the book covered all that Nantong had to offer, the preface stressed that changes and improvements were taking place in Nantong with each passing day (*rixin yueyi*), and that new developments after October 1920, when the manuscript went to press, were not included. The preface also pointed out that the book contained high-quality photographs, but was being sold at a discount price so that all the "admirers" of Nantong could travel through the pictures to learn about the place. Such self-promotion had a serious intention, which was to lure potential investors for the much-needed capital to sustain Nantong's development. Unlike other tour books, this one, in fact each of its pages, came with a price tag. The skillfully composed captions provided a rather complete sketch of each project in a limited space: its starting date, its scale—in the case of a school, it was about how many grades, students, and graduates the school had—and its significance. It also indicated the initial capital invested in the project or its current annual operating budget. For instance, it stated that the initial investment in the Dada Company was 130,300 taels, and that the normal school's annual expenditure was over 33,400 yuan.[96] The reader learned the exact cost of all the projects featured in the book (Fig. 10).

Details of this sort fulfilled a dual purpose where investors were concerned. On the one hand, the information illustrated the overall scope of Nantong's development and the success the elites had achieved, which served to impress potential investors and give them confidence. On the other hand, it showed Nantong's need for outside capital to support all these very beneficial yet costly projects. It is this balancing act that the *SJCF* tried to perform. In order to boost investors' faith, the authors often went out of their way to construct a cheerful picture. The introduction for Zhang Jian, for instance, not only identified his initiative as a cause for China entering upon "her present career of industrial development," but also stated, "The capital for all these enterprises was easily forthcoming because of the integrity which was a well-known and widely respected trait in Mr. Chang's character and secured for him the confidence of the investing public." In the next paragraph, the writers once again emphasized how Zhang Jian enjoyed "the confidence of the public."[97] The story told here was contradictory to what was established in Hanmolin's three landmark publications, in which—and in reality as well—Zhang Jian experienced a great deal of difficulty in raising funds for the early projects, and the "investing public"—that is, the merchant community—initially had little faith in him. What the authors intended to do, obviously, was to present what Zhang Jian had achieved as a way of ensuring investors' trust, even if they had to rewrite some of the facts.

It is in this context that some of the unique features of the *SJCF* become understandable. The use of the English language was not only to accent the cultural sophistication of Nantong and its connection to the outside world, but also to speak directly to potential foreigner investors. Such purposes were served by the nature of the contents of the book as well. For instance, things that were familiar to Westerners, such as "modern instruments and appliances," were prominently featured, as in the case of the hospital and the museum; and the photograph of

THE NANTUNG GIRL'S VOCATIONAL SCHOOL.

FIGURE 10. Sample page from *Nantong Industry, Education, Philanthropy* (1920). This picture book, prepared in anticipation of a flood of foreign visitors in 1922, spotlighted Nantong's modern institutions. It typically ran pertinent data for each institution, in this case the annual budget for the girls' vocational school—3,000 yuan. Source: *Nantong shiye jiaoyu cishan fengjing fu canguan zhinan*, p. 44.

the Dutch engineer was intended to demonstrate Nantong's cosmopolitanism. The *SJCF* also included pictures of the head office of the Nantong Embroidery and Lace Works in Nantong city, its Shanghai office for export, and its branch office on Fifth Avenue in New York City.[98] Zhang Xiaoruo's name in English, "Chang Chien, Junior," reflected a customary practice in the West. All of this conveyed the message that Nantong, though not a treaty port, was readily connected to the world not only by transportation facilities but also by institutional, personnel, and cultural linkages, something that would be particularly attractive to foreign investors.

However, not all things and people foreign were included. Here once again what was absent was telling. The first Western-style hospital in Nantong, for instance, was built by a Christian church in 1907 and expanded into a popular memorial hospital in 1913, and it was headed by a Stanford-trained American doctor. That hospital started using an x-ray machine only a year after the Nantong County Hospital, which at the time was a major local news item.[99] The *SJCF* contained no information about either the church or its hospital. It only recorded the modern projects established by the Zhangs.

Of course, the book itself—its contemporary packaging by a major Shanghai publishing house, its advertisement of modern staples, its use of a foreign language, and its hundred-odd well-made photographs— was a strong statement of Nantong's status. There is no evidence to suggest that the preparation of the book was aided by people outside Nantong. By the late 1910s, Nantong had a significant number of returned students from overseas on the faculty of various schools, including English majors from London University and graduates of Columbia University and the University of Wisconsin. Zhang Xiaoruo himself had also traveled extensively in the West.[100]

The photographs, the main body of the book, were also locally produced. There were at least six photo studios in Nantong at the time. The one responsible for the *SJCF* was named Erwu (meaning "the two mes," one outside the camera and the other inside). Erwu started business in 1913. Like many local photo studios of the time, it was operated as a second business by a dentist. With the increasing demand in Nantong for group photographs and visual presentations after 1914, Erwu quickly began importing advanced equipment. In its advertisement in the *SJCF*, it claimed to own an American-made high-speed camera to capture action in movement, as in sports and dance, and wide-angle lenses capable of photographing groups of a hundred people and distant scenic vistas. Erwu also made hundreds of pictures of Nantong's scenic and monumental spots, which were sold in major hotels and bookstores; provided photos for other local publications; and served as the official photographer for local ceremonies. Erwu's success apparently owed to its manager, the dentist Luo Xinquan, whose ad in the *SJCF* revealed him as a sophisticated businessman, astute enough to promote his dental practice as well as his photo studio; fittingly, he completed the ad with two pictures, one for each of the two trades, as well as with his office phone number. In contrast, another photo studio that advertised in *SJCF* provided neither a picture nor a phone number, though it did use its new location on Mofan Road as a sales pitch.[101] Clearly, while capturing the image of a new Nantong, Erwu itself became part of that new image.

Unlike the three publications discussed earlier, the *SJCF* was considered lightweight and often discounted, perhaps because as a picture book it was by definition seen as trivial.[102] But photography, a Western invention of the mid-nineteenth century, was to become a fashionable medium in the early twentieth century. Some of the leading intellectuals of the day considered it to be an answer to their long search for a universal language, unbiased and neutral, one that reflected accurately its subjects, and was thus perfect for communication transcending geographical and cultural boundaries.[103]

But the pictorial language is plainly yet another particular form of knowledge that can be manipulated to mediate impressions. By appealing directly to the sense of sight, and especially by appearing to mirror what was real, the picture was an influential instrument used widely, for instance, in colonial conquest, as well as in domestic politics.[104] In early twentieth-century China, photography became a new ritual for certain official occasions to lend them importance and novelty. In 1913, for instance, it was listed as one of the ten items on the formal agenda of Nantong's celebration of foreign recognition of the new Republic of China.[105] Studio pictures also began to be used for practical purposes, such as for screening future marriage partners.[106] More important, they came to be considered appropriate and precious gifts for family, relatives, and friends, as well as a new device for social networking, and were exchanged in ways much like, and often along with, correspondence, calling cards, poems, and other gifts of various kinds.[107] In 1910, for instance, Zhang Jian sent the picture that had been taken of him at his fifty-seventh birthday to a friend in Shanghai, requesting 100 copies with his name, occupation, and birthplace written on the back in both Chinese and English. Clearly, those photographs were for socializing purposes.[108] Photographs, however, were not commonplace and available to everyone. They bore the imprint of the modern and signaled social privilege and difference. Indeed, pictures could be intensely charged with meanings, not only in how to photograph a certain subject, but also in whether or when to photograph it.[109]

If a picture is worth a thousand words, then the photograph collection of the *SJCF* was of inestimable value from the elites' point of view. It helped define the vanguard position of Nantong by displaying the rich material establishments and by connecting them with the prevailing cultural values, a characteristic of what Chandra Mukerji has termed modern materialism.[110] Moreover, its visual property not only made reading unnecessary while transmitting impressive messages, but also gave concrete shape and scope to the claim of a progressive Nantong.

Although details on the circulation of the *SJCF* are not available, it announced in its own advertisement that it was being distributed in Shanghai and other cities. Furthermore, it is certain that, as was intended, the book was disseminated overseas, mainly as gifts. Students from Nantong took copies of the book with them to their foreign destinations. Indeed, there was probably no better way for those students to introduce their hometown to their new friends.[111] Moreover, when, in 1923, Zhang Xiaoruo was appointed by the Beijing government to lead a Chinese delegation on a nine-country tour of industrial investigation in North America and Europe, his immensely proud father wrote to the Chinese ambassador in each country, as well as to his foreign acquaintances in those countries, and enclosed copies of the *SJCF*, along with pictures of himself, in his letters. Though he did not explicitly appeal to foreign investors in those letters, he did state China's need for foreign support.[112] That he did not particularly emphasize the needs of Nantong in the letters demonstrated Zhang Jian's statesman-like quality; he understood that Zhang Xiaoruo was on a mission representing the Chinese government instead of his hometown. The *SJCF* nevertheless spelled out what the letters could not: it at once showed off Nantong's accomplishments and indicated where foreign investment could be most beneficially used.

Other Media

Other local media outlets served similar purposes of promoting Nantong. Newspapers and magazines, films, and other seemingly insignificant yet far-reaching everyday printed materials were all an integral part of the Nantong story.

The Zhangs' Newspapers

Nantong's first newspaper, the weekly *Xingbao* (*Star News*), edited and printed by the Hanmolin Publishing House, started in 1907 at the high point of constitutional reform. Its mission was to educate the community on nationwide constitutional currents, to promote reform and local self-government in Nantong, and to support Zhang Jian's activities. It printed the Qing court's documents on constitutional reform and reprinted some articles and news items from *Shenbao*, on which it was modeled. It also covered major local self-government events (*dashi*) in the prefecture. Zhang Jian's articles and speeches frequently appeared on the front page. Assuming the status of a regional newspaper, *Xingbao* had special columns on news in Haimen and Rugao counties. Its circulation was about four hundred. It was distributed every Sunday to governmental offices, professional institutions, factories, schools, companies, and big shops in Nantong, and a small number of copies were shipped to areas outside Nantong.[113]

Xingbao was created by the Hanmolin Publishing House and, like it, was thoroughly enmeshed in local politics. Although the publishing house was founded primarily to meet the needs of local schools, it quickly became a political tool of the Zhang family. In 1903, at the onset of the constitutional reform, Hanmolin published Zhang Jian's *Diary of Travels East*. Not by coincidence, it started *Xingbao* in 1907, when Zhang Jian was becoming an important figure in the constitutional movement.

This relationship is best illustrated in the career of Zhu Zongyuan, the first editor-in-chief of both Hanmolin and *Xingbao*. Zhu, a native of Zhejiang province, was a talented man of letters. He was recruited by Zhang Cha to work in Hanmolin. If the size of one's library is a measure of cultural status, then Zhu must be ranked at the top. His private library was said to have contained more than ten thousand volumes. Like most of the active members of the upper gentry class, Zhu had broad political, social, and cultural contacts. He socialized with and befriended politicians such as Ma Xulun, onetime Minister of Education in the early Republic; famed men of letters such as Liu Yazhi and Wang Guowei; and artists such as Wu Changshuo and Mei Lanfang. In 1909, Zhu, together with Liu Yazhi, created the renowned South Society (Nanshe), an influential literary society with a distinctly anti-Manchu flavor. He was also an active member of the Association for Preserving National Learning and engaged in the publication of its journal, *National Learning* (*Guocui xuebao*). In addition, Zhu belonged to the group of professional journalists that was gaining much ground in the public arena. He was particularly familiar with publishing in the lower Yangzi region, since the members of the South Society were all active in that business. Zhu's reputation made Hanmolin a gathering-point for local and visiting reform-minded scholars who supported Zhang Jian's activities. Because of Zhu's status, Zhang Jian allowed Zhu to keep his position at Hanmolin even after he took a job with the China Book

Company (Zhongguo tushu gongsi) in Shanghai.[114] Zhu exemplifies the successful transition of a traditional gentryman to a modern professional. His social station and connections were a great asset to Zhang Jian and Hanmolin.

Despite the best efforts of Zhu and the Zhangs, *Xingbao* did not last. Imbued with the spirit of constitutional monarchy, it closed down shortly after the 1911 Revolution.[115] However, the end of *Xingbao* did not discourage the Zhangs from further flirtation with the newspaper business; on the contrary, they had just begun to explore the power of the press.

The post-1911 environment provided many advantages for strong local leadership. As Zhang Jian once again actively involved himself in national affairs and accepted central government posts, his brother Zhang Cha became increasingly influential on the local front. Zhang Cha had already become the most prominent figure next to Zhang Jian, thanks to his longtime control of local institutions such as the chamber of commerce and the Erosion Protection Society. The 1911 Revolution made him all the more visible because he held some key positions in the transitional period. To accentuate his rising status and to serve his political needs, Zhang Cha created *Tongbao* (*Tong News*), the second local newspaper, in March 1912, three months after the closure of *Xingbao*. Sun Liyan, secretary of the chamber of commerce, took charge of its editorial board. To the local people, *Tongbao* was the chamber's house organ. Published twice a week, it had a circulation of about five to six hundred, more than that of *Xingbao*. Later, when Sun Liyan resigned, Xue Heng took over as editor. Xue, a juren degree-holder trained in the traditional eight-legged essay style, was said to be unqualified to operate the newspaper. *Tongbao* closed in March 1914.[116]

The creation of *Nantongbao* (*Nantong Times*) in 1919 by Zhang Xiaoruo reflected a transition of power within the Zhang family. The Zhang brothers were in their late sixties and wanted to pass the torch to Xiaoruo. As *Xingbao* served Zhang Jian in his career, and *Tongbao* Zhang Cha in his, so *Nantongbao* was primarily Zhang Xiaoruo's tool to build his influence. The newspaper operated in the office of Zhang Cha's agriculture society, free of rent for the next ten years. It was published every other day.[117]

Established at the high point of Nantong's reputation, *Nantongbao* initially seemed to have many advantages. Supported by his father and uncle, Zhang Xiaoruo was extending his reach in politics and finance at both the local and the provincial level. We have seen that, among other things, he was the president of several local and regional institutions, had reinstalled the Nantong county Local Self-government Association with himself as the director, and was on the standing committee of the Jiangsu Society, which included the most prominent elites in the province. Xiaoruo's career is detailed in Chapter Five, but suffice it to say here that the political and financial power he gained in these years justified his need for a media outlet of his own.

Indeed, *Nantongbao* was completely at Xiaoruo's service, and he freely used it in those eventful years. Newsworthy items were plentiful—the operation of the new county Local Self-government Association, the activities of the Jiangsu Society, the ongoing preparations for the 1922 convention, and the election of the provincial assembly were among the highlights. The Zhangs' activities, speeches, and writings were reported in especially flattering tones. *Nantongbao*'s publication of the new gazetteer in installments in 1920–21 was itself an important boost for Zhang Jian. To attract readers and to display the prestigious social group Zhang Xiaoruo belonged to, every month the newspaper's masthead was written by different celebrities in their own distinct style of calligraphy. This promotional tactic, together with the threat of war that generated much interest in news, helped increase *Nantongbao*'s circulation, which allowed the newspaper to make a profit.[118]

In fact, *Nantongbao* alone seemed an insufficient forum to cover the new wave of local self-government. In 1920, Yu Weiting, a supporter of the Zhangs, started *Nantong zazhi* (*Nantong Magazine*), which was exclusively devoted to the idea of local self-government. It reported on the inaugural meeting of the Jiangsu Society, with the full text of Zhang Jian's speech. Another issue was dedicated to the establishment of the county Local Self-government Association, detailing its first meeting, regulations, and leadership arrangements, and printing the congratulatory speeches made by local institutions to show the broad support for Zhang Xiaoruo. The magazine also printed celebrity speeches and writings on local self-government by, for instance, Liang Qichao.[119] In short, *Nantong zazhi* was a cheerleader for Xiaoruo and his new ventures.

Publications under the Zhangs' control tried to maintain the established order and reacted negatively toward radical social movements. *Nantongbao*, for instance, did not cover the May Fourth demonstrations promptly, because the Zhangs considered them a threat to their interests. After Zhang Jian's death in 1926, *Nantongbao* overwhelmed its readers with Zhang Jian's posthumous glory. Telegrams and messages of condolence from Zhang's distinguished friends were published daily; many articles were printed in praise of Zhang Jian.[120] All this was an attempt to capture Zhang Jian's memory and to keep his Nantong alive. During the uncertain years from 1927 to 1930, *Nantongbao* carefully watched the ups and downs of the political thermometer and adjusted its attitudes to protect the interest of the Zhangs, but its high point had irreversibly passed.[121]

Tonghai xinbao

The Zhangs were not alone in recognizing the value of newspapers, and at times their control over the local press was challenged. At the time Zhang Cha established *Tongbao*, another important newspaper was founded by Chen Chen (alternative name Chen Baochu), the first person besides the Zhangs to operate a newspaper in Nantong. Chen, born into a landlord and merchant family in Nantong, started as a village head (*jiazhang*). He was sufficiently wealthy but did not have much influence beyond his village. Chen was ambitious enough, however, to grasp opportunities when they were presented to him. First, he established some connections with county merchant elites such as Liu Yishan and the Zhang brothers through the Erosion Protection Society. He was the head of a petition group for government funding of water control, which later landed him the position of assistant director of the society. Chen thus earned himself a second-class elite status in the county and later became a member of the provincial assembly.[122]

That accomplished, Chen now wanted to establish a base of his own. The opportunity came in 1913. Zhang Cha was then in the process of closing down his office because his position as general commander of Nantong had been abolished. Learning that Zhang Cha wanted to get rid of the ten telephones he had installed but refused to give them to the county magistrate's office, Chen Chen came up with the idea of forming a telephone company. He persuaded Liu Yishan to present the idea to Zhang Cha, and Zhang Cha accepted it.[123] Chen became the director of the telephone company, thereby substantially expanding his financial base.

He also tried to build his political influence. In 1912, Chen, together with a Nantong man named Lin and two friends from Haimen county, by the names of Liu and Zhang, created *Tonghai xinbao* (*New Tonghai Newspaper*). Not well educated, Chen left the paper's day-to-day operation to its chief editor, Liu Wei. Liu initially hired a few assistants and some local reporters in Nantong and Haimen counties, and then, when the newspaper expanded to cover a greater part of the Jiangbei region, employed additional staff in Rugao, Taixing, and Chongming counties. The paper started with two pages every other day, but it did not do well and had to close down in late 1913 because of financial difficulties. The shutdown was only temporary, however. In the end, *Tonghai xinbao* lasted for sixteen years. It expanded to eight pages, and it became a daily in 1924, with a circulation of almost one thousand.[124]

The newspaper stated its mission in its inaugural issue: "The establishment of the Republic should be attributed first to the power and influence of newspapers. In the future it will also depend on newspapers to monitor local politics and reform social customs. This is why Chen, Lin, Liu, and Zhang have founded *Tonghai xinbao*."[125] Chen and his associates were plainly aware of the functions of newspapers and intended to use *Tonghai xinbao* to shape local political, social, and cultural life. This required *Tonghai xinbao* to follow developments in the community, which meant reporting on the Zhang brothers and the local self-government activities.

The May Fourth movement provided an opportunity for the newspaper to distinguish itself and gain an identity of its own. Zhang Jian, as an established authority, considered social stability a priority. He punished students who participated in the movement by expelling them and closing down some of the schools.[126] Accordingly, newspapers controlled by the Zhangs tended to cast the student demonstrations in a negative light to discourage anyone from getting involved. In contrast, *Tonghai xinbao* allocated a great deal of space to the protests at the local and national levels. It sympathized with the students' point of view. *Tonghai xinbao* published follow-up reports on local students' activities and also printed news of the movements in other regions. In the month after the May Thirtieth Incident of 1925,[127] the newspaper published twenty-seven special reports on the event. It also stopped printing advertisements for foreign goods in response to the students' call for a boycott. Moreover, it exposed and criticized the Nantong Chamber of Commerce for not sincerely participating in and supporting the boycott. The newspaper's clear stand was encouraging to the students, some of whom highlighted its reports to show that public opinion was on their side.[128]

Tonghai xinbao's rather radical view had much to do with its chief editor, Liu Wei. Liu, after being educated in the classical tradition, had traveled to Beijing and other cities, where he experienced first-hand the rising tide of modern culture that was to characterize the May Fourth era. He was among the new cultural elites of the time who acted as cultural brokers to produce and transmit fashionable concepts and practices. In doing so, Liu not only created an aura of social prestige for himself, but also lent *Tonghai xinbao* a fresh outlook. By providing a different voice from the Zhangs, *Tonghai xinbao* gained popularity among radical intellectuals and students long after the May Fourth period.[129]

Overall, however, *Tonghai xinbao* strengthened rather than undermined the Zhangs' authority for a number of reasons. First, many of the Zhangs' activities were newsworthy items, and the newspaper had to cover them. Even if there were times when *Tonghai xinbao* disagreed with the Zhangs' conduct and opinions, it still had to report them to maintain its credibility as a newspaper.[130] Though at the time, notions such as "any publicity is good publicity" had yet to gain currency, such exposure no doubt helped keep the Zhangs in the spotlight and thus reinforced their domination. Moreover, as a pro-reform newspaper, *Tonghai xinbao* was in agreement with the Zhangs most of the time, because the schools, factories, and many of the other projects the Zhangs engaged in bore the mark of modernity and progress, a position the newspaper tried to seize for itself. In doing so, it directly or indirectly brought attention to the Zhang family, as well as to Nantong's image. On 21 April 1924, for instance, its second page was dominated by two news items. One was an announcement that Zhang Xiaoruo had been invited to give a speech at several prominent institutions. The other was a report on the grand welcoming ceremonies for two foreign groups, one led by a Chilean ambassador and the other composed of Japanese YMCA members from Shanghai.[131] The report detailed the stream of events arranged for the guests, emphasizing their impression that after seeing Nantong with their own eyes, they believed that it lived up to its reputation as a model city.

There were also personal reasons why *Tonghai xinbao* was generally friendly to the Zhangs. Although Chen Chen was unwilling to be swallowed up by the Zhangs, he tried to remain close to them, for association with the Zhangs was a shortcut to power. The masthead of *Tonghai xinbao* was in Zhang Jian's calligraphy, thereby connecting the newspaper with the most powerful man in the community.[132] On 12 March 1924, when *Tonghai xinbao* became a daily, it printed a poem by Zhang Jian especially written for the occasion, though by that time Zhang had become cynical about the press (*yulun jie*) and used words such as "absurd" to describe it. His poem lectured the newspaper more than it congratulated it.

The Zhang brothers, especially Zhang Cha, were not particularly fond of this self-made country lord. Chen thus turned to the inexperienced Xiaoruo. In 1921, as a member of the provincial assembly, Chen maneuvered for the election of Xiaoruo as speaker to fulfill his own political ambition. Although not an official voice of the Zhangs, *Tonghai xinbao* nevertheless contributed significantly to the building of the Zhangs' power and Nantong's fame.

Film Production Companies

The founding of two film companies in Nantong was another measure of the local ambition. Movies were introduced to China in 1896, one year after their birth, but only to a privileged few.[133] In the early twentieth century, interest in movies, whether making or watching them, was mainly an urban phenomenon even in the West. As late as the 1980s, movie theaters were still a rarity in rural China, strong testimony to the continuing cultural gap between the city and the countryside. However, in the 1920s, some people in Nantong were adventurous enough to flirt with every imported novelty of the time, including film making.

The first film company, the Nantong Film Company, was created in 1920 by Lu Chunlian, a Ford automobile comprador in Nantong. He had family roots in Yangzhou, a more bustling city in Jiangbei. Lu became rich in the car business and bought a movie theater in Shanghai. Inspired by the local theater events, which brought to Nantong the best opera actors and programs in China, Lu decided to make movies himself. At the time, some cultural enterprises, such as the Commercial Press in Shanghai, had filmed famous opera plays, turning stage performance to movies for the first time in China, and Lu wanted to follow suit. His company was meant to record the colorful theatrical events in Nantong. Lu discussed the project with Ouyang Yuqian, the director of the local acting school, since his films would involve the school's students. Ouyang initially rejected the idea on the ground that the students' performance was not good enough to be preserved on film. After much negotiation, Lu was granted permission to make two movies, and in the summer of 1921, they were shown in the Gengsu Theater. Despite their poor quality, they exposed the local audience to the silver screen and generated much amusement. Since Chinese-made films were still rare, Lu's filmed operas had their share of fame; they were shown in Shanghai and Nanjing, and even across the ocean in New York City.

However, Lu was ill equipped to support such a costly enterprise on his own. In 1921, he invited Zhang Jian and other elites to invest in movies. Together, they formed the Chinese Film Production Company, Ltd. As the majority shareholder, Zhang Jian became the company's chairman. Ironically, the film company, which was meant to capture Nantong's glory, was created at a time when Zhang's enterprises were declining. Despite that situation, or perhaps because of it, it seemed all the more important for Zhang Jian to capture the spent glory in a permanent and tangible manner; in this case, it was through movies that could be shown repeatedly and to everyone. The film company had an office in Shanghai, but its production facilities were located in the East Park, Nantong. It stopped production only one year after it started because of the lack of technicians, professional actors, and financial resources.[134] To meet the now high local interest in film, Zhang Jian rented some Chinese and foreign films from Shanghai to be shown in Nantong. Efforts to revitalize the company completely failed after Zhang Jian's death in 1926.

Though short-lived, the film company did serve the purpose of its sponsors. Its very existence highlighted the new Nantong, because visitors found it amazing that people in such a peripheral county had made films about their community. The company left some memorable products, and their quality was said to be better than Lu's first attempts. It screened, among other things, "Zhang Jian's Visit to the New Market" and "Scenery of the Five Hills [in Nantong]." Zhang Jian was the central figure in both documentaries. The new market in question was located near the South Gate, one of the projects designed to commemorate the 1922 convention. Thus Zhang Jian's visit to it was not an ordinary act. The film connected him, through the new market, with the celebration. The five hills were similarly filmed as a showpiece of the modern Nantong. Zhang Jian paid a great deal of attention to developing them as scenic spots and tourist attractions. The film on the scenery of those hills thus was not only a record of Nantong's natural beauty, but a commemoration of the human capacity to command nature. In 1922, Zhang Jian delighted the delegates of the Chinese Science Society with these films.

Popular Print Culture

Though films were considered a novelty, and newspapers mainstream, the printing world in Nantong did not stop there—its presence was also felt in the vast zone in between. Picture postcards of Nantong's scenery, for example, were distributed everywhere, in local hotels, bookstores, and tourist attractions. One could buy a piece of Nantong's impressive landmarks inexpensively and take it back to show family and friends. In addition to *Nantong zazhi*, there were other regular periodicals, such as *The Journal of Nantong Normal School Alumni Association*, and special issues, such as the one that commemorated the establishment of Nantong University in 1928.[135] They were effective ventures to spread information on Nantong and the Zhang family. Advertisements that circulated information far and wide were another marvelous invention of the modern world. The picture of the imposing multistoried building of the Huai Hai Industrial Bank advertised in the *SJCF*, for instance, was a declaration of the political and financial power possessed by the Zhang family.

Modern print technology allowed the mass production of textbooks that played a key role in strengthening the established order. Information on Nantong as a model, for instance, was included in school textbooks and read by thousands of students across the region.[136] Easy access to printing also helped simplify and expand the use of personal cards. Calling cards, or name cards, as they were generally known, were widely used by officials and literati in traditional China. In the Qing dynasty, the most common type was a slip of paper enclosed in a piece of red paper shaped like a big envelope. After the 1911 Revolution, people handed out small cards with white or red printing, which were both easy to store and to carry.[137] Zhang Jian and Xiaoruo both had their own personal cards. Zhang Jian disseminated his widely, sending them with gifts or handing them out to visiting guests.[138] During Zhang Xiaoruo's campaign for the speaker of the provincial assembly, his associates carried his cards on his behalf to influence the course of the election.[139] The Zhang family also had its own stationery, printed with the characters for Haonan Villa, as did many of the offices and institutions in Nantong, such as the Club Hotel. As evidence of how widely available such printed material was, at least in certain circles, on one occasion, Zhang Jian's cards were misused without his knowledge, and on another, someone used his office stationery to send out a telegram in his name. Zhang Jian protested both incidents.[140]

The impact of printing was reinforced by the intersection of various media outlets, as when, for example, the *Illustrated Gazetteer* was printed by *Nantongbao* in installments and then by Hanmolin in its entirety. Advertisements of books were another channel that used different printing businesses. Hanmolin's publications, the *SJCF*, and Zhang Jian's writings were routinely advertised in local newspapers.[141] The Nantong press also converged with other forms of information dissemination. For instance, Zhang Jian's long essay on how to regulate the Huai River was intended as a proposal for the central government, but it was also printed in installments in *Tonghai xinbao* during May 1913. His speech at the opening ceremony of the normal school in 1903, before any of the local newspapers appeared, was reprinted by *Nantongbao* on 17 May 1931 with editor's comments. Poems and couplets composed during Mei Lanfang's visits were not only recited at banquets and parties, but also printed by local newspapers,[142] which furthered not only Mei's name but also the influence of his trips to Nantong.

The proliferation of publications in combination with oral and other communication channels stimulated further demand for printing facilities. Nantong's few traditional printing shops continued to operate alongside Hanmolin, but together they still could not handle the increasing needs. Some customers took their business as far away as Shanghai. Several new printing companies started up when the demand for services became apparent. The most important was the Tongxing Printing Company, Ltd., created in 1918. Chen Chen was involved in that company, and he switched *Tonghai xinbao* from Hanmolin to patronize the new endeavor.[143] The company advertised its capacity to produce fifteen different items in full color, including newspapers, family histories, trademarks, leaflets, invitations, funeral announcements, stationery, and personal cards. That advertisement not only reflected the growth of local business, but also indicated the crucial role printing had come to play in both public and private lives.

Of course, those who had their cards or announcements printed were not typically ordinary people, but the ordinary people too were part of the printing world; they composed a reading public that rose steadily in Nantong throughout this period. To be sure, there were major regional discrepancies in the degree of literacy and availability of print materials in China. In 1924, Xu-pu in Hunan province, an area of 300 square miles with a population of 300,000, had only nine copies of a Shanghai newspaper, which often arrived a month late; teachers were said to be ignorant of current events. In some rural towns of Sichuan province, textbooks were five years out of date.[144] But in the mid-1910s, a reading room in the capital city of Shandong province attracted two hundred visitors daily. The city's public library housed seventy different newspapers and magazines with about one thousand readers daily.[145]

If these figures are accurate, Nantong was somewhere in between. Although it was not a provincial capital, education had been a priority since the late Qing. Its modern schools significantly raised the rate of literacy. Other cultural outlets, such as the library and the museum, bookstores, mobile book stations, and newspaper reading rooms also stimulated and promoted the spread of literacy. Some major shops in Nantong set out ten or so local and regional newspapers on their counters for customers and neighbors to browse.[146] Reading rooms, sponsored by public as well as private funds, were considered such a common part of a town's cultural life that Guanyinshan, a town long on shops but short on reading rooms, was publicly criticized as backward by local newspapers. As a remedy, the Nantong Educational Association initiated a reading room to "increase local people's knowledge."[147]

The illiterate could not escape from printed matter entirely. The pictures in advertisements and other publications did not require literacy. The illiterate were also indirectly exposed to printed materials through public speeches and daily conversations. After all, in China as in Europe, a "hearing public" had always been part of the oral tradition.[148] Still, even those who had no interest whatsoever in opening a newspaper or attending a public gathering could be part of the printing world. A primary example in Nantong was the paper money the Zhangs printed. As in the case of the newspapers, each of the Zhangs issued paper money in his own time. The practice started in 1911, when Zhang Jian tried to establish a bank. One-yuan bills, imprinted with Zhang's picture, were issued in the name of the No. 1 mill as a test for the bank idea. They stopped circulating after one year with the establishment of the Dasheng Savings Bank. In 1917, when Zhang Cha's land reclamation company was short of capital, it issued some paper money as working funds in the hope of speeding up capital turnover. The currency, bearing Zhang Cha's likeness, circulated within the reclamation area for about two years. With the precedents set by his father and uncle, Zhang Xiaoruo, in the name of the Huai Hai Industrial Bank, printed several hundred thousand yuan of paper money in one-, five-, and ten-yuan denominations. In light blue, they bore Zhang Xiaoruo's picture on one side and, depending on the denomination, a picture of Langshan or of the bank on the other (Fig. 11).[149] Though the paper

FIGURE 11. One of the paper bills printed by the Huai Hai Industrial Bank in 1921. Zhang Xiaoruo's picture was on the face of all the notes, printed in three denominations, with various pictures on the back, here a scene of Langshan. The money was never circulated. (Courtesy of Jiang Ping)

money Zhang Xiaoruo printed never entered circulation for reasons that will be spelled out later, the bills printed by his father and uncle reached thousands of hands in Nantong, schooled or not. Those who used them would have likely learned the identity of the men depicted on the money and thus perceived, at least to some extent, the messages it conveyed.

Although printing in Nantong became an all-pervasive force that penetrated the everyday lives of ordinary people, its immediate political function was most prominent. This was demonstrated in the production of the landmark publications—the *Documents*, the *Achievements*, the *Gazetteer*, and the *SJCF*—at each of the critical moments of Nantong's development. It was also evident in the fact that each of the three main figures of the Zhang family felt compelled to have his own newspaper. In this connection, we must highlight the significance of the paper money the Zhangs printed. Money is not merely an economic object. Numismatic scholarship often takes for granted that issuing currency is a function of the state, and that has usually been the case.[150] Therefore, money of various kinds inherently carries with it an aura of authority at the highest level; in fact, it is a "minor monument,"[151] and a matter of sovereignty: when money makes the world go around, it also makes the power of its sponsor go around in the world in which it circulates. That Zhang Jian, his brother, and his son all printed currency bearing their pictures testified to the breakdown of the Chinese central government, on the one hand, and the tremendous political ambition and influence of the Zhangs, on the other. With the control of the printing presses, the Zhangs were undoubtedly major opinion makers and the political powerhouse in Nantong; and the two were closely intertwined.

Roger Chartier has pointed out that printed words always aim at installing or reinforcing an order.[152] The publications discussed in this chapter certainly did that. They reflected the consistent intentions of their authors or sponsors. In the last few decades, postmodernists have called our attention to the many factors other than the author that affect the meaning of a book. However, any construction and negotiation of meaning is conditioned as much by the author's intention as by the printing process and the reader's experience. Furthermore, the author's participation in a book is essential to an understanding of the historical context in which it was produced. Justifiably, in recent years, the author has returned after going through a postmodernist "weight watch" program.[153] In Nantong, the elites used the print media to define the history of their community in ways they saw fit. In doing so, they built a master narrative about the Nantong model and their role in achieving it, and disseminated the narrative beyond the county boundaries. The Nantong story effectively demonstrated that in early twentieth-century China, printing had begun to alter the conditions under which power was exercised. Moreover, politics had come to depend on the dissemination of information on a massive scale; printing had become power.

CHAPTER 4

The Model on Display

There is nothing natural or necessary about the way museums are organized or works of art displayed within them. Nor are museums neutral spaces: they "frame" their contents as certainly as a picture frame circumscribes a canvas.

Andrew McClellan, *Inventing the Louvre*

DURING THE EVENTFUL years of the late 1910s and early 1920s, Nantong experienced an endless flow of public ceremonies, celebrations, exhibitions, conferences, speeches, shows, banquets, and athletic contests. Virtually all of those events were publicized in the local newspapers—the public was informed, and in some cases invited to observe, participate, and learn something new. Though some of the activities were traditional in form, they were repackaged as public spectacles to promote modern, progressive purposes. Those events are another key to understanding Nantong's rise from obscurity.

One of the distinct marks of the modern era is what might be termed public-mindedness—a population's awareness of its importance in the political and social life of a nation. When the private people began to recognize their shared interests and to invent their own representations,[1] the state was compelled to acknowledge that rising force and adjust its policies accordingly. As a result, early modern Europe witnessed the evolution of a more open, representative government, as well as more government regulations to assert state power in the public domain. But direct regulatory control was only one way, and not even the best way, to govern, according to the Enlightenment scholars of the eighteenth century. They advocated a liberal government that emphasized public instruction—to educate and enlighten the public through arts and other cultural means.[2]

The conviction of the importance of public education began to gain currency during the late eighteenth century in Europe and the United States. The result was not only the institution of official bodies for the oversight of public instruction, but also the emergence of a host of new cultural instruments designed for public consumption, such as museums, libraries, and reading rooms. The public museum, which turned magnificent princely collections into public treasure, had become a fixture in every European capital by 1850 and grew to be one of the most important cultural institutions of modern times.[3] Public libraries sprang up in major urban centers and gradually found their way to provincial towns as well. These new institutions did more than just raise the level of education; they also came to redefine leisure activities and public behavior. Through these "instructive entertainments," to use the term of the nineteenth-century British visionary social reformer James S. Buckingham,[4] the public was instilled with the ideas, values, and tastes that were essential to the strengthening of established authority. In a more open, mobile, and commercialized world, such seemingly invisible yet wide-reaching means of governance were more effective than naked force and strict regulation, and were thus sanctioned by the state. The state has been directly involved in the processes through which modern nations accumulated and created rich symbolic inventories of cultural institutions and artifacts for public consumption.

Public consumption is indeed another angle from which to understand the public-mindedness of the modern era. Aside from its commercial value, public consumption provides a channel to exhibit and validate modernity. In the West, this exhibitory modernity was most evident in the wave of major expositions that began in the mid-nineteenth century.[5] In the following years, countries in other parts of the world tried to claim their own progress by imitating this exhibitory modernity. They embellished themselves with modern staples and showed off at world fairs.[6]

Chinese politicians, master performers of ancient ceremonies, quickly caught on to this modern exhibitory culture. From the last years of the Qing dynasty on, various exhibitions were held at national, regional, and local levels. The Qing court, together with important merchants, sponsored the 1910 Nanyang Exhortation Fair (Nanyang quanye hui) in Nanjing, and in 1913 Beijing hosted the first national Children's Art Exhibition.[7] China also began to participate in international fairs, such as the 1876 American Centennial Exposition in Philadelphia and the 1915 Panama-Pacific International Exposition in San Francisco.[8] Regional exhibitions were often held in preparation for the national fairs. For instance, the Tongzhou General Chamber of Commerce organized a local display in 1909 to collect items for the

Nanyang Exhortation Fair, and the Jiangsu Educational Association ran
a provincial exhibit in 1912 to select works for the Children's Art Exhibition.[9] The awareness that such exhibitions were a global phenomenon
was evident. The medals for the Nanyang Exhortation Fair, for instance, bore a picture of a soldier standing on the globe,[10] which of
course also symbolized military power. All this indicates that China
had begun to join a world culture that focused on collecting and showing, with the public as the target.

In this, Nantong was certainly a leader. After 1914, Nantong was
made into a showcase where every elite effort at modernization was
carefully collected, displayed, and therefore magnified by the available
means and resources. The very publicity of the Nantong story helped
"give what goes on there its aura of being not merely important but in
some odd fashion connected with the way the world is built";[11] the way
the *modern* world was built, one might add, for the local elites used the
same new cultural institutions that were publicly recognized as progressive to broadcast Nantong, relating the county and themselves to
the new and modern.

The best known of the new institutions was the Nantong Museum,
initiated in 1905. It was considered a supplemental educational institution for local schools. In this connection, the schools, their students'
achievements, and their sports activities were also offered to visitors to
demonstrate the progress of Nantong. Thus schools served as exhibitory sites as well, in addition to their many other functions. Moreover, there were periodic events with an exhibitory quality. Some were
locally oriented, such as anniversary celebrations of landmark projects,
whereas others took place on a grand scale and involved nationally
recognized celebrities, such as the theater reform in the early 1920s that
brought renowned actors to Nantong. There were also public lectures
given by major opinion makers. Around these events were welcoming
and farewell ceremonies, poetry and couplet compositions, and banquets, the so-called *mingren shenghui* (celebrity gatherings), which became part of the unfolding drama on the local scene.

This chapter visits the institutions and events that were engineered
to show, in myriad ways yet not always consciously, the new Nantong.
If showing is telling, there is much to learn from the narrative of those
exhibitions and performances about the struggle for power and fame,
and about the common ground of modernity and tradition that was cre-
atively used to serve pragmatic local interests.

The Nantong Museum

The Nantong Museum was a byproduct of Zhang Jian's trip to Japan for the Fifth Industrial and Agricultural Exposition. That he should be convinced of the country's need for a public museum after his return is hardly surprising, for he was deeply impressed by the public nature and educational orientation of the national and local museums he visited there.[12]

Zhang Jian's Initial Proposal

At the outset, Zhang Jian was persuaded that so unprecedented and grand (*shengju*) an undertaking as the creation of the first Chinese public museum had to be sponsored directly by the Qing court and located in Beijing, the political center. He lobbied for the project at the highest levels of government. In 1905, he wrote to the Education Ministry and also to Zhang Zhidong, proposing the establishment of an imperial institution that combined the forms and functions of the museum and library. He called this a *dishi bolanguan* (literally, imperial museum-library), a term borrowed from Japan.[13] Though the idea of public libraries in China can be dated back to the nineteenth century and was supported by some other prominent Chinese,[14] Zhang Jian's proposal was the first in China that systematically set forth the essence of the museum as a modern institution and is thus worth exploring.

By all accounts, Zhang Jian's understanding of the museum institution was quite up-to-date. His argument centered on education, an urgent concern in 1905, when the Chinese educational system was undergoing a historic transition away from the civil service examination system. "The reason that those initially backward countries in the East and West have now become the leaders of civilization lies in the popularization of education," he declared. But he quickly added that schools alone had their limits; "that is why there are libraries and museums to supplement and support the school system."[15] To Zhang Jian, the museum was an integral part of public education. He emphasized its conservational and public nature—its purpose was to conserve artifacts and books of historical significance for the benefit of the public. Accordingly, the Qing court should open its treasures to "all under Heaven" and gather valuable items from private people to enrich the museum. He used Japan as an example. There the Imperial Museum-Library was said to have put on display "every piece of the centuries-

old palace collections, as well as contributions from private people."
Zhang Jian obviously understood the two basic functions of the museum: to conserve and to educate.

Why did the museum have to be named "Imperial" and be located in the capital? In suggesting this, it is clear that Zhang discerned the political function of the museum. Aside from the fact that the existing courtly possessions of artworks, artifacts, and books could be easily converted into a public museum, Zhang Jian argued that since the main purpose of a museum was to cultivate morality and proper behavior, it had to start at the top, for the court was the highest moral authority. An imperial museum would spread the Emperor's moral influence all over the country. He expected this museum to serve as a model for all the provincial and county museums, so that people everywhere could benefit from this institution. The other all-important political role of a museum in China's capital, according to Zhang, was to impress visiting foreign dignitaries, so that they would report on China's glorious past and its magnificent architecture and culture. To Zhang Jian, as to the creators of the Louvre, the proposed museum was to be an integral part of the political structure, "a source of national pride as well as royal glory," and "a state institution occupying center stage in the public life of the capital."[16]

Zhang Jian went on to discuss the technical aspects of the museum, from its architecture to its classification system, management, collections, and rewards for private contributions. He envisioned the museum as a magnificent seven-story building with three main halls to exhibit objects on nature, history, and the arts. Interestingly enough, though Zhang thought that the exhibits in natural history should be arranged according to the regions where they were discovered or produced, he insisted that the history and art collections should be arranged in chronological order to illustrate long-term trends in the development of civilization. Clearly, Zhang Jian grasped the representative quality of the museum and intended to use it to teach the process of evolution, a main theme in contemporary Western museum work.[17] But Zhang was not a believer in linear progress; he emphasized the importance of showing both historical progress and historical degeneration. This notion of nonlinear history in fact became popular in China during the May Fourth movement under the influence of Western fin-de-siècle thought, but there is no evidence to suggest that Zhang's understanding of history was swayed by that intellectual trend. More than likely, he came to this conclusion on his own as an avid reader of Chinese history. Also absent in Zhang's thinking was the pessimistic view of history that characterized the fin-de-siècle.[18] To Zhang Jian, it was a simple fact that history passed though both progressive and regressive stages, which the museum ought to reflect. To increase the prestige of the museum, Zhang insisted that its director be a distinguished person-age (*mingliu*) and appointed directly by the Emperor himself, and that its staff should include people skilled in foreign languages. Being a hands-on person, he also gave instructions on details such as the height of the display shelves (not too high for exhibiting and cleaning) and the number of exits (not too many to compromise security). He anticipated that the project would take five years to complete.

Written in classical Chinese with frequent reference to Confucianism and ancient Chinese dynasties, Zhang Jian's proposal nevertheless em-bodied the very spirit and knowledge of a professional, standard mod-ern museum. In assessing the significance of the museum, Zhang did not go as far as some European cultural reformers, who believed mu-seums had the potential power to save a monarchy politically or to lead a person to heaven privately.[19] But just as the opening of Louvre in 1793 was tied to the birth of a new state,[20] Zhang Jian conceived the im-perial museum to be an "important aspect of modern politics in China" (*woguo jinzheng zhi yaoduan*). For him the urgency for China to catch up with this modern politics was self-evident. "Considering the current situation," Zhang argued, "[we] cannot afford to wait to implement the museum idea."[21]

The Creation of the Nantong Museum

The Chinese government waited another twenty years to implement Zhang Jian's plan: the Palace Museum of Beijing opened in 1925. In the meantime, Zhang Jian, realizing that an imperial museum was a dream at a time when the Qing dynasty was struggling for its very political survival, chose to found a museum in Nantong instead.[22] In 1904, the normal school drew up a plan for a botanical garden where students could be instructed in the natural sciences. The following year, Zhang Jian decided to modify the plan and turn the forty-eight-mu piece of land into a museum instead. This he called a *bowuyuan*, or "museum-garden," a combination of a Western-style museum and a traditional Chinese garden. In 1912, after a seven-year effort, the museum was complete.[23]

The garden area in the south was dotted with picturesque stones, lily ponds, water fountains, artificial hills, an herb garden, and decorative and functional pavilions and halls. Zhang Jian gave poetic names to the pavilions and halls, and adorned their door frames and entryways with his own poems and couplets. There was also a zoo of moderate size with birds, deer, monkeys, and other animals. The garden proper was beautifully landscaped and was designed to please not only the eyes, but also the nose. A variety of flowers, trees, and herbs from as far away as Germany were planted, so that no matter what the season, there would always be some in bloom and some releasing heady fragrances. All the trees were classified and labeled with their Latin names.[24]

The museum initially had three exhibition halls: the central, southern, and northern halls. An eastern hall was subsequently added as an office and reception area. All four halls were built in Western-style, were designed by Sun Zhixia, and were constructed by a local company (Fig. 12). The exhibits were organized under the rubrics of nature, history, arts, and education. The central hall housed metals, minerals, and stones, including inscribed ancient bronzes and stone tablets. On its roof was an observatory, the first meteorological station in Nantong.[25] The southern hall stored historical objects upstairs and specimens of animals, plants, and metals downstairs. Artworks were displayed upstairs in the northern hall, and the aforementioned giant fish skeleton occupied the downstairs. Between and around the halls were large Buddhist and other sculptures in iron and stone.[26]

In time, the Nantong Museum expanded. It grew to cover sixty-six mu of land and possessed nearly three thousand types of objects. With multiple items of each type, it had a considerable number of holdings. The items came from many sources: the museum's own purchases and productions; donations from private individuals, private and public institutions such as local temples and schools, and government offices; and gifts from Chinese and foreign guests. Zhang Jian himself donated his lifetime collection of paintings, calligraphy, and other artifacts.[27] Today, any museum can regularly count on at least some of those channels for their acquisitions, but in the early twentieth century, for a remote Chinese county museum to accumulate such a large collection in a matter of a few years was most unusual. This had much to do with Zhang Jian's prestige and his broad social contacts. Some of the gifts to the museum were specifically meant to please him.[28] Zhang also had substantial power over the local community. In 1908 and again in 1915, he wrote open letters to encourage people in Jiangsu province to contribute to the museum. To assure the public that anything stored in the

FIGURE 12. The southern hall of the Nantong Museum. (Courtesy of the Nantong Museum)

museum was safe, and in fact safer than if kept in private hands, he referred to the international law that protected museums during warfare.[29]

Zhang Jian's ambition for the museum was clearly expressed in his instruction that it should search out objects from deep antiquity and from foreign lands. As a result, the museum had live and fossil specimens of various animals from Russia, America, Australia, and Asia. Not surprisingly, given the contemporary emphasis on the natural sciences, scientific objects constituted the museum's major holdings, about 63 percent of the total. Historical objects included ancient musical instruments, stone tablets, weapons, and a relatively recent piece, a flag of Yuan Shikai's "Imperial China." The artworks included paintings, calligraphy, sculptures, and various kinds of stationery. Educational objects were initially kept in the history hall. The purpose of setting up a separate educational exhibit was to provide a special focus for research. It contained materials on the civil examination system, private academies, and new schools in the form of tests, homework, and copybooks from different time periods.[30]

The museum was quite professional by Western standards. Specialization and classification are the essence of modern museology, which is expressed in the development of both specialized groupings of objects within a given museum and a range of specialized museum types.[31] Systematic specialization and classification imposes "stability and order on bodies of knowledge" and thus allows us to make "intelligible a scientific view of the world."[32] The Nantong Museum clearly followed the contemporary general principles of classification by dividing its objects into science, history, and art.

The other important part of modern museology is the catalogue, without which no museum is complete.[33] For the Nantong Museum to claim to be a modern institution, it had to develop a catalogue on the Western model. That was not an easy task, for there were few available references in Chinese. In 1912, Zhang Jian invited six Chinese, Japanese, and Korean experts on history, art, and natural science to take on the job. They checked the Latin names for plants and animals. In history and arts, they examined the authors and time periods for the holdings. Since the Japanese were ahead in introducing Western museology, the Nantong Museum subscribed to and purchased Japanese science magazines and books. In 1914, after two years of effort, the *Nantong Museum Catalogue* came out in two volumes, one for natural science and the other for history and art, and was distributed to libraries in and outside Nantong.[34]

Though Zhang Jian was involved in all this, much of the museum work was under the specific supervision of Sun Yue, the first and long-term director of the museum. Sun Yue was the brother of Sun Zhixia, the architect who designed the museum. The Suns came from a humble local family but, benefiting from the new educational system, both brothers became prominent professionals in Nantong. Attracted by the so-called new learning, Sun Yue interrupted his schooling in classical Chinese in 1903 and entered a Japanese school in Nanjing, where he excelled in the Japanese language. One year later, because of financial constraints, he was forced to transfer to the Nantong Normal School, where he immediately became a favorite of his Japanese teachers. When Zhang Jian started the museum garden, Kimura Tadajiroo, a Japanese science teacher, recommended Sun for the job of assistant. With the completion of the museum, Zhang made Sun the director, a position he held until 1933.[35]

The Control of the Museum

Like many of the new institutions of the period, the Nantong Museum, for all its outward Western trappings, was operated in the traditional way that long prevailed in China: it was strictly controlled by one man, Zhang Jian, who considered the museum not only the crown jewel of the new Nantong, but also his personal property. Before Zhang Jian built his own house in the city in 1914, he lived in the museum and made it both his home and his office. The Flower and Bamboo Well Hall in the museum was built specifically to help one of Zhang Jian's wives recover from her illness, though she died before the hall was completed.[36] Zhang constructed his Haonan Villa next to the museum and had the two buildings connected. There was no clear divide between the Zhang family's property and the museum. When, in 1913, the Jiangsu Provincial Educational Bureau reconstructed all the schools and, in the process, put the normal school under provincial administration, Zhang Jian immediately divorced the two institutions, so that the museum would remain in his hands.[37] Early on, when the museum was considered a part of the normal school, the school, by unspoken agreement, never made major decisions about, for instance, the appointment of the museum's director and its regulations. Zhang Jian was the one who decided all this, including when and to whom the museum was open. In fact, though the avowed purpose of the museum was public education, its ownership was not clearly spelled out. In various documents, it was listed as part of the Dasheng complex, as a component of the local self-government establishment, and as Zhang Jian's private property.[38]

One major difference between the Nantong Museum and its European counterparts is that it was never open to the general public during Zhang Jian's lifetime. During the seven years when the museum was being built, it was gradually made available to the students at the normal school. In 1912, when the basic construction and organization were complete, the museum allowed other local schools and institutions to visit, though limits were set on the number of daily visitors. But Zhang soon put a stop to this when some unpleasant incidents occurred. As it happened, the culprits were certain students of the normal school, who picked flowers, damaged the lawn, jumped out of windows, and beat the gardeners who tried to stop them. Though these were the typical acts of mischievous students, Zhang Jian was greatly upset.[39] To some extent, he took it as a personal insult—disrespect for all his hard work that had brought the museum into existence. In his own words, his heart was attached to every blade of grass and tree on the museum grounds.[40] He immediately wrote and posted a set of "Museum Visitor Regulations."[41]

In the regulations, Zhang Jian sharply criticized the students and expressed his bitter disappointment at their actions. As a justification for the regulations, Zhang mentioned that when Westerners visited Japan, they laughed at the sign "Do Not Damage Flowers and Trees" in Japanese parks, for the need for such a sign betrayed the lack of public morality among the Japanese. "Now what happened in this museum is worse than what happened in Japan," Zhang said. He then went on to emphasize the need to treat such a "disease" with "medicine"—the regulations. That wording offended some of the teachers and students, who, instead of confronting Zhang, took it out on the museum staff. Zhang Jian, outraged, posted a "Temporarily Closed" sign as a punishment for the rebellious students and teachers.[42] The museum reopened late that year, but as in the past, to only a limited audience, as now specified in the regulations.[43]

The visitor regulations say a good deal about the museum's operation. The seven provisions were both punitive and discriminatory.[44] Visitors were to come only as a group from organizations and institutions, not on their own as individuals. There were two kinds of visitor passes, one regular and the other special, which were unevenly distributed to local institutions. The normal school was privileged to receive twenty passes, but the other schools and organizations were assigned only four to twelve each. The museum was open to the normal school on Wednesdays, Saturdays, and Sundays, but to the others on Wednesdays and Sundays only. During the designated days, groups of twenty or fewer would wear regular passes. Their captain wore a special pass, and without a captain, a group, even with regular passes, would not be admitted.[45] Only one of the seven regulations concerned "outsiders" (*wairen*)—a telling term referring to those who did not have any institutional affiliations in an age that was prolific in associations. They were required to provide a reference in order to get a regular pass and to be accompanied by a person from the normal school who held a special pass. The captain or anyone who was provided with a special pass was to police his group and to take responsibility for any wrongdoing. The punishment for violating the rules was severe. For instance, if the captain failed in his duty, no pass would be issued to his school for a month. But the bar was set much higher if the captain was a normal school student: his name would be recorded, and he would be banned from obtaining a pass for three months. Should someone enter the museum without a proper pass, that person would be permanently expelled, and his or her name would be printed in the newspapers, together with a description of the infraction that was deemed "lawless and harmful to the public interest." With their detailed restrictions and harsh penalties, these regulations tended to deter and exclude, instead of encouraging and inviting the public to visit.

The regulations give the impression that Zhang Jian was more concerned with protecting the museum than using it to educate the public, an anxiety shared by other such institutions elsewhere.[46] Part of this was of course dictated by a legitimate concern about museum security. Then and now, the burden falls on the institution to protect its holdings and environment. Today, museums have various high-tech security devices at their disposal, but in Zhang's time, the main protection was the human eye. It was therefore understandable that he tried to put pressure on the visitor so that the museum staff could do their job.

Public behavior was a frequently discussed issue in the development of museum culture in the West as well. More precisely, with the growth of public institutions and spaces after the eighteenth century, behavior management—regulating the conduct of visitors—became an urgent concern. This was reflected in the museum practice of guided tours and restricted rights of entrance. Gradually, aside from architectural and technological solutions, a public culture regarding crowd behavior took shape to set the standards for civilized, acceptable conduct. The museum was one of the first institutions to reshape and manipulate what were later to become general norms of public behavior. Ideally, museums, according to the noted museum administrator and ichthyologist George Brown Goode, should be "passionless reformers"—the high culture offered by the museum should itself be a force to transform people into rational, self-restrained human beings. This "modern-museum idea" expected visitors, through cultural cultivation, to become self-monitoring, and thus a regulatory force in themselves. By the early twentieth century, Goode's ideal had become a reality in the West, where public warnings such as "Do Not Pick the Flowers" were no longer necessary. This was achieved, however, only with a century of improvements in education and parallel developments in architecture and technology.[47]

The Nantong Museum's need for stringent rules was not due merely to the lack of appropriate technology; it was also due to the fact that in a provincial town like this, a "museum public," let alone an educated museum public, was virtually nonexistent. When the idea of the museum was being discussed, Nantong's earliest modern schools were only three years old. Those students, few in number, were the first generation of the local people who would someday probably appreciate the museum. Moreover, it was unlikely that students outside the city could regularly attend the museum, thus further reducing the pool of potential museum-goers. There was a disproportionately large number of professionals in Nantong, but very few visited the museum more than once. Unlike the theater, where new plays were staged from time to time, the exhibits in the museum were mostly fixed and therefore did not invite revisiting. Given that the museum could not even handle the behavior of its targeted audience, it was understandably all the more worried that admitting the general public might bring in rowdy crowds, and thus opted to exclude the general public altogether.

As for the general public, what happened in the museum was essentially irrelevant to the daily lives of most ordinary people. If in Paris, the art capital of Europe, the museum public was "divided by degrees of visual competence" because people varied in their level of artistic and literary sophistication,[48] that was hardly the case in Nantong: the majority of the public simply had no interest in the museum. Some people might have looked at it from a distance with admiration for its novelty, others might have felt intimidated by its claim of culture and science, and still others, probably only a few, might have been alienated by Zhang Jian's sudden shutdown of the museum in 1912, but their lives were largely unaffected by that institution.

Thus when Zhang Jian discriminated against ordinary people, they repaid him with indifference. That, of course, was a great irony: Zhang Jian started the museum to support the schools and to educate the people, but only a small tier of the public—the schools and professional institutions—had access to it. Though in the West, at least in theory, the museum was a public space in which rights were supposed to be universal and undifferentiated,[49] entering the museum in Nantong was a privilege that was granted, and thus could be taken away, by Zhang Jian. It was not until after Zhang's death in 1926, and in the aftermath of the Northern Expedition, that the museum became open to anyone who wished to visit.[50]

The Exhibitory Function of the Museum

If the modern museum means a public museum,[51] then whether the Nantong Museum qualified as a modern institution invites debate. But that the museum was used as a modern instrument to serve the elite interests in various capacities, as a privileged space, a powerful platform, a celebrity-drawer, and above all, a representation of modern Nantong, is not in any way in doubt. In addition to storing regular museum objects, the precious space in the museum was devoted to displaying personal items of the Zhang family. Since Zhang Jian practically owned the museum, anything he deemed valuable would be exhibited. All of the objects related to the Zhangs were housed in the southern hall, the key exhibition room. One of the main items there was a set of Korean ceremonial robes, a gift from the Korean king to Zhang Jian as a reward for his assistance in handling the 1882 Korea crisis, a major event that distinguished Zhang in his early political career. The other objects from foreign lands included a gilded city key from a Boston mayor and a two-inch piece of wood, said to be from President Lincoln's bed; both items were obtained by Zhang Xiaoruo during his visit to the United States.[52] From the father's early distinction to the son's recent honor, time was accumulated in a rearranged space that spoke about the lasting, marked eminence of the Zhangs.

Along with family glory, national pride was on display, implicitly. In 1910, Zhang Jian helped organize the Nanyang Exhortation Fair, which included a unique twelve-piece embroidered screen by a famed embroidery school in China. A Japanese intended to purchase the screen, but Zhang made a bet with him and won. To many this was a rare instance in the early twentieth century when a Japanese lost to a Chinese. The screen was extravagantly framed and prominently placed in the southern hall.[53]

The museum proved to be an influential image-making platform for Zhang Jian in other ways as well, most notably through its catalogue. A catalogue not only lends a coherent historical narrative to separate pieces and gives voice to objects that cannot speak for themselves. It also provides the author with great authority, through his interpretation of its contents, to influence the ways in which the museum is perceived. After all, a catalogue is a presentation that can be manipulated.[54] Zhang Jian himself wrote the preface to the *Nantong Museum Catalogue*, in which he first stated how his initial proposal for creating an imperial museum in Beijing had been ignored and how this led to his own effort to establish the Nantong Museum. He also pointed out that in other countries museums were supported by the state and founded with national revenue, to emphasize the extraordinariness of a locally sponsored museum.[55] Implicit in all this was the idea that Zhang Jian and Nantong had accomplished a modern project of great significance while the Chinese government had failed.

Zhang then proceeded to highlight the richness and significance of the museum holdings, which included objects "from thousands of years ago and foreign countries."[56] Things from distant space and time, no matter how insignificant on the surface, often convey special values and command unusual attention.[57] For instance, a gilded key from as far away as the United States, awarded in symbolic welcome to Zhang Xiaoruo by a mayor there—who, like his country, was exotic and mysterious to a Chinese—carried a whole different new meaning. It instantly invoked the feelings of amusement, curiosity, admiration, and respect that turned it into an irreplaceable sacred item. Such feelings were naturally transformed to Zhang Xiaoruo himself. The closest thing to that key, he now personified everything the object represented. Zhang Jian's preface, as well as the catalogue itself, mediated the message in the museum exhibition to satisfy both Zhang's political ambition and his personal vanity.

Such ambition and vanity were greatly embellished by a number of famous people, including two talented foreigners who came to be associated with the museum. One of the foreigners was Kimura Tadajiroo, a Japanese teacher at the normal school and Sun Yue's mentor, who served as an adviser to the museum. He specialized in biology and taught Sun Yue and others how to make specimens. The other was Kim Changkang, a writer and poet who held a jinshi degree in Korea.[58] In 1882, during Zhang Jian's mission to Korea, Kim and Zhang became friends out of mutual admiration for each other's literary talent. When Korea lost its sovereignty to Japan after the Sino-Japanese War, Kim, filled with grief and indignation, left Korea for Shanghai with his family. Zhang Jian welcomed his expatriate friend and offered him a job in the Hanmolin Publishing House. Kim was well known for his patriotic writings and activities during his years in Nantong. His knowledge of literature and art was a great asset in the preparation of the museum catalogue.[59]

The best-known person among those who played an important role in the museum was Chen Shizeng (1876–1923), also known as Chen Hengke. Chen was from a highly recognized official elite family. His grandfather Baozhen, a former Hunan governor and a noted reformer, had recommended four of the "six gentlemen" whose deaths marked the tragic end of the Hundred Days Reform to Emperor Guangxu. Chen's father, Sanli, a late Qing jinshi and onetime Minister of Ritual, was also a well-known reformer and poet, and Shizeng's younger brother Yinke was one of the most respected historians in China, a scholar who excelled at Sanskrit, Turkish, Uighur, and several other languages.[60]

It was said that Chen Shizeng gained his reputation as a poet, artist, and calligrapher at the age of ten. He socialized not only with official elites but also with noted men of letters and artists. In 1902, while studying in Japan, Chen shared a dormitory with Lu Xun, an eminent writer of modern China, and the two became close friends. In 1909, Chen accepted Zhang Jian's offer of a teaching post at the normal school. Though Chen's "great name" (*daming*) initially intimidated the students, he was well respected and received on campus. In fact, Chen was perhaps the ideal teacher for the moment when schools in China were trying to hold onto the traditional learning while embracing the new. Chen's own body of knowledge was a mix of the old and new, a fact that the students could relate to, and his overseas experience had given him an edge in the age of reform. The subjects Chen Shizeng taught included mineralogy and zoology. When the Nantong Museum needed to examine and catalogue its specimens for exhibition, Chen became a natural candidate to join Kimura and Kim in the project. He left Nantong in 1914, right after the completion of the catalogue, for a post in the Ministry of Education in Beijing. Soon after Chen's death in 1923, the Palace Museum in Beijing published *Shizeng Yimo* (*The Ink Shizeng Left Behind*), a ten-volume work that included only a small portion of his paintings and calligraphy.[61]

Chen Shizeng was not particularly close to Zhang Jian personally and found Zhang's vanity especially distasteful.[62] But he enjoyed his work in the museum and his newly formed friendship with Sun Yue, a bond that was strong enough for the two to correspond after Chen's departure.[63] To be associated with the name of Chen Shizeng was of endless benefit to Nantong. He lent credit to the museum catalogue by being one of its researchers and producers. His prestigious family background and his social contacts, as well as his learning and reputation, were all powerful decorations to the museum and the school where he worked, and thus to Nantong in general.

Of all the renowned people that became linked to the Nantong Museum, one was a female, the embroidery expert Shen Shou (1874–1921; Fig. 13). Known as a "world-class artist, " the so-called "divine needle" flattered the museum with her own internationally acclaimed works.[64] The daughter of a scholarly family in Wu county, Jiangsu, Shen gained national attention in 1904 when she was commissioned to create some embroidered screens for Empress Cixi's seventieth birthday celebra-

FIGURE 13. The embroidery expert Shen Shou. Source: *Nantong shiye jiaoyu cishan fengjing fu canguan zhinan*, p. 45.

tion. The eight pieces selected for the occasion delighted Cixi, who awarded Shen the character "shou" (longevity), which she promptly adopted as her personal name. When, with Cixi's support, the Ministry of Agriculture, Industry, and Commerce established a female embroidery department, the Empress invited Shen Shou to be its master teacher. Shen and her husband taught court ladies there until the fall of the Qing dynasty. In 1914, Zhang Jian invited Shen to start a girls' vocational school in Nantong as part of his educational program for women. She worked there until her death in 1921, training more than 140 students from Nantong and beyond.[65]

Shen produced some award-winning embroidery pieces. Her portrait of the Italian queen claimed the first prize at the Nanyang Exhortation Fair and again took top honors at the following year's Italian Exposition. The portrait was presented to the Italian queen as a gift. Shen's masterly portrait of Jesus won first place at the 1915 Pacific International Exposition. The portrait was said to be worth $13,000. The Nantong Embroidery Bureau capitalized on her international fame by setting up a branch office on Fifth Avenue in New York City to display her works. Both Zhang Jian and Shen Shou considered those works national treasures. In her will, Shen left them to the Nantong Museum, where they were cherished as the most prized of possessions.[66]

It was to Zhang Jian's credit that Nantong, a small pond by any measure, was able to attract such big fish as Shen Shou and Chen Shizeng. They became part of the Nantong experience, for they would not have come were it not for Zhang Jian's many pioneering projects and his determination to hire the best-qualified people for those projects.[67] The unique talent and extraordinary accomplishments of people like Chen and Shen added great substance to the claims of the new Nantong.

What the Nantong Museum represented above all else, however, was modern culture and science. Zhang Jian and most of the other local elites were traditional scholars at heart who were not ready for the wholesale application of Western culture and science in China. Nevertheless, they realized the need to adopt certain aspects of Western learning to improve China's condition, especially to educate the young generation on whom the future of the nation rested. This was the reason why the education exhibit, for instance, included modern industrial tools and models of various machines, steamships, and trains.[68] Like museums in the West at the time, the Nantong Museum emphasized natural history and the sub-disciplines of anthropology, archaeol-

ogy, biology, and botany. The giant fish skeleton was prominently exhibited in the north hall for the very reason that it exemplified most of
those areas of scientific knowledge.[69] Other claims to modern science
were achieved with less effort and expense than that one. For instance,
a tree is just a tree, but a tree labeled with its Latin name suddenly carries a scientific aura. Terms in Latin, the universal language in the classification of plants and animals, were by definition scientific terms.
Even today, literature on the Nantong Museum tends to dwell on the
fact that all the specimens in the museum were classified and labeled
with their Latin names to underscore the scientific nature of the institution.[70]

In this connection, the promotion of science also had other agendas.
Local elites used the "respectability of science in areas having little
bearing on science itself," a phenomenon known as "scientism" that became popular among Chinese intellectuals in the early twentieth century.[71] Of course, the Chinese were not the only ones who mustered
"science" to curious causes. Michael Smith has studied the rise of "commodity scientism" in the United States, where science and technology
were repackaged and put on display for advertising products that "revealed less about the design of the new device than about its sponsor."[72]
Likewise, the Nantong elites considered the museum to be a decoration
of the model. They made it part of important local events and confidently presented it to almost every celebrity visitor. In 1920, the delegation of the Jiangsu Society took a tour of the museum during its first
meeting. A visit to the museum was also scheduled for John Dewey's
trip. Other foreign visitors included a German professor from Hamburg
University, the general editor of *Millard's Review*, contributors to *Asia*,
and a Japanese delegation led by the cultural entrepreneur and writer
Uchiyama Kanzoo, a friend of Lu Xun.[73]

This city showpiece was valued also for its unique structure as both
a residential and a cultural complex. It sometimes hosted special guests
and served as a conference hall for grand events. After 1918, with the
rise of Nantong's reputation, the museum increasingly became a center
of entertainment for banquets and other social functions. For instance,
the actor Mei Lanfang was lodged in one of the museum halls during
his performances in Nantong. In 1922, the Chinese Science Society held
one of its meetings in the museum. The delegates also visited the museum as part of the conference program.

Perhaps overwhelmed by all the new things they experienced in
Nantong, often during a short trip of a few hours or a few days, none of

the visitors left an extensive account specifically about their impressions of the museum. From what they did mention, however, it is not difficult to see how the museum affected their overall view of Nantong and Zhang Jian. Recalling his trip to Nantong, Uchiyama Kanzoo made a long list of the places he saw, and the museum was one of them. He concluded that Nantong was an "ideal cultural city."[74] One of the five photos Sites chose for his 1918 article about Nantong showed a "well-kept corner" of the city that encompassed Zhang's private garden, an "ivy-covered museum," and the Nantong Library. In the article, Sites passionately described this corner and its "charming group of buildings." To Sites, this was an artistic representation of the "spirit of progressive enterprise" at work.[75] If in museum-rich America today, a museum was able to save a dying town and to bring a renaissance to a community,[76] then it is not so surprising that the Nantong Museum, the first Chinese-sponsored museum, should impress visitors and contribute to the image of Nantong. In 1905, when Zhang Jian launched this project, there were just a few museums in the whole of China, all of them foreign-sponsored.[77] In 1916, when the Jiangsu Provincial Educational Bureau took an inventory of popular educational facilities, Nantong was still the only county in the province with a museum.[78] It was not until the 1920s that Chinese-sponsored museums of various types began to emerge. Whether they were influenced in any way by Zhang Jian's experience is not clear, but Zhang is recognized in China as the father of the Chinese museum.[79] Nantong's relative autonomy from the central government and Zhang's control over local affairs allowed him to dabble in costly foreign toys like the museum that gave Nantong a patina of modernity.

The museum did meet one of its stated goals, notably in serving as a place of learning for students, despite the strict rules. But since it denied the public access, it failed to achieve its other stated goal—to educate the local people in general. Its other notable, but unstated, function was political. To be sure, to make political use of the museum was not Zhang Jian's invention. Museums present accumulated time, framed space, and thus a mediated message. Only the specifics vary: how the technical details are manipulated and what message is emphasized. But what was striking in the case of the Nantong Museum was how, with the increasing visibility of Nantong, it changed from an institution of enlightenment into one of the city's entertainments. In Zhang Jian's initial proposal for an imperial museum, he had pointed out that museums should be different from commercial conference halls or fairs. The former were sites for scientific and scholarly research.[80] The Nantong Museum indeed placed emphasis on science and education. In time, though, Zhang Jian commercialized its scientific contents and used the museum as a showcase for his achievements. Like many of the great American museums,[81] the Nantong Museum was in essence Zhang Jian's personal monument.

Schools as Exhibitory Institutions

The museum was arguably the most legitimate exhibitory institution in Nantong, but by no means the only one. The land reclamation companies, the Dasheng mills, and local public institutions all had designated office space for presenting pieces of their histories and achievements.[82] There was also a commercial exhibition hall for displaying local products and new purchases from Shanghai.[83] Of all those institutions, however, the schools were by far the most important in their exhibitory function.

In 1912, the county educational association initiated an exhibit of achievements in primary education. In 1913, a summer educational research project involving sixty teachers and graduates set up a showroom (*chenlie shi*) for schoolwork. Individual schools had their showrooms as well.[84] In 1918, the Nantong Agricultural School started a cotton production exhibit to promote new methods in cotton planting. It attracted three hundred visitors, mostly peasants, that year, but three thousand the next year. It soon became an annual fair.[85] There were also special exhibits and small school fairs. In 1915, the first autopsy performed at the Nantong Medical School was put on display to show the progress in Western sciences. A formal ceremony was held, and speeches were made in front of eight hundred invited notables.[86] Nantong schools were not alone in all this. At the time, educational associations and new schools all over China were using the exhibition form to present their achievements and to gain public support for the modern school system. The Jiangsu Educational Bureau, for instance, sponsored exhibitions that involved reviews and rewards.[87] Sometimes, it was not only the students' textbooks, class work, and handicrafts that were on display, but also their performative talent expressed through band, dancing, and singing.[88]

The school was also an arena where many other new activities first took hold, including sports meets, excursions, and public speaking.

These activities quickly became extremely popular, in part because schools had a concentration of impressionable youth who were excited with novelty, but perhaps in greater part because they were one of the things that distinguished the modern school from the traditional academy. Though education reform and its impact on early twentieth-century China have been extensively studied,[89] little attention has been paid to the implications of the school as an exhibitory institution. Even when exhibitory activities at the school are acknowledged, they tend to be considered "informal,"[90] when they were in fact part of the very essence of modern education.

New schools began to appear in China at a time when the country was in a crushing crisis, crystallized by its defeat in the Sino-Japanese War. Their development was thus inevitably associated with the mission to strengthen China, as reflected in the widespread slogan, "Education to Save China" ("Jiaoyu jiuguo"). To accomplish this mission, however, the Western-style school was supposed to do more than merely reform the content and methods of the old academy. It was expected to create a generation of new men and women who would rekindle the nation's spirit and represent modern China. In other words, the new school was expected to remake the image and identity of China as a nation. To that end, education was no longer limited to the classroom; performance outside the classroom became as important as that within. The clear intent of emphasizing student participation in competitive sports, for instance, was to produce a disciplined and public-minded citizenry, and thus convey the image of national strength and unity.[91] Such events attracted considerable community attention. Student sports meets and outings were frequently covered in Nantong newspapers.[92] One reporter, in describing a school outing, noted that the students walked in "neat lines, singing along the way with good spirit," and that the onlookers gave them "warm applause."[93] To be sure, these performative activities and the concepts behind them were not exactly Chinese inventions. The idea that there was a connection between a healthy body, a healthy mind, and a strong national spirit, for instance, was deeply rooted in the culture of modern Britain and other Western nations. The Chinese were trying to adopt this institutional and cultural package from them.

In Nantong, Zhang Jian directly involved himself in the new schools and their activities, as did some of the other important members of the new elites, in part because they were sure to advance the county's reputation. As the hallmark of a successful local self-government, Nantong's modern school system, with the normal school as the crown, attracted many noted educators from the outside. Some of them were hired to teach, and others came to visit and give lectures. Any positive publicity about the schools was associated with the achievements of the local government and its leaders. Not incidentally, since Nantong schools emphasized practical training to meet local needs, they were meant to turn out just the kind of disciplined, hardworking, and public-minded people who were necessary for local development, and more specifically, for the continued progress of Zhang Jian's enterprises. As a result, Zhang was greatly interested in innovative school activities. Here we focus on sports meets, public speeches, and celebrity visitors to illustrate how, through these activities, local schools effectively contributed to the rise of Nantong.

Sports Meets

In early twentieth-century China, sports meets had a certain connotation of progress, something that both the state and the educated elites were eager to claim.[94] Early sports meets were typically more performative than competitive and often included plays, acrobatics, and the other sorts of non-sports activities that were seen routinely at a traditional county or temple fair. In Nantong, as elsewhere, organized sports came only with the establishment of the new schools.[95] Periodic or annual intramural games became regular student activities there, but more influential were the school union sports meets (*lianhe yundong hui*), where some or all of the local school teams competed with one another. Rarely would the students play against teams from outside the county.[96] Several large school union games took place in Nantong; each had an agenda beyond the sports arena, reflecting the evolution of both modern sports and the model.

Nantong held its first school union sports meet in 1905. It was one of the earliest intermural competitions in Jiangsu province.[97] Its purpose, however, was not to promote sports as such, but rather to educate the public about the new school system, which, at its inception, was opposed by conservative forces.[98] To add prestige to the meet, Zhang Jian invited officials from the prefecture and county, as well as influential local elites, to attend. Their support of the modern school system, as he recognized, was crucial to its success. The games themselves were rather uneventful, with only freestanding exercises, military drills, and boxing matches of Chinese style. But as the first of its kind, it was a local sensation; the townspeople were said to have rushed to the arena to cheer for the students.[99]

Two years later, in 1907, there came a "model sports meet" (*mofan yundong hui*), an event organized by the normal school alone, although it was not treated as such. About fifty new schools had been added to the local map since 1903.[100] Held on the instructions of Zhang Jian, this event was meant to showcase the normal school as an example for those new schools. Hence its identification as a "model sports meet." Among other things, the program included the first-ever track-and-field competitions in the county. Another new item that greatly excited the audience was the bicycle, which had just begun to appear in Nantong. Before each game, several students, each riding a bicycle and carrying an eye-catching white board on their backs with the next event written on it, rode around the arena to announce what was to follow. Zhang Jian and Zhang Cha strove to become models in sports as well. The high point of the day, reserved as the next-to-last spot on the program, was their heel-and-toe walking race to the finish line holding a dish with an egg in it. As the younger brother, Zhang Jian invited Zhang Cha to start first, and the latter modestly declined. In the end, Zhang Jian still let his brother take the first step and win the game, an example of how modern sports could not only accommodate Confucian morality but even emphasize it.[101]

If these early sporting events were meant to further modern education, and appeared to be more performative than competitive, the later ones had a different emphasis. After 1914, as Nantong's reputation was being transformed, sports meets were consciously used to shape its identity as a modern community and to cultivate a competitiveness that would represent its spirit. A case in point was the sports meet the normal school held in 1918 to celebrate its fifteenth anniversary. The event was a rehearsal for the grand convention of 1922. Zhang Jian was meticulously involved in its preparation. In one of his letters to the teachers in charge, he discussed the kind of games suitable for competition, how to select the student participants, when and where they should go to register, what songs were to be sung at the ceremony, and so forth. Evidently, he had watched the students rehearsing, because he mentioned a particular song that the students had learned to sing.[102] At the meet, Zhang began his speech by pointing out that Nantong's recent achievements had attracted Chinese as well as foreign visitors. He went on to exhort the students to do their best, saying, "This meet is to test and encourage your competitive spirit as a preparation for the 1922 celebration, when we will invite people from all over China to observe Nantong. It will be shameful if our future guests think that you are only mediocre."[103] Clearly, what was utmost in Zhang Jian's mind was how the 1922 convention would affect visitors' impression of Nantong. He expressed such concerns at other sports meets as well.[104] This was typical of Zhang Jian's thinking after 1914, when building Nantong's reputation became a priority.

Recognizing the important role of sports events, local elites invested heavily in them. In addition to playgrounds at most schools, two public stadiums were built to accommodate large sport spectacles.[105] In 1919, seven local schools participated in a track-and-field meet. Two thousand students and eight thousand spectators were said to have participated.[106] To further the cause of Nantong, the elites also looked for high-ranking official patrons for local sports games. At the 1919 meet, provincial military officers were among the honored guests on the reviewing stand of the newly built public recreation arena outside the South Gate. They were reportedly impressed by, among other things, the military drills performed by the students (Fig. 14).[107]

Indeed, military drills were prominent in all these sports meets and were taught at the schools as part of physical education. A national military education (*junguomin jiaoyu*) program, complete with drill instruction and weapons training, was heavily promoted in the late Qing and early Republican period. Its advocates hoped to instill the military spirit and the attributes of loyalty, discipline, and physical strength in the young, so that China would not only shake off the image of the "sick man of Asia," but also achieve national unity. But military education had a decided downside for the authorities. It made students more aggressive and prone to disruptive, collective action such as strikes; the spread of Western ideas of democracy and freedom only added to this tendency.[108]

In Nantong, education was designed to meet local needs in economic and social development, as envisioned by the elites. A disobedient student body would not only nullify all the investment the elites had made, but also pose a political challenge to the established order. Although Nantong's campuses remained calm during the 1911 transition, schools elsewhere were scenes of anarchy and unrest. Aware of this situation, Zhang Jian handled it by emphasizing strict military training. In the immediate aftermath of the 1911 Revolution, he equated the schools with the army, where "there is no greater catastrophe" than indiscipline.[109] For him, strictness, order, and morality were of the ut-

FIGURE 14. Nantong students in military drill at a public stadium, 1919.
Source: *Nantong shiye jiaoyu cishan fengjing fu canguan zhinan*, p. 54f.

most importance for success in education. Such thinking reflected both
the influence of current ideas such as "national militarization" (*junmin
zhuyi*) and "military citizenry" (*junguomin*) and Zhang's own conviction of the need to protect the existing order in Nantong.[110]

Though Zhang Jian's preaching of discipline was not exactly successful, and the students did rebel later, his championing of military education led to the requirement that all local schools include military
drill. It was often taught by retired soldiers. The Seventh Middle School
chanced to have the man who was locally recognized as the best military teacher in Nantong, a former officer in the 1911 Revolutionary
Army by the name of Lu. Some schools had outdated but real guns for
training purposes. After the May Fourth movement, Japan's ambitions
in China were further exposed, and nationalism was running high in
China. The Nantong schools responded by holding an open war exercise, a so-called *yinjiaolian* (battalion training), in 1920. After three
months of preparation, the military maneuvers took place in a sports
stadium. Some one hundred students selected from four schools were
organized into a battalion of four companies. They were in uniform and
given real bayonets, rifles, and bullets. Lu, in the yellow uniform of an
officer, commanded the event on horseback. Accompanied by loud, au-

thoritative orders, bugle calls, drumbeats, and flag-waving, the war exercise was declared a huge success.[111]

Modern sports were new, with few items available for competition, but the techniques of the military drill could be easily borrowed from the army to become a mainstay of sports education. In time, the drills performed at sports meets became more elaborate. They added spectacle to athletic competitions and excited the audience. More important, although sports were supposed to heighten the spectators' sense of cohesion and unity, team sports were still unfamiliar to many. Military drill thus became a tangible representation of the spirit of unity.

School songs at sports meets also served to boost the collective spirit. Like sports, popular songs were considered educational instruments. Other significant events were also often occasions for songs.[112] Student singing, for example, was frequently written into the formal agenda of local ceremonies.[113] Though other, more conservative officials were concerned that singing and dancing might adversely affect the students' classroom performance, Zhang Jian himself wrote song lyrics for at least fourteen local schools.[114] Those songs, like the mottoes he created for some of the key schools, were supposed to reflect each school's specific mission.

In reality, the songs also helped promote Zhang Jian and Nantong as the pioneers of the new schools. One of the songs for Tongzhou's primary schools, for instance, goes like this:

> The highest mountain in the south of the Huai River is Langshan.
> The earliest schools were in Tong prefecture.
> Every town and village has schools.
> Mountains are built of stones, and citizenry on primary school students.
> Patriotic students must have knowledge.[115]

Some songs celebrated the history of a school, which often understandably had something to do with the Zhangs or one of the other elite families, since they sponsored most of the local schools. Other songs expressed Zhang Jian's personal feelings. The song for the Zhang-Xu Private Girls' School in Changle, Haimen county, for instance, reflects both elements:

> Trace girls' schools in Haimen,
> Changle's was the first,
> Created with private funds according to Mrs. Zhang's wishes on her
>   deathbed.
> Mrs. Zhang was a woman conscious of righteousness . . .

What a glorious history the Changle Girls' School has!
Young generation, please rise up![116]

The Mrs. Zhang referred to here (Xu was her maiden name) was one of Zhang Jian's wives, who before her death had asked Zhang to establish a girls' school in her hometown with her lifetime savings.[117]

Singing songs and other performative activities including sports inevitably invited different reactions from the local people. At the 1905 event, a prefectural official and a gentryman arrived near the end of the game with their entourages. One of them, named Liang, was known for his indifference to modern schools. Their tardiness was probably an expression of resentment toward Zhang Jian and the new schools, a not-uncommon reaction in that early stage of Nantong's development. Furthermore, members of their entourages bullied the students at the gate by insisting on carrying their sedan chairs into the arena and refusing to take the designated entrance route. The students, aware of Liang's reputation, ended up beating Liang's men and destroying their sedan chairs.[118] This incident was resolved with Zhang Jian's apology on behalf of the students. Zhang later decided to use the police to enforce order at public functions.[119]

Conservatives may have disapproved of the games, but the students of rural areas considered it a privilege to attend a major sports event in the city. In 1919, Zhang invited a higher primary school in Changle to send a sight-seeing delegation to a three-day track-and-field meet in Nantong city. The excited students were said to have run around spreading the news. Some of the forty students selected had never been outside of their town. Though they had to travel all day on foot and by boat, burdened down with their school flag and luggage, to get to the city, their spirits were never higher. The students were impressed by the opening ceremony, where a military band performed and Zhang Jian, in black Western garb, made his grand entrance. Zhang also treated them to a play at the Gengsu Theater, another first for many of these country children. Reportedly, as a direct result of the trip, the students were inspired to develop better sports activities at their school. They were all aware, in any event, that the trip was something special because their school's sponsor, Zhang Jian, had shouldered all the costs. The sports games in this case strengthened patron-client ties and reinforced loyalty. One of the students, in his old age, still considered it the highlight of his life, thanks wholly to Zhang Jian's personal kindness.[120]

The impact of these sports events is difficult to measure. Sports meets certainly added to the array of leisure activities available to students in this provincial town and helped them gain physical strength and a competitive spirit. Some developed a lasting interest in sports and went on to become professional athletes, and a few even succeeded in national and international games.[121] But organized, and therefore modern, sports in Nantong, as elsewhere, were also assigned important political, social, and cultural functions.[122] Sports clearly embodied moral values, such as the collective spirit, and above all, patriotism; and spectator sports were an ideal device to cultivate those new values in the general population. The relevance of sports to politics and political posturing is also obvious. These sports meets were controlled by the local elites and officials. Major public sporting events had to be approved by Zhang Jian.[123] He and other local officials and elites were often honored guests seated prominently in the reviewing stand. The sports arena was thus a perfect place to display and exercise political power.[124] As "vehicles of identity,"[125] sports were equally effective in projecting preferred individual, community, and national images. In Nantong, they were used to portray the collective identity of a modern city. With the open arena, military drills, colorful flags, well-dressed notables, uniformed athletes, an excited audience, and even the tension between the old and new forces generated by such events, sports meets created a dramatically sanctioned opportunity that validated the model claim.

Public Speaking

Although public speaking occurred sporadically in imperial times, often during popular riots, Chinese culture was not known for its strong oratory tradition. The introduction of Western-style public speaking (*yanshuo*) to China was closely associated with the almost uninterrupted string of rebellions, reforms, and revolutions that shook the country after the mid-nineteenth century. The large open-air assembly preaching of the Taiping leaders reflected the influence of the Western oratory tradition, which probably first found its way into China via the missionary schools along the southeastern coast.[126] The activists of the 1890 reform were early promoters and practitioners of the new craft. In the last decade of the Qing, as the establishment of political assemblies at various governmental levels shifted the legitimacy of the state from Heaven to "the people," their leaders quickly learned that speaking effectively to a crowd was essential to winning popular support.[127]

During the May Fourth era, speechmaking was conducted in an increasingly more professional and organized fashion. Meetings, assemblies, and other formal activities became regular occurrences for many people. Foreign and Chinese celebrities were invited to give lecture tours, and students formed speech societies and sent their groups into the countryside.[128] The Jiangsu Provincial Educational Bureau, for instance, sponsored a popular course in public speaking. In 1916, twenty-two of its graduates made the rounds in Jiangsu to demonstrate their newfound skills. In three months, they reportedly traveled to sixty counties and made three hundred speeches, attracting an audience of 166,500.[129] Public speeches sometimes interacted with other modern spectacles. In 1914, at the first school union sports game in Jiangsu province, for instance, two American Ph.D.s and their Chinese counterparts, Kang Youwei and Liang Qichao, were invited to speak as special guests.[130] With practices like these, speechmaking not only became a significant component of the public arena, but was also perceived as a necessary means for both building a modern nation and improving the quality of the citizenry that was required by the imagined new China.

In the late Qing, at a time when speechmaking was still considered a novel, mostly urban, phenomenon, it had already become fashionable in Nantong. Speechmaking started during the constitutional reform movement, when teaching the people basic modern political and legal principles was considered part of the preparation for local self-government and a constitutional monarchy. In 1906, the Nantong elites invited teachers from outside to speak on the subject; more than one hundred people attended the first session. Soon after, three local students were sent to Shanghai to study public speaking. Upon their return, they formed the Law and Politics Lecture Bureau (Fazheng jiangxisuo), the first institution to teach the specialty in Nantong. About four hundred people graduated from the bureau in the next three years and later became activists in the self-government movement.[131] Evidently, that was where Nantong's "schoolhouse politicians," to borrow Helen Chauncey's term, got their first training in political involvement.[132]

In 1909, with the rapid progress of the local self-government movement in Nantong, this institution was converted into the Local Self-government Research Bureau. Despite its expanded responsibilities, which included, for instance, providing guidelines for local elections, its members continued to give public lectures on issues related to self-government.[133] The demand for more lecturers on those issues grew to the point where, in 1911, a new unit, the Propaganda and Speech Practice Bureau (Xuanjiang lianxisuo), was formed to train graduates from local

schools who were "good at speaking."[134] Clearly, it was well understood at this point that if speakers were to "move" their audience, they
had to be trained.[135] In addition to refining their skills in speechmaking,
the members of the bureau were supposed to establish rules and principles for public speaking and propaganda,[136] an indication that this exercise had become more professional and institutionalized. Indeed, the
bureau constituted a permanent organ of the local self-government establishment in Nantong until it was dissolved, along with all the other
self-government institutions, in 1914.[137]

Public speaking was considered part of social education and thus
was appropriately emphasized by the county educational association
and practiced at schools.[138] That connection illustrates the political dimension of modern schools, on the one hand, and the schools' unique
role in promoting speechmaking, on the other. All the speech-related
bureaus mentioned above were sponsored by the educational association. Their offices were located in various schools, and their members
were students or graduates of local schools. Schools were also the first
places to develop their own speech groups, one of which was the
Women's Speech and Propaganda Society formed in 1911 by the students at the women's normal school.[139] Some schools even held debates
in English and invited foreigners to their campuses to speak in their
own tongues.[140] One Nantong student, Jiang Xizeng, became a star
speaker. During the high tide of the Japanese boycott, in 1918, Jiang
made speeches at streets and temple fairs. He is said to have held the attention of his audience for an hour in the heat of the summer sun.[141]
Jiang also translated an article, "The Art of Speaking," from English to
Chinese, which argued that a person did not have to be a lawyer, minister, or politician to learn the skills of speaking, and that in fact everyone needed those skills, for they were essential in making a living, in
expressing one's self, and in serving society. Jiang's translation was immediately printed by a local journal.[142] All this made Nantong known
for its student speechmaking. In 1923, the Jiangsu Provincial Educational Association selected the city to host a provincial middle school
speech contest. Zhang Jian chaired the review committee, and students,
as well as some prominent educational leaders from all over Jiangsu, attended.[143]

The popularity of speechmaking was due in part to the introduction
of a uniform "national language" at schools in the late Qing dynasty
that relied on a new phonetic system.[144] Concerned elites of the time realized the importance of establishing a uniform spoken language to

overcome the difficulty in popular education created by the numerous local dialects, and thus promoted the phonetic reform.[145] Such a reform also indicated a new perception of the audience as a national entity instead of local fragments. Teaching the phonetic system bore fruit in Nantong, for it was mentioned that one of the members of the Nantong delegation accurately spoke "the national language" (*guoyu*) during the 1923 provincial speech contest.[146] Furthermore, though political developments in early twentieth-century China brought public speaking to new heights, the schools were probably the most fertile ground of all for the new venture. The opening and closing ceremonies in each semester, graduation celebrations at the end of each school year, new and traditional festivals, sports games, school anniversaries, alumni gatherings, and daily morning meetings were only some of the regular school occasions that called for and indeed demanded speechmaking. In Nantong, such opportunities were well utilized to inculcate student morality and to promote elite power, as well as local autonomy, as exemplified by Zhang Jian's participation in speechmaking.

With the many political and public positions Zhang Jian held, often simultaneously, he was a speaker in much demand, and he used the platform effectively to serve his purposes. There are roughly seventy pieces in his *Complete Works* that have either the word *yanshuo* (speech) or the word *jianghua* (talk) in the title, and another dozen speech texts that are not identified as such. Zhang made speeches at political, business, educational, and ceremonial functions in Beijing, Shanghai, Nanjing, Nantong, and elsewhere in China, to groups numbering from a few thousand to an intimate luncheon of a dozen. Both the sheer number and the broad range of topics of his speeches attest to the popularity of the new medium and the decisive advantage the elites held in using it to influence the public. In perhaps no other realm was this better reflected than in education.

About forty of Zhang Jian's eighty-odd recorded speeches were delivered at schools or at education-related events, mostly in Nantong. He dwelt on different recurring themes, depending on the period in which he spoke. From 1903 to 1907, when the Qing court was tottering under the weight of foreign and domestic crises, his message was national unity: "All under Heaven is one family; and China is one person."[147] He emphasized that the educated—students in this case—should shoulder the mission of strengthening China.[148] After 1907, education became more geared to producing the requisite talent for the county's social and economic transformation, leading to specialized majors and schools. Zhang Jian's speeches were now more hopeful and filled with specific instructions to the students involved. For instance, addressing students majoring in banking, he emphasized that business ethics and credibility were a key to succeeding in the financial world.[149] The overall theme, though, was self-government. As he pointed out, "education would allow everyone to support and thus govern himself."[150] Since local self-government was then still part of the constitutional reform, Zhang did not explicitly treat the Qing government as an alienated "other," as he did later. Nevertheless, an abstract national interest represented by the Qing court was clearly fading away from his speeches; in its place was an increased emphasis on local affairs.[151] In the meantime, Zhang had begun to present the Nantong story as his personal success. In his 1911 speech at the Commercial School of Beijing, Zhang offered a detailed account of how he, a "poor scholar," through "a firm will and arduous effort," built factories and new schools, all with sincere motives.[152]

After the fall of the Qing, and especially after 1914, the increased number of visitors provided Zhang with an expanded platform and audience. He could now address an outside and local audience at the same time. More important, what visitors saw and heard would reinforce each other, thus adding to the effectiveness of his speeches. In this period, he dwelt on three related themes. First of all, he continued to promote his own virtues as the key to Nantong's success. As mentioned, he usually presented those virtues by speaking of his humble beginnings and the hardship he endured in creating local enterprises. In one typical speech, he began with the remark, "I was poor and started with only a few hundred yuan," and then noted that the several thousands of yuan his Nantong enterprises now owned were the "results of my longtime self-sacrifice" (*ziku*). He also mentioned that people first laughed at him for the idea of building a normal school, "but I did not retreat and succeeded in the end."[153] Through such speeches, Zhang Jian created for himself a "representative personality," whose moral authority was the center of progress in the community. Here what Edward T. Channing said in 1856 about the modern leader as an orator still applies: "It is his virtues, his consistency, his unquestioned sincerity that must get the orator attention and confidence. . . . His hearers must believe that his life is steadily influenced by the sentiments he is trying to impress on them—that he is willing to abide by principle at any hazard, and give his opinions and professions the full authority of his actions."[154] Zhang Jian might not have been familiar with the principles of Western rhetoric, but he did not have to be. His instinct and experience made him an effective speaker who knew the art of persuasion.

In sharp contrast with this self-made, public-minded, moral man of word and action was the image of a corrupt central government that was impotent in, and even opposed to, modern ventures, the second of the three themes that ran through Zhang Jian's speeches during this period. He claimed that "all the Nantong schools were created by myself and not supported by the government."[155] Zhang once made a comparison between the Chinese and Japanese governments and concluded that the former lagged way behind the latter in supporting local development. Hence came the third consistent theme in Zhang's speeches: that local autonomy was both the means and the end of Nantong's achievement. He expressed this in terms of "pure Village-ism," as discussed in the first chapter.

Zhang Jian also used public speeches to control students and instill a moral order that would maintain his authority in Nantong. That intent is obvious in the speeches he gave during the unsettled beginnings of the Republic, in which he promoted discipline as a principle and compared the schools with the army, and even more so in his speeches from the May Fourth movement in 1919 through the May Thirtieth Incident of 1925, when he preached strict discipline, or "strict-ism" (*yange zhuyi*).[156] His purpose amid those stormy times was to confine the local students to campus and isolate them from any type of social unrest. Such preaching was often accompanied with threats of punishment for anyone who participated in that type of event.[157] Public speaking in this case became a mechanism for behavior management and for suppressing local dissidents.

Celebrity Speakers

"Celebritydom" in the modern sense was something altogether new to the late Qing and early Republican Chinese, a byproduct of mass communication, where fame could be created and cashed in on instantly. Among its many advantages was the power to sway people to a cause. A big name gave authority and persuasiveness to almost any cause. Modern-day celebrities also typically served as role models, particularly for students.[158]

Nantong students were privileged to hear a number of national and international celebrity speakers. Such distinguished foreign and Chinese scholars, social reformers, and opinion makers as John Dewey, Huang Yanpei, Tao Xingzhi, and Liang Qichao, to mention only a few, were invited to lecture at various schools. Not surprisingly, the largest class of invited speakers consisted of educators who were keenly interested in Nantong's new school system.

In 1919, following his lecture tour in Japan, Dewey came to China for a short visit, arriving in Shanghai in early May, a tension-charged time. That short trip turned into a two-year stay when he was offered a visiting professorship at National Peking University. At the time, many returned students from overseas, including Dewey's former students, had become important professional educators in China. Those returned students, who constituted "a definite category" in China, as Dewey himself recognized,[159] not only worked out an invitation for Dewey to teach in Beijing, but also arranged for him to go out on the lecture circuit. Because of the promotion efforts of those students and the hunger for Western ideas among young Chinese, Dewey became an instant celebrity, and his lectures were widely publicized. Some students even followed him from city to city. Among other things, these "groupies" reflected the increasing mobility of Chinese society. To them, Dewey, like Bertrand Russell, who was also lecturing in China in 1920, was a modern-day sage.[160]

In the spring and summer of 1920, while Dewey was a visiting professor at Nanjing Teachers' College, he made a six-week tour of thirteen cities and towns of such varied size and developmental levels as Shanghai and Nantong.[161] Sources do not indicate exactly how Nantong came to be on the list of scheduled stops, but considering the city's reputation and the Columbia graduates teaching there, its inclusion is not surprising.[162]

Accompanied by his wife and daughter, Dewey stayed in Nantong for four days in early July and gave four speeches—two at the Gengsu Theater, one at a park in the industrial town of Tangzha, and one at a middle school. There was some tension between Dewey and Zhang Jian, however. Dewey, falling back on well-developed material from his lecture tour in Japan and elsewhere in China, spoke about the relationship between education and Western democracy and freedom, a subject that the students, in the immediate aftermath of the May Fourth movement, were bound to find inspiring.[163] The students were also excited about meeting such a famous American scholar and hearing him in person. Zhang Jian had a different agenda. In his introductory speech at one of Dewey's appearances, he first praised Dewey's learning and the

American political system, and then launched into an attack on the local May Fourth activists. Zhang expressed his hope that Dewey could
guide them to focus on the classroom, a subtle warning to Dewey not to
say anything radical.[164] Zhang Xiaoruo was said to have explicitly told
one of the interpreters to advise Dewey not to talk about democracy.[165]

The tension between the two apparently did not dissuade Zhang
Jian and other elites from taking this opportunity to show off Nantong.
They arranged an exhausting schedule for Dewey. The Nantong newspapers had extensively covered Dewey's life and work before his arrival, which gave him instant fame in a community where the general
public had known little about him. He was lodged at the Youfei Hotel
right on Mofan Road. During the four days of his stay, he was invited to
visit dozens of schools, factories, and other institutions in Nantong city,
Tangzha, and the Langshan area. The Zhang brothers held banquets for
him in their homes. He was treated to an evening show at the Gengsu
Theater featuring Ouyang Yuqian.[166] Dewey seemed reasonably impressed, recognizing that Nantong was "known popularly as the model
town of China."[167]

Huang Yanpei, one of the most important educators in twentieth-
century China, was a frequent guest and speaker in Nantong. Inspired
by his 1915 trip to the United States, Huang in 1917 initiated the China
Vocational School in Shanghai.[168] He directed education in Jiangsu and
had been a close associate of Zhang Jian since the constitutional reform.
Both men shared a conviction in the importance of practical and vocational education. Huang especially appreciated how Nantong schools
were meeting local needs. He visited Nantong five times between 1917
and 1923 out of an eagerness not only to promote his own ideas, but
also to investigate the practice in Nantong, though in one instance the
principal reason for his visit was to accompany Dewey. In addition to
vocational education, two of Huang's favorite themes were personal integrity and the importance of libraries, clubs, and sports stadiums in
student development. In 1923, he gave a presentation at the women's
normal school on the topic "The Ideal Woman." Some of his speeches
reportedly went on for three hours and drew crowds of three hundred
to six hundred people. Huang's idea of vocational education left a visible impact on Nantong. Aside from its many vocational schools, in 1917
the Vocational Research Center was formed as a direct result of
Huang's work.[169]

Important speakers also came to Nantong in groups, mostly through
organized activities such as conferences, a new phenomenon of the

twentieth century that gradually came to attract celebrated participants and, with them, increasing prestige. The 1922 meeting of the Science Society of China, for instance, brought some men to Nantong whose renown the local community took full advantage of. Among the delegates, Liang Qichao was probably the best-known opinion maker. He was also somewhat familiar with Nantong, having been invited by Zhang to speak there the year before. In that speech of 1921, he had immediately endeared himself to the Nantong elites by praising the city as the "birthplace of the local self-government movement" and a source of "endless hopes" for China.[170] No doubt because of their particular fondness for this friendly, eloquent speaker, he was invited to give a public speech during the science society conference. It was a major event organized by *Nantongbao* and three educational institutions and attended by seven hundred people. There, taking his theme from the conference, he expressed the hope that Nantong would continue to lead China in education and particularly in the domain of the sciences.[171]

The practice of speechmaking in Nantong illustrates that in early twentieth-century China, with the recognition that the people were the source of political legitimacy, political life had acquired a public dimension. Politicians, understanding the capacity of the people to influence social and political life, had to persuade them through direct appeal in a face-to-face setting. Hence the large investment in new forms of propaganda such as speeches. Participatory politics and its vehicles, however, could be potentially turbulent and anarchic. Some Nantong students, for instance, made public speeches in an attempt to mobilize the people during the May Fourth movement, speeches that the elites quickly suppressed. Clearly, speechmaking was a politically contested ground. In controlling that ground, the elites made speechmaking, a potential instrument for freedom and democracy, into a monopoly that reinforced their domination. Furthermore, by selecting the celebrity speakers or manipulating the content of their speeches, local elites capitalized on those famous names to raise Nantong's status.

Theater and Performance

In the 1910s, popular cultural institutions and forms, such as theaters, teahouses, and novels, were considered primary targets for social reform, arenas where a healthy and productive modern culture would replace corrupt and superstitious tradition. It was hoped that social education would allow a stronger China with a progressive citizenry to emerge.[172] Zhang Jian was convinced that his model community should reform social customs along with other things, and he believed that the theater was the most effective means to accomplish that.[173] With more and more Chinese and foreign visitors flowing in as the decade wore on, Zhang came to consider it especially important to promote new customs so that the local people would behave like model citizens. Theater reform in Nantong took place against this background, a development that both provided a dramatic public exhibit of the new Nantong and provoked sharp clashes among various social and cultural forces.

A Perfect Match

To realize his plans for theater reform, Zhang Jian initially sought the advice and assistance of the celebrated star of Chinese opera Mei Lanfang, a close friend. In 1918, he wrote to Mei to announce his intention to build a new theater in Nantong and to train new actors. He asked if and how Mei could help him in this venture. Mei, sensing the difficulty, did not seem to be particularly enthusiastic about being part of Zhang's plans. If Zhang Jian was disappointed, he did not show it.[174] His idea of building a major theater and creating a new acting school was finalized in the spring of 1919, when the famous actor Ouyang Yuqian (1889–1962) came from Shanghai to perform. Zhang invited him to manage the future acting school, and Ouyang accepted. Things moved quickly thereafter: construction of the theater began that summer, and a simultaneous search for recruits for the acting school was initiated in both Beijing and Nantong; the school (its formal name was Linggong xueshe) opened in September with about twenty faculty members and staff and sixty students, ranging from ten to thirteen years of age; and the appropriately named Gengsu (literally, Change of Customs) Theater was launched in October with grand ceremony.[175]

On the surface, it was puzzling why Ouyang, already a prominent actor, would settle in a small town to build an acting school from scratch. Later developments would justify such doubts. But at the outset, it seemed a perfect match: Ouyang could not have found a better place to reshape the Chinese theater in the way he envisioned; and Zhang Jian, on his side, could not have chosen a better person to start the local theater reform.

Ouyang was a different actor from most of his colleagues. The reason he jumped into the reform while Mei Lanfang shied away from it was deeply rooted in his background and experience. Born in 1889 of an elite-official family of Liuyang, Hunan province, Ouyang, unlike most of his fellow actors, was college educated. He first became involved in modern drama while studying in Japan, where he was an active member of the Spring Willow Society (Chunliushe), a reform-oriented drama group.[176] Ouyang began his career in Chinese opera upon his return from Japan in 1910. Gifted and hardworking, within a matter of years, he established himself as a master of the southern school of Chinese opera, in contradistinction to Mei Lanfang, the premier performer of the northern school.

Ouyang's career represented a major departure from tradition. Typical of the May Fourth generation and from a family associated with the prominent late nineteenth-century Hunanese reformers Tan Sitong and Tang Caichang, Ouyang was sensitive to social issues and concerned about the ordinary people.[177] In the same vein, he took seriously the social significance of his profession. Yet, retaining a profound sense of elitism, Ouyang often stood aloof from politics and practical matters. He loved the stage, but he was also acutely aware of the antitheatrical attitude of elite society, a prejudice that his own family shared.[178] His profession defined him as an entertainer with commercial values, but he never had Shakespeare's sense of playwrights as pleasure deliverers.[179] Ouyang considered his work too "sacred" (*shensheng*) to be judged by profits or audience tastes alone.[180] From a "good" family, yet engaged in a career with a "bad" reputation, Ouyang had the primary aim of reforming the theater from within. Much like the pioneers of modern drama in the West who engaged in "combating this decaying theatricality,"[181] Ouyang saw himself as a combatant against the traditional Chinese theater.

As a starting point, Ouyang, like other radical playwrights of his time, attacked the old Chinese opera. His critical attitude is evident in his 1918 essay, "My Opinion on Drama Reform." He pointed out that, in sad contrast to Western plays, which demonstrated a knowledge of literature, aesthetics, music, art, and acting techniques, Chinese opera did not even have scripts, let alone a grounding in theory, and was completely dissociated from reality. The profession, he said, was corrupt, and the actors were encouraged to be narrow-minded and tradition-oriented. Consequently, Chinese opera had no position in the domain of world performing arts, and in fact China had no drama (*xiju*) at all.[182]

Ouyang suggested three ways to change all this: to develop written scripts (*juben wenxue*, "script literature"), beginning with the introduction of vernacular language and the translation of Western plays; to foster criticism and knowledgeable critics; and to train a new generation of actors who, rather than just memorizing a few plays as a lifetime "rice bowl," would be educated in literature and social affairs. To be sure, Ouyang recognized that the old-style Chinese opera had reason to survive. The problem for him was that it had to be cleansed of its decaying elements: its traditional subjects, fixed formalities, unreality, and obscure language.[183] An avant-garde in the performing arts, Ouyang wanted to modernize old opera, both artistically and socially.[184]

He was aware, although not fully, of the difficulty of carrying out such tasks. In his experience, it was the very elements he criticized in Chinese opera that were most appealing to the audience. "What can I do?" he sighed.[185] Between 1912 and 1918, Ouyang had performed with various troupes in Changsha, Shanghai, and other cities, and found no suitable place to experiment with his ideas.[186] The theaters in Beijing, Ouyang pointed out, were controlled by the rich and the powerful. To Ouyang, the situation in Shanghai was no better, for the theaters there were in the hands of gangsters.[187] Under the circumstances, it is not surprising that he should buy into the carefully cultivated image of Nantong as a community that was uniquely committed to and capable of modern ventures.

The established sources of patronage for itinerant entertainers in China were either *shenshi* (gentry) or *zibenjia* (capitalists).[188] They usually provided financial means, as well as protection against local bullies, who typically harassed actors. Now along came Zhang Jian, arguably one of the most respected elites and one of the richest capitalists in China. He claimed to support not only theater but also reform, and extended to Ouyang a potentially long-term offer that could free him from the day-to-day struggle for sponsorship and provide him with a favorable environment to implement his reform program. In a 1919 letter addressed to Zhang Xiaoruo, Ouyang could hardly contain his excitement: "Even in my wildest dream, I could not find anyone outside Tongzhou [Nantong] who would nurture the new performing arts." He fully expected that "the theater in Tongzhou will not only represent one region's popular education, but also mark a new era of literature and performing arts."[189]

The Reform

The school and the theater were financially supported by the No. 1 mill and other local resources. A six-year system was set up for the acting school; the students would study for the first four years and serve the school for the remaining two, with pay. The education was free, as was practically everything else the students might need. The school was given a monthly budget of 800 yuan. In July 1920, less than a year after its founding, the school moved from the South Park to a new campus of fifteen mu outside the South Gate. It now had a small theater, a sports stadium, dormitories, and more than sixty classrooms and offices, and was equipped with pianos, gramophones, and other musical facilities.[190]

Zhang Xiaoruo was the nominal director, and Ouyang the executive director, with authority over the hiring and firing of the faculty and staff, as well as the admission of students. Ouyang certainly took his job seriously and set high standards for the students. For instance, two years of primary education were a prerequisite for admission. Three months after the school opened, more than ten students from the Beijing area were dismissed because of their lack of talent. To help the students practice Mandarin, necessary for learning Beijing opera, a Beijing native was added to the faculty. Ouyang also invited experts from Shanghai, Beijing, and other cities to teach, including some of his colleagues from the Spring Willow Society.[191]

The Nantong school was distinctly innovative. In contrast to the traditional acting troupes, which were essentially schools of hard knocks, Ouyang treated his actors-to-be with respect. He banned physical punishment and insisted on patient and civilized education. There were courses in Chinese, mathematics, English, history, geography, painting, and gymnastics, in addition to acting classes. Ouyang himself taught courses on the history of Chinese and Western operas, and introduced the students to Ibsen, Shakespeare, and other Western writers. A good actor, Ouyang believed, should be well versed in both Chinese and Western culture, and this idea was symbolically reflected in the school badge, which showed a stave with a pen and a brush across the center.[192] He created a music class and an orchestra, requiring the students to study dance and Western music. To expose the students to concert music, the class was later sent to study in Shanghai. Beyond all this, he took care to see that the school showed the same social commitment as he did. In 1921, Ouyang, together with the students and staff, took the stage in Changsha to raise funds for famine relief.[193] Two central themes

Ouyang emphasized for the school were to train new actors for drama reform, not to create traditional troupes, and to breed artists, not privately owned entertainers.[194]

What most distinguished the school was Ouyang's attempt to reform Chinese opera by combining it with Western music and dance and to promote spoken drama. He created and adapted more than seventy works and staged them in Nantong. Among the fifty whose titles are still known today were nineteen traditional operas, twenty-one spoken dramas, six song-and-dance dramas, and four modern-dress plays (*xizhuangxi*). In terms of subject matter, twenty-three plays were traditional, twenty-two modern, and five Western borrowings, including *Uncle Tom's Cabin*.[195] Although Chinese operas, most of them based on traditional novels such as *Dream of the Red Chamber*, accounted for half the repertoire, Ouyang reinterpreted them to reflect new values of anti-traditionalism and women's rights. For instance, the pursuit of love by female characters such as Lin Daiyu and Qing Wen in *Dream of the Red Chamber* was passionately praised, and their tragic lives attributed to the darkness of China's past.[196] Ouyang's works on women seem to reflect the "male-dominated feminist" discourse that emerged in the May Fourth era.[197]

Social issues were the main subjects of the rest of the repertoire. Some plays denounced the warlords or class oppression, and others applauded freedom and democracy. In one play, *The Pure Heart of a Newborn Babe* (*Chizi zhi xin*), written by Ouyang, a little rich boy condemns his mother's abuse of her maid. The play represented the author's own cry for a better society.[198] In another play, *The Tears of a Famished Refugee* (*Anhong lei*), Ouyang portrayed a female victim who, after months of flight from famine, was "rescued" by a so-called philanthropist and died outside a warlord's home. In this play, Ouyang satirized the warlords and those who got rich by pretending to be philanthropists, and sensitized his audiences to the plight of the poor, who were doubly victimized by natural disasters and human evil.[199] In *The Hater of Black Slaves*, a story based on *Uncle Tom's Cabin*, Ouyang recast the character Tom as a slave who no longer meekly submitted to oppression but was animated by a spirit of resistance.[200] These performances for the first time introduced spoken drama and Western plays, along with new values, to the Nantong audience.

Ouyang also tried to create an orderly theater environment. The Gengsu Theater, modeled on the China Theater in Shanghai, was located in the new downtown southwest of the city. Outside its front gate stood two garden terraces, and next to it was a large parking lot. The four characters for Gengsu Theater (Gengsu juchang) inscribed above the front gate were in Zhang Jian's own calligraphy. The two-story theater's 1,200 folding seats were numbered and organized into three price ranges. All the seats had baskets underneath to hold hats, and long tables in front for teapots. Next to the entrance were seats set aside for drivers and maids. Tables were scattered in the hallway for intermission activities—the theater's small shop offered coffee, tea, cocoa, wine, fruit, and snacks. Restrooms were available for both men and women on both floors. The main stage, large enough that a car was once driven onto it as a prop, was covered with a custom-made red carpet. Electric lighting was provided. It was said to be one of China's best theaters, costing more than 60,000 yuan (silver) to build.[201]

Ouyang made strict rules for the theater. Order was one of the main concerns. Each ticket showed the number of the theatergoer's assigned seat. To keep the theater quiet, infants were not allowed. People who brought servants and drivers had to purchase tickets for them in the designated area. Some of the rules show that Ouyang's commitment to "clear the stage" was more than symbolic. The theater floor was washed daily. And eating melon seeds and spitting were prohibited; anyone who brought seeds along would be asked to leave them with the gate guards until the show was over. This proved to be a tough rule to enforce. Ouyang then proposed to have two children walk around the theater, wearing eye-catching red vests with the characters "Please Do Not Eat Melon Seeds" on their back. If they saw someone eating seeds, they would sweep the floor right away with an attractive small broom and dustpan. The purpose, Ouyang said, was to shame people into changing their bad habits.[202]

There were also rules governing the staff and actors. According to an old custom, when a theater was built, a rite was performed to "open the stage." All sorts of deities would dance on the stage to drive evil spirits away and ensure the theater's safety and prosperity. Ouyang abolished that practice. Another custom that he considered superstitious was maintaining a shrine in the theater. Because the majority of the staff insisted on having one, however, Ouyang had to allow it. Real guns and knives were banned as stage props. In the past, backstage staff had the responsibility of "hurrying the actor up"(*cuixi*) if it looked like he might miss his entrance. Under Ouyang's new regime, all the actors themselves were responsible for being on time. He also disapproved of the habit of staff and actors peeking from backstage while the show was on, which he considered disturbing to the audience.[203]

These rigid rules represented Ouyang's determination to remake the theater. They naturally met resistance. Once, a star actor tried to challenge Ouyang's authority by claiming that all the other rules were fine with him except for the one prohibiting spitting. He then spat right on the stage carpet. Ouyang was determined to confront that kind of "lower class" attitude (*xialiu piqi*) as damaging to the prestige of the theater. Threatened with dismissal, the actor cleaned the carpet; after that, it was relatively easy for Ouyang to discipline others.[204] As a result of these efforts, it was said that one could not find any more pleasant a theater in China than the Gengsu.[205]

The other integral part of the theater reform was the publication of a small newspaper, *Gongyuan ribao* (*Park Daily*), beginning in 1919. It had a threefold mission: to develop dramatic criticism, to provide up-to-date information on the performing arts, and to promote civilized theater behavior. Gengsu audiences received the newspaper free with the purchase of their tickets. Regular contributors included Ouyang himself; Wu Wozun, a member of the Spring Willow Society who taught at the acting school; and Xu Haiping, a Nantong native and a theater activist who helped manage the school. The paper was edited at first by Wu Wozun and later by Zhang Xiaoruo.[206]

With the training of new actors, the promotion of new plays and customs, and the nurturing of dramatic criticism, Ouyang's three-part reform program seemed to go well. The years from 1919 to 1921 were the high point of Nantong's theater. Two plays were staged daily, one from one o'clock to five, and the other from seven o'clock to midnight. In the first months, Ouyang paired a Chinese opera with a spoken drama. Tickets were priced from two *jiao* to seven yuan, allowing even students to attend.[207] So great was the prestige of Zhang Jian and Ouyang Yuqian that fifty-seven famous professionals, including Mei Lanfang himself, came to perform in Nantong in the years 1919–22. The theater also attracted many amateur actors, the most notable of whom was Yuan Hanyun, Yuan Shikai's son.[208]

The guest actors who came to Nantong for the first time must surely have been impressed to find in this provincial town a new-style acting school, a magnificent modern theater, and an unexpectedly enthusiastic and polite audience. But their presence in turn was a great boon to the local theater. Their performances not only gave the acting students a rare learning opportunity, but also exposed the Nantong audience to the very best that Chinese theater could offer, a rich variety of styles and plays that was rarely afforded to any but metropolitan audiences. The school and its students, the famous performers, the new and different plays—all this stirred great interest in theatrics. Theatergoing became a new vogue in this small town.[209]

Setbacks

In early 1922, Ouyang resigned from his posts at both the school and the theater and left Nantong. Although his departure was not the only reason for the decline of local theater, it certainly started that decline. From this point on to 1926, the position of the acting school's director was rotated among other actors. After Zhang Jian's death in 1926, the school was dissolved, and the Gengsu Theater had to contract with outside troupes in order to survive. Consequently, Zhang Xiaoruo considered the name Gengsu no longer appropriate and even ridiculous, and so renamed it the Nantong Theater.[210]

What happened to Ouyang and, perhaps more important, to theater reform in Nantong? Little is mentioned about Ouyang's departure in Zhang Jian's recorded writings, and other relevant works have often downplayed the issue.[211] But in his autobiography, Ouyang devoted a full chapter to his three years in Nantong, in which he bitterly complained about his experience there. As biased as it may be, that chapter, fleshed out with other sources, provides a glimpse of the struggle behind the ostensible theater reform.[212]

The problem was multilayered. On the surface, financial difficulty was the main issue. The acting school depended on the No. 1 mill and the other local companies that were part of Dasheng System Enterprises. With the decline of the Dasheng enterprises in 1921, the school, an expensive institution, lost its funding. In 1921, Ouyang's monthly salary went unpaid for a year, and by 1922 the school was 2,000 yuan in debt. Zhang Jian then decided that the school should support itself by performing at the Gengsu Theater, even though the students had only studied for two years out of the designated four.[213]

The monetary pressure was of course unpleasant, but its consequences were not what bothered Ouyang the most. In late 1921, he took the students to perform in Hankou for the sole purpose of making a living (*mousheng*). He even spent 7,000 yuan of his own money to support the school.[214] What did deeply disturb him was that, because of the financial woes, the students had to turn professional before they were ready for the stage. Since making money became a priority for the school, the original goal of training a new breed of actors had to be put aside. The students were no longer able to concentrate on their classes, and worse, began to compete for fame and pay, much like the actors of the old troupes. Ouyang proposed that the acting school take control of Gengsu in the hope that the theater would support the school, an idea that Xue Bingchu, Gengsu's manager and a Zhang Jian confidant, strongly opposed. This and other professional and personal conflicts greatly discouraged Ouyang.[215]

What also disappointed Ouyang was an obvious gap between his ideals for the theater and the social reality in Nantong. Ouyang's effort to reshape Chinese opera and to promote spoken drama did not go as well as he had expected. His introduction of Western dance and music into Chinese opera was not accepted by the Nantong audience, who found the musical instruments incompatible with the Chinese vocal music. The situation with spoken drama was worse. The audience quickly lost interest in it.[216] Various reasons lay behind the unpopularity of spoken drama.

Modern drama, initially referred to as *wenmingxi* (civilized play) or *xinxi* (new play), was introduced to China by the Spring Willow Society in 1907.[217] In part because of the society's promotion efforts, modern drama flourished in China from 1913 to 1917. During those years, new professional acting groups mushroomed; the new drama spread rapidly from the lower Yangzi region to various parts of the interior; huge crowds attended the plays; and the actors received the same pay as actors of traditional opera.[218] The New People Society, a professional acting group managed by the critic-turned-businessman Zheng Zhengqiu, and other troupes with a similar focus on family stories enjoyed a sustained success, at the expense of the self-proclaimed progressive and reformist Spring Willow Society,[219] a shift in popularity that indicated the rise of a commercial entertainment market and its power to reward and reject.

The May Fourth movement, ironically, witnessed a temporary setback for modern drama. Though the movement encouraged intellectuals to go to the people, it also alienated them from the people with its strong anti-traditional and pro-Western tone. In drama circles, some of the activists, Ouyang included, turned to aestheticism (*weimei zhuyi*) and to the development of aesthetic plays (*aimei ju*), forms that did not suit the popular taste. In addition, those dramatists, dissatisfied with the restriction on artistic expression by the market forces, launched a so-called nonprofessional drama movement (*fei zhiye xiju yundong*).[220] Like many avant-garde artists, the pioneers of modern drama were extremely conscious of the individual self, a core concept of modernity. They were thus at odds with the trend toward cultural commercialization, which was also part and parcel of modernity. Consequently, the "nonprofessional drama movement" was too idealistic to be successful. The experiment of modern drama came to an end during the Northern Expedition. Facing the grim reality of the mid-1920s, dramatists, like their counterparts in other fields, became more practical. They tried to relocate themselves among, not above, the people, and to reconnect their profession with the social concerns of the day.[221]

Thus when Ouyang came to Nantong in 1919, the high tide of the new drama movement had already begun to recede. But Ouyang's overall experience with spoken drama thus far had been positive, which initially gave him confidence. He chose to put a spoken drama on for Gengsu's opening night. The play, *Yurun Zhuyuan* (*Moist Jade and Round Pearl*), described the forced separation and much-delayed reunion of two young lovers, and their devotion to social causes. According to Ouyang, only a few people applauded at one point, and most reacted to the play with silence. Worst of all, he felt that there was a seemingly "organized indifference" (*you zuzhi de lengdan*)—no one said a word to him about the play even when asked.[222] *The Tears of a Famished Refugee* received the same treatment, and Zhang Xiaoruo apparently was not pleased with its implied criticism of current affairs. Unlike some of the Chinese operas Ouyang authored, these spoken plays were never staged again at the Gengsu Theater after their debut.[223]

This lack of repeat performances had much to do with the composition of the audience, the popularity of Chinese opera, and the way Ouyang used spoken drama as a didactic instrument to convey social messages. The members of Nantong's elite society, though small in number, had an enormous influence over the theater. Some were in the habit of booking the whole building when their favorite actors came to perform.[224] The elites could make or break a play, and their particular passion was the sophisticated Kunqu style of opera that originated in Jiangsu.[225] Lacking the dramatic singing, literary lyrics, and elegant moves of the Kun opera, spoken drama was too plain for this group. Perhaps more to the point, although the elites could relate to the importance of educating the people, they had little sympathy with Ouyang's use of drama to attack the rich and to expose social ills.

The majority of the theatergoers, the townspeople, shared this indifference toward spoken drama and passion for traditional Chinese opera. They departed from the elites only in their fascination for adaptations from certain popular works; a particular favorite was *Strange Stories Written in the Liao Studio*.[226] They came to the theater for the operas that they were accustomed to and for the kind of plots that would take them to fantasyland. They were thus hardly likely to be enthusiastic about getting a realistic education from new drama, especially when it was presented in a way that sacrificed the kind of entertainment and artistry they delighted in.[227]

Ouyang's eagerness to educate the people laid bare his arrogance as a self-appointed enlightened cultural leader. He clearly underestimated the popularity of traditional Chinese opera. Developed through the past few centuries, Chinese opera had become one of the favorite performing arts, enjoyed by the elite and the ordinary folk alike. Both the educated and the unschooled felt at home with it. The distinction between the so-called highbrow and lowbrow was blurred in this case. Spoken drama was ill-prepared to compete with such a deep-rooted tradition. Thus, even when the theater was at the peak of popularity, the plays staged at Gengsu had little to do with "gengsu," changing the customs, a fact that at least one local reporter was ready to acknowledge in 1920. "The old Chinese opera has been criticized for lacking the spirit of freedom and equality, and moral principles," he stated. "Our Gengsu Theater was meant to change that, but little has been accomplished so far."[228] When the change of the theater's name and the disbanding of the acting school were announced in 1926, it was generally conceded that after seven years of effort, the stated mission of the theater and the school had yet to be realized.[229] Ouyang himself also acknowledged that his dramatic experiment in Nantong was a failure.[230]

By 1921, Ouyang was no longer in a position to reform the theater and to teach the students the way he wanted. He also lost *Gongyuan ribao*. Like many other periodicals that emerged during the May Fourth era, that local newspaper, though initiated to promote the theater, soon began to print essays attacking the corruption and superstitious practices of the local elites. When it made so bold as to single out Zhang Cha in late 1920, he ordered the newspaper to shut down. Its editor, his nephew Zhang Xiaoruo, dutifully complied, reflecting the censorship that came with patronage.[231]

One Man's Theater

Though all of this greatly frustrated Ouyang and impaired his reform effort, his departure from Nantong, like his arrival, was mostly due to Zhang Jian, the principal patron of the theater. Zhang disagreed with some of Ouyang's ideas about student training and opposed some of Ouyang's new rules,[232] but it was their differences over the purpose of theater reform that finally led to the split.

On the surface, Zhang's belief in theater as a vehicle to influence social customs remained unchanged. To prepare for the 1922 convention, Zhang paid a visit to the Gengsu Theater in 1921 to investigate whether local customs had progressed by observing audience behavior. Did people take seats according to the numbers on the tickets? Were they polite and disciplined? Observing some shortcomings, Zhang Jian wrote an open letter to the community with suggestions for improvement. This letter reveals that Zhang's support for theater reform was in part motivated by his concern to present Nantong in the best possible light to outside visitors. What he wanted to show off, as he stated, was not only the county's material progress but also evidence of its modern culture; otherwise it would be a "great shame" (*dachi*) to Nantong. To Zhang Jian, it was a matter of local self-government whether the audience took their assigned seats, but "very few people understand [the relevance between the two]." Perhaps frustrated by this situation, Zhang implied that those who failed to follow rules in the theater meant to "destroy" (*pohuai*) local self-government in Nantong.[233]

In short, Gengsu was a ticket that Zhang Jian meant to use in support of his claim of modern culture and a small stage for a rehearsal of his own grand performance in 1922. Though such major celebrations occurred rarely, and the one in question was in fact canceled, Zhang felt a constant need to display Nantong's achievements, of which modern culture and civilized behavior were important components, to impress visitors and maintain the city's image. The Gengsu Theater, a prominent cultural institution and surefire attention-getter, was an ideal instrument to meet that need.

Let us take Mei Lanfang's visits as an illustrative case. Zhang Jian was a combination of godfather, mentor, patron, and bosom friend to the celebrated opera star. Their extraordinary friendship started in Beijing in 1914, when Zhang Jian began to attend Mei's performances. Zhang, sixty-two years old, was then Minister of Agriculture and Commerce; Mei, just twenty-one, was a rising star of the Beijing stage.[234] In the following decade, Zhang composed numerous poems for Mei and his family and friends, as well as essays about Mei's performances, and there were dozens of letters between the two, with more from Zhang to Mei than the other way around. Those letters show that Zhang cherished Mei's divine beauty in both his appearance and his art, and that he closely followed news reports of Mei's activities. He sent Mei poems, paintings, and other artworks as gifts. In return, Mei sent him fans and his stage photos, which Zhang used to decorate his villas. Zhang was extremely protective of Mei, constantly asking his "art friend" (*yiyou*), "little friend" (*xiaoyou*), and "younger brother" (*di*) for details about his health, his spirit, his travels, and his work.[235] Concerned that Mei would get a big head from all the praise, he advised him to paint daily, a practice, he counseled, that both required and cultivated the virtues of patience and unostentatious hard work.[236] Zhang also encouraged Mei to become more literate, offering to correct his writing: "I would not show your writing to anyone [so you do not have to feel embarrassed]."[237] In 1924, Zhang drafted a fifteen-point set of guidelines for Mei's planned American tour, covering everything from expenses to makeup.[238]

Mei performed in Nantong three times between 1920 and 1922, for a duration of a few days to about two weeks. All of his visits were publicized well beyond Nantong. Many of the offstage activities organized to honor Mei were as theatrical as his stage acting (Fig. 15). In anticipation of Mei's first visit, a "waiting pavilion" (*houting*) was built near the dock, and the Gengsu Theater was colorfully decorated. Zhang arranged for a special ship to pick up Mei and his staff of more than thirty in Hankou. On the day of Mei's arrival, Zhang Jian and other elites and a local band awaited him at the new pavilion for a formal welcoming ceremony. Pictures of Mei and his elite hosts were taken in front of the pavilion before they were driven away through the crowd of curious townspeople to Zhang's villa for a banquet.[239]

Zhang Jian set aside a room on the second floor of the Gengsu and named it the Mei-Ou Chamber (Mei-Ou ge) to show his fondness for Mei Lanfang and Ouyang Yuqian. The room was embellished with Zhang's couplets and calligraphy, pictures of both actors, and photos of them with various Nantong elites (Fig. 16). To ease the possible tension between the two famed actors, Zhang arranged for Mei and Ouyang to share a performance. This was an unusual treat. People, including some Westerners, came from as far away as Shanghai to see the two masters at work, and the news quickly spread to other parts of China.[240]

FIGURE 15. Welcoming ceremony for the opera star Mei Lanfang in front of
the Gengsu Theater, January 1920. (Courtesy of Zhang Xuwu)

Mei's visits were obviously as much social as cultural events. Banquets were held, and gifts exchanged.[241] Zhang Jian invited renowned
men of letters to compose poems commemorating the visits. Zhang
typically made his own contributions, and Mei sometimes responded in
kind. Their poems, mostly mutual flattering between the host and the
guest, were printed in *Gongyuan ribao*. In one of his poems, Mei called
Zhang his "heart-to-heart friend" (*zhiji*) and said that his Nantong trip
was more valuable than gold, since his returning luggage was full of
Zhang's poems.[242] Zhang Jian later published the poems, a fashionable
thing to do at the time, under the title *Poems of the Mei-Ou Chamber*.
Ouyang considered this sheer vanity and tried to squash the idea.[243]

Mei came to Nantong for the third time in 1922, supposedly to celebrate Zhang's seventieth birthday (which was actually the year before).
He brought his troupe of more than sixty people, which included some
well-known actors and personalities. Public and private banquets were
held in Zhang Jian's villas, the Club Hotel, and parks day after day. The

FIGURE 16. Zhang Jian with two of the Gengsu Theater's star performers, May 1920. Zhang (4th from the left), is flanked by Mei Lanfang (on the right) and Ouyang Yuqian (on the left). Zhang's son, Xiaoruo, is standing next to Ouyang. The building behind them is the Southern Hall of the Nantong Museum. (Courtesy of Zhang Xuwu)

public banquets, or *gongyan*, were usually hosted by local officials, and the private ones, or *siyan* and *jiayan* (house banquets), by individual elites. Zhang Jian, his brother, and his son were always among the hosts at both the public and the private banquets. Oftentimes, Mei and other actors would perform exclusively for the elites gathered at the banquets.[244] Mei staged a special play about birthday celebrations at the Gengsu in honor of Zhang.[245] Zhang built a villa in Nantong for Mei, named Mei-cha; the grounds contained thousands of plum trees (*meihua*) and herds of sika deer (*meihualu / Cervus nippon*), both of which shared the character for Mei Lanfang's family name,[246] but there is no indication that Mei ever stayed in the villa.

Despite the social prejudice against the acting profession, it was not uncommon for prominent actors to establish close relationships with politicians and elites for patronage and other reasons.[247] In most cases, such relationships were kept private, or, more precisely, were not intended for public consumption. Zhang Jian, however, went overboard in conspicuously displaying his fondness for and friendship with Mei. He arranged for their letters to each other to be printed in *Tonghai xinbao* in a special column, "Mei Xun"("Correspondence with Mei").[248] Zhang's own love of the theater and his admiration for the artist were only part of the reason; the high marketability of Mei Lanfang's name was another.

In fact, while the Gengsu Theater was still under construction, Zhang Jian had already thought about how he might capitalize on Mei's name to boost the new theater, in part out of financial concerns. "To promote the theater, your help is essential, which means you must come [to perform]," Zhang stated in his invitation to Mei in 1919. He went on to speak of the huge cost of building the theater, funded mostly by private loans, which the theater would eventually have to repay. "Without your help, there would not be a speedy result [in making profits]," Zhang stressed.[249] Most of all, Zhang hoped to boost the theater by having Mei perform at its opening in September, but that plan fell through because Mei could not make it until November. In 1922, when Ouyang's departure left Gengsu in disarray, Zhang once again thought about having Mei rescue it, for a while at least. While Mei was performing in Shanghai, Zhang first sent Gengsu's manager and then his son, Zhang Xiaoruo, to Shanghai to persuade Mei to make yet another trip to Nantong. The result, as discussed above, was Mei's third visit, ostensibly for Zhang's belated birthday celebration.[250]

Mei's marketability went beyond profit making. His appearances were arguably great public relations campaigns that created a local, regional, and even national sensation, putting Nantong in the media spotlight. As the most popular ticket of the day, Mei's performances attracted opera fans from all over the lower Yangzi region to Nantong, many for the first time. Some convoys on the Yangzi River had to add as many as five ships to accommodate those fans.[251] There were people from Shanghai, too, including the owner of the noted Tianchan Theater.[252] Tickets were in short supply. Some patrons had to settle for temporarily added seats on the sides of the stage and in the aisles; others had to stand through the show; and still others waited outside in the hope of getting in.[253] Once there were about four thousand people packed in the 1,200-seat theater.[254] Some people even came as much as three hours early to secure their seats.[255] Both as an advertisement and as a solution to the high demand for tickets flooding in through the mail, by phone, and in person, Gengsu designated four staff members to help with in-house ticket reservations. In addition, it sent its repre-

FIGURE 17. *Gongyuan ribao* ad for the performances of Mei Lanfang, Ouyang Yuqian, and other actors, Jan. 18, 1920. (Courtesy of Zhang Xuwu)

sentatives to some of the ships making the run to Nantong on the Yangzi River to handle ticket booking, so that the fans could secure their tickets before landing.[256] As in the case of Dewey's visit, Mei's performances heightened a celebrity culture, in which a local event gained wide exposure, and fans traveled to follow media stars. Such mobility—in terms of both information and people—was made possible by the advances in transportation and communications.

Indeed, Gengsu and its in-house voice, *Gongyuan ribao*, together with other local newspapers, did an outstanding job in promoting Mei and his shows (Fig. 17). They presented Mei not only as a superstar of Chinese opera, but as an artist of international stature. One of the *Gongyuan ribao* ads stated that millions of Mei's stage photographs had been sold in America, and that the world was in love with his talent.[257] In Nantong, each of Mei's visits was reported as headline news days before his arrival, and the public was urged to make tickets reservations as early as possible.[258] There was daily coverage of Mei's activities during his stay. Theater programs gave detailed information on the content and texts of Mei's plays, as well as on the other actors' backgrounds. Following each show there were stories about the audience and its reactions. Every last detail, no matter how trivial, was reported: the appearance of Westerners among the Gengsu crowd, a blind man's joyful response to Mei's performance, a fan's carelessness in putting a lit cigarette into his hat while applauding Mei, a banker's mistake in making a check payable to "Shanghai Mei Lanfang," because he had nothing but the actor's name on his mind.[259] When Gengsu gave Mei's stage photographs to its first-class ticket holders, a local photo studio immediately cashed in, putting a set of thirty pictures of Mei on sale.[260] Traditional means of advertising were also used. Gengsu had its staff walk the streets with a board on their backs to spread word about Mei's performances.[261] Mei's plays became popular topics of conversation in local teahouses and taverns.[262] With all the sensation created about Mei, even the local people who could not get into the theater gathered in front of the Gengsu or at one of Zhang Jian's homes to get a look at the famous actor—Mei and his entourage were quite a spectacular sight for the townspeople.[263]

If before the theater reform, Nantong's reputation was mostly pertinent to educated people, Mei's trips changed that. For he attracted to Nantong not only his and Zhang Jian's *gaopeng*—friends in high places who filled those VIP banquet rooms—but also an unprecedentedly large number of local and regional people. In other words, Mei's performances carried the message of an advanced Nantong to the sphere of everyday life and sold it to ordinary people. Moreover, as a national figure closely followed by the print media, Mei helped Nantong gain more nationwide exposure. Aside from performing and socializing, Mei and his staff, like all other distinguished guests, were given a tour of all the new landmarks in the city and its vicinity. With Mei's relatively large entourage and the sizable number of local notables and officials who accompanied the visitors, the long motorcade tours made a mighty impression as they wended their way through the rural landscape.[264] The tours apparently persuaded Mei that Nantong was so perfect it would surely become a "gentlemen's kingdom" (*junzi guo*) in the future.[265] Though these tours were meant for Mei, the newspapers' coverage of them afforded Nantong a much broader audience. Major newspapers' reports on Mei's Nantong trips resulted in much admiration for and even envy of Nantong, especially from bigger cities.[266]

In addition, Mei's visits caused a chain reaction in the acting profession that kept Nantong in the spotlight. It was not a coincidence that, following Mei's appearances, more than fifty famous actors performed in Nantong. The new theater instantly became a big draw for other actors; associating themselves with it was certain to raise their social and professional status. When Cheng Yanqiu, for instance, performed in Nantong in 1920, local newspapers lavished praise on him. He was delighted to gain such "face" (*mianzi*).[267] Some actors came with a small entourage to stage only one or two shows, and pay was not their main concern. The real purpose for them was to be talked about as having been in Nantong. They all tried, using Mei Lanfang as a precedent, to get examples of Zhang Jian's poems, couplets, and calligraphy to show off. Zhang was of course aware of the impact of his writings on their careers and usually granted their requests.[268] For one actor, he wrote: "Your name is waiting for my poem to disseminate it and you will be well known in the country."[269] The reverse was also true: the stardom of these actors in turn gilded Nantong's reputation. Their profession made them one of the most geographically mobile segments in society. When they shared their Nantong stories with others for self-promotion, they propelled the image-building process for Nantong.

As symbolized by the Gengsu, Zhang Jian turned the community into an open theater whose main function was to publicize Nantong and in which Zhang himself was the star. Zhang's ambitions and vanity eroded his initial intention to reform the people through theater. Though Ouyang was more of a reformer than Mei, Mei was more useful to Zhang's purposes. Consequently, the small stage of Gengsu was reduced to a prop for the larger show as a disillusioned Ouyang finally realized that his difference with Zhang Jian was in ideas, and that in the end the theater and the acting school had become merely an "embellishment [*zhuangshi pin*] for the 'model county.'"[270]

The kind of exhibitory and performative institutions and events discussed in this chapter both reflected and shaped several emerging tendencies in early twentieth-century China. To begin with, those institutions and events were new and bore a distinct mark of the time; even the traditional operatic theater was made to absorb new elements. As such, they were part of the modernization process. Behind this effort was the reconfiguration of social boundaries, which not only allowed new social forces such as professional educators to promote their causes, but also allowed traditionally marginal groups such as actors to negotiate a space with elites to influence social change. Though the lack of a clear, unified vision for modernization among these groups proved to be costly for China's struggle, their paths did cross at one point or another, producing some temporary alliances on the issue of reform. Largely because of their combined effort, the social educational movement, for instance, bore some fruit.[271] Also because of their effort, modern culture was no longer merely an urban monopoly but reached China's hinterland and gained some momentum.[272] Despite their indifference and even resistance to modern culture, the people in provincial towns like Nantong were given an opportunity to stretch their minds and to taste something new.

The arrival of competing political players coming from various channels and equipped with new instruments broke the traditional power monopoly and further compelled politicians and reformers to appeal directly to the people. Mass mobilization and public orientation, trends that started in the late Qing, became increasingly visible. Zhang Jian once said that what he did in Nantong would remain a private matter if it was only recognized by a few, and that it would become a public matter only when it was evaluated and confirmed by every county, province, and country.[273] Zhang was clearly aware that public recognition was the ultimate validation for the model, which partially explains his motives in promoting these performative activities. Here lay the implication of exhibitory modernity: it reflected the existence of a market that was ready to consume images of the modern. In light of this interconnected mass society and a commercializing political culture, it was crucial for the elites to polish their image and to target that market for political gain. In the meantime, the elites also felt an urgent need to influence the previously invisible masses, not only in how they should think, but also in how they should behave in public. The museum, schools, and the theater thus became new arenas of control for the elites.

The Nantong case also illustrates how personal politics cast an intense shadow on the path of China's modernization. After all, Nantong, the "Mecca of Chinese progress," was Zhang Jian's personal kingdom at the time; Zhang was practically a local emperor (*tuhuangdi*). Yet this accomplished reformer was himself in a state of social and cultural transition. Though the enlightened side of the "local emperor" was forward-looking and experimental, his arbitrary side was self-serving, turning new cultural inventions into personal possessions and to an extent suffocating them. Perhaps the dark side of this personal politics was a necessary evil of the time: the lack of a central government cried out for local strongmen to take charge. However, Zhang Jian, unlike the May Fourth radicals, drew no clear line between the traditional and the modern, even in the case of the novel institution of the museum. Instead, he moved comfortably among various, sometimes opposing, forces. Perhaps he did not see that there was a conflict, or perhaps he understood that not all conflicts had to be resolved.

CHAPTER 5

The Model in Decline

Failure often strikes at the height of success.

Zhang Jian, *Complete Works*

IN 1920, WHEN Zhang Jian urged his associates to be mindful of the ups and downs of industrial adventure,[1] he little dreamed that the aphorism quoted above would prove him a prophet. The No. 1 mill had experienced a steady growth in profits for twenty years, a success that struck some as at once exciting and frightening. But this would be the last time local elites would rejoice in their good fortune. The year 1921 was a turning point for Zhang and Nantong. The cancellation of the 1922 convention that fall, an event so optimistically anticipated only a few months before, marked the beginning of a downward spiral from which Nantong never recovered. The local elites blamed the violent autumn floods for causing much damage and the end of World War I for terminating Dasheng's profitable years. That narrative neutralized the role of the social agent, the Nantong elites in this case, in the failure, since neither natural disaster nor the war was susceptible to local control. But floods were a familiar enemy, and the dependence of local growth on the No. 1 mill was itself a symptom of a serious structural problem. Just as the rise of Nantong was due to the specific political, social, economic, and cultural environment of the first two decades of the twentieth century, so its fall was conditioned by some of the profound changes that marked the 1920s on both the national and the local stage.

Politically, though the conflict between the existing political forces and their various competitors—the warlords, the Nationalist Party (or the Guomindang, GMD), and the Chinese Communist Party (CCP)—further destabilized China, it also brought a renewed desire for national reunification, an aim that threatened the existence of local self-government. Economically, the effect of the re-entry of foreign competitors into the China market after the war was compounded by the elites' long-term mismanagement of the Dasheng System Enterprises, a lesson Nantong's first generation of capitalist entrepreneurs were about to learn, years too late. Socially, a young generation of intellectuals, trained in the new schools Zhang Jian created and influenced by the May Fourth movement, began to search for its own identity by challenging the established order. Culturally, the nationwide rise of nationalism, fueled by the media and spread through ever more wide-reaching communications channels, inevitably penetrated and divided the local community. On one side were the youth, who wholeheartedly embraced nationalism and joined in demonstrations and strikes on its behalf. On the other were the dominant elites who, frightened by the social unrest that came with student radicalism and the boycott of foreign goods, tried to put out the nationalist fire. In the end, the elites' attempt to impose their vision of local progress without national policies was unable to withstand the youth's nationalist drive.

With all these forces at play, the influence of the Zhang family was shaken on every front. The deep financial troubles of the Dasheng enterprises strained the relationship between Zhang Jian and the stockholders to the breaking point. In 1921, Zhang Xiaoruo's campaign for speaker of the provincial assembly suffered intense media scrutiny and ended in a scandal, damaging the Zhangs' political reputation and moral authority. Zhang Jian's suppression of student protests during the May Fourth movement and the May Thirtieth Incident severely alienated the local youth, on whom Zhang had placed so much hope for Nantong's future. These crises tested Zhang Jian's strengths and exposed his weaknesses. He fought tenaciously to rescue his enterprises and his vision of the county, but he proved to be too caught up in his own vision to adjust to the changing times. Though his worst fear was being controlled by circumstances, a legacy of his youth, he spent the last years of his life once again trapped in situations that he had no power to alter. But this time, in contrast to his years as an examination candidate, the problem was partly of his own doing. Zhang Jian died in 1926, a deeply disappointed man, barely missing the further trauma that the Northern Expedition was about to inflict on his family and the community. Zhang Cha and Zhang Xiaoruo labored to carry out Zhang Jian's legacy, but to little effect. By the end of the decade, the relevance of the Nantong model to the nation, as well as the relevance of the Zhang family to the community, had become a thing of the past.

Economic Crisis

The financial difficulties that beset the Dasheng System Enterprises in 1921 were the first indication that Nantong's fortunes were on the ebb. By then, the system included four textile mills and more than forty other enterprises, with the No. 1 mill as the financial core. Its prior success was due mainly to the prosperity of the textile industry. In fact, the No. 1 mill was the only one out of the sixteen Chinese-owned cotton mills established since 1896 that was still operating with the same ownership on the eve of World War I.[2] The war provided a golden opportunity for the No. 1 mill's further growth. Except for 1916, the factory reported an annual gain in profits from 1900 to 1921.[3] But the mill, and therefore the Dashing System Enterprises as a whole, went into deep debt after 1921 and steadily declined thereafter. Various factors contributed to that fatal turn of fortune.

Causes of the Mill's Financial Troubles

Natural disaster did play a role in the mill's downfall, as the elites contended. Though much emphasis is put on the 1921 floods, the previous year was not disaster-free either. The annual typhoon season delivered on its usual promise in July 1920. Its effect was compounded by a plague of locusts that resulted in widespread crop failures. A two-month epidemic of cholera followed, which kept part of the Dasheng workforce at home and forced the No. 1 mill to temporarily close down.[4] Then came the 1921 floods. From June to August, the Jiangbei region was repeatedly buffeted by torrential rains and raging tides. Both the river and the ocean rose beyond the embankments. The areas in Nantong county that were near waterways were completely submerged. Barrages, dikes, and other water control facilities built in the past two decades were destroyed, and much property and many lives were lost. The floods not only deprived Nantong of a fall harvest, but also affected the next spring's planting, for some of the fields that had been under seawater could not be cultivated until the salt was removed from the soil.[5] Furthermore, many of the land reclamation companies scattered in the Jiangbei region that were financed by the No. 1 mill were devastated by the floods. The disaster placed dual pressure on the local economy—it suffered a tremendous loss in labor, raw material, and investment but still had to manage flood relief and to rebuild dikes and levees.

Foreign as well as domestic competition also had a negative impact on the Dasheng enterprises. Though the Western companies that re-entered the China market after the war were a major source of competition, the impact of Japan's wartime economic expansion in China cannot be overlooked. Not only did the Japanese textile factories in China increase their productive capacity to the point where they outproduced the Chinese-owned factories, but with their up-to-date machines and advanced technology, they turned out high-quality products at a lower cost, and thus had a market advantage. The No. 1 mill competed with Japanese mills to hold onto the northeastern market, a traditionally strong area for Nantong cotton products, but eventually lost it.[6] In the meantime, the war encouraged Chinese in their industrial ventures, and new factories sprang up rapidly, putting further pressure on the already competitive market.[7] The Nantong mills were part of this problem; they expanded production significantly during the war.[8] The Chinese factories ended up nullifying each other's opportunity and profit. In 1922, the National Association of Chinese Textile Merchants had to repeatedly advise factories to limit or terminate altogether their production.[9] This situation reflected not only the steep competition among Chinese and foreign enterprises, but also the overall decline of the Chinese economy and industry because of changes in the international market and the renewed political instability caused by warlord conflicts.

What the decline of the Dasheng system revealed, ultimately, was its own lack of a safety net, an especially surprising weakness given the No. 1 mill's impressive record of profits. The mill's inability to weather the financial and natural storms was due in equal parts to long-term mismanagement, undisciplined growth, and the abuse of power by the majority stockholders, including the Zhang brothers. If Zhang Jian's personal flaws included being overconfident, wartime prosperity further encouraged his unrealistic ambitions. Among other things, he involved the Dasheng System Enterprises in a host of new business ventures, including real estate, hotels, and a new power station. Because of the lack of capital, which was compounded by corruption and mismanagement, some of the enterprises were in debt or closed down soon after their birth, and others never took off.[10]

Of the aborted plans, those related to the cotton mills were perhaps the most revealing of the wartime overgrowth. In addition to the two existing mills, Zhang Jian and his associates decided to build seven more in Jiangbei and Shanghai. But because the Dasheng system was

perennially short of capital, any new factories had to start on government and private loans, and most struggled in the beginning. Moreover, lenders were often difficult to find. Even during the war, the
Zhang brothers had a hard time coming up with loans to finance the
No. 3 mill, which took seven years to complete and was soon in debt.
The No. 8 mill, started in 1920, was mortgaged even before production
started. Plans for the other five mills were terminated, resulting in the
loss of the deposits already made to purchase machines and the money
spent on the construction of workshops.[11] Though these factories were
supposed to raise their start-up capital on their own, their failure nevertheless affected the No. 1 mill. The problem was that the Zhang brothers were involved in most of the new ventures and also in control of the
No. 1 mill. The majority of Dasheng stockholders, after their unsuc-
cessful attempt in 1907 to limit Zhang Jian's power by forming the
Tonghai Industrial Company, basically took a free ride during Dasheng's profitable years but little responsibility. As a result, the Zhang
brothers continued to treat the No. 1 mill as their personal property.
They often tapped its capital holdings or used its assets as collateral in
securing loans for other projects. For instance, when the No. 8 mill went
broke, the No. 1 mill as its guarantor eventually had to take it over and
deal with its creditors. Often the factory lent money that it did not have
and then borrowed more from banks. Before 1921, investors trusted the
factory because of its sustained profitability and the inflated reputation
of Nantong and Zhang Jian.[12] In this case, the model that he and the
other new local elites so eagerly cultivated contributed to financial irre-
sponsibility and economic strain.

The profits of the No. 1 mill were also directly used for many local
projects. In principle, Zhang Jian understood that the annual budget for
local development should be based on the previous year's profits, but
he was dreaming big dreams and was often willing, as he himself said,
to "go into debt" to fulfill whatever he was determined on.[13] Unfortunately, his determination could not overcome economic constraints. A
case in point was the land reclamation companies, the most costly of all
the projects and with the least possibility for a quick return. Worse yet,
the growth of those companies had spun out of control because of the
Zhang brothers' ambition. By 1921, they had involved themselves in
sixteen such companies in Nantong and neighboring counties in Jiangbei, some of which were far away from Nantong.[14] All of them were
founded on borrowed money.

By 1922, the No. 1 mill, the star factory of the Dasheng System Enterprises and the life support of local development for decades, was 12,428,720 liang in debt. Its loans to the land and salt reclamation companies alone amounted to 1,334,215 liang, and other local projects accounted for another 1,753,243, all with no hope of repayment.[15] As it happened, the land reclamation projects worked out, but only in the long run. Reclamation involved vast tracts of non-arable land that required tremendous long-term (15 to 30 years) investment in infrastructure and irrigation work before they became productive. The companies were located near water and thus especially vulnerable to floods; the peasants who worked for them were often among the poorest. Furthermore, the company managers had little or no training, and some of them were corrupt.[16] The reclamation program was thus a serious financial and administrative challenge to the Dasheng System Enterprises. It also affected the Huai Hai Industrial Bank. Having lent money to local factories and land reclamation companies, the bank was now forced to deal with its own tremendous debt.[17] Not surprisingly, many of Dasheng's majority stockholders quickly became disenchanted with the reclamation companies. In the past, such discontent was neutralized by the success of the No. 1 mill, but now, with the mill in crisis, they spoke out. In 1923, Zhang Jian was compelled to defend the investments in reclamation at a meeting of the Dasheng board of directors. His explanation—that the mills had benefited from land reclamation over the years by obtaining a large cotton supply, and that the current financial problem was merely the result of natural disaster—was hardly a consolation when the mill was nearly bankrupt.[18]

The distribution of the Dasheng System Enterprises' interest and profit was as arbitrary as the top leaders' investment decisions. Some of the No. 1 mill's unprecedented wartime profits were simply issued as dividends or lent out to majority stockholders. To be sure, such financial mismanagement, as John Dewey observed, was common during China's early industrialization, when "a short life and a merry one was the usual motto."[19] In the Dasheng case, by 1922, five of the majority stockholders had misappropriated 1,012,692 liang, and the Zhang brothers had borrowed 1,400,000 liang.[20]

Evidently, it was rather common for those in power in the Dasheng system to take advantage of its many loopholes. Zhang Jian was aware of the problem. In 1920, he twice appealed in writing to his colleagues to respect regulations for the sake of the long-term interest of the companies and not to misappropriate or borrow any factory money for private purposes.[21] But his effort to tighten the loopholes was in vain, not least because he and his brother failed to follow their own advice. In 1922, when the No. 3 mill was finally brought into being, it was already 800,000 liang over budget. Even so, the board of directors, noting that Zhang Cha had worked hard during the eight-year building process without pay, decided to reward him with 20,000 yuan. They also gave Zhang Cha the authority to reward his staff in whatever amount he saw fit. In this case, arbitrary bonuses replaced a formal payroll system. Zhang Cha eventually donated his bonus to sponsor an old people's home,[22] an example of how what the Zhang brothers claimed to be private donations to local projects were actually monies obtained directly from the factories they controlled. In 1923, when the Zhangs were forced to mortgage the No. 1 and 3 mills to deal with the financial crisis, several of the stockholders turned on Zhang Jian and demanded an audit of the accounting records.[23]

Casualties of the Dasheng Decline

Zhang Jian was consumed by the financial crisis throughout this period. If the wartime encouraged his unrealistic ambitions, the crisis reconnected him with his pragmatism. In his correspondence, he continuously mentioned the grave difficulty he was having in maintaining the status quo.[24] Realizing the planning mistakes (*yunchou shice*), especially in capital accumulation and overdevelopment, Zhang Jian tried to "change the way things were run" (*gaixian er gengzhang*).[25] He had to manage the debts first, however, and he did so by downsizing the existing programs and by looking for new investors. He also seems to have made a pass at least of cutting down himself. In 1921, he wrote to Liang Qichao to cancel a promised purchase of some foreign books because of the huge debts.[26] This cancellation was only a small sacrifice compared with other critical setbacks.

The first major casualty of the crisis, ironically, was the much-anticipated 1922 convention. In the immediate aftermath of the 1921 floods, Zhang Jian announced that the event would be postponed to 1927 for a thirtieth anniversary celebration instead.[27] The self-congratulatory mood early on was quickly replaced by the desperation to retrieve the community from the disaster. Zhang Jian gave two reasons for the change of plan. One was the lack of funds. According to him, to rebuild the water control system alone would cost 300,000 yuan. "My brother and I looked at each other helplessly and could find no way to come up with the money," he said. As it happened, that was the very amount budgeted for the convention, and as Zhang Jian was forced to admit, "Comparing famine relief and water control with the convention, the former was more urgent and important." Facing a grave situation, Zhang's vanity finally gave way to his sense of responsibility to the people and the community.

On the other hand, Zhang Jian understood very well that the floods made the celebration practically impossible anyway. The land reclamation and water control projects, considered unprecedented achievements of local self-government in Nantong, were planned as key components of the convention. With both of them under water and with little hope of recovering them in time for the convention, the grand exhibition of Nantong would not only be incomplete but worse, reveal failures. "If all the self-government did in terms of water control could only handle ordinary natural disasters but not the extraordinary ones, then how can we call it self-government and what do we have to report to the outsiders?" Zhang Jian became self-examining in the crisis.

Failed ceremonies can be as significant as successful ones in affecting political image. In this case, the failure was a wake-up call for the elites to realize not only the fragility of their success, but also the limits of their capacity, although that realization came a bit too late to do them any good. One of Zhang Jian's main concerns was the damage to Nantong's reputation. The 1922 convention had been much publicized. The Beijing government and the foreign and Chinese press had all been informed; thus the news about the convention had spread far and wide to become common knowledge. Accordingly, Zhang had little choice but to publicly announce the cancellation. His statement was carefully worded to save face and to forestall any doubts about Nantong. He first pointed out that the preparations for the 1922 event had all been going well as planned and had fallen through only because of the floods. He then went on to stress the magnitude of the floods and the suffering of the community, in effect glossing the cancellation as a laudably noble act. He concluded with the reassurance that the convention would take place after all, in 1927, and so implied that the preparations were not all wasted. What he failed to mention, however, was that the convention was already problematic before the floods because of the county's financial woes. Moreover, since the promised 1927 event never took place, all the construction that had been completed did indeed go largely to waste, including an exhibition hall and a conference hall. Zhang decided to halt all the planned projects that had not been started but to carry through the half-completed new market and sports stadium. Finished or not, the convention facilities bore witness to the disappointment over the failed project and served as a reminder of a past ambition.

The fate of this grandiose, highly anticipated, and intimately personal celebration of Zhang Jian was an ominous portent. The financial crisis could not be resolved by eliminating a single event. Other local projects began to suffer and die as well. Tellingly, the way in which they were affected, just as the way they were built in the first place, reflected the inner logic of the model. New-style entertainment facilities became a priority only at the height of Nantong's reputation. Like the plans for the convention, those facilities mirrored the model at its peak and the elites' vanity. Consequently, they were among the first to lose funding in 1921. The acting school, for instance, became an immediate victim of Dasheng's financial troubles. The Club Hotel's so-called high-class facilities—the tennis and baseball courts, bar, restaurant, music room, opera room, reading room, and gardenlike bath house—were built mainly for the accommodation of prestigious foreign and Chinese guests. The hotel fell into deep debt before it could complete the new facilities. As a result, Zhang Jian appealed to local elites for help.[28] In the meantime, the hotel began to advertise its restaurant and sell itself to the general public, emphasizing sanitation as its unique, civilized feature.[29] The fate of these leisure institutions and facilities illustrated the trouble Nantong faced. Perhaps because of its broad impact, Nantong's financial problem was apparently common knowledge at the time.[30]

Financial Maneuvers

The cancellation and downsizing of certain projects were passive reactions to the financial difficulties. Zhang Jian and others did, however, try to raise funds at the local, provincial, and international levels and through both regular and speculative channels. In the past, he had sold his calligraphy to sponsor charitable projects. He would typically make a public announcement in the Shanghai newspapers, as well as the local ones, to trade in on his reputation in the lower Yangzi region, listing the price range and the conditions for his work. In 1922, he once again declared that, in light of the natural disasters, he would donate two hours every day for a month to write for anyone who was willing to pay for his labor.[31] Noble as Zhang Jian's action was, it was an utterly inadequate measure considering the scale of the problem.

Government was another source Zhang approached for help. Immediately after the floods, he wrote to the provincial officials asking them to inspect the disaster areas and to allocate emergency funds.[32] He also pondered issuing local bonds as a long-term solution. In 1920, he wrote enthusiastically about the benefit of the bonds and tried to involve the community.[33] It became a hard sell in 1921, when the economic slowdown was all too apparent.

The most risky of all of the financial maneuvers at the local level was the creation, in September 1921, of the Combined Stock Exchange of Nantong Cotton, Yarn, Securities, and Grains (Nantong mianye, shaye, zhengquan, zaliang lianhe jiaoyisuo). At the time, there were many stock exchanges in Shanghai, promoting a culture of speculation.[34] The Nantong exchange was the work of Zhang Xiaoruo and his associates, and its staff was trained by people from one of the Shanghai organizations.[35] As pointed out earlier, Zhang Xiaoruo was then on the rise to power, in control of both the Local Self-government Association and the Huai Hai Industrial Bank. He and his associates saw the stock exchange as a golden opportunity to capitalize on his rising reputation for political and financial gain. The merchant community, for its part, faced with the economic recession and looking for new ways to make quick money, enthusiastically embraced the idea.[36]

The stock exchange had all the appearances of a legitimate organization. It was located in the chamber of commerce building and functioned as one of its subordinate offices. Zhang Cha was the director, and Zhang Jian the honorary director. As executive manager, Zhang Xiaoruo answered to a twenty-man board for the daily operations. The stock exchange had detailed regulations regarding its practice and a group of legal and business advisers. Most of the stockbrokers were local cotton and yarn merchants, some of whom were on the staff of the No. 1 mill.[37] Zhang Jian was at first concerned about the pitfalls of financial speculation—he emphasized the need for the brokers to follow the regulations and warned them of the consequences if they did not—but it was not long before he too was persuaded that the exchange could be potentially helpful to the economy.[38]

In fact, the stock exchange proved to be a disaster. Zhang Xiaoruo left the operation to his associates, who plotted to control prices and lure gullible investors. For a brief moment, the highways from several neighboring counties to Nantong were crowded with cars and buses taking profit-seekers—peasants, women, and nuns included—to the chamber of commerce building. Various related activities, such as banking, gambling, fortune-telling, and loan-sharking, boomed. The general market was inflated as well. By the end of 1921, the prices of rice and firewood had risen sharply, severely affecting the basic living standards of peasants and townspeople alike.[39] All this caused public panic and complaints. Zhang Jian's worst nightmare came true. He banned the companies and people within the Dasheng system from trading on the exchange,[40] even though his own brother and son, both top leaders in the system, were deeply involved. In the winter of 1921, a manipulative scheme by some of the board members was exposed, causing strife among the staff and indignation among the public.[41] By then, the big market bubble had burst.

How best to deal with this situation tested the unity of the Zhang family. Blaming the chaos on the greedy public and bad influences from Shanghai, Zhang Jian wanted to close down the stock exchange immediately, but was concerned about Zhang Cha's prestige and Zhang Xiaoruo's reputation. Both Zhang Cha and Zhang Xiaoruo agreed with Zhang Jian that the stock exchange would have to go, but they sharply disagreed on the timing. Zhang Cha considered an immediate shutdown inevitable, whereas Zhang Xiaoruo preferred a gradual phaseout.[42] That preference may well have had something to do with Xiaoruo's associates' alleged use of the money they controlled through the exchange to finance his campaign for speaker.[43] At any rate, all three Zhangs were quickly tarred with the same brush. The spread of rumors about the family's wrongdoings called for urgent damage control. In January 1922, Zhang Cha asked the Beijing government to issue an order to close down the stock exchange, ending the difference between him and Zhang Xiaoruo.[44] Zhang Cha also gave away his personal profits from stock trading to calm public outrage.[45] By then, hundreds of people and businesses, including seven traditional banks, were bankrupt. Some people committed suicide, and others were sent to jail. Gone almost as soon as it appeared, the stock exchange not only failed to rescue the local economy, but left a huge debt of its own and a lingering public relations nightmare.[46]

In the end, Zhang Jian pinned his hope of reviving his enterprises on foreign loans, even though that was a highly sensitive issue in this time of rising nationalism. Zhang had been both open-minded and prudent when it came to dealing with foreign nations and foreign aid. A pragmatist at heart, he prized political stability at almost any cost as essential to economic development. For that reason, he condemned the Boxer violence and was even apologetic to the foreign countries affected, and later, in 1905, would support only a "peaceful" boycott of American goods.[47] Again, with economic development always uppermost in mind, Zhang realized the importance of foreign capital, whether from friendly or hostile nations, to China's economic growth. In 1913, as Minister of Industry, he provided a detailed guideline for Yuan Shikai's initial policy of "opening the door and utilizing foreign capital to strengthen Chinese industry."[48] He also proposed involving American banks in his ambitious plans to control the Huai River.[49] Nevertheless, before the 1921 financial crisis, Zhang Jian was wary of foreign loans and the motives of the lenders. For instance, in 1911, he questioned the Qing court's decision to borrow money from foreign banks on the ground that the loans lacked a clearly defined purpose and were thus fiscally irresponsible.[50] In 1912, he argued against a proposal to have the Japanese share the ownership of a major mine company for fear of Japan's gaining control of Chinese resources.[51] All this illustrated Zhang Jian's pragmatic yet cautious attitude toward the role of foreign capital in China's economic life.

But the financial crisis of the early 1920s tipped that balance. Thereafter, economic pragmatism came to dominate Zhang Jian's thinking, primarily for two reasons. The end of the war encouraged his illusion about a world of "great harmony" or "unification" (*datong*). He envisioned that in such a world all the countries would, or should, help one another for the common good of industrial development. He fully expressed this view in an extensive article, "On the Demands and Supplies of World and Chinese Industry," published in 1923, in the midst of his loan negotiations with Japan.[52] That title was misleading, because the article was not about industry as such, but exclusively about the textile industry, something of particular importance to Nantong. Filled with statistics of cotton production in major industrial countries, as well as in Nantong, the article argued that international cooperation was the only way to deal with an unpredictable market that could threaten world peace in the future. By international cooperation, Zhang Jian meant that countries should make use of one another's strengths and make up for one another's deficiencies. He used his ambitions for the reclamation of land to demonstrate how this kind of trade-off could work: China had great resources in cheap land and labor that could ensure the cotton supply of other nations, and they, in turn, had the wealth to lend China the capital it needed to realize the full potential of those resources through land reclamation and other measures. Zhang Jian proposed that a world bank be formed to oversee this economic cooperation.

Clearly, Zhang Jian's article was meant to persuade foreign investors to rescue his troubled enterprises, especially the land reclamation companies. If the postwar era allowed Zhang Jian to think in terms of international cooperation, the financial crisis in Nantong gave him no choice but to seek foreign aid at any cost. Zhang realized how land reclamation had become a fatal financial burden for the local economy and regretted being too ambitious. He understood that without major, long-term loans, his reclamation companies would fold. On the other hand, born a peasant, he sincerely believed that land reclamation was a key to China's future economic well-being and thus stubbornly tried to hold onto the enterprise.[53] Of course, to give it up would also mean a waste of all previous investment, a denial of his lifetime work, and a blow to his ego. In his desperation, Zhang Jian became dangerously single-minded. While negotiating with Japan for a loan, Zhang Jian was pointedly asked by the Japanese representative how he would feel if he was criticized by the Chinese public for depending on foreign money. He answered, "I am seventy years old. My only concern is to complete the local enterprises I started; I seek nothing else."[54]

In 1921, two returned students from Japan who were involved in Zhang Jian's reclamation companies put him in touch with several Japanese banks. His purpose was to borrow 8,000,000 yuan to complete the reclamation projects already in progress. Those involved in the negotiations included Komai Tokuzoo, a Japanese China hand, who visited Nantong in the winter of 1922 to size up the whole situation and, in particular, to investigate Zhang Jian and high-ranking officials of the reclamation companies and the No. 1 mill. What apparently attracted the Japanese bankers most was the promise of an abundant cotton supply from the reclaimed land, should the project be successful. Komai spent most of his time during his twenty days in Nantong studying the land reclamation companies, but he also visited the industrial center of Tangzha and other local attractions. He was treated as a prestigious guest and lodged in the Club Hotel; both Zhang Jian and Zhang Cha held banquets for him in their homes.[55]

The trip resulted in a detailed report by Komai on Zhang Jian's career and reputation, as well as Nantong's investment environment. Komai had nothing but good to say about Zhang himself. He considered Nantong the "capital" (*shoudu*) of Jiangbei, and Zhang Jian the "head" (*yuanshou*) of the Jiangbei region, and emphasized his influence and connections in the business community in Shanghai.[56] To demonstrate Zhang's political reach, Komai mentioned that, though Zhang did not hold any formal government position, the central and provincial governments consulted him on important policy issues. He pointedly highlighted Zhang's relationship with the warlords Zhang Zuolin and Wu Peifu, who controlled Manchuria and China's northern plain. According to Komai, both warlords, who were engaged in a military conflict at the time, tried to rally Zhang's support, in part because they needed the financial backing of industrialists and bankers in Shanghai.[57] Portraying Zhang Jian as an influential, skilled politician, the report implied that Zhang could be useful to Japan's ambitions in North China.

Komai had mixed feelings about Zhang Jian's economic ventures. Like most visitors, he was reportedly impressed by what he saw. He was also aware of Zhang Jian's missteps in management. Komai pointed out that two-thirds of Dasheng's investment was in sixteen reclamation companies, all but one of which were in debt. He considered it a typical case of wartime overgrowth. "Had Zhang Jian taken a gradual approach then," Komai wrote, "he would not need to borrow any money from Japan today." But Komai also emphasized that since cotton was in much demand in East Asia, he was hopeful about the future of Zhang's reclamation companies.[58]

Probably because of Komai's report, the prospects for a loan were promising for a time. Negotiations continued from 1921 to 1923 in Nantong, Shanghai, and Tokyo. It was in the midst of them that Zhang Jian published the article on world industry discussed above. He clearly had the loan negotiations in mind when he wrote it. The article especially played on Japan's sense of insecurity about its lack of land and raw material. It also pointed out the high cost and difficulties of land reclamation in Japan to show the comparative advantage of reclaiming land in China.[59]

Zhang's article created a public stir, because it promoted an economic structure in East Asia that consisted of an agricultural China and an industrial Japan. In 1923, the CCP, in its official magazine *Guide* (*Xiangdao*), criticized Zhang as an example how the capitalist system would inevitably reduce Chinese-owned factories to a mere attachment of foreign capital.[60] That criticism, however, did not deter Zhang Jian. His only concern was whether the deal with Japan would come to fruition. Unfortunately, the negotiations eventually collapsed, in part because the great 1923 Tokyo earthquake put pressure on the banking community to meet Japan's own financial needs.

Zhang Jian also sought American funding. He was convinced that the United States was the only country aside from Japan with the potential to aid Chinese enterprises, primarily because of its economic strength and its seemingly friendly attitude. Zhang Jian had previously had a number of opportunities to discuss forming a Sino-U.S. economic development plan with American businessmen. According to him, the two countries shared common ground both geographically and politically. As two Pacific countries, they were like brothers, and as two republican countries, they were like student and teacher, for the Chinese had learned the republican system from the United States. "With these close connections," Zhang Jian reasoned, America naturally should "guide and support" China's development.[61] His 1923 article was particularly targeted not just at Japan but also at the United States as a future investor in his companies. It frequently cited American economic data and hinted that cooperation with China would be beneficial for American manufacturers.[62] In 1924, when news came that the U.S. government intended to return the Boxer indemnity to China, Zhang wrote to Washington requesting that three-tenths of the indemnity be used to support cultural programs in Nantong. The letter was an excellent example of a grant proposal.[63] In two pages, it summarized Nantong's unique success in following "the trends of the world" in developing cultural and educational programs. It emphasized that private, not government, funds had supported all the projects. To highlight the impact of supporting Nantong, the proposal especially pointed out that students from all over China came to attend schools in Nantong. In conclusion, Zhang Jian listed the programs in need and their cost to justify his request. In the end, the American aid that Zhang so hoped for never came.

The Changing of the Guard

By 1925, the Dasheng enterprises were 6,000,000 yuan in debt with no relief in sight, and were under mounting pressure from both their stockholders and their creditors. In 1924, nine local traditional banks (*qianzhuang*) that had invested in the No. 1 mill took steps to make sure their money was repaid. Forming what they called a preservation association (*weichihui*), they simply took over the factory for three months.[64] This damaging blow to the Dasheng reputation intensified the concern of other creditors. In 1925, those creditors, including four banks from Shanghai, formed a consortium to take over the four existing Dasheng mills.[65]

Because of the huge debt, the consortium could not afford to simply shut down the factories. Zhang Jian's friends and associates in the financial and industrial community also hoped to prevent his enterprises from being dissolved. It was, therefore, in the best interest of both parties to find a way, or rather, a suitable person, to revive the factories. Li Shengbo, the twenty-nine-year-old son of a banker from Zhejiang province who was a major creditor of the No. 1 mill, emerged as the right man at the right time.[66] A graduate of the Pennsylvania Textile Institute in the early 1920s, Li had just that year returned from an inspection of the textile industry in Europe, North America, and Japan. He was full of ambition and eager to practice in China what he had learned abroad. He was contemplating his options in Shanghai when he was asked to pay Nantong a visit.[67]

Li's trip proved to be crucial for the future of the Dasheng mills; it also changed his own life for the next thirteen years. It turned out that Zhang Jian was Li's hero. On a field trip during his middle school years, Li had a chance to hear Zhang speak at the Nanyang Exhortation Fair and was moved by Zhang's devotion to China's development. Nantong's reputation and its textile industry were also known to Li. Zhang and his associates, however, were understandably skeptical about Li's intentions in the beginning since he was sent by Dasheng's creditors. Upon Li's arrival, Zhang Jian introduced him to Dasheng's history and then sent him on an extensive guided tour of various local enterprises. The tour convinced Li that the factories were worth saving. He immediately proposed an eight-item program that would at one and the same time reorganize the cotton mills and allow the No. 1 mill to continue its support of local educational and cultural institutions. Needless to say, Zhang Jian was pleased. Li's plans also satisfied the banks. On Zhang Jian's subsequent trip to Shanghai to meet with the bankers, they together decided that Li Shengbo would be both the general director of the bank consortium and the executive manager of the No. 1 mill, and that the other banks in the consortium would send their representatives to manage their respective debtor factories.[68]

As a new-style entrepreneur, Li Shengbo had the banks' trust. He was able to persuade them to grant him a 7,000,000-yuan loan at a reduced interest rate to turn the Dasheng factories around. Li's first step was to modernize the management methods at the No. 1 mill. He brought in a group of textile experts trained in the West and Japan and made them responsible for key operations in the factory. This system of accountability gradually ended the personnel system of thirty years that was based on personal connections with the Zhang brothers. Li also imposed fiscal discipline and took a number of measures to ensure cost effectiveness. In the meantime, he made some drastic changes in Dasheng's production, including importing new automatic textile machines from Japan and developing new products to increase Dasheng's competitiveness in the market. His reforms were by and large successful. Li was able to regain a degree of control over the No. 1 mill's production and marketing, and kept the plant in operation into the 1930s. He himself remained in Nantong until 1938, after the Japanese occupation.[69] The No. 2 mill, however, was forced to close down in 1934, unable to unburden itself of a huge debt.[70]

Thus, after 1925, the Dasheng System Enterprises began to dissolve, and the control of the mills was shifted from Zhang Jian to the Shanghai banks and their representatives, who were mostly young and foreign-educated. The fact that the banks refused to provide loans to Zhang Jian yet wholeheartedly supported Li's reforms was telling. It reflected the depth of Nantong's financial trouble and Zhang's deflated reputation. It meant a rejection by the Shanghai financial capitalists of the old-fashioned managerial style of China's earliest industrialists, which is to say, in the manner of a feudal lord running his domain.[71] The Shanghai banks now placed their trust and capital in the hands of a new generation of Chinese industrialists and entrepreneurs, men who had specialized training and technical expertise gained from Japan and the West. The changing of the guard at Dasheng exemplified a turning point in China's industrialization.[72]

The Political Demise of the Zhang Family

Unfortunately for Zhang Jian, just as financial difficulties were dashing his hopes for his Nantong model, Zhang Xiaoruo's campaign for speaker of the provincial assembly came along to weaken the Zhang family's political dominance. Scandals about Zhang Xiaoruo's attempt to buy votes provoked popular demonstrations and one protest suicide in Nanjing. Xiaoruo was hounded by newspapers for his alleged corruption, which damaged his political career beyond repair. Both he and his father were forced to defend their political motivations and moral principles. The entire episode devastated Zhang Jian as a father and as the creator of the Nantong model who had expected his son to carry his torch.

Little has been written on Zhang Xiaoruo's campaign or, for that matter, anything else about him, primarily because of his larger-than-

life father, his own undistinguished career, and perhaps equally important, his tragic death. After 1930, Zhang Xiaoruo spent most of his time
in his Shanghai home, working on a biography of his father and editing
his father's writings. In 1935, at the age of thirty-eight, he was shot to
death in bed by one of his father's bodyguards.[73] The murder was headline news throughout the Shanghai-Jiangsu region. The Nantong community was shocked by the loss of a favorite son.[74] In time, memory be-
got more sympathy for the Zhang family. Moreover, the fact that some
of Xiaoruo's children have become influential in local and national politics has rendered it difficult for Chinese authors to closely examine
Xiaoruo's life.

But it is eminently clear that Zhang Xiaoruo's rise and fall were intertwined with the rise and fall of the Nantong model. His 1921 campaign for speaker reflected some important regional and national
trends. It revealed geopolitical tensions in terms of the political challenge the Zhang family, a powerhouse in northern Jiangsu, was facing,
especially from elites in southern Jiangsu; it illustrated the penetration
of money into the political process and the public's objection to the
commercialization of politics; and it indicated a shift in the political and
cultural climate, a point when the public demonstrated a greater political consciousness than ever before and proved to be an active force in
pursuing democracy. Simply put, without an exploration of Xiaoruo's
career and especially his campaign, the erosion of Nantong's reputation
cannot be fully understood.

The Rise of Zhang Xiaoruo

Zhang Xiaoruo (1898–1935) was Zhang Jian's only surviving child,
borne by his fourth wife when Zhang Jian was forty-six years old.[75] The
Zhang family considered Xiaoruo an answer to its years of prayer to the
goddess Guanyin, a debt that, as we earlier saw, Zhang Jian later repaid
by renovating her temple. Despite all the wives and household servants
on hand, Zhang Jian paid meticulous personal attention to his precious
son's daily needs when he was a child. With an eye to Xiaoruo's future
responsibility, Zhang Jian tried to provide him with both a Chinese and
a foreign education, hiring private tutors from Japan and America.[76]
Wealthy, handsome, and well connected, Xiaoruo had the makings of a
future political heavyweight and was known as one of the "Four
Princes of the Republic" (*minguo si gongzi*).[77] But as a child brought up
in privilege without any pressing responsibilities of his own, Xiaoruo

lacked his father's substance and ability. He did not accomplish much in school either. In 1917, he was sent to the United States to attend college. His father expected him to stay for three years and learn something substantial; he returned in a year.[78]

Ready or not, Xiaoruo was the heir apparent of the Zhang family. As mentioned earlier, during Nantong's heyday and supported by his father and uncle, Xiaoruo was extending his reach in several directions— at local and provincial levels, in politics and in finance. In addition to controlling the county Local Self-government Association, he was the president of five institutions: the administrative board of Nantong Industrial Enterprises, the Nantong Colleges' Faculty Union, the Nantong District Educational Association, the Huai Hai Industrial Bank, and the Da Yu Land Reclamation Company. He was also on the executive committee of the chamber of commerce.[79] Some of those positions were once held by his father, and all of the institutions were created and controlled by either his father or his uncle.

Unlike his father, who had had to pioneer his way every step forward, Xiaoruo had an established base to build upon. In 1920, at the inaugural meeting of the Jiangsu Society, Xiaoruo was made a member of the standing committee. His election to that position at the young age of twenty-three was most telling—he was now among the highly respected Jiangsu politicians and elites. Chu Nanqiang, a former Nantong magistrate, and Sha Yuanbing, who passed the jinshi examination in the same year as Zhang Jian and was an eminent leader in Rugao county, were among those who failed to attain enough votes to be on the committee.[80] In addition, Xiaoruo was a member of the provincial assembly.

As the president of the Huai Hai Industrial Bank, Xiaoruo controlled significant financial resources. The bank was created in 1920 by Zhang Jian with a claimed capital of 1,000,000 yuan. The head office was in Nantong, and it had five branches in Shanghai, Zhengjiang, Yangzhou, and other parts of Jiangsu.[81] Its main mission was to help develop textile, reclamation, and other enterprises in the Jiangbei region. The bank purchased a multistoried building in Shanghai, where its opening ceremony attracted the rich and famous of the business world of Shanghai, and even guests from a number of foreign embassies.[82]

Though the bank depended heavily on Zhang Jian's reputation and enterprises, Xiaoruo as its president came to be perceived as a financial power in his own right. He began to use his various positions to make a splash in financial circles to further his political ambition. Aside from the Nantong stock exchange, in 1920 Xiaoruo, in his capacity as the head of the county Local Self-government Association, issued bonds of 20,000,000 yuan for the development of local factories, long-distance telephone companies, and highways. The bonds were handled by the Huai Hai Industrial Bank.[83] In the meantime, the bank printed several hundred thousand yuan of paper money bearing Xiaoruo's portrait on the face.[84]

The political and financial ground Xiaoruo gained in these years seemed to promise him a bright future. Though he still needed the elder Zhangs' support on virtually every front, he was anxious to emerge from their shadow and to become his own man. To that end, he gathered a group of young and energetic professionals, politicians, and returned students in the Jiangbei region to serve as his own power base. In 1921, when the third provincial assembly of Jiangsu was about to convene, Xiaoruo and his friends and colleagues, who were mostly members of the assembly and the Jiangsu Society, organized the Jinling Club in Nanjing for the purpose of electing Xiaoruo speaker, a position that would have given him virtual control of the assembly. However, these helpful activities came back to haunt Xiaoruo in the campaign, which proved to be the first and fatal setback in his young and promising life.

The Assembly and Speaker Campaigns

On October 1, 1921, when the Third Jiangsu Provincial Legislative Assembly convened in Nanjing, electing the speaker was the first order of business for the 120 assemblymen (in a total of 160) who had arrived to attend the session. There were two candidates, Zhang Xiaoruo and Zhang Yicheng. Zhang Yicheng (1867–1943), a contemporary and colleague of Zhang Jian's and a senior member of the assembly, was from Wu county in southern Jiangsu. A politician of national stature, he served Yuan Shikai in the late Qing and headed the Education Ministry of the Republican government in 1915. Because they bore the same surname, the two Zhang candidates were variously identified by their colleagues and the press as "Little Zhang" and "Old Zhang" or "Northern Zhang" and "Southern Zhang," a subtle indication that the contest between them was at once generational and geographical.[85]

Events leading up to the opening session assured that the election would be tense. As early as May, newspapers in Jiangsu and Shanghai had begun to level serious accusations against Zhang Xiaoruo. They alleged that during the elections for the general assembly, Xiaoruo had misappropriated 3,000,000 yuan from the Nantong stock exchange for his campaign, and that he and his followers had promised to pay likely winning candidates for their votes for Xiaoruo as speaker. The papers further charged that the office of speaker was only a springboard for Xiaoruo's ambitions, and that it was not just the provincial assembly but the governorship of Jiangsu that was at stake. Several papers revealed details of meetings of Xiaoruo and his trusted followers to select future cabinet members from the Jinling Club and claimed that Zhang Jian was at those meetings and thus part of the plot;[86] the whole Zhang family, it seemed, was poised to take over the Jiangsu provincial government.

The accusations linking Xiaoruo's financial speculation with political wrongdoing evoked not only jealousy among other assembly members, but also public outrage. The "Money Speaker" ("Jinqian Yizhang"), a label that the newspapers pinned on him in the spring, and that would dog him for the rest of his campaign, brought down many of those connected with him. With highly inflammatory accusations like these flying around, it is small wonder that the reputations of various close colleagues and assistants, including Chen Chen, the co-owner of *Tonghai xinbao*, and Xue Bingchu, the stage manager of the Gengsu Theater, were badly damaged.[87]

Against this background, the ordinarily simple procedure for electing a speaker became tension-charged. The assemblymen could not even agree on a date to hold the election. Xiaoruo's faction wanted a speedy resolution in hopes of a fait accompli, while Zhang Yicheng's group held out for a longer process so that Xiaoruo might be further investigated and exposed. As a result, members of the assembly engaged in heated debate and fistfights for days over the matter of a date.[88] Only five days into the session, *Shenbao* already depicted the election as a battle of "Money vs. Conscience," which quickly became a widely accepted characterization.[89] The next day, through *Shenbao*, Xiaoruo made the first of many public announcements withdrawing his candidacy,[90] but his exit proved to be as controversial as his entry. His opponents criticized his resignation letter as insincere, and his followers insisted it was forged; they could not let Xiaoruo retreat with their own interests so closely tied to his.[91] Xiaoruo renounced his candidacy time and again, often with contradictory messages about his true intentions, but he remained a central figure in the race for the remaining two months. On November 28, one day before the assembly was supposed to close, this toxic issue was finally resolved when Xu Guoren, who was close to the Jinling Club, emerged as a compromise.[92]

The high drama of this two months of political theater prevented the assembly from addressing some urgent tasks. The assembly convened at a time when Jiangsu had just suffered unprecedented flooding. It was supposed to deal with disaster relief, as well as the expected revenue shortage caused by the floods.[93] Instead, the members spent the entire two months accomplishing nothing. More than a dozen scheduled voting dates were aborted, and the assembly was forced to close down at one point because of the members' violence. Then came the dramatic ending. With only one day left in the session, the members still could not agree on the voting procedure. Hundreds of people, students among them, protested inside and outside the assembly, demanding a result. They claimed that if the assembly failed to produce a speaker by the end of the day, they would beat the members to death. A senior assemblyman, on his knees and in tears, begged his colleagues to cooperate. Some members started to cry with him, but others continued to attack their opponents and promote their own candidates. One assemblyman who voiced his support for Xiaoruo was immediately beaten and silenced by several of his colleagues. When the final votes were counted, only one was for Xiaoruo.[94]

This was not the outcome that Xiaoruo and his supporters had expected. At the opening of the assembly session, Xiaoruo was said to be ahead in the race. Despite negative publicity over the summer, in early October Xiaoruo reportedly commanded eighty votes against Zhang Yicheng's sixty. Xiaoruo's advantage was ascribed to his spending 2,000,000 yuan on bribery.[95] But Xiaoruo had the edge also because Zhang Yicheng, though a stout advocate of provincial self-government, was not a committed, active candidate. At the time, Zhang Yicheng was engaged, together with Li Yuanhong, Wang Jingwei, Zhang Jian, and other prominent politicians, in trying to mediate among the warlords and restore peace.[96] Zhang Yicheng's activities for both peace and self-government won him much publicity and admiration. Indeed, some thought that the office of speaker was unworthy of his talent and status,[97] but his prestige was precisely what the anti-Xiaoruo forces needed. Concerned with the prospect that Xiaoruo and his followers were going to take over the provincial government, those groups persuaded Zhang Yicheng to contest Xiaoruo's candidacy. Zhang Yicheng apparently agreed, but he did not arrive in Nanjing until one day before the assembly convened, and he left for Shanghai five days later without attending any of the meetings. He remained absent from Nanjing during the heat of the election and spoke publicly in Beijing and elsewhere of his lack of interest in the position. Perhaps he had better things to do than engaging in this distasteful election, or perhaps he was aware that his direct involvement would compromise his statesman-like image. His campaign was consequently run by others in his name, which made it difficult to find allies among the assemblymen.[98]

If Xiaoruo's rivals were not particularly strong, neither were his supporters, who consisted in the main of the few core followers in the Jinling Club, or the Nantong Clique, as it was sometimes known. Though some representatives from southern Jiangsu were also on Xiaoruo's side at one point or another, the majority of his supporters were from northern Jiangsu, a geographical dimension that was not lost on the media from the beginning of the election. Depending on such factors as the amount of bribes supposedly offered, the degree of public pressure against Xiaoruo, and the strategic weighing of their bargaining power, they switched their position frequently.

These factional changes not only added more confusion and drama to the process, but also denied Xiaoruo's campaign a stable, consistent majority. Tao Baojin, an assemblyman from Nanjing, was set on the vice-speaker position. Over the summer, Tao decided to form the Ning Society (Ningshe; Ning is an alternative name for Nanjing) to launch his own campaign and compete with Xiaoruo's Jiangsu Society–based operation. The Ning Society soon vanished without a trace, however, and Tao and twelve of his supporters joined the Jinling Club instead. Newspapers speculated that Tao had been bought by Xiaoruo with both money and promises to make him the vice-speaker.[99] With the increased exposure of Xiaoruo's purported corruption and protest from their home districts, eight of the twelve men in Tao's camp defected to the Southern Zhang faction. They allegedly told Tao that they would support him for vice-speaker as a fellow native of Nanjing, but they would have to cast their vote for speaker on the basis of their conscience. In the meantime, ten representatives from Zhengjiang in northern Jiangsu also abandoned Xiaoruo to support Zhang Yicheng. According to newspaper reports, the hidden cause for their defection was that the Jinling Club offered more money to some than to others, causing strife in a fragile alliance.[100] Though such reports further exposed both the extent and the limits of Xiaoruo's alleged bribery, they were also damaging to the assembly members who supported him. Thanks to their links with Xiaoruo, they were called "money assembly members" (*jinqian yiyuan*).[101]

Evidently, Xiaoruo's age was also an issue. Opponents questioned whether Xiaoruo met the age requirement for an assembly position: twenty-five. He was only twenty-four, but the controversy about the legal requirement somehow just gradually faded away. The age issue nevertheless lingered on. Xiaoruo was routinely portrayed as young, arrogant, and superficial, and easily manipulated by others, while Zhang Yicheng was frequently praised as a seasoned politician with a long record of public service and a national reputation. One reporter openly advised Xiaoruo to protect his "feathers" until they became full-fledged, implying that he was not mature enough to be pursuing such a responsibility. Newspaper articles pointed out that it would be a grave injustice if Xiaoruo became the speaker while many far more experienced and reputable candidates were waiting in line.[102] He was said to be frivolous and thus unreliable, as evidenced by his alleged close relationship with the actor Ouyang Yuqian.[103] This particular attack demonstrated both the social prejudice against the acting profession and the opponents' determination to bring Xiaoruo down. He was called Little Zhang not just to distinguish him from Zhang Yicheng, but also to emphasize that he was the son of an "elite giant" (*jushen*), who took advantage of his father's reputation for his own gain.[104]

Exactly how much Zhang Jian knew about his son's activities is unclear. From early October on, newspapers outside Nantong printed open letters and telegrams from "citizens of Jiangsu," as well as civic organizations, requesting Zhang Jian and Zhang Cha to take action to discipline Xiaoruo and his club members,[105] but whether Zhang Jian read them is a question. For one thing, Zhang Xiaoruo tried to control the flow of information. Obviously, anything he did not want his father to know would not be printed in his own newspaper. At the height of public outrage against Xiaoruo throughout Jiangsu and Shanghai, some people sent letters directly to Zhang Jian, but Xiaoruo and his associates reportedly tried to prevent them from reaching his father.[106] It was said that he even printed false news to deceive his father.[107]

Nevertheless, some of Zhang Jian's close friends and associates felt obligated to alert him to the controversy surrounding his son. Meng Sen, Zhang Jian's chosen author for the final version of the *Illustrated Gazetteer*, was one of them. Responding to Meng Sen's concern, Zhang Jian simply dismissed reports of his son's bribery. "I have a deep distaste for those who use money in assembly elections. Even if my son is not perfect, he can still tell right from wrong. Besides, how is it possible for my son to come up with 2,000,000 yuan [to buy votes]? We were 1,000,000 yuan in debt last year and need 3,000,000 yuan next year [for the convention]. My brother, my son, and I are worried day and night [about money]. How could we have the extra money [for bribery]?" He then said that he had advised his son to resign from his candidacy and to support Zhang Yicheng instead,[108] a piece of advice that his son was reported to have overtly accepted but covertly ignored. On October 8, the Zhang brothers sent a telegram to the assembly requesting that Xiaoruo's name be removed as a candidate. "He [Xiaoruo] has formally renounced his candidacy; why haven't you gentlemen heard about it [and so leave him alone]?" they asked with "indignation."[109] Because of his defense of his son, resentment toward Zhang Jian built up. He was depicted as an irresponsible father and a hypocritical politician who criticized lack of virtue in others yet tolerated his own son's corruption. Some newspapers, as noted, alleged that he was his son's co-conspirator. Even the Nantong model and his motive for creating the Jiangsu Society were questioned and at times attacked.[110] These articles reflected the anxiety over and objection to what was seen as the Zhangs' enduring ambition to take over the highest provincial government office, first through the Jiangsu Society and now through Xiaoruo.

Popular Protests

The severity of the damage Xiaoruo did to himself and his family was perhaps most evident in popular protests. The thousands of college and middle school students in Nanjing were among the first to react to news of Xiaoruo's alleged corruption. On October 6, when the members of the assembly were first scheduled to cast their vote for speaker, more than six hundred students, male and female, occupied the visitors' gallery in the assembly hall. They made it known that they would do everything in their power to block the influence of money and to defend the election as a democratic process.[111] Throughout the two months, students continued to take seats in the visitors' gallery whenever a vote was scheduled, carrying their books and homework with them. They cheered when anti-Xiaoruo speeches were made and booed when Xiaoruo's supporters rose to defend him. Some members of the assembly who tried to win the students' approval in their speeches were roundly criticized by others, dismayed by such circus-like, crowd-pleasing behavior.[112] Students also sought out individual members in Xiaoruo's camp to argue their case, causing several direct confrontations. Xiaoruo's supporters often required extra police protection. The area surrounding the assembly hall was under heavy armed police guard.[113]

Street protests began on the very first day of the session, October 6. Accompanied by their bands, students from various schools of Nanjing carried flags with slogans such as "Down with the Money Speaker!" and distributed leaflets along the way.[114] Disturbed by the protests, some of the Jinling Club members reportedly went to see the Jiangsu governor and handed him Xiaoruo's calling card, with a request that the governor ban students from auditing assembly meetings.[115] The Nanjing Student Union immediately took the case to the public by mounting a large street demonstration involving thousands of students from twenty-four schools. The union also sent a petition to the governor.[116] The debate over the right to be present at the assembly meetings led to a major confrontation, in which the students beat some assemblymen, whose hired bodyguards, said to be gangsters, retaliated. Policemen were involved in this fierce brawl. In the end, a dozen students and several assemblymen were injured, and the alleged gangsters were arrested. The assembly was forced to shut down as the students and assemblymen launched lawsuits against one another. Fear of the students kept those "dog-headed assemblymen" (*goutou yiyuan*), as their contemptuous opponents called them, at home or in hiding. When the assembly reconvened, fewer than half the members attended, which once again made a vote impossible.[117]

The student actions were supported by the people of Jiangsu, judging by the media reports. The news that the assemblymen fought among themselves for money and power while ignoring the people who were suffering from the floods was seen as disgraceful. During the two-month debate, newspapers received hundreds of letters and telegrams from various counties in Jiangsu protesting against the "money assembly speaker and members." They were signed by individuals and organizations such as county local self-government associations and educational bureaus. Some of the assemblymen received letters from their home districts condemning them as scum and demanding their recall. A few writers even threatened their representatives who supported Xiaoruo.[118]

The high point of popular indignation came when Ye Limin, a man from Huai'an of northern Jiangsu, committed suicide in protest of the alleged widespread political corruption. He was a former staff member of a government office and happened to be in Nanjing for other matters. Ye was intensely distressed by the news of Zhang Xiaoruo's conduct and the paralysis of the assembly. On November 21, he took his own life in his hotel room, leaving behind six letters variously addressed to the assembly, certain newspapers, and his family and friends. In each, he announced his intention to "use his corpse as remonstrance" (*shijian*), a traditional extreme means to express one's will. He hoped that this drastic action would wake up the assembly members and compel them to consult their consciences and reject the influence of money. Ye also requested that his corpse be placed near the assembly hall, where every member would have to pass it to enter the hall, a request that was honored. Ye's death further heightened emotions and fueled public outrage.[119]

The popular protest surrounding this election revealed, above all, that the people now identified themselves as citizens (*gongmin*) and considered this a new era. "This is a democratic era in which the rich and noble mean nothing unless they have the support of the people," one person wrote to *Shenbao* in condemning Xiaoruo.[120] Politics and government were no longer a matter purely for the officials, they held, now that they had power to influence the political process. The changing times provided even the most humble with many effective means to make their voices heard. They could involve themselves directly by coming to Nanjing to sit in the assembly's visitors' gallery, join street protests, distribute leaflets, or simply exchange information. They could also send telegrams and letters to their representatives or to newspapers from home. The election illustrated the rising citizen consciousness and the evolving participatory politics. Students came to the assembly hall to "keep watch on" (*jianshi*) the politicians. They were not, however, neutral or passive monitors; they were ready to take action and to change the course of the event. Ye Limin committed suicide because he believed that his death could make a difference, and it probably did, for the display of his corpse must have unsettled many assemblymen enough to press them into acting. The people did not seem to doubt that they could prevent Xiaoruo from being elected, and they persistently fought for their cause to the end. At the same time, they were deeply distrustful of not only the reportedly corrupt politicians or politicians in general, but also the political institution itself. They did not have faith in the assembly as a legislative body to resolve the election justly; instead, they were convinced that they had to be physically present to stop any illegal conduct.

What troubled the public most was the kind of political wheeling and dealing they did not expect to see in elections. The involvement of hard cash, in particular, caused the greatest apprehension, fear, and outrage. The "large sum of money" (*jukuan*) that was allegedly handed out by the son of one of China's leading industrialists was considered "capital." Xiaoruo had thus used "capital to suppress justice,"[121] for if he were indeed qualified, he would not have had to pay for any votes. To the public, that use of capital in the "sacred" election represented the invasion of the worst vice of the West, where money seemed to be omnipotent. The fact that Xiaoruo visited America only further fueled this assumption. He was criticized for imitating American political campaigns in which big money was essential for candidates to win. At a time when the Chinese had a difficult time resolving their ambivalence toward the West—admiration for its strength and distaste for its seeming moral decay—their fears about the penetration of money into politics were made real by the election. The defined danger was that politicians would lose integrity, and that people would no longer trust the political process. Painfully aware of how government offices and academic degrees had been routinely sold in imperial China to perpetuate the elites, the public now refused to accept the involvement of money in politics. Clearly, these Chinese were both idealistic and uncertain about the republican system and representative government. They saw the new system as a sharp break from the past, and money politics and democracy as incompatible. They also made a shift in their emotional commitment to the new system. But they were apprehensive about how democracy really worked. As a result, the public tried to uphold moral standards to defend the idealized version of the Republic, while the election system, like the imperial system in the past, continued to favor those with money and power.

The public condemned the corruption that had reduced politicians to merchandise, to the shame and misfortune of the entire people of Jiangsu.[122] Some became cynical. One man wrote that he understood what a disappointment it would be for Xiaoruo if he lost the election after spending 2,000,000 yuan, but, he reasoned, "you can just treat it as an unexpected business loss": politics was regarded as the same as business. Psychological pressure was also in play. The same person advised the assembly members who had reportedly taken Xiaoruo's money to anonymously donate it to flood relief for their own peace of mind.[123] The unequivocal message in all this was that big money and politics were a fatal mix.

Impact on the Zhangs

Entangled in the storm, Xiaoruo stayed put in Nantong, continuously sending out public statements to protect himself by announcing that he was relinquishing his candidacy. He was apparently torn between his political ambition and the harsh reality, and felt ambivalent about the prospect of being forced out of the race. In a confidential, emotional letter to Chen Chen in October 1921, at the height of the election, he complained that the public misunderstood his goodwill for Jiangsu and Nantong, expressed his concern for his father's position, and apologized to his associates for his possible retreat. But he was quick to add that such a retreat would only be a temporary sacrifice for a comeback in the future (Fig. 18).

All the while that Xiaoruo was publicly announcing his withdrawal, the Jinling Club was said to be working overtime on his behalf. The discrepancy between Xiaoruo's public posturing and the Jinling Club's underhanded maneuvers only provoked more suspicion and outrage. Even some people from Nantong began to criticize Xiaoruo, exposing him as an opium addict and calling him scum.[124] Xiaoruo categorically denied any involvement in bribery or any other wrongdoing. But his campaign had been doomed almost from the start, from the moment when the newspapers began to call him the "Money Speaker." The Chinese people were not ready to embrace a politician with a reputation that implied injustice, immorality, and the worst vice of Western politics. The tragedy was that neither Xiaoruo nor his associates had enough political wisdom to see that.

In the end, Xiaoruo was held responsible for the assembly's failure to accomplish anything for two months. Some considered him to have committed a crime against the people of Jiangsu for all the controversy he had caused and for the time wasted.[125] He was practically booted out of the assembly, and that setback was compounded by the collapse and subsequent legal troubles of his Nantong stock exchange and the downfall of the Huai Hai Industrial Bank in the same year.

Once Zhang Jian understood that the 1921 election had fatally wounded Xiaoruo's political career, he became an overprotective father, determined to save his son from further damage. In the following years, though Xiaoruo was offered several political positions, including being an adviser to the governor of Jiangsu and ambassador to Chile, Zhang Jian declined them all. Even after Zhang Jian's death, Xiaoruo's mother continued to restrict Xiaoruo's contact with his friends in poli-

南通俱樂部賓館
NANTUNG CLUB HOTEL
NANTUNGCHOW, CHINA

FIGURE 18. Letter from Zhang Xiaoruo to Chen Chen, October 1921. Xiaoruo, then in the midst of a scandal-ridden assembly campaign, tries to explain himself to one of his confidants. (Courtesy of Jiang Ping)

tics.[126] In 1923, Xiaoruo did make another splash when he was named by the Chinese government to lead an industrial delegation overseas. Zhang Jian was overjoyed to have an opportunity to reclaim Xiaoruo's name in this mostly honorary position.[127] Upon his return, Xiaoruo made a number of public speeches in Nantong and Shanghai.[128]

Zhang Jian was devastated by Xiaoruo's campaign. Though he openly acknowledged that he had severely disciplined his son and forbidden him from even mentioning the election ever again, he attributed most of the failure to Xiaoruo's associates and an unfriendly political and public climate.[129] He frequently expressed his bitter disappointment with politics.[130] Wounded by the accusation that the Jiangsu Society was a Zhang-controlled organization that supported Xiaoruo's campaign, Zhang Jian decided to resign from his position as its president and to decline all other "empty titles," which he indeed did.[131]

From 1921 on, exposés of the Zhangs' various financial and political misfortunes and questions about Zhang Jian's personal integrity continued to appear in the press. The main problem, of course, was the falloff of his enterprises, which fueled much speculation and doubt. With his financial power gone, Zhang Jian was regarded as a spent force and thus became vulnerable to unfriendly political forces and the watchful eye of the media.[132] He was often compelled to respond to rumors and defend himself and his son in public.[133] Consequently, his early positive view of the press changed dramatically; he now saw newspapers and magazines as irresponsibly "mixing black and white" and "siding with their copartners and attacking those who disagree."[134] Discouraged by all this, Zhang Jian expressed his desire to retreat to a quiet life in the countryside.[135] He did continue to build his villas in the Langshan area and to hold poetry and wine parties there, but the unsettling time and Zhang's own perseverance denied him the luxury of withdrawing. In addition to the pressing financial difficulties, new invasive political and ideological forces were posing unprecedented challenges to the image of Nantong that he so cherished.

Political and Social Instability

Throughout Zhang Jian's career, his authority in Nantong was challenged by other political forces within and without elite society. Those confrontations even led to bloodshed on more than one occasion.[136] But none of the previous challenges were as potent as the ones he faced in the 1920s. In the past, he had alienated social conservatives who opposed his reform programs. Now he encountered a new generation of opponents with a radical social, political, and ideological agenda. Furthermore, that new generation was produced, ironically, by the schools and factories he created. By 1920, Nantong had a formidable industrial workforce. Tangzha alone had more than ten thousand workers. The majority were from rural Nantong and the surrounding counties. In addition, there were thousands of current and past students who had been exposed to modern sciences, ideas, and culture; many still stayed in touch with the Nantong graduates who had spread all over China and overseas. Under the explosive circumstances of the 1920s, the presence of a disproportionately large number of workers and students and their networks made Nantong a fertile ground for social unrest.

Campus Unrest

Large-scale organized student political activities started in Nantong during the May Fourth movement. Influenced by student protest in China's urban centers, nationalist-minded local students quickly staged their own demonstrations. Cartoons and popular slogans such as "Return Our Qingdao!," "Down with Japan!," and "Boycott Japanese Goods!" were posted on the streets. The students searched stores and burned or hung up in public any Japanese merchandise they found. They also performed spoken dramas that mocked the failed diplomacy of the warlord government.[137] In the process, the Nantong Student Union was formed, with representatives from the normal, textile, agricultural, commercial, and medical schools, and the provincial Seventh Middle School.[138] The textile school and the middle school were the most involved. Both student bodies staged strikes on their campuses and clashed with the local police when they came in to maintain order. The principal of the Seventh Middle School, under student pressure, promised to raise the teachers' salaries and grant more freedom to the students.[139]

These developments connected Nantong students with the larger student community beyond their county, helping awaken them to nationally significant aspirations that were diametrically opposed to the message of local self-government that Zhang Jian had been preaching. The new cultural tide that started in major cities before the May Fourth incident finally began to reach the Nantong shore. Magazines such as *New Youth* became available in some of the school libraries and in local bookstores.[140] If Zhang Jian's reforms in the early twentieth century started the provincial town on the path of modernization, the May Fourth movement marked another turn that brought national politics into that locally oriented modernization process.

The May Thirtieth Incident of 1925, in which British police in Shanghai opened fire on Chinese protesters, provoked another high tide of nationalism on and beyond the various campuses. As soon as the news reached Nantong, the students at the ringleading textile and middle schools organized other campuses into a support society for the protesters in Shanghai, with six departments in charge of public speech, fund raising, communication, and other areas. The society sent telegrams to the Beijing government, Shanghai newspapers, and the Shanghai Student Union to express their opinions and support. The students also started a magazine pointedly titled *Blood Tide* (*Xuechao*), which quickly became widely read. They went on speaking tours to the city, towns, and the countryside, trying to involve every social group in the protest. In early June, they held a public meeting in Tangzha, to report to a crowd of more than a thousand people the details of the May Thirtieth Incident. A second meeting, which drew four times as many people, was held in the city, followed by a protest march. Leaflets with anti-imperialist slogans were handed out along the way. The support society raised more than 6,000 yuan for the families of the victims of the May Thirtieth demonstration, sent representatives to the conference of the National Student Union in Shanghai, and pressed the local chamber of commerce to boycott British and Japanese goods.[141]

Thanks to Zhang Jian's stringent control, the Nantong students met greater resistance than demonstrators in other Chinese cities. Zhang opposed any social unrest that would scare away potential investors and tarnish the image of a peaceful and prosperous model county. The divide between Zhang Jian and the students was also ideological. Zhang was hostile to radical Western political ideas, bourgeois freedom no less than Marxist communism;[142] both were gaining currency among the young generation. In the six years from 1919 to 1925, Zhang wrote more than a dozen essays that directly or indirectly addressed the issue of student agitation. They included open letters to local and national students, to the Beijing government, and to provincial and local educational administrators. He also made a number of public speeches on the topic. Those writings and speeches reflected not only Zhang's deep disappointment in both the government and the students but also his new ambivalence toward his own lifetime devotion to education and local affairs. Furthermore, they revealed a profound sense of defeat. Although he still tried to run Nantong the way he wanted, he felt increasingly hopeless about the future.

Zhang Jian believed that one purpose of education was to inculcate a morality of loyalty and obedience. He considered student protests a challenge to that purpose. During the May Fourth movement, in a letter to all students of China, Zhang stated, "The government is like the father or elder brother, and the students are like the son or younger brother. Even if the father makes a mistake, the son should help remedy the defect instead of hating his father." He went on to explain the background against which Japan proposed the Twenty-One Demands and the reason China lost Qingdao at the Paris conference. His point was that there were other contributing factors to those crises besides the government's failure, and that even when the government was chiefly at fault, the problem should be kept within the "family." Nevertheless, Zhang Jian himself did not truly believe that the government could be helped. One of the reasons he opposed the student activities was precisely his lack of faith in government politics. "I was once involved in political affairs," Zhang said in a speech to students, "and made a number of suggestions to the government, but none of them was accepted. Therefore I decided to engage in local projects." He further pointed out, "Whether the government is good depends on Heaven; whether diplomacy is sound depends on the government. If the government remains corrupt forever and diplomacy fails forever, can you hold a strike forever?"[143] Though this line of argument was meant to turn the students away from politics, it also mirrored Zhang Jian's despair about the government and his bitterness over his own shattered political ambitions.

Zhang tried to persuade students to remain in the classroom regardless of what was going on. He invoked patriotism to make his argument convincing. Since the competition in the world today was a "competition of knowledge," and students were "supposed to obtain knowledge in school," it followed that, "If you love your country, you should first love yourself. If you love yourself, you should then love to learn. If you love to learn, you must value your time. The only way to value your time is to study at school. To waste your time in demonstrations is no different from committing suicide." This logic was consistent with Zhang's view that the student activists were troublemakers. He was puzzled by the students' failure to see his point. As he complained, "I, my brother, and my associates have spent millions of yuan to train you with useful knowledge for the country. My patriotism is no less than yours; but you have no understanding of it!" But Zhang Jian defined his patriotism by localism and personal loyalty to him. He insisted that since all the schools in Nantong were created by him without government support, the students in Nantong should stay out of national issues. This version of local progress without national politics was not only unappealing to the students, but also unrealistic under the new circumstances of the 1920s.[144]

The gap between the competing patriotic claims—the students' and Zhang Jian's—was of course more than rhetoric. At issue was not only Zhang's feeling of personal betrayal by the local students, but also his deep concern—the core of his patriotism—over the impact of student activism on the social and economic order in China and in Nantong in particular. His instincts as an entrepreneur told him that protecting business interests demanded a stable social environment. He believed that the strikes by workers and merchants during the May Fourth movement had caused tremendous financial losses throughout China, and "yet all you got in return was the resignation of Cao [Rulin], Zhang [Zongxiang], and Lu [Zongyu]. How sad!"[145] To many at the time, the forced resignation of those officials responsible for China's diplomatic failure was symbolically significant—it demonstrated the power of a united people and the force of nationalism—but to Zhang, it was not worth the economic price.

Representing the established order, Zhang Jian had an inherent distrust of any revolution and attributed all the current social chaos to the May Fourth movement. He was convinced that the students were being used by people with ulterior motives, namely, the radical intellectuals who were experimenting with their ideas. As a result, his positions on many issues were the opposite of those of nationalistic demonstrators. During the May Fourth movement, Zhang Jian defended the government and even the Twenty-One Demands, and criticized the students for being too ambitious in demanding the abolition of the foreign imperialists' unequal treaties. During the May Thirtieth Incident, he went so far as to say that both sides, the foreigners and the Chinese, should bear responsibility, and that he did not feel compelled to defend the Chinese involved. Mindful of the Boxer Rebellion and its impact, Zhang was especially concerned about how foreign countries would react to student protestors.[146]

Zhang Jian was least of all willing to accept the demonstrations in Nantong. After all, local student protests were a direct challenge to his authority. After treating Nantong as a personal domain for two decades, Zhang was shocked that outside influence was able to penetrate the local campuses and bring about changes beyond his recognition. Indeed, one of the things that most disturbed him was that the local schools, a centerpiece of the model, had now become a source of trouble. He considered this a weakness in the local self-government idea. Zhang labored hard to dissuade the students, even threatening them with legal punishment for their actions. "Destroying a shop for no reason is a criminal offense. It will involve the police, and you could be sued. Rejecting foreign products is against international law and can cause diplomatic confrontations. Nantong is not [a suitable place] for such incidents." For Zhang Jian, Nantong was special because of its localism; and being local in Nantong meant being under his control.[147]

Zhang Jian thus took an ever-harder line against the student activists in Nantong. In 1919, to prevent other schools from joining the strikes at the textile and Seventh Middle schools, Zhang Jian immediately closed down the textile school, expelled the students, censured the principal, and put the school under martial law. The Seventh Middle School was administered by the provincial educational bureau, and so was not under Zhang's direct control, but that did not stop him from exerting pressure. He sent letters and telegrams to provincial officials, demanding that the students be immediately expelled, and the principal fired. Zhang accused the principal of several serious wrongdoings, including "shamelessly compromising his dignity" in allowing more freedom to the students and granting higher salaries to the faculty. Fearing further student agitation in such a tense time, the provincial officials had doubts about the wisdom of firing the principal and put off doing anything about the matter. Zhang had no tolerance for such indecision and even threatened them with legal and political repercussions for their delayed response. When the provincial government finally decided to take action, Zhang Jian argued that "Strict-ism" with the students was a key qualification for selecting the next principal. In the aftermath of the May Thirtieth Incident, this Strict-ism was reinforced at all Zhang Jian–funded schools through longer class hours, more homework assignments, and new rules to prevent networking and organized political activities on campus. None of this was open for discussion or negotiation. "If anyone disagrees with these policies, be it students or teachers, please go elsewhere," Zhang said.[148]

In reality, though, Nantong had become a more open and complex community with the influx of new people, ideas, and social trends. Though Zhang Jian was quite aware that relatively developed and complex societies were prone to social disorder,[149] he still considered any undesirable incidents to be a challenge to his personal authority and reacted accordingly. In Nantong, the campus was one of the most sensitive indicators of social change. It was inevitable that the spread of the ideas of freedom and individualism, compounded by youthful energy and sexual tensions, would come to shake the foundation of one-man rule.

And incidents of social unrest were clearly on the rise. Some of them were apolitical but equally chaotic. In 1920, a group of male students on bicycle broke into the East Park, a playground for women and children where men were banned. Ignoring the objections of park staff, the students used the exercise facilities there and tore up the posted rules. The park administrators immediately sent a warning to local schools. A month later, the primary school attached to the women's normal school had a campus gathering for its students and teachers. More than one hundred male students from various campuses forced their way into the primary school, harassing the girls and their teachers. Zhang Jian was deeply disturbed to see the school rules he had helped to institute breaking down under his very eyes. "Each school has rules. If students leave the campus, they should get a permit; if they travel, they will be assigned a leader; if they visit a place, they should obtain a pass. [With such rules in place,] how could such an incident ever take place?" He ordered the school officials to record the names of all the miscreants and to expel the worst offenders.[150]

In 1925, rumors about two sexual scandals involving Nantong students spread as far away as Nanjing. One involved several male students from the commercial school, who were alleged to have gang-raped a student of the women's normal school at a hotel. The other involved a sexual encounter between two students, also in a hotel. Zhang Jian considered the rumors a plot to destroy Nantong's reputation and was incensed. At age seventy-two, he worked like a detective in investigating every detail of the stories. After checking records at the schools, the hotels, and the police department, Zhang wrote an extensive report to dispel the rumors.[151] That such incidents took place in 1920 and 1925 was not coincidental. Nationally, the overall social atmosphere encouraged disorder; locally, Zhang Jian's authority was in decline. Indeed, in 1925, in the midst of the rape scandal, an anonymous letter was sent to the women's normal school that criticized Nantong schools for training slaves instead of independent individuals. "The youth are innocent; the responsibility is on the false leaders who

are ignorant of education," the writer asserted.[152] Zhang Jian was almost certainly one of the targets of this criticism.

Struggling unsuccessfully to maintain local order, Zhang Jian critically reflected upon his own journey and his early convictions about
education, reaching some unexpected conclusions. "I am heartbroken
to see my twenty-odd-year effort in local self-government go in the opposite direction of my intentions," he stated. Consequently, his views
on education took a sharp turn. To Zhang Jian, the civil examination
system now looked better than the new school system because it was
stricter and compelled students to learn. Zhang Jian, who initially invested in schools because of his hope for the young generation, now
considered the students not just disappointing but positively harmful
to China. Furthermore, recalling his former belief that education could
save China, Zhang Jian bitterly sighed in 1925, "How could I ever imagine that education might also destroy the country?" Though these
thoughts are untypically extreme, recorded, we may guess, in moments
when he was at his lowest, they do reflect Zhang Jian's profound pes-
simism at a time of great uncertainty.[153]

Political Parties

The beginning of political parties in Nantong paralleled the student
movements. The activities started at the normal school, which, more
than anything else, illustrated the diminution of Zhang Jian's influence.
Zhang Jian considered the normal school his precious asset, and his authority at the school had been undisputed, especially because it was
managed by people he appointed. Because of extreme pressure from
Zhang, the normal school acted with restraint during the May Fourth
movement and was the first to resume classes.[154] The May Fourth era,
however, could hardly leave a place like the normal school untouched.
The school's reputation in the region and the extensive networks built
by its graduates and faculty over the years made it a focus of attention.
Different political forces tried to penetrate this local ivory tower.

Communist Party agitators became active in the school in 1924. In
1925, a student named Wang wrote to Yun Daiying, the head of the
Communist Youth League and a teacher at the Shanghai University,
asking to join the youth league. In 1926, the youth league was formally
established at the normal school.[155] If Nantong was the hub of early
CCP activity in northern Jiangsu,[156] the normal school was the hub
within that hub. It produced many CCP activists and some well-known

party leaders who were instrumental in the establishment of the Four-teenth Red Army in the Nantong region in 1930.[157]

In 1926, several of the activists of the May Thirtieth movement es-tablished a CCP branch at the normal school. As elsewhere in China, the normal school students formed various societies, such as Chen-guangshe (Dawn Society), which generally issued their own maga-zines. The students also went to rural areas to mobilize peasants and help organize peasant societies.[158] As a result of all these activities, the school came to be known as Hongse tongshi (Red Nantong Normal),[159] a name that quickly attracted the GMD's attention. In 1927, several members of the GMD's Nantong branch entered the school to keep an eye on the students and also to offer courses on GMD doctrines. Once, when a package was sent to a student from Mt. Jinggang, a Red Army base in Jiangxi province, three hundred GMD soldiers surrounded the school and searched the dormitory and classrooms. In the end, they ar-rested a student who happened to have a book with the letters "C.P." on the cover. The irate teachers and students fought for six months to obtain the student's release and finally forced the GMD to give in. In re-venge, the GMD Educational Association created difficulties for gradu-ates of the normal school to find jobs, turning more students into CCP sympathizers.[160]

The normal school was of course not a red island. The textile and Seventh Middle schools, the leaders of the May Fourth and May Thirti-eth protests, also had direct contacts with the CCP. In 1924, two gradu-ates of the middle school went on to attend Shanghai University, where they were influenced by the Communist Youth League's Yun Daiying. Yun instructed them to return to Nantong to start organizational and propaganda activities among the students. Upon their return, the two students, together with a CCP member at the textile school, met with student activists at the normal school to plan a grass-roots movement to popularize CCP ideas.[161]

The CCP also penetrated the factories and rural Nantong. Qiu Huipei, a Jiangxi native and graduate of the textile school, was a staff member at the No. 1 mill when he joined the CCP. In 1926, he rounded up five others to form the first independent CCP branch in Tangzha. In the spring of 1927, peasant associations (*nongmin xiehui*) and similar or-ganizations promoted by the CCP appeared in many rural districts. They successfully led some rent-resistance movements against land-lords. Later, in the fall, the CCP established a county committee in Nan-tong (and also in Rugao and Haimen counties), which engineered worker strikes and peasant riots. Far less successful was the Fourteenth Red Army, created in 1930, which after a few skirmishes in the Nantong region was defeated by GMD troops in October of the same year and subsequently left the area. The power of the CCP declined in Nantong until 1937, when the war with Japan broke out.[162]

During the 1920s, despite the CCP's vigorous attempts to mobilize students, workers, and peasants, it was the GMD that emerged as the central player in the political life of Nantong. In 1927, after the Northern Expedition Army (Beifajun) swept away the army of the warlord Sun Chuanfang, the party took over Nantong and reorganized the county administration. New offices were created, and some office names were changed. In 1928, all existing city, town, and rural administrative units were replaced by administration bureaus (*xing-zhengju*). The following year, a ward system was established in Jiangsu province. Nantong's twenty-one districts were thereupon consolidated into eighteen wards, each managed by a newly trained ward head (*quzhang*).[163]

Before the arrival of the GMD, the local elites had had a relatively smooth relationship with the warlord Sun Chuanfang. That continued to be the case even after Zhang Jian's death in 1926. Zhang Cha continued to provide supplies for Sun's army in exchange for peace in the region. Though Zhang Cha no longer directly controlled the Dasheng factories, the chamber of commerce and other local institutions remained in his hands, and he still had great influence. May 1927 brought a quick and dramatic change: Sun's army fled and the Northern Expedition Army marched in. Zhang Cha, scared by the Northern Expedition slogan "Down with Local Bullies and Evil Gentry" ("Dadao tuhao lie-shen"), resigned from his post in the chamber of commerce and fled to Shanghai. Other prominent local merchants and elites either stayed put or went to Shanghai, awaiting developments.[164]

The GMD encountered great difficulty in controlling the county, as the rapid succession of magistrates—a total of eight from 1927 to 1930—attests.[165] The first county magistrate appointed by the GMD army was a young man named Zhong, who had no experience, no financial backing, and no local knowledge. He got some help from Zhang Xiaoruo, who had stayed in Nantong, where he played the role of the leading elite, but only briefly. Not seeing any immediate danger, Zhang Cha returned to Nantong in July. (His properties in Haimen had been seized by the GMD county magistrate, but that apparently did not trouble him.)[166] In mid-August, local elites were excited by rumors of

Sun Chuanfang's return.[167] Nantong newspapers ran daily reports tracking Sun's advance, stirring the elites' hope of reestablishing their power. Even the GMD county magistrate who had succeeded Zhong, a political opportunist by the name of Zhuang, changed his tone and prepared to welcome Sun's arrival. Zhuang held a meeting with local elites, where they decided to borrow money from public funds as "gifts" to welcome Sun.[168]

Looking forward to restoring his authority, Zhang Cha regained control of the chamber of commerce and tried to operate as before. But Sun did not come, and Zhang Cha's hopes were shattered. The performance of Magistrate Zhuang during this period, especially his handling of public funds, caused much anger among the Nantong people, who lodged complaints against him. Zhuang was arrested by the GMD provincial government for collaborating with the warlords and embezzling public funds. Zhang Cha quickly fled again and later died in Shanghai.[169] Zhang Xiaoruo continued to hold leadership positions at the local educational and cultural institutions established by Zhang Jian, but only in name and only briefly. He soon moved to Shanghai, where he occupied himself writing a biography of his father and editing his father's works until his death in 1935.

The beginning of the Nanjing decade in 1927 spelled the end of Nantong the model. In 1929, the GMD municipal government issued a city planning document that referred to Nantong as a model in the past tense. It also held that the Zhang brothers' enterprises were doomed to fail because they were promoted by only "one or two private persons," a situation that the new city administrators vowed to correct.[170] Three years after Zhang Jian's death, his lifetime achievement had already become a thing of the distant, problematic past.

Although it is convenient to regard a failure as doomed, the question remains: why did the Nantong model fail? Or, could the model have survived throughout the 1920s and beyond? An educated answer will have to be negative.

On the surface, the Nantong model bore distinct similarities to the kind of planned social order that James Scott has described. According to Scott, such an order is characterized by four elements that, if combined, inevitably lead to disasters: an administrative ordering of nature and society, a high-modernist ideology blindly believing in the rational design of society, an authoritarian state, and a civil society incapable of resisting state power. What is lacking in this kind of social order, Scott maintains, is the practical knowledge, informal processes, and improvisation that are crucial for any successful social transformation.[171]

The Nantong model was clearly socially engineered. Although it was not imposed by the state, the elite *was* the state for all practical purposes. In Nantong, elite authoritarian rule was evident; so was the lack of democracy and dissenting voices, at least before 1919. The similarities between the Nantong model and the designed society Scott describes, however, end here. The major difference is that the Nantong model was based on local resources and practical knowledge. One can even argue that the elite depended too much on informal processes and improvisation, and not enough on institutional mechanisms and discipline, as in the case of the handling of Dasheng's finances.

At the time, the design of a model community under elite leadership—a self-sufficient economic structure accompanied by progressive social, educational, and cultural programs—was doable. In fact, Zhang Jian carried out much of it. Nantong's decline resulted from a number of intertwined factors, not all because of flaws in the design. In essence, the model depended on Zhang Jian's ability to control the community and on the financial well-being of the Dasheng System Enterprises. In the early 1920s, both were eroded by internal and external forces.

Zhang Jian certainly bore partial responsibility for the financial difficulties of those enterprises. However, his plans were utopian only in that he underestimated the time and resources to realize them. The eagerness to be modern and to exhibit the modern also in turn hurt Nantong's economy. Zhang Jian wanted to include all the possible modern institutions and inventions in Nantong. But some of them, such as the museum, the acting school, and the film company, pulled capital and energy away from more practical and reasonable investment. In this and other cases, most notably in the management of the No. 1 mill, the inevitable lack of experience was also an important factor. Under other circumstances, Zhang Jian might have been able to learn from his failures and improve his skills, but he was not given the chance. Wartime overgrowth was part of the problem but hardly unique to Nantong.

The financial crisis undermined the prestige of the Zhang family, a fact that only became clear to Zhang Jian and his brother in Xiaoruo's tumultuous campaign. Understandably, Xiaoruo's ambition caused resentment, but Zhang Jian was also attacked. It is possible that in Zhang Jian's long political career he had made a good number of enemies who were ready to take advantage of an opportunity to discredit him, or that some men were simply jealous of him. But those possibilities notwithstanding, it is clear that the erosion of Dasheng's financial strength weakened the foundation of Zhang Jian's power. Xiaoruo's campaign further damaged the Zhangs politically and morally.

In simple fact, most of the political developments of the time, even the campaign to a considerable extent, were out of Zhang Jian's control. The rise of a new generation with radical ideologies, the emergence of political parties, and the tendency toward national reunification, all belonged to a larger trend with which Zhang could not compete. Yet he refused to understand it, stubbornly and hopelessly trying to convince the students that his formula of local progress without national politics was the best solution for the country. Consequently, he became increasingly irrelevant in the political swirl of events. Despite his deep aversion to subjecting himself to circumstances, he could not escape from them. Indeed, changed circumstances are a key to understanding the downfall of the Nantong model. We must distinguish between what is successful and what is lasting—the Nantong model was successful in its own time, but it did not last. In fact, models are a reflection of a particular, and therefore temporary, circumstance; they are not meant to last.

CHAPTER 6

The Model as Past

Memories of the past . . . return not as unreflected traditional-ism, but as conscious and calculated ways of controlling the modern.

Børge Bakken, *The Exemplary Society*

HOW HAVE HISTORY and memories treated the Nantong model and Zhang Jian? Remembering that past is in itself not difficult. Zhang him-self had a special interest in preservation—the parks and his villas were monuments, the *Gazetteer* and other publications historical records, and the museum and library "memory-institutions."[1] Nantong's past, as well as Zhang Jian's legacy, inheres in the physical structure of the city and in written texts, which we may call silent memory.[2]

To activate this memory—to articulate, communicate, study, and give meaning to the past in some tangible fashion—requires certain conditions. The war years of the 1930s and 1940s permitted little atten-tion to the past as people struggled for survival. With the restoration of peace in 1949, Zhang Jian was gradually brought back into contempo-rary debate, a process that was dictated by the ever-changing political atmosphere. It started in the tension-filled late 1950s, went through the Cultural Revolution (1966–76), and continued on in the post-Mao era. During those forty-odd years, the debate took sharp turns that were as dramatic as Zhang Jian's own changing fortunes in life. It helped make and break careers and at times even endangered lives, and it also di-vided the Nantong community and generated tensions. The right to re-member is not automatic; it has to be fought for and earned.

The new wave of modernization in the post-Mao era made the Nan-tong experience of the early twentieth century highly relevant, and Zhang Jian once again a fashionable figure. Renewed interest in Zhang was expressed in conferences, publications, monuments, and other commemorative events. In this way, the past became a vital part of modern-day Nantong. Yet the present also invades the past; for that reason, memory is selective and demands invention as well as suppression. Though Chinese writers tended to emphasize the aspect of modernity of the Nantong model because of its contemporary relevance, Village-ism, the other facet of the model, was largely buried because promoting local autonomy was politically incorrect. This tailored memory made the closing decades of the twentieth century look much like the early years when Nantong was distinguished because of Zhang Jian. It also reintroduced the past as a compass to provide direction, order, and thus control for the current modernization, a process that was bound to generate dramatic social change and was thus potentially turbulent.[3]

The Right to Remember

The human activity of remembrance requires not only distance in time, but also resources such as spare time, money, and energy. In that sense, to be able to express and experience the past is a luxury. The decade immediately after Zhang Jian's death, when the GMD was trying to consolidate its rule, was not an ideal time to remember him. And the wars that followed—first the anti-Japanese war (1937–45) and then the civil war (1945–49)—made it virtually impossible to indulge in memory. The wars destroyed many of the accomplishments of the earlier decades. For instance, Nantong University, created in 1928 by incorporating the existing local colleges, was forced to take refuge in Shanghai and elsewhere. When it finally returned to Nantong, it returned to a campus with broken windows, empty classrooms, and little teaching equipment.[4] The Nantong Normal School underwent a similar experience.[5] The No. 1 mill also suffered much damage at the hands of the Japanese. During the final days of the civil war, when the GMD began to ship some of the No. 1 mill's equipment to Taiwan with a view to moving the entire factory there, six thousand Dasheng workers, organized by the CCP, went on strike and occupied the premises to prevent the equipment from being removed.[6] But this show of loyalty to the mill arose in the workers' support of the CCP and their desire to protect their own jobs, not from lingering feelings for Zhang Jian. All the same, the wartime suffering did add to the general population's appreciation, in retrospect, of the Zhangs' accomplishments and nostalgia for a better time. The popular consensus in Nantong was that what Zhang Jian did was good for the community and he thus deserved respect. Zhang continued to be viewed favorably there in the post-1949 era.

The CCP benefited from Zhang Jian's legacy in a number of ways. During the "socialist reform" of the 1950s that eventually brought the nationalization of private industry,[7] the Dasheng factories were taken over by the state. Zhang Jingli, son of Zhang Cha, who had been the director of the No. 1 mill during the war, continued to hold that position until the mid-1960s, when all "capitalist" directors and managers were swept away. Zhang Jian was also a useful connection for the CCP's united front policy. Many of his former colleagues and students—either men of property or experts in various fields who now fell into the category of "democratic personages" (*minzhu renshi*)—were eagerly courted by the CCP in the early 1950s, when the party was struggling to gain political legitimacy and economic control. Zhang Jingli himself was a longtime member of the Chinese People's Political Consultative Conference (PPCC) and was more than once invited to have dinner with Mao Zedong and Premier Zhou Enlai.[8] He was later made the assistant director of the Department of the Textile Industry of Jiangsu province. At the local level, the CCP accorded proper respect to Zhang Jian's legacy and his descendants. In the early 1950s, the city government helped restore some of Zhang's projects, including the museum, that were ruined during the war. Zhang's tomb in the southern outskirts of the city, which Zhang himself started constructing in 1923 and where his son was also buried, was listed by the Jiangsu provincial government as a historic site and cultural relic for preservation. Mr. Se's Tomb (Segong mu; Se was Zhang Jian's alternative name), as the area was called, included the Zhang Jian Memorial Hall that Zhang's descendants had built in 1956.[9] One of Zhang Jian's granddaughters, Zhang Rouwu, was a long-time member of both the municipal and the provincial PPCC,[10] a mostly powerless but prestigious position.

But the fact is, in the immediate postwar years, when both the state and the community faced numerous urgent tasks, Zhang Jian and his legacy were not a major concern. Little new work was done on the mainland to supplement the biography Zhang Xiaoruo had published in the early 1930s and the compilations of his writings that appeared before 1949,[11] nor had any special institutions been established to honor him. Without conscious effort to remember and celebrate him, Zhang was no longer the dominant figure he once was. Yet the memory of Zhang Jian was ever-present. The many edifices he left behind were inescapable reminders of his life and his time, and were only waiting to be rediscovered and reinterpreted.

In the highly politicized society of the People's Republic, what brought Zhang Jian's memory back to life was politics. Concerns about Zhang were first raised during the 1957 anti-rightist campaign.[12] Under the influence of Mao Zedong's leftist ideology, Zhang, a capitalist of "old" China, was naturally regarded as in the wrong camp. The Zhang family had tried its best to be cooperative with the CCP. For instance, in the early 1950s, as a way to dissociate themselves from the past, the family gave several of its properties to the city and donated some precious artifacts, including Zhang Jian's collection of 180 artworks, to the museum.[13] All this, however, did not help to dispel the CCP's distrust. On the other hand, the target was not exactly Zhang Jian himself; rather, it was the high esteem that he still enjoyed in the community, which in some cases amounted to worship. Such views were deemed politically undesirable by the CCP in a period when it was attempting to establish itself as an absolute authority commanding the undivided loyalty of the people. To contain Zhang's influence, in 1958 the party decided to rename his tomb Southern Suburb Park (Nanjiao gongyuan). Before the name change took effect, Hu Yaobang, a high-ranking official from Beijing who became the general secretary of the CCP central committee in the early 1980s, paid a visit to Zhang's tomb on a trip to Nantong. Hearing about the decision, Hu pondered the matter and then allegedly said, "Even the First Emperor's tomb is preserved." But Hu's subtle rejection of the change did not prevent the renaming.[14]

In 1959, at the height of the "rightist tendency" (*youqing*) purportedly represented by Peng Dehuai, a member of the central committee and an accomplished general,[15] the Nantong community's pro–Zhang Jian attitude, the "lingering ghost" (*yinhun busan*) of Zhang Jian, was imputed to this rightist tendency.[16] The same year, the central government's Industrial and Commercial Bureau (Gongshang ju), headed by Xu Dixin, a noted economist, initiated a project to study how socialist reform could be implemented in capitalist-controlled industrial and commercial sectors. The bureau instructed the Nantong city government to prepare documents on the Dasheng System Enterprises. The result was a work called "A History of the Dasheng Capital Group" ("Dasheng ziben jituanshi"), the first attempt after 1949 to study the Nantong experience. One chapter was to be devoted to introducing Zhang Jian, a difficult and delicate task for the person who drew the assignment: in piecing together the history of the Dasheng system, it would be impossible not to make Zhang Jian a central figure, but to emphasize Zhang's role was to risk being criticized as a rightist. Understandably, the chapter was left blank in the early drafts.[17]

Fortunately, in Nantong the anti-rightist movement, superficial at best, evaporated before causing much damage. By 1960, the central committee had begun to correct the leftist bias, and the overall political situation was loosening up. As it happened, this change in the political climate roughly coincided with the fiftieth anniversary of the 1911 Revolution. In October 1961, Chinese scholars held a conference to commemorate the anniversary in Wuhan, where it started. The conference raised several issues, including how to evaluate historical figures such as Zhang Jian. Later that year, two Shanghai-based scholars published articles about Zhang. Both authors tried to sort out where Zhang stood politically in standard Leninist-Maoist terms, such as "bureaucratic capitalist class" (*guanliao zichan jieji*), "national bourgeoisie" (*minzu zichan jieji*), and "imperialist" (*diguo zhuyi fenzi*). Though the two disagreed on whether Zhang belonged to the national bourgeoisie, which the CCP preferred, or to the bureaucratic bourgeoisie, which the CCP rejected, both writers concluded that he was a reactionary because he represented the upper layer of the capitalist and landlord classes, and that he had colluded with Western imperialists.[18]

That view of Zhang, clearly reflecting the influence of the anti-rightist movement, was perceived in Nantong as a gross injustice, and counterarguments soon appeared. In a 1962 article, members of the Jiangsu Institute of Philosophy and Social Sciences argued that, even though Zhang had never been a revolutionary, his contributions to industry, education, and local affairs were important, and that any evaluation of Zhang should take his whole career into consideration. At the same time, scholars began to take a close look at Zhang's industrial activities. At the Nanjing Historical Society's annual conference, members discussed these and other issues related to Zhang Jian with invited scholars from Beijing and elsewhere. All this marked the beginning of a series of studies on Zhang that engaged scholars from all over China, and that began to focus on Zhang's overall career.[19]

The timing seemed perfect. In January 1962, the CCP central committee held a meeting in Beijing with seven thousand cadres to redirect the party toward economic recovery after the grave failure of the Great Leap Forward.[20] This reorientation was accompanied by a certain degree of political freedom, which encouraged scholars to take more balanced approaches to their subjects. The fact that sensitive issues such as

Zhang Jian's class identity could be freely debated as academic questions was inspiring to some organizations and people in Nantong. The Nantong CCP municipal committee, especially its propaganda department, the museum and the library, the Dasheng factories, and local scholars and historians all closely followed the development of outside scholars' interest in Zhang Jian. Mu Xuan, who was at the time in charge of editing material on the CCP's history in Nantong, was instructed to write a detailed report on that trend. His report was circulated among the city leaders,[21] who decided to study Zhang Jian in historical terms, above and apart from the political issue. Realizing the importance of mastering historical source materials and the unique advantage Nantong had in this regard, Cao Congpo, head of the propaganda department, set his staff to work collecting and publishing material about Zhang and his times. Reflecting the increasing interest in Zhang Jian, editors and historians from various places came to Nantong to search for publishable material and to investigate Nantong's past.[22]

The result was stunning. In the short span of ten months, Jiangsu People's Publishing House printed Zhang Jian's diary; Cao Congpo published an article, "The Tragedy of Zhang Jian," in a scholarly journal; and the "History of the Dasheng Capital Group" went through a second draft when the prestigious China Bookstore expressed an interest in publishing it. Zou Qiang, former mayor of Nantong and onetime CCP representative at the No. 1 mill, took charge of the writing project. The missing introductory chapter on Zhang Jian was now completed by Zou Qiang himself; it was an extensive piece based on substantial research, as we will discuss later. Much more took place during this same period. Guan Jingcheng, a learned local historian and teacher, produced some well-documented studies on Zhang. The Nantong Archives managed to collect the vast and invaluable documents about Dasheng enterprises that had been scattered in various factories and in the Shanghai office. The Nantong Library organized and transcribed Zhang's unpublished letters, telegrams, and other writings. The Committee on Cultural and Historical Material of the Municipal PPCC published a special issue on Zhang, which was based on materials its members had contributed. Cao Congpo initiated a lecture series on Zhang at the library, where Guan Jingcheng and others reported their research results. And professional historians in Jiangsu and elsewhere were contemplating long-term, major research projects on Zhang.[23]

This "short spring of academic study," as some people in Nantong called it,[24] ended in October 1962, when the political winds shifted following Mao Zedong's warning "Never Forget Class Struggle" at a central committee meeting. More political campaigns ensued, culminating in the chaos of the Cultural Revolution, which did not end until 1976.[25] Zhang Jian studies were immediately affected by this turn of events. In 1963, the CCP Jiangsu Provincial Committee criticized the publication of Zhang Jian's diary. The new head of the propaganda department in Nantong questioned why material about a capitalist was kept in the local archives. The publication of "A History of the Dasheng Capital Group" was put off indefinitely. During the Cultural Revolution, Cao Congpo, Zou Qiang, Mu Xuan, and Guan Jingcheng, and indeed anyone else who had actively pursued Zhang Jian studies, were attacked by local radicals and Red Guards. Cao was criticized as representing Nantong's "Three-Family Village."[26] One of his alleged crimes, as pointed out in the first big-character poster targeting him, was that he helped reverse the judgment (*fan'an*) on Zhang Jian; Cao suffered for ten years. Guan Jingcheng, refusing to take the abuse, committed suicide, together with his wife.[27]

The Red Guards destroyed the tombs of both Zhang Jian and Zhang Xiaoruo and searched the Zhangs' villas. Their descendants were summarily thrown out of their homes.[28] As in other Chinese cities and towns, the Cultural Revolution brought to Nantong a massive change of street and building names. In 1966, at the height of the revolution, Haonan Road, where Zhang's famous villa was located, was renamed Liberation Road (Jiefang lu), implying that the true liberation of Nantong would come from a thorough criticism of Zhang Jian.[29] Zhang's literary handwork on the city landmarks, such as the couplet on the fire and clock tower, were plastered over with white lime.[30] His accomplishments were forgotten, or, more accurately, were forbidden to be remembered, and his lifetime experience was recast to serve as an appropriate backdrop to a triumphant "revolutionary" history.

But this forced amnesia and distortion were only successful on the surface. Underneath the madness, an equally strong drive to preserve the memory of the Nantong of old was at work. Concerned local people took extraordinary measures to protect the history of their community, and some even quietly continued to collect material on their own. The library and museum both stored precious classics and artifacts in locked rooms shut off from all public access. The museum took the further precaution against radical invasions of putting a large X on Zhang Jian's pictures and works to indicate that they had already been deemed to be among the "four olds" (Fig. 19).[31] But even some radicals, it was said, understood why classics and Zhang Jian's artifacts should not be touched.[32] Like archive offices all over China, the Nantong Archives, which housed the all-important Dasheng documents collected from Shanghai and local factories in the early 1960s, was under military protection, as ordered by the CCP central committee. As a result of these deliberate and chance events, throughout the Cultural Revolution what had been compiled in the early 1960s was kept safe in various Nantong educational institutions or in private homes.[33] Looking back, involved local people were convinced that the Dasheng documents would have been destroyed had they been left in Shanghai and the factories. They considered what they did on the eve of the Cultural Revolution uncanny; "as if Heaven had willed it [*tianyi*]," one said with rejoicing and pride.[34] Indeed, this is the very epitome of what Rubie Watson has described—of how, under state socialism, "small acts" and "unsanctioned remembrance" by ordinary people kept alive memories and histories—though one must add that state socialism is not the only circumstance under which such remembrance takes place.[35]

The first three years following Mao's death in 1976 brought both hope and uncertainty. The CCP central leadership was in transition from Hua Guofeng to Deng Xiaoping. People who had been wrongly accused, dead or alive, during the previous decades were gradually being rehabilitated at every level of the government. All signs pointed to the possibility of reclaiming Zhang Jian's name. But in Nantong, as elsewhere, no one was clear about the CCP's new direction. The CCP municipal committee was hoping the provincial committee would instruct it how to handle the image of Zhang Jian.[36] When the provincial authorities did not follow through, the local people took the initiative, which led to an ironic development.

Although the criticism of Zhang Jian by and large resulted from the extremist ideology of Mao Zedong, it was Mao—in death—who finally legitimated the remembrance of Zhang Jian. In September 1978, Mu Xuan, who had been the party branch secretary at the Nantong Museum since 1972, arranged an interview with Zhang Jingli, then the vice-chairman of the Jiangsu provincial PPCC. Mu hoped to learn from Zhang Jingli what Mao Zedong and Zhou Enlai had said to him, if anything, about Zhang Jian. Mu took the precaution of making the interview a matter of record by inviting others to sit in; in addition to two colleagues from the museum, the head of the municipal United Front Committee was present. During the interview, Zhang Jingli recalled

FIGURE 19. Defaced picture of Zhang Jian. During the Cultural Revolution, museum workers put an X mark on anything attaching to Zhang to deceive local radicals. The mark was meant to indicate that they themselves had already rejected the material as reactionary. (Courtesy of the Nantong Museum)

that he had had four meetings with Mao and Zhou between 1953 and 1956, a period when the CCP was eager to gain the support of prominent democratic personages like him. According to Zhang Jingli, he spoke directly with Mao and Zhou at two of the meetings. Both Mao and Zhou appeared to be familiar with Zhang Jian's life and writings and reminisced a bit about them, but the focus of their conversations was the ongoing socialist reform.[37]

Zhang Jingli's recollection showed that Mao was at least not hostile to Zhang Jian. In fact, it was unthinkable that Mao would criticize the renowned uncle of an invited dinner guest, especially when he not only controlled a major factory but also represented a political force that the CCP wanted on its side. This commonsense assumption was precisely what the interviewers banked on; they expected to hear that Mao had made some positive remarks about Zhang Jian at those dinner parties. Though Zhang Jingli failed to provide any direct, definitive comments by Mao, he did not disappoint the interviewers completely. He told them what he heard from Huang Yanpei, the noted educator and colleague of Zhang Jian we met in Chapter Four. As another prominent democratic personage, Huang had been invited to several of Mao's Chinese New Year's parties in the early 1950s. According to him, Mao once mentioned that four historical figures were worth remembering for their contributions to China's national industrialization, including Zhang Zhidong for heavy industry and Zhang Jian for light industry.[38]

Huang Yanpei turned out to be the sole witness to Mao's comments, though he had reportedly repeated them to others on different occasions. By the time of the interview, in 1978, Huang and most of those who were said to have heard his recollection had passed away, but Mu Xuan and his colleagues did manage to contact a few people who confirmed what Huang said. That apparently was all the interviewers were looking for.[39] Now they had a "mandate of Heaven" to remember Zhang Jian: to them, Mao's comment indicated that he considered Zhang Jian a "national bourgeois," not a "reactionary bureaucratic bourgeois," who had contributed importantly to China's industrial development. The fact that Zhang Jingli could not verify Mao's words to Huang did not bother the interviewers, who treated the interview notes as an authentic record and immediately sent an account to the municipal CCP committee.[40] The account was subsequently published as an important historical document.[41] In time, the details faded and what was remembered in the community was that Mao directly told Zhang Jingli, a most intimate, logical, and thus seemingly reliable source, that Zhang Jian was not to be forgotten.[42]

Obviously, the intention behind the interview was to use whatever favorable remarks Mao had made to rehabilitate Zhang Jian's image. In retrospect, the reform of the 1980s proved that Mao's protection was not needed. However, in 1978, especially in light of the Central Committee Chairman Hua Guofeng's "two whatevers"—whatever Chairman Mao instructed and approved was correct[43]—the Maoist umbrella was useful to break the taboo and to protect the process of reclaiming Zhang's name against the lingering fear of leftist ideology. It would also provide cover for them against a shift in the political winds, the interviewers hoped, so that their work on Zhang would not again be interrupted. This case nicely illustrates the "weapons of the weak"—how the less powerful can manipulate the powerful to legitimize an intensely disputed memory and thereby sanction their work. Memory control cuts both ways.

The museum's involvement in the interview was not a matter of chance. In the post-Mao era, the museum was looking for a way to assert its special position among the numerous museums in China. But if it was to promote itself as the first Chinese museum, and deserving of acclaim as such, the clouds surrounding Zhang Jian's name had to be dispelled. As Mu Xuan once argued, referring to the inevitability of dealing with Zhang, "If the person, that is Zhang Jian, who started the first Chinese museum was a taboo subject [*jinqu*], then how is it possible to write the history of the museum?"[44] Furthermore, the museum was now located in Zhang Jian's Haonan Villa and housed a great many artifacts and materials from the Zhang family and the early twentieth century. All this made the museum a valuable institution, but only if the subject of its founder was open for discussion.

Mu Xuan was the right person to pursue this interest. A Nantong native, Mu was born in 1924, two years before Zhang Jian's death. Like many of his colleagues, he attended schools Zhang had created and became an active member of the CCP-led student movement. After 1949, he had a series of positions in the municipal party's various organizations—the department of propaganda, the Editing Office for Historical Material, *Nantong ribao*, the Writers' Association, and the Nantong Museum[45]—from which he emerged as the city's well-respected veteran leader on cultural affairs. Long-term experience in the field of culture not only sharpened his political sensitivity, but also gave him a greater appreciation for history. A productive writer and researcher in his own right, Mu Xuan became a driving force in promoting local culture and supporting studies of Zhang Jian.

Mu arranged the interview with Zhang Jingli just at a time when China was becoming a more open society. Soon thereafter, the restoration of Zhang Jian's good name was well on its way. With the local PPCC beginning to function again, members of the Zhang family re-emerged on the local political scene. Zhang Rouwu was allowed to move back to her own home, which had been confiscated during the Cultural Revolution; and her younger brother, Zhang Xuwu, had returned from a position in northeastern China to become deputy mayor of Nantong. The museum and library were planning a number of writing projects about Zhang Jian; further systematic and institutional efforts to re-examine Zhang were also under discussion.[46] Thus, at the beginning of the 1980s, the Nantong community, after almost thirty years of struggle to contest the official memory, was finally able to embrace and engage Zhang Jian without undue fear; a taboo was broken.

Mechanisms of Memory

The policy goals of the post-Mao government provided a ready connection to the early decades of the twentieth century. Modernization again became an overarching objective, making Zhang Jian's efforts extremely pertinent. After all, what the CCP now strove to do was to realize the dream of the previous generations—to make China an advanced nation comparable to the West and Japan. The four modernizations outlined by the CCP—industry, agriculture, technology, and defense—were remarkably similar to the goals set by Zhang Jian and his fellow reformers almost a century earlier. The specific means to achieve the four modernizations, such as improvement in education and culture, had also been emphasized in the past. The Nantong community thus found in Zhang Jian and the past associated with him not only practical experience to borrow, but also a source for rhetoric and inspiration. He came to be honored in particular for his patriotism, his belief in the crucial tie between industry and education, his practical and pragmatic style, and his pioneering spirit.[47]

The instruments that the community employed to remember and promote Zhang Jian's legacy were almost identical to those Zhang himself used to fashion the Nantong model: institutions, conferences, ceremonies, monuments, tourism, spatial enhancement, the media, and social contacts. In terms of institutions, the most important by far was the Center for Zhang Jian Studies, founded in 1984 as an outgrowth of the special office the Nantong Library formed in 1979 to gather material on Zhang. A host of organizations and individuals were involved in its creation: the CCP municipal committee and its propaganda department, the city government, the museum, the library, and Zhang Jian's grandchildren, as well as academic institutions beyond Nantong, such as the Historical Research Institute of Nanjing University, and some noted historians. Cao Congpo was its first director. The center identified itself as an academic institute and defined its mission as the study of Zhang Jian, the Dasheng enterprises, and the part Nantong's early efforts played in the current drive for modernization.[48]

From the start, the center saw its main task as gathering material in preparation for the publication of the *Complete Works of Zhang Jian* (*Zhang Jian quanji*). Even with all the efforts of the library and the museum, which had long seen their main contribution to the study of Zhang Jian as gathering, preserving, organizing, editing, and publishing historical materials,[49] this was a daunting task, not only because of the sheer volume of the work, but also because of the difficulties created by the war years and the chaos of the Cultural Revolution. A great deal of material was scattered in private hands, and some of it turned up in unlikely places. For instance, Komai Tokuzoo's 1924 report about Zhang Jian's loan negotiations with Japan was rescued by Guan Jingcheng in the early 1960s from a wastepaper station in Nantong city.[50] Twelve volumes of the originals of Zhang Jian's telegrams and correspondence had been kept by his secretary, Guan Guozhu, and then forgotten after Guan's death. But Cao Congpo happened to be Guan's nephew and eventually helped to recover this important material.[51] Between the work done in the early 1960s and its own initiatives, the center managed to overcome the difficulties. In 1996, after twelve years of effort, the *Complete Works* came out in six volumes. It was considered a publishing event in Nantong.[52]

Publishing in fact became an important channel for promoting Zhang Jian's legacy and Nantong's past. In the 1980s and 1990s, various local organizations, institutions, and individuals turned out more than a hundred books on their own or in collaboration with outside institutions, including such invaluable historical sources as the *Selected Archives of the Dasheng Enterprises* (*Dasheng qiye xitong dang'an xuanbian;* 1987) and *A Chronology of the Dasheng Textile Company: 1895–1947* (*Dasheng fangzhi gongsi nianjian;* 1998). "A History of the Dasheng Capital Group," started in the early 1960s, was finally published in 1990 under a new title, *A History of the Dasheng System Enterprise* (*Dasheng xitong qiyeshi*).[53] The change in the title from the politically colored word "capital" (*ziben*) to the neutral term "system enterprise" (*xitong qiye*) testifies to the political transformation that had taken place during the past thirty years. "System enterprise" has since become the standard way of referring to Zhang Jian's businesses.

Many of the locally edited and published books were distinctly promotional in nature. Some of these were produced for commemorative events, and some were distributed as souvenirs. Like Eastern Europe after the fall of the Berlin Wall, post-Mao China employed the technique of commemoration as both a correction for the political persecution and memory suppression in the previous decades and an effort to control the interpretation of the past.[54] In the course of time, the wrongly accused were rehabilitated; funerals, often long overdue, were held, and victims remembered. Forgotten birthdays, anniversaries, and names were rediscovered or, if need be, invented.[55] All this tended to be accomplished through public ceremonies, which sometimes produced monuments as well as publications. In 1993, sponsored by the Center for Zhang Jian Studies and other institutions, Nantong held a conference to commemorate Zhang Jian's 140th birthday. The conference led to the publication of *Pioneering and Development: The Today and Yesterday of Zhang Jian's Enterprises* (*Kaituo yu fazhan: Zhang Jian suochuang qishiye jinxi*).[56] The book covers twenty-seven of his enterprises and their development from the early twentieth century to the 1990s. It thus emphasizes the relevance of Zhang's work to today's Nantong. Three international symposiums on Zhang Jian were held between 1987 and 2001; each resulted in a conference volume, complete with congratulatory speeches from high-ranking CCP officials.

In 1997, Zhang Xuwu arranged for the Nantong Museum to work on a publishing project with the Mei Lanfang Memorial Hall in Beijing, which housed a number of Zhang Jian's letters and gifts to Mei and Mei's stage pictures in Nantong. The result, in 1999, was a large hard-cover picture book, *Zhang Jian and Mei Lanfang* (*Zhang Jian yu Mei Lanfang*), edited by Zhang Xuwu and one of Mei Lanfang's sons. The same year, China Central Television (CCTV) introduced the book in its "Reading Time" ("Dushu shijian") program, together with footage from Nantong.[57] Meanwhile, various other local institutions held their own commemorative events and published mementos. In 1987, the Nantong Textile School celebrated its seventy-fifth anniversary with a large picture book on its history and famous alumni. Like the publications produced under Zhang Jian's direct control more than half a century earlier, all these books begin by introducing Zhang and his achievements.

The effort to correct the decades-long destruction of history and to control the narrative of the past is also evident in the CCP-sponsored history writing projects that became popular in China after Mao's death.[58] In 1986, the Nantong city government started an office to produce a local gazetteer covering the period from 1912 to 1985. The office decided to mobilize the community in gathering material, to which end it began publishing, in 1987, *Nantong jingu* (*Nantong Past and Present*), a bimonthly magazine that treats practically any topic, from mayors' speeches to reminiscences about a particular food of earlier times. This magazine, like the yearbook *Material on the Culture and History of Nantong*, which started earlier, in 1981, is rather informal. Many local people who were once directly or indirectly related to Zhang Jian published articles on their experiences in the two outlets. In some cases, the same story was told differently by different people.

To support the writing of the new gazetteer, some local institutions undertook to write their own histories. Many of these private and public memories were incorporated into the new gazetteer, which, after several drafts, was published in 2001. A significant portion of it is devoted to the early twentieth century. Like Zhang Jian's 1922 gazetteer, it presents that period as the beginning of modern Nantong. The chapter on the textile industry begins, for instance, with the history of the No. 1 mill, and the chapter on the electric industry, not surprisingly, starts with an account of how an electric generator was installed at the No. 1 mill in 1899.[59] Zhang Jian has imposed his historical periodization from the grave.

Meanwhile, another media outlet had picked up the Zhang Jian story. In 1993, the Nantong television station, Nanjing University, and CCTV together produced a TV program documenting Zhang's life and work. Titled simply "Zhang Jian," the film started with Mao Zedong's remarks on Zhang and proceeded on to an interview with Zhang Xuwu, who recalled that Jiang Zemin, the CCP's general secretary, had reminisced with him about Zhang Jian's literary talent. The filmmakers clearly believed that presenting Mao's and Jiang's favorable views of Zhang at the very beginning of the program would provide a political license for promoting him. The mention of Jiang especially highlighted the relevance of Zhang to the post-Mao reforms and his own timelessness. The film took up several themes in turn: Zhang's academic success, political career, industrial and educational activities, public projects, and openness (*kaifang*). All these were familiar except for the last, which had to do with Zhang Jian's importation of foreign equipment for his factories and his employment of foreign experts, something that was especially in tune with the opening of China after Mao's death. The Nantong Museum and the Gengsu Theater received special attention in the TV program, the one because it established Zhang as the creator of Chinese museums and the other because it revealed him as an all-around reformer who used theater to "promote social progress."[60]

Targeting a broad audience in China and overseas, the film included information on Zhang's contributions beyond Nantong, such as his part in establishing schools in Nanjing and Shanghai. The film contained interviews with several well-known scholars, which not only lent Zhang's story academic authority but also underlined his impact still further. Fei Xiaotong, a sociologist well respected in China and abroad, praised Zhang's practice of township and village industries (*xiangzhen qiye*), an important theme in the new reform era. To accent the fact that Zhang Jian had attracted international interest, the filmmakers interviewed overseas scholars, including Samuel Chu, whose 1965 book introduced Zhang to English readers.[61] The film was shown by various television stations in China and the United States, and some transcripts of it were published.[62]

Conferences played a similarly critical role in propagating the Zhang Jian story. They ranged from local informal tea parties to international symposiums at China's major campuses. In between were meetings commemorating things like the anniversaries of Zhang's birth and death, the anniversaries of landmark projects such as the museum, the publication of the *Complete Works*, and the unveiling of new monuments. One early gathering was particularly important—the preparatory meeting of China's Natural Science Museum Association, which was held in 1979. Nantong was the chosen location for the obvious reason that it was the birthplace of Chinese museums. The meeting was a sign of China's recovery from the previous decades. At the time, the clouds surrounding Zhang Jian's name had not been fully cleared, and the recognition the conference brought provided much-needed hope for the local people who were eager to rehabilitate Zhang.[63]

The international symposiums were attended by government officials, celebrity guests, and Zhang family members, groups that were typically allotted the whole of the first day to give flattering speeches on Zhang Jian. In 1995, at the second symposium, invited guest speakers included Wang Guangying, vice-chairman of the standing committee of the National People's Congress with a powerful family background, and Hu Deping, one of the vice-chairmen of the All-China Federation of Industry and Commerce and a son of the former CCP general secretary Hu Yaobang. At the time, Zhang Xuwu was also a vice-chairman of the federation, so he and Hu Deping were colleagues. Among the guests were J. de Reike, nephew of the Dutch engineer Hendrik de Reike, who reminisced about his uncle's friendship with Zhang Jian, a topic that was also highlighted in Zhang Xuwu's speech.[64] Across time, space, and political background, the symposium provided an opportunity for the mutual promotion of political figures and for the renewal of the friendship between the families of de Reike and Zhang that started two generations earlier.

But these conferences were much more than just occasions to affirm political connections, renew family ties, and forge new social networks. Small or large, their main purpose was to review past accomplishments and propose new directions. In 1998, at a tea party sponsored by the Center for Zhang Jian Studies to celebrate the Chinese New Year, twenty representatives of several local cultural institutions expressed concern that Nantong was not doing enough to make use of Zhang Jian's name. They suggested that, in addition to supporting scholarly research, they should channel their propaganda efforts into popular enterprises, such as publishing children's picture books, erecting a statue of Zhang Jian in a public square, and producing a TV series based on his life.[65]

Today as in the past, many conferences and symposiums make time for participants to tour the host cities. Nantong sponsors typically made a special point of this. In 1997, a conference was held in Nantong to launch the Zhang Jian Research Foundation, a project Zhang Xuwu initiated to help finance studies, publications, and exhibitions on his grandfather. During the conference, forty delegates from all over China toured Nantong, visiting Zhang Jian's tomb, Langshan, and factories in Tangzha.[66] In 1999, members of the Nantong PPCC met to investigate available local resources for cultural tourism. The Center for Zhang Jian Studies prepared a road map for them and identified forty locations related to Zhang Jian. The PPCC concluded that the development of local tourist resources should focus on Zhang Jian.[67] In essence, this amounted to commodifying Zhang's memory.

In fact, the local tourist resources had begun to be enriched many

years before, in the early 1980s, when various old monuments were restored, and new ones erected. Haonan Villa, for instance, where more
than two hundred pictures about Zhang's life were once on display,
was opened to visitors as Zhang Jian's former residence.[68] In 1987,
Zhang Jian's birthplace, Changle, Haimen county, started a permanent
exhibition about him; by 1997, it had become a locale for "patriotic education," attracting ten thousand visitors, including overseas Chinese
and foreigners, over its lifetime.[69] In 1983, Zhang Jian's tomb was re-
built and regained its original name; new trees and other works were
added to improve the appearance of the grounds. Two years later, a
bronze statue of Zhang, which had been installed in 1928 and destroyed
in 1966, was restored in the cemetery. More than two hundred people,
including provincial and local government officials, attended the unveiling ceremony.[70] Though the erection of a monument serves as a
"central means of shaping memory,"[71] it is also an occasion to define the
future. The unveiling of Zhang's statue was reported in the news as a
sign of a "complete repudiation" of the Cultural Revolution, a reflection
of a "truthful view" of Zhang, and the "will" of all the people, including overseas Chinese, who "care deeply about the development of today's Nantong."[72]

If restoring this statue was a symbolic act, the Nantong Textile Museum built in 1987 represented a more substantial monument to Zhang
Jian. Mu Xuan brought up the idea at the 1979 conference of the Natural
Science Museum Association, and the delegates were quick to support
it; so were the city's textile bureau, science association, and cultural bureau, all important municipal organizations. The following year, the
Nantong Museum held a workshop to further the project. Among those
who attended were potential contributors and beneficiaries from various municipal organizations, including the propaganda department,
the construction and economic committees, and the cultural and textile
bureaus.[73]

The workshop justified the project on four grounds, namely, that
Nantong was the earliest textile industry base in China, that the Nantong Textile School had since 1912 trained a great many of the country's
experts, that the textile industry remained a dominant force in the local
economy, and that Nantong was the birthplace of the Chinese museum.
The participants pointed to the vital role the new museum would play
in preserving historical and cultural materials, in history education and
scientific research, and in promoting tourism. They argued that the time
was right, because the old machines and the rich archives left by the

Dasheng factories were ready for exhibition. Once the matter was settled, the group decided that the new museum would be located in the Cultural Peak Compound (Wenfeng yuan) in the southeast of the city. With space, buildings, and materials for display not an issue, the project was considered low cost and thus feasible. That year the construction of the museum was included in the municipal urban plan. The sponsors expected to have the job nearly finished by 1985, when the Nantong Museum, which was now listed as a key national cultural and historic relic for preservation, would celebrate its eightieth anniversary.[74]

A committee was soon formed to oversee the project, and Zhang Xuwu, assistant director of the Nantong Textile Bureau at the time and an engineer himself, was among those in charge. In 1982, to publicize the new museum, the committee organized an exhibit on the history of the textile industry in Nantong; a book based on it, the *Illustrated Record of the Textile Industry in Nantong* (*Nantong fangzhishi tulu*), soon followed. Both the exhibition and the publication helped gather material for the new museum. Funded by several of the institutions that had participated in the workshop and some overseas Chinese, the construction was pushed through expeditiously. By 1985, as planned, the main exhibition hall was open to the public. A ceremony was held to celebrate the opening and the eightieth anniversary of the Nantong Museum, and the resonance between history and reality was not lost on those who attended. Two years later, in 1987, an annex was added to the new museum.[75]

The textile museum sits on thirty mu of land and houses five thousand items. The main exhibition hall consists of six parts arranged in chronological order. The annex was an attractive addition. It traces the history of local cotton handicraft production and distribution before the modern era through miniature replicas of, for example, a field where various kinds of cotton were planted, farmhouses in which old ladies are weaving cotton, and the street in old Tongzhou city where the ten best-known cotton shops were located. Behind this miniature exhibit stands a reproduction of early twentieth-century Tangzha in a large hall. Inside it are displays of Dasheng workshops, imported and locally made textile machines, Zhang Jian's couplets on the Dasheng clock tower, and material about the Nantong Textile School.[76]

The museum exhibits run the gamut of the industry's history, from primitive textile tools such as bone needles and clothes unearthed in Ming dynasty tombs, to drawing frames by Hetherington & Sons of

Manchester dating back to 1895 and Toyoda looms made in the 1920s, to the latest textile goods being produced in Nantong for export. Its pictures of female and child workers operating the machines, and of the Nazi swastika painted on a Dasheng factory in the hope of warding off Japanese bombers during the war, bear witness to the political and human drama of the last century.[77] The museum's unmistakable star, however, is Zhang Jian, a situation not much different from the first museum under his direct supervision. From the main hall to the exhibition on Tangzha, the museum is filled with Zhang's influence. In addition to artifacts directly related to the No. 1 mill and the textile school, the museum includes materials on the enterprises and projects operated or otherwise financed by the No. 1 mill, thereby intensifying the focus on Zhang.[78] He is ever-present, in a large iron machine and in a small piece of paper: his picture, together with his brother's, is printed on a graduation certificate of the textile school that is on display (Fig. 20).[79]

The new museum, like the old one, serves Nantong well. It not only reaffirms the stature of modern Nantong in China's textile industry and museum development, but also improves the image of the city as a whole. By the end of 1987, several thousand people had come to visit, including hundreds of foreigners.[80] The museum also helped to connect Nantong with the outside world. In 1986, the grandson of the founder of Toyoda, after seeing the machines produced by his family two generations before, wanted to make a donation to the museum. Though the donation did not materialize because the museum lacked a procedure to handle it, that incident had an important consequence. It inspired Zhang Xuwu to create, in 1987, the Zhang Jian Research Foundation, for which the Zhang family provided seed money. That year, he also formed a fund-raising group, the General Office of Nantong Textile School Alumni.[81]

The Issue of Preservation

While the reform era has allowed new landmarks that commemorate the past such as the textile museum to emerge, rapid economic growth has also disadvantaged the past, for old buildings have to compete with the new. This is a common paradox city planners wrestle with throughout China. Nantong is no exception. After 1984, when Nantong, as part of the Shanghai economic zone, gained the status of an open coastal city, it began to expand dramatically. It established various joint ventures with more than five hundred foreign companies.[82] New hotels of

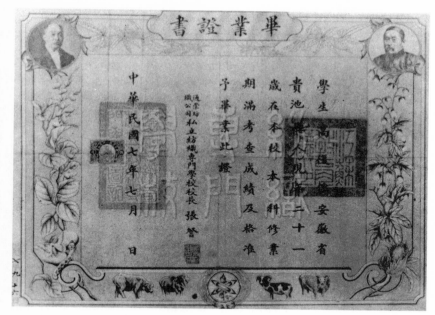

FIGURE 20. Graduation certificate of the Nantong Textile School on display at the textile museum. Zhang Jian (left) and his brother Zhang Cha were prominently featured as founders of the school. (Courtesy of Jiang Ping)

international standard, a new airport, more office and apartment buildings, larger shopping centers, wider roads, and better entertainment and other service facilities sprang up; skyscrapers became a familiar scene. Most of the new construction was outside both the old and the new downtown of the early twentieth century, which allowed the area to maintain its earlier character. But it was inevitable that this would be challenged, especially considering the prime land that the two downtowns occupy. Indeed, as 1990 approached, the entire area had already been encircled by high-rises from all directions, and plans were under way for its reconfiguration.

This prospective move forced the community to deal with the tension between the old and the new. People were deeply divided. Some considered it a crime to destroy historic remains, and others saw little value in old houses and narrow alleys. Among the most vocal of the preservationists, known as "cultural workers" (*wenhua gongzuozhe*), were Mu Xuan and his colleagues in the museum, the library staff, members of the city cultural bureau, and groups of teachers. Their pro-development opponents included young upwardly mobile entrepreneurs, outside developers, and some municipal leaders who wanted to speed the city's economic growth.

In 1991, the municipal government applied to the provincial government to have Nantong declared a "famous city in history and culture" (*lishi wenhua mingcheng*), a special honor bestowed on cities with a unique history and rich culture. Since such an identity would lend legitimacy to the cultural workers' resistance to the demolishing of old historic buildings, they fully supported the city's effort to gain Nantong this status. In 1993, Mu Xuan wrote an essay titled "From Model County to Garden City" ("Cong mofanxian dao huayuan chengshi") to argue the uniqueness of Nantong city. Referring to Shanghai's reputation as an "international architecture museum," he proposed naming Nantong an "architecture museum" as well. As justification, Mu pointed to the still-standing residences from the Ming and Qing dynasties and the buildings constructed on either side of the Hao River in the early twentieth century. According to Mu, both Northwest Camp (Xi'nan ying), a small lane in the new downtown (where Mu's own house happens to be located), and Temple Street (Shijie), a typical traditional alley in the old downtown, also deserved protection. Both neighborhoods had important houses, including those that belonged to the Korean scholar Kim Changkang and the contemporary Chinese movie star Zhao Dan, that made the area doubly important in qualifying Nantong as a famous city in history and culture.[83] In another, related article, Mu suggested a number of specific measures to recapture the past, such as restoring the People's Theater to its original name, Gengsu, promoting ten famed historical figures, and systematically identifying all historically significant remains in the city and the surrounding area. To conclude, Mu stressed the need to consider preservation part of the city's long-term planning.[84]

Although the municipal government wanted Nantong to be honored as a famous city, it lacked the determination, to the dismay of the cultural workers, to take forceful measures to make it happen. Economic development was an overwhelming focus nationwide, and its seeming inevitability put the municipal government in a dilemma. In the absence of regulations, construction that was considered damaging to historic sites moved forward. Tellingly, the first major site involved was the Nantong Library, which lay in the heart of the new downtown, with Zhang Jian's Haonan Villa and the Nantong Museum as close neighbors. The area was regarded as the main target of cultural preservation.

The library lacked strong leadership. The Department of Ancient Books (Gujibu), for instance, had five staff members, but only three came to work regularly; the department head was not among the three. The librarians, especially the young ones, were frustrated with their low pay, a reflection of the under-funding that plagued most Chinese libraries. Their frustration became more intense as the growing market economy made inflation a problem. To help repair the situation, the library rented out some of its rooms to outside companies as offices; the rentals became a source of supplemental income for the library and of bonus pay for the staff. By 1994, one-third of the library's space had reportedly been rented.[85] This side business was quietly tolerated because it benefited the library and because the same practice was also occurring in other government and official institutions where the pay was generally low.

In 1994, however, a brash local entrepreneur, who also happened to be the brother of a young librarian, decided to take the bold step of starting a nightclub in the library. He intended to rent the entire first floor of an adjunct called the Calm Sea Chamber (Jinghai lou), and refit it for his business. The leaders of the library, despite disapproval within and without, agreed to the deal. As a result, construction started quickly; existing walls and structures were removed, and neon lights, TV rooms, and other entertainment facilities were on the point of being installed.[86]

The construction set off a great storm on the "Calm Sea," both literally and symbolically. This was not an ordinary library. One of the first local libraries in China, it was built in 1912 by Zhang Jian. At the time, it housed some 150,000 books in the Chinese language, 600 books in Western languages, and 300 in Japanese. Two-thirds of those works, including a significant number of valuable classics, were donated by Zhang Jian. The name Nantong City Library, in the calligraphy of Guo Moruo, a prominent contemporary writer, was inscribed on the front gate.[87]

But the Calm Sea Chamber itself was a late addition, a three-story building that had been constructed only in 1983 to house the library's 60,000 ancient books. The name Calm Sea Chamber on the front door was in the calligraphy of Li Yimeng, a scholar of some repute and head of the National Committee on Ancient Books. In fact, only the second and third floors were used as stack rooms; the first floor was designed as a lecture hall with a stage for conferences and other cultural and educational events. Nevertheless, converting any part of this historically significant library into a nightclub outraged the cultural workers. They could hardly believe that the city authorities were allowing this to happen, and as soon as construction started, five former library heads fired off letters to the cultural bureau, the municipal office in charge of the library, and to the municipal government itself.[88] "We are shocked and saddened to see that this conference hall was broken to pieces and is now beyond recognition," they wrote. They especially questioned how, after the municipal government disapproved the project, "certain people" in the library dared to "ignore heaven and earth" (*tian bupa, di bupa*) and continued the construction—a not so subtle criticism of the weak leadership in both the library and the municipal government. They emphasized that such money-driven conduct was utterly wrong and tried to invoke a sense of responsibility and guilt among those in charge: "If we fail to protect the only building for ancient books in the only library of the city, what are we going to tell the several hundred thousand readers in Nantong as well as future generations?" They also compared China with other countries to exert political and moral pressure: "Even in capitalist countries such as Japan and the United States, libraries when facing budget cuts would not start strange things such as nightclubs [to make money]. How can we, a socialist country, do such a thing?" They demanded that the cultural bureau halt the construction, restore the building, investigate the incident, and punish those involved.

This letter was only one of many that were sent to the appropriate government offices. Local newspapers and TV stations also condemned what was dubbed the Calm Sea Chamber Incident. Critics framed the issue in the context of the so-called two civilizations (*liangge wenming*)—material and spiritual (*wuzhi* and *jingshen*)—that the CCP emphasized as crucial for realizing the four modernizations. The two civilizations were supposed to go hand in hand, but in reality economic development, or the material side, was often at the expense of improvements in education and cultural life, the spiritual side.[89] The Calm Sea Chamber Incident was criticized as a violation of spiritual civilization that upset the balance between the two. Under tremendous pressure, the cultural bureau and the municipal government finally took the matter seriously. In the end, the standing committee of the municipal PPCC, after a series of meetings, decided to stop the conversion.[90] The first floor was then turned into a newspaper and periodical reading room. No one, though, was punished.

The battle between past remains and current needs, however, had only begun. The cultural workers were highly sensitive to the alarming rate at which the old city was being damaged. They consistently fought for the survival of Temple Street, the old city temple, and the fire and clock tower, among other historic places. They made their opinions known by holding meetings to rally support, sending letters of protest to the municipal government, and publishing articles and conducting interviews in the local press to appeal to the public. Some municipal leaders criticized the cultural workers as "troublemakers" who held "narrow, selfish compartmentalized ideas" (*benwei zhuyi guandian*).[91]

In the summer of 1994, urban planning experts from a dozen cities in the Yangzi region held a conference in Nantong to discuss how to deal with old city structures in the face of rapid new development. They suggested preserving old cities while also reforming them. That suggestion inspired *Nantong ribao* to run a front-page article under the headline, "The Reform of Old Cities Should Not Be Like Having One's Head Shaved: Experts Appeal to Leave Cities with [Their] History."[92] At the time, the municipal government, ignoring a protest from the cultural workers, had decided to demolish the old city temple to make space for a public square. Seeing allies in the *Nantong ribao* report, Ji Xiufu, a retired teacher of the normal school and a lover of local history and culture, immediately sent a clipping of the article to the municipal government, together with a note of his own: "This is the opinion of experts on urban planning, not of 'cultural workers.' [These experts] do not have 'narrow, selfish compartmentalized ideas.'"[93]

By then, Ji Xiufu had become a leading voice for preserving the city's past. He spent most of his time and energy in retirement making sure that his rapidly growing city embraced its past while moving forward. Ji published numerous essays in the local press on Nantong's history and culture, arguing that the city's old houses and streets must be preserved because they were filled with local flavor and provoked a deep sense of nostalgia. He also bombarded the city government with letters to register his objection to policies that he did not like. Ji Xiufu routinely kept copies of his letters and essays, which by the late 1990s made up several volumes.

One of Ji Xiufu's most important battles began in 1995, when the mayor of Nantong decided to demolish the city's fire and clock tower. As earlier noted, the tower dates back to the Yuan dynasty, and the clock was added in 1914 as a symbol of the modern era. Much as the tower's arched gate once led into the prefectural yamen, the CCP municipal government chose to establish its offices in a group of buildings behind the tower. Over the years, the buildings were expanded to accommodate more offices and people, and more and more cars were in regular use. The tower's arched gate, however, remained dark and narrow and only allowed one car to pass at a time. The clear need to improve the traffic flow to the busy offices beyond seemed a compelling argument for leveling the tower, and the issue had been raised several times before 1995. But the symbolic meaning of the tower escaped no one's attention. It was part of the "municipal emblem" (*shihui*), approved by the city's People's Congress. Anticipating resistance to the demolition, the mayor allegedly instructed the local media not to print or broadcast opposing voices. Ji Xiufu, one of those who were expected to protest, was advised by his former employer not to make his opinion known to the public.

Ji was not intimidated. He sent a letter to the deputy mayor, who was said to be in charge of the demolition.[94] The letter first criticized the reported attempt by the mayor to repress public opinion: "How could you not let the Nantong people speak [on this matter]? Where is democracy?" Ji then expressed his shock at the matter in question: the municipal government's order to demolish the tower was comparable to "the Chinese government ordering the demolition of Tiananman Gate. It is unthinkable; it is unreal!" He continued, "It only takes dozens of workers ten days to destroy the tower, but the symbol of Nantong, which represents the [cultural heritage] of the city, and which the people are most familiar with, would be gone forever. Even if afterward some people would admit it was a mistake, no one can ever bring the tower back!" The point Ji Xiufu tried to make is that for something as significant as this tower, the municipal leaders must think hard before taking any action that would result in an irreparable loss. Ji did suggest an alternative way to improve traffic. For the most part, however, his letter reflected his misgivings and frustration: "I cannot understand how this humble idea of mine about preserving the tower is not shared by the mayor, the 'people's servant' [*renmin gongpu*]! Am I just an old diehard who is far too long-winded? But I love my country and hometown, and my heart refuses to be as dead as ashes!" In the end, the retired teacher, feeling powerless yet aware of a valuable resource at his disposal, issued a warning: "Being a teacher of forty years, I have students all over China. Some of them now enjoy a high reputation and positions as ministers of various government departments and presidents and professors of prestigious universities. I am contemplating a signature drive to see if they approve of the demolition. I am confident that they will respond to my call." To preempt any potential threat, Ji invoked the constitution to protect his right to take that action and then added, "I am not afraid of any attack or punishment; I am too old to care about that!" The old teacher also proved that he was strategically alert: "Whether I will do this [the signature drive] depends on how you respond to my letter. Please do not think that I am just complaining; I await your reply." He completed the letter with his name, his home address, and his phone number, but received no response from the deputy mayor.

Ji Xiufu was not the only one who protested the leveling of the tower. Ding Hong, a seasoned journalist and retired professor, also spoke out on its behalf. He argued that if Americans would pay a high price to purchase a brick from the fallen Berlin Wall, how could the municipal government destroy a historic site of eight hundred years?[95] Letters like these reflected the cultural workers' attachment to the city's past and their determination to protect it. Most of them were retired and thus no longer had any decision-making power. But they were highly experienced in propaganda and persuasion, and also resourceful and influential partially because of the social networks they built in their lifetimes. They constituted a force that the municipal government could not simply ignore. Largely because of their efforts, the fire and clock tower still stands today (see Fig. 8).

The Meaning of Remembrance

Clearly, the methods the Nantong community employed to remember Zhang Jian—institutions, print and other media outlets, conferences, monuments, and spatial arrangements—bore a distinct resemblance to those Zhang Jian used to promote Nantong. The similarities, however, did not end there. Those familiar instruments were used to underscore some familiar themes. To be sure, Nantong was no longer known as a model of any type. Zhangjiagang, a once small rural community across the Yangzi to the south, rose to replace it in the 1990s as a national model of "county-level cities" in both its economic and its "spiritual" development.[96] Despite being in the shadow of this star neighbor, or perhaps because of it, the Nantong community tried to hold onto its glorious past and to make it part of the city's new identity by, among other things, emphasizing its own uniqueness.

One way the community did this was to highlight Nantong's connection with celebrities. The establishment of the Center for Zhang Jian Studies, the unveiling of monuments, and especially the international symposiums all involved the politically powerful and academically and socially prominent. *Nantong jingu* introduced two special columns, "Nantong Celebrities" ("Nantong mingren"), which focused on successful people of local origin, such as Sun Zhixia, and "Celebrity and Nantong" ("Mingren yu Nantong"), which reported on renowned people related to Nantong, such as Guo Moruo, who wrote inscriptions on the Nantong Library and a local water control project.[97] Both kinds of stories reinforced each other to convey the message of an extraordinary community that not only was capable of producing its own talented and influential people, but also had the privilege of being connected with the nationally powerful and famous. New connections were also explored. Jiang Zemin, the general secretary of the CCP, was said to have a special relationship with Nantong, because both his grandfather and his father worked in Zhang Jian's Dada Shipping Company.[98]

By the same token, Zhang Jian's relevance to the wider world was also explored. Stories about foreign visitors Zhang received were repeatedly told. The first major conference on Zhang Jian was proclaimed an international symposium, although only a small number of participants were from overseas.[99] Foreign studies on Zhang Jian and Nantong were regularly reported and collected by the Center for Zhang Jian Studies. In 1996, Zhang Xuwu arranged an exhibit in Tokyo of Zhang Jian's collection of Chinese artworks; the Center for Zhang Jian Studies immediately reported the exhibition.[100] The emphasis on Nantong's ties to celebrities and the outside world across time and space was meant not only to underscore its cosmopolitan flavor, but also to establish the continuity between the past and the present—that the previous model city still somehow stands out among China's numerous cities, for very few Chinese cities of the same size have attracted so much attention from abroad for their cultural and historical heritage.

This uniqueness as part of the community identity was reinforced in the stress on "Nantong's utmost" (*Nantong zhi zui*)—the ground-breaking contributions Nantong had made to China's economic and cultural development. *Nantong jingu* launched a special column tracing all the "firsts" that belonged to Nantong.[101] According to one tabulation, there was a total of nineteen firsts—the first normal school, museum, observatory, highway in Jiangsu, shipping company, kindergarten, etc. The TV program on Zhang Jian picked up on this story, concluding the film with the same impressive list of firsts. All this put that period and

Zhang Jian into sharp focus. By referring to these firsts, the community not only kept the past alive, but used it to promote its current status. Over time and by repetition, the local people took the firsts for granted, although, in fact, Zhili in North China was equally a pioneer region in training teachers, and the Baoding Normal School also started in 1902.[102]

Embedded in this seeming obsession with firsts and celebrity contacts was a profound sense of local pride. The people believed that what was special about their community was above all the high value it placed on culture, knowledge, and education, and its ability to achieve and to be distinct. They attributed these local qualities to the early twentieth century. To them, the fact that Nantong produced someone like Zhang Jian and attracted intellectual giants like John Dewey and Liang Qichao was proof of its uniqueness.

And Nantong also had Zhang Jian's descendants, a legitimate linkage to the past and a living reminder of its own distinctiveness. Encouraged by the city and motivated by their own interest, the third generation of the Zhang family became actively involved in enhancing Zhang Jian's image, perpetuating a family tradition of self-promotion. Zhang Jian was hardly cold in his grave before Zhang Xiaoruo began to write the first biography of his father and edit his father's writings. Though Zhang Jingli, Zhang Cha's son, did play a small role in this regard,[103] the most visible keeper of the flame after 1979 was Zhang Xuwu, Zhang Xiaoruo's son and Zhang Jian's grandson.

Zhang Xuwu, born in 1928, initially took a path in life that his grandfather and father would have disapproved of. As a middle school student in the mid-1940s, Xuwu and his mother used their home to help underground CCP activists. In 1946, Xuwu attended college in Shanghai. The following year, to fulfill his mother's wish, Xuwu transferred to Nantong University to major in textile engineering. He graduated in 1950 at the age of twenty-two, only to find himself left alone in Nantong to deal with the vast uncertainty that the changing times had imposed upon his family. (His mother had died three years earlier, and his three surviving siblings had scattered to Hong Kong, Taiwan, and Shanghai.) Xuwu chose to run away as far as possible from his "exploiting class" family background so that he could start anew. In 1950, he ended up in a textile factory in Jiamusi, a city in China's far northeast, leaving his sister, who had returned from Shanghai, to handle the family property in the only way possible under the circumstance—donating all of it to the municipal government. In the next thirty years, Xuwu worked first as an engineer in Jiamusi and then, after being classified as a rightist in 1958, as a worker.[104]

In 1979, the Nantong city government invited Zhang Xuwu to return home, where he was soon offered the position of assistant director of the city's textile bureau. His political career quickly took off from there: he was elected deputy mayor of Nantong in 1981, was elected deputy governor of Jiangsu in 1983, and moved to Beijing in 1988 to become vice-chairman of the All-China Federation of Industry and Commerce.[105] He subsequently became active in the National People's Congress as a member of the standing committee and deputy director of the fiscal and economic committee.[106] After a long detour in life, Zhang Xuwu came to occupy a position that was appropriate to his family tradition.

Not coincidentally, the return and growth of Zhang Jian's reputation paralleled his grandson's steady promotion. Xuwu was a driving force behind many of the projects and events discussed above, most notably, the establishment of the Zhang Jian Research Foundation, the publication of *Zhang Jian and Mei Lanfang*, and the founding of the textile museum. He sponsored a number of the conferences devoted to Zhang Jian's memory and had the clout to get many distinguished guests from Beijing and abroad to take part in them. As an important official, he could now play the celebrity card to validate his family legacy better than the local people. In 1985, Zhang Xuwu tried to capitalize on the name Dasheng for practical economic reasons. He formed the Dasheng Industrial Company, Ltd., and started joint ventures with foreign companies.[107] Though settled in Beijing, he maintained close contact with Nantong and remained interested in developing Zhang Jian's image to the maximum. The local people, for their part, tried to keep him involved in their work to the same end.[108]

Though one can only speculate on the degree to which Zhang Xuwu's rapid rise up the administrative ladder owed to his being Zhang Jian's grandson, it is clear that Zhang Jian's rehabilitation afforded Xuwu a unique opportunity to increase his own visibility and prestige. By the 1990s, because of who he was, his appearances at various events remembering Zhang Jian were much sought after, especially on ceremonial occasions, where he represented legitimacy and authenticity. Zhang Xuwu was often referred to in the media as Zhang Jian's "blood grandson" (*disun*) to underscore the direct line of descent, and thus the unique honor he brought to the events. Over the years, his calligraphy graced the covers of several publications; he also wrote introductions for some of them. In his many speeches about Zhang Jian, he was wont to emphasize that the most important value his grandfather passed down to the Zhang family was serving the public.[109] All this worked to significantly enhance his own image and to assure him a public forum for airing his private memories.

Indeed, the issue of what the past does or does not mean to those who try to keep it alive is an intriguing one. In the case of Zhang Jian and Nantong, the meaning of remembrance evolved over time. Before 1980, local people who were interested in Zhang Jian generally believed that he had both merits and flaws, and that it was wrong to only criticize him. As a result, some of them treated Zhang Jian relatively dispassionately as a historical figure. Such an approach is best reflected in Zou Qiang's introduction to the early 1960s work "A History of the Dasheng Capital Group." Forty pages in length, with 176 notes that cover an additional ten pages, Zou's essay, "Zhang Jian: The Founder of the Dasheng Capital Group (Dasheng ziben jituan de jianlizhe—Zhang Jian)," is a solid piece of research. Despite the inevitable mark of "class analysis" that was characteristic of history writing in the Mao era, this article remains, to my mind, the best scholarly work on Zhang Jian that has ever come out of Nantong. Unlike the bulk of local authors before and after, Zou was not interested in either attacking or flattering Zhang. The introduction was meant to provide a context for the history of the Dasheng enterprises. It covers the major aspects of Zhang's life and work and connects them with the developments of the late Qing–early Republican period. In doing so, it brings out the dynamics of the time. The article includes some critical and insightful points. For instance, Zou contended that the difference between Zhang's autonomy, which was based on economic and cultural means, and that of the warlords explained why the central government, as well as various warlords, supported or at least tolerated Zhang; and that the fact that they found Zhang's practice non-threatening in turn explained why Nantong thrived as it did in so chaotic a time.[110] On this and other issues, Zou showed considerable discipline and distance in his historical treatment of Zhang Jian. In 1979, just before his death, Zou Qiang received news that a scholarly journal was interested in publishing his article. Revised by Mu Xuan, it finally came out in 1980.[111]

What was acceptable in 1979, however, was apparently not suitable a decade later. In 1979, in Nantong and the academic field generally, the concern about Zhang Jian was mainly to break the taboo and to bring him back for study and remembrance. In fact, Zou's article was the first publication on Zhang Jian after the Cultural Revolution. Ten years later, the lavish praise of Zhang Jian that had become the norm made Zou's view out of date. As a result, in 1990, when *A History of the Dasheng System Enterprise* was finally published, Zou Qiang's original introduction was dropped. Instead, Xu Dixin, the initiator of the writing project in the 1960s, was asked to write the introduction. In less than two pages, Xu simply emphasized that what Zhang Jian did was patriotic and progressive; his piece showed no trace of the critical analysis that characterized Zou's essay.[112]

This one-sided approach is not surprising. After 1980, Zhang Jian's legacy became increasingly useful to the community in both symbolic and tangible ways. As some of the cultural workers in Nantong put it, Zhang Jian was "invisible capital" (*wuxing zichan*) that could be used to raise the visibility of the city. They argued that some cities would even invent celebrities to attract attention, and that Nantong should do more to promote what it already had.[113] Indeed, politicians, entrepreneurs, and cultural workers all found in Zhang's memory an almost inexhaustible source for exploitation. Changes in party line also provided chances to keep Zhang Jian's image alive. For instance, when the CCP emphasized the two civilizations—material and spiritual—Zhang Jian's attention to both industry and education was referred to as a perfect example of the two civilizations "harmoniously combined."[114] Politicians and cultural workers used this reference not only to advance the CCP's propaganda agenda, but also to provide a new framework for viewing Zhang Jian. Thus we find the head of the municipal CCP proposing this dedication for the second international symposium on Zhang: "Study Zhang Jian to serve the construction of the two civilizations in Nantong."[115]

Zhang Jian in fact was made relevant to almost every issue raised in the reform era, from openness, market economics, township and village industries, and regional economic growth, to foreign investment, urban planning, the rule of law, and even religion. New topics were still being developed at the close of the twentieth century. Zhang's close relationship with Mei Lanfang, for instance, had been ignored by his biographers in the past. Now, with corporate sponsorship for cultural events becoming increasingly important in China, their relationship was framed as an example of how entrepreneurs could make friends with artists.[116] In 1999, to prepare local authors for the third international symposium, the Center for Zhang Jian Studies provided forty-one topics as a guidance for study. As befitted the current structural reorganization of Chinese enterprises, the center stressed that Zhang Jian's thought and practice in joint-stock enterprises and in joint ownership (state and private) should be one of the main focuses for the conference.[117]

Remembering Zhang Jian was also important to many for personal reasons. Whether they study Zhang or propagandize him, many people in Nantong have a vested interest in the "Zhang Jian industry."[118] At least some members of the staff of the textile museum, for example, owed their employment to the renewed interest in Zhang. That renewed interest not only created new institutions and thus jobs, but also opportunities for promotion. The conferences and publications discussed in this chapter became forums for local authors, who might be teachers, professors, librarians, museum workers, and editors who needed to provide evidence of their research ability for promotion. To them, presenting a paper at an international symposium would be the most prestigious item on their résumé. The fact that a symposium was not truly international in scope and that some papers lacked scholarly quality was not important; what was important was the name. About a dozen local authors presented their papers at each of the symposiums. Though some of these people, university professors, for instance, needed this "international" stage, others, such as a museum staff member, would be satisfied to give a paper or a speech at local gatherings or to publish an essay in *Nantong jingu*. To them, those arenas were big enough.

Of course, not all of the local writers chose to cover this topic to advance their careers. Ordinary people, including retirees who were not necessarily former cultural workers, were also engaged in cultivating the Zhang Jian legend by writing and other means. Perhaps this was a fulfilling way for them to spend their spare time, to gain recognition, to show off, or to contribute, as they understood it, to the history of home. Or perhaps this was a reminiscence therapy that everyone could take advantage of after the brutal control of memory under Mao. During my 1996 fieldwork in Nantong, my guide, a retired cadre from a mine, spent a week at the height of summer helping me to find suitable subjects for interview. He knew every alley of the city and people who were old enough to provide the kind of material I needed. He cut his noon nap short and enthusiastically volunteered information. Before my departure, my guide gave me a unique teapot as a gift but would accept nothing from me in return. He was not the only one in Nantong who was enthusiastic about the history of the city for no apparent concrete reason. Whatever the reasons were, remembering the past and Zhang Jian had in a sense become both a pragmatic and a sentimental community enterprise.

The consequence was to make Zhang Jian's image increasingly popular and positive. For example, the number of ceremonial speeches by special guests at the symposiums rose from six in 1987, three of which were delivered by the Zhang family, to fourteen in 1995, only one of them made by a Zhang. The rest of the guest speakers included, besides some nationally renowned scholars, the president of Nanjing University, where the conference was held, the deputy governor of Jiangsu, and the vice-chairman of the standing committee of the National People's Congress. More than half of these people were government and party officials from Beijing. If the first symposium was still a provincial event in its ceremonial representation, the second one made it to the national scene. Likewise, where the first conference volume contained fifty-eight papers, the second one contained 102. The sheer increase in number indicates the degree of Zhang Jian's popularity. Because of all the energies and resources invested in his promotion, Zhang Jian had reportedly become the most-studied figure of the Republican era next to Sun Zhongshan.[119]

Unfortunately, the quality of Zhang Jian studies suffered as a result. The general tendency was to make Zhang a pioneer of virtually everything the new reform era encountered. In doing so, critical analysis of the kind found in Zou Qiang's work, or indeed anything that was critical of Zhang, became extremely rare. To be sure, information about Zhang Jian's mismanagement of the Dasheng enterprises and his suppression of student movements came out, but only in fragments. In 1994, an oral history, *Investigation of the Life of Workers in the Dasheng Mills, 1899–1949* (*Dasheng shachang gongren shenghuo de diaocha: 1899– 1949*), was published.[120] That book, the fruit of Mu Xuan's work in the 1960s, when he was gathering material on the history of the CCP, was based on interviews with more than two hundred former Dasheng workers, most of them women. Their reports of poor factory conditions, extremely low pay, and frequent physical abuse, as well as job-related illness, injury, and death, are totally inconsistent with the image of a thriving model Zhang Jian presented. But that publication did little to damage Zhang's reputation, perhaps because of the understanding that the suffering of workers was a universal phenomenon and so Zhang bore no particular responsibility. The book, the only one in the numerous publications about Dasheng that reflects the voice of an otherwise silent yet indispensable group in the history of modern Nantong, was largely ignored by the local as well as the scholarly community in China.

Indeed, history and memory are selective, and remembrance means negotiation with the past that often requires re-invention and forgetting. Understandably, in the study of Zhang Jian, distortion and the neglect of some basic historical facts were common. This happened not only in the writings of local amateurs, but also in the works of trained professionals. Topics such as Zhang Jian's attitude toward freedom, equality, gender issues, and Confucianism, for instance, are sensitive ones. Credit must be given to those who try to tackle them. But, like any topic, they can be interpreted to fit into the mainstream view. One college professor from Nantong took up all these topics in a paper presented at the second international symposium. Denying that Zhang was a conservative who opposed freedom, equality, and women's liberation and promoted Confucianism instead, he argued that Zhang was only against "extremely individualist behavior" that threatened the rule of law and social stability.[121] In other words, Zhang in fact promoted the rule of law and social stability, politically correct themes in post-Mao China. The author made no mention of Zhang's suppression of the students during the May Fourth and other movements. He also used the example of Shen Shou, the embroidery expert, to illustrate that Zhang made a "significant contribution" to women's liberation,[122] omitting the fact that Zhang had several concubines and employed a distinctly double standard for male and female students—conduct and notions that were perfectly acceptable in his time. As for Zhang's affinity with Confucianism, the author suggested that Zhang meant to absorb the moral excellence from Chinese tradition to vitalize China, which proved that Zhang was a patriot, not a conservative.[123] This article demonstrates the limits (or lack thereof) of strained interpretation and artful forgetfulness.

Though it seems that there was nothing about Zhang Jian that could not be reinterpreted positively to fit current needs, one central theme of his work was conspicuously missing—the idea and practice of local self-government, or Village-ism. According to Zhang Jian himself, everything he did, factories, schools, and charitable work, was meant to build a self-sufficient local unit. In fact, he emphasized that it was because of his focus on Village-ism that he was able to achieve in all those areas. After all, Nantong was known at the time as a model of local self-government and modernity. After 1980, however, the moder-

nity aspect of the model was overly stressed, and Village-ism was suppressed. Though Zhang's idea of local self-government was mentioned
in various works, very few confronted the issue directly. For instance,
only one of the 160 articles collected in the conference volumes from
the first two international symposiums mentioned local self-government in its title. And that article dealt mainly with urban planning and
treated self-government as a marginal issue. Moreover, the author was
only interested in the social and economic aspects of Zhang's local self-
government. He made no attempt to examine the tension between the
state and local society and Zhang's critical view of the central government.[124] In fact, to highlight Zhang's patriotism, it was said that Zhang
demonstrated how love for one's country and love for one's hometown
could be perfectly combined.[125] According to these writings, Zhang was
motivated purely by his patriotism; he had no ego, no concerns for self-
interest, and no localism either. Though patriotism is always in fashion,
localism is not. So long as the CCP imposes its central leadership in the
current modernization process, Zhang's idea and practice of local self-
government will remain a neglected issue.

Also condemned to obscurity are matters relating to the decline of
the Dasheng System Enterprises and the Zhang family. As pointed out,
the 1921 flood and the end of World War I have been used as standard
scapegoats for Dasheng's downfall. To be sure, Zhang Jian's mismanagement has been cited as a contributing factor, but the issue has not
been well studied or squarely addressed. For instance, it is taken for
granted that Zhang Jian and his brother personally financed many local
educational and charitable projects,[126] but questions about the source of
their extraordinary wealth and how they benefited from the Dasheng
enterprises' arbitrary distribution of dividends have not been raised.
Furthermore, the controversy surrounding Zhang Xiaoruo's campaign,
though still recollected by local people, has never been investigated in
depth. The Nantong library and museum have abundant material on
the story, a fact that was known to some local as well as outside authors. But for all that writers seem to have tried to exhaust every possible topic related to Zhang Jian and that time period, no one has touched
this story. The story, of course, is inconsistent with the larger-than-life
image created for Zhang Jian. It was therefore perceived as not only an
irrelevant and useless past, but also a painful memory for both the community and the Zhang descendants. On Zhang Xiaoruo's untimely
tragic death, too, till recently, there was a determined silence.[127] By unspoken community consensus, to revisit Zhang Xiaoruo's failed cam-

paign would be to show grave disrespect toward both Zhang Jian and Zhang Xuwu. For that reason, no local people showed any interest in exploring the topic. Indeed, unpleasant, unfortunate, and unfitting stories of any sort must be buried in order to maintain an "appropriate" and coherent memory of Zhang Jian and his time, and to move the community forward; remembering, after all, demands forgetting.

Looking ahead, there are challenges and obstacles in remembering Zhang Jian. Family ties usually fade over time. It is questionable whether the fourth generation of the Zhangs will take as much interest as the previous generations in promoting their family legacy. In Nantong, the generation that was familiar with Zhang and his time is aging rapidly. The youngest among them were reaching the seventy-year mark by the end of the twentieth century. They had long been retired and were playing less and less of a role in the community. The younger generation will more likely invest their energies in ways other than advancing Zhang's memory. Already in 1998, the Center for Zhang Jian Studies warned that local people under fifty years old knew little about Zhang Jian and showed slight respect for the past.[128]

As for the center itself, since the publication of the *Complete Works*, it has not found another project to focus on. Cao Congpo passed away in 1998. The new director was regularly absent from the center. The center had no regular staff, office hours, or telephone. A professor at a local college was supposed to take charge of its day-to-day operation, remotely. Anyone who wished to visit had to make an appointment first. But there was little to see. Most days, the center's small one-room office on the second floor of the Calm Sea Chamber was closed. Inside, the two desks and a few chairs, along with remaining copies of the *Complete Works* and other materials, were collecting dust. In 1997, it started a monthly two-page newsletter that was meant to exchange information about studies on Zhang Jian and report relevant events. But its publication soon became ever more infrequent, reflecting the decline of reportable events.

The center has tried to shift its attention to "studies on Zhang Jian studies," which is to say, the scholarship on Zhang Jian.[129] But since the explosion of hundreds of articles and books in the 1980s and 1990s, substantial new research on Zhang Jian and his time has been rare, especially at the local level. It is also not clear how this focus on scholarship will serve the interest of the community.

Financial support is a major issue. Like many educational and cultural institutions in China today, the library, the museum, and the tex-

tile museum are all chronically under-funded. Creating additional income on their own has been difficult. For instance, charging admission
fees has had virtually no effect on the financial well-being of the textile
museum. There have been few regular local visitors in recent years. The
museum depends on conference participants and leisure travelers from
the outside. The former are infrequent, and the latter scarce. Located between Shanghai, the most cosmopolitan city in China, and Nanjing, the
capital of six ancient Chinese dynasties, Nantong has difficulty attracting regular tourists. Two of the three times that I was at the textile museum, I was the only visitor. The other time, the only other visitor was
also an outsider, a high school student from Ohio brought there by a local student. The textile museum, like the library, has had to rent out
space to get by financially. In fact, neither the two museums nor the library had a single computer in 1999. In 1996, a young librarian took
evening classes to study computers on his own. Upon his graduation
and with a certificate in hand, he had no machine to operate on in the library and, frustrated, left for another job. In the summer of 1999, the entire Nantong Museum staff was redoing the catalogue by hand. Because
of the lack of financial resources, none of the three institutions had an
air conditioner either. The hot, humid air in summer has contributed to
the rapid deterioration of the precious materials housed there.

Rescuing them by modernizing these institutions is an urgent task,
but in 1999, it was not on the agenda of either the municipal government or the Zhang family, both of which, according to employees at
these institutions, have exploited their resources without offering substantial support in return. There have indeed been tensions between the
Zhang family and those institutions. The library's administrative office
building was donated by the Zhang family in the 1950s. The library
wants to expand the building, but the Zhang family wants to keep it in-
tact. The consensus seemed to be that during Zhang Xuwu's lifetime,
the building is unlikely to be touched. In the meantime, the Zhang family was in the process of negotiating with the municipal government for
the return of the Haonan Villa.[130] All this suggests that the next phase of
Zhang's memory will unfold with uncertainty.

The flourishing of Zhang Jian's memory in the reform decades benefited from a combination of various factors, both national and local. The
grave injustice the CCP did to culture and history under Mao called for
compensation. This opened up many areas for exploration and created
a culture of commemoration, for which Zhang Jian seemed an ideal fit.

The new tide of modernization put China in somewhat the same position as it was in the early twentieth century, and Zhang's experience became a political commodity for the CCP to exploit in advancing its own agenda. Rapid social and cultural change threatened existing lifestyles, as well as familiar landscapes, intensifying the sentiment of nostalgia and bringing the issue of community identity into focus.[131] Remembering Nantong's past both satisfied the community's longing for another time and afforded the city a ready means of distinguishing itself. Also, the longtime neglect and destruction of the large amount of invaluable source material Zhang Jian left behind provided legitimate reason for investing time and money in rescuing his work. As a result, the kind of material Nantong was able to offer not only promoted studies on Zhang Jian, but also increased the visibility of the city itself. Zhang Jian and the Nantong he built were still within the living memory of the old generation. Some, like Mu Xuan, had a sufficient appreciation of history and significant capacity to shape local events. Zhang Jian's grandchildren, especially Zhang Xuwu, were in positions of influence to advance Zhang's image. All this contributed to a renewed interest in Zhang Jian. Consequently, the old master lives on.

And he lives on in many ways. The return of Zhang Jian's memory was part of the effort to settle accounts with the recent past—the Mao era when the community was deprived of the right to remember him and when his image was severely bruised. As a result, the re-articulation of Zhang Jian's life was intensely political—it was a validation of the community's entitlement to its past, a rejection of the forced amnesia and a denial of the politics of the Mao era. Also, as Nantong (and China at large) tried to reprocess its past to fit into the new framework of economic reform, Zhang's modernization effort was made into an economic model. Furthermore, Zhang's memory was commodified to attract visitors. His houses and his tomb all became tourist resources. Indeed, as Jonathan Boyarin has pointed out, "Memories once evoked may be employed in infinite and unpredictable ways."[132] As a ceaseless dialogue between the present and the past, remembrance makes the past as unpredictable as the future. In the case of Nantong, the re-creation of the past magnified its modernization projects and discounted its autonomous status.

This reformulation of Zhang Jian's memory to serve late twentieth-century modern development nicely illustrates Børge Bakken's point about the relationship between tradition and change in China. According to Bakken, Chinese modernization follows a pattern of "controlled

change . . . with tradition and modernity interlinked in a system of social control where 'tradition' can also serve transforming purposes and
'modernization' can mean stability and order."[133] In this process, memories provide a useful past with exemplary norms and behavior to direct current change. Bakken considers such memories "practical strategies" designed to bring order to a process that can otherwise be
disorderly.[134] Clearly, the emphasis on Zhang Jian's modern projects
and the suppression of his localism serve to reinforce the CCP's control
of the reform.

The irony of this latest manipulation is that whereas the Cultural
Revolution blindly attacked Zhang, the post-Mao era has just as blindly
elevated him. In a sense, the former provoked and enabled the latter.
The difference is that where praising Zhang was forbidden during the
Cultural Revolution by political force, criticizing Zhang has now become unacceptable largely by self-censorship. If the two periods share
anything in common in this regard, it is the existence of taboo and the
absence of critical analysis. Thus, when we celebrate the unleashing of
repressed memory in post-Mao China or in the post-Communist world
generally, we must be aware that political suppression as well as its op-
posites, such as freedom and openness, can all produce restriction, distortion, and blindfolds in memory in both overt and subtle ways.

Conclusion

History is nothing if not a master narrative.

George Lipsitz, *Time Passages*

THE INITIAL PURPOSE of this study was to examine the model claim—not to argue that Nantong was not a model, but to explore how the image was constructed. In the process, I became aware of my inevitable dependence on Zhang Jian's own work and the rich local material produced during the period under consideration. Thus the extent to which my study has been influenced by Zhang's interpretation is a legitimate concern. To gain perspective on my own work and to ensure a fuller understanding of my subject, I searched for competing narratives, or a "counter-memory," which, in Michel Foucault's words, records events outside of any "monotonous finality."[1] This has proved to be difficult.

Whether from the assessments of Frederick Sites and Liang Qichao or from the writings of ordinary local people (and my conversations with them), the opinions on Nantong consistently confirm Zhang Jian's view rather than challenge it. Even as critical a mind as John Dewey's seemed to be mainly convinced. Here is Dewey's impression of Nantong from his 1920 visit, quoted in its entirety to capture his view in full (the italics are mine):

The entire development [of Nantong] has been in the hands of a single family, two brothers. And the leading spirit is one of a small group of men who vainly and heroically strove for the reformation of the Manchu dynasty from within. Finding his plans pigeon-holed and his efforts blocked, he retired to his native town and began *almost single-handed* a course of industrial and economic development. He has in his record the fact that he established *the first strictly Chinese cotton mill in China* and also *the first normal school*. And since both were innovations, since China had never had either of these things, *he met with little but opposition and prophecies of disaster* to himself and the district. Now the district is known popularly as *the model town of China, with its good roads, its motor buses for connecting various villages, its technical schools, its care of blind and deaf, its total absence of beggars.* But the method is that of old China at its best, a kind of Confucian paternalism; an exhibition on the small scale of the schemes for the reformation of the country which were rejected on the large scale. The combination of the new in industry and the old in ideas is signalized in the girl and woman labor in the factories, while the magnate finds it "inconvenient" that boys and girls should be educated together after the age of ten years, with the usual result that most of the girls receive no schooling.[2]

Dewey's main criticism of Nantong and of Zhang Jian—Confucian paternalism and gender discrimination, where he saw old China at work—was rare at the time and indeed contradicted Zhang's own claim that Nantong represented the embryo of a new world. That these supposed shortcomings were not pointed out more frequently was largely because they were, to most contemporary observers, acceptable. In that sense, Dewey's disapproval does not add to our understanding of Nantong. The main body of his account, however, is remarkably similar to Zhang Jian's own presentation and to other visitors' impressions—it belongs to a prevailing narrative. In that sense, Dewey seems to disappoint us again.

It is of course unfair to blame Dewey or anyone else for being part of this large narrative, and to ignore it would be ahistorical. My difficulty in finding a counter-memory of the Nantong story reveals a number of issues concerning historical study in general and the Nantong model in particular. In examining the records of a 1922 anti-police riot in north India, Shahid Amin expressed a similar frustration in his failure to find an alternative representation of the event. According to him, the overriding power of judicial and nationalist discourse produced "hegemonic master narratives" that "tainted or vitiated or colored" even peasants' views.[3] He further pointed out how "the process by which historians gain access to pasts is richly problematic."[4]

Indeed, we work with what is available to us. The powerful, by and large, control the making of historical records, as well as memories, and thus influence our thought. In the case of the Nantong story, the lack of competing interpretations indeed indicates the success of a hegemonic power in constructing an indisputable narrative. This power derived from the political authority, social status, and financial strength of the Zhang brothers and other local elites, as well as from politicians and intellectuals beyond Nantong; both groups controlled the press and other public forums and thus were able to influence public opinion. The operative specifics of this power in effectively shaping image and reality, as this study has tried to show, provide invaluable access to the past but also render that access highly problematic. Both the advantages and the limitations challenge us to maintain the kind of healthy skepticism that is conducive to a more nuanced understanding of history.

The consistent representation of the Nantong story also sheds light on the meaning of the model as its contemporaries understood it. Both Chinese and foreign observers identified the same set of institutional, material, and cultural establishments—factories, up-to-date transportation and communication facilities, urban planning, and Western-style schools and other educational and charitable organs—as representative of the modern and the progressive. In the early twentieth century, beyond the treaty ports and even in some rural areas, the pursuit of modern culture had to some extent become fashionable, which, to the Chinese, was a departure from the Self-strengthening movement.[5] When modernization was understood in a much broader sense, China's dependency on foreign patterns for its own development deepened. Even though modeling itself on other nations proved to be difficult in the ensuing decades, the belief that China should do so became increasingly strong. What Zhang Jian did in Nantong was, after all, to imitate the success of the Japanese and to adopt institutions and practices that had become staples of advanced Western countries. In Nantong and elsewhere in China, the development of steamships, railroads, factories, and new schools was thus accompanied by a deepening admiration of the modern and a growing sense of Chinese cultural inadequacy, an inferiority complex that has characterized Chinese nationalism to this day. The Nantong model reflected and reinforced both sentiments.

The meaning of the Nantong model, however, goes beyond that. Shanghai was recognized as more modern than any other Chinese city, yet it was not considered to be a positive model by the Chinese of the time. While the image of Shanghai was appealing to other Chinese cities, certain elements of the "Shanghai modern," such as those described by Leo O. Lee, were essentially alien to most Chinese.[6] Moreover, Shanghai's modernity was perceived as associated with moral decay and vice. Aside from an inherent bias against the city in an agrarian society and anti-foreign nationalism, there is another key reason why Shanghai failed to attain the lofty status of a model—it was simply too diverse and thus potentially too chaotic to be an ideal example.

Børge Bakken points out, in his recent study of contemporary Chinese society, that the process of modernization can generate "mounting disorder" and requires exemplary models as a control mechanism. He considers China an "exemplary society," where exemplary norms and behaviors were a matter of paramount importance. Such norms and behaviors distinguish the rights from the wrongs and thus provide direction and stability to a changing society.[7] Although Bakken's work is long on theoretical analysis and on various individual models, studies of model units shed further light on both the controlling nature of model building in China and the broader implications of the model phenomenon.

Model units of various kinds have existed throughout Chinese history. In the Republican period, there were many other models besides Nantong, notably Tao Xingzhi's model teacher-training school in Xiaozhuang, near Nanjing, James Yen's model village in Ding county, Hebei province, and Liang Shuming's Rural Reconstruction Institute in Zhouping, Shandong province, to name but a few.[8] The Mao era produced Dazhai and Daqing, much-publicized models for agriculture and industry, respectively.[9] More models emerged during the post-Mao reform, such as Zhangjiagang village in the south and Daqiu village in the north.[10]

These model units differed in many ways. For one thing, some of them were initiated by individuals, and others sponsored by the state. But they shared at least four characteristics. One is that they were all in small, and in some cases remote, rural locations. In other words, compared with China's urban centers and treaty ports, they were in a relatively controlled, closed environment. Just as exemplary models are designed to regulate social change, the experiment and production of such models must also be a controlled process, which requires a manageable size and locale. Another similarity is that they were led by strong, visionary, and resourceful men: Zhang Jian in Nantong, James Yen in Ding county, and Yu Zuomin in Daqiu. These two characteristics—restricted location and strong leaders—are related, for the former enables the latter. The combination of the two is requisite for the kind of social laboratory that is necessary to culturing any model, because it eliminates undesirable and unpredictable elements and ensures order and control in the process of model construction. In the case of Nantong, both Frederick Sites's praise of Zhang Jian's "guiding hand" and John Dewey's criticism of his "Confucian paternalism" reflect this laboratory condition and Zhang's role in creating it. Not surprisingly, the political integrity of the model began to unravel partly because of the increased outside influence that shook Zhang Jian's authority.

If the combination of these two elements constitutes the internal ingredient of an orderly model production, the other two provide models with external appeal; otherwise there would be no models. Thus, the third characteristic in model building is the imaginative power invested in it that allows a local practice to attract a broad audience. There is an irony in this, of course. On the surface, models are meant to be imitated, but they are often a distortion of reality, based on active imagination and a specific set of circumstances and resources that might be "unreal" in another place or another time. In essence, the appeal of a model is not that it is real, but precisely the fact that it is richer and more colorful than the real world—it returns our calls and grants our wishes.

In the case of Nantong, the reform programs created a preferred reality, so to speak, that was, in Dewey's words, "rejected on the large scale." This preferred reality therefore caught the fancy of the public— what would China have become had the Nantong experience been reproduced in other regions or in China as a whole? Politicians, industrialists, educators, and ordinary people could all come up with their own grand or trivial wish lists. To all of them under the warlord government, however, this progressive and, equally important, orderly community under local leadership had special appeal. It was telling that Nantong's reputation took off precisely at a time when the collapse of the Yuan Shikai government finally destroyed any hope of an effective, centralized state and long-term stability. Nantong provided a successful example of modernity and order achieved by local initiative for other regions that were struggling on their own to ensure social stability and to promote economic development. At a time when mistrust of the central government intensified with each passing crisis, and the course of China's modernization was unsettled, there was a ready market for such an emblem: a symbol of progress and stability in an otherwise depressing era.

The appeal of any model, however, is not automatic. Models demand conscious promotion, the fourth element that characterizes all models. Tao Xingzhi, for instance, wrote extensively to propagandize his Xiaozhuang School. He also had powerful patrons such as Feng Yuxiang, a warlord in North China, to help extend the influence of his school.[11] James Yen was a polished public speaker and master promoter of his mass education program and rural reconstruction project in Ding county. His background as a Yale graduate gave him unique advantages in raising funds and gaining support from foreigners. Yen's success was inseparable from the many channels through which he and his colleagues publicized the Ding county model: organized tourism, greeting cards, traveling lecture teams, slide shows, soccer matches, village theaters, magazines, and press exposure by the journalist Edgar Snow, among others.[12] Liang Shuming and his associates, eager to restore traditional Chinese values, nevertheless adopted modern forums, such as newspapers, pamphlets, journals, and agricultural fairs to advertise their ideas.[13] In fact, Liang's reputation was itself a valuable commodity that drew attention and support for his experiment.[14]

The Nantong story especially illustrates how, in early twentieth-century China, using new commercial means to exhibit modernity and promote political images was taken for granted. First, there was the involvement of money. Money was behind virtually every major institution and event that gave Nantong positive public exposure—the Gengsu Theater, the conference of the Science Society of China, and celebrity banquets. However, before the allegations of bribery in Zhang Xiaoruo's campaign, no questions were raised about the possible connection between money and the model. Furthermore, advertising and the other forms of publicity we find in Nantong indicate that a certain degree of magnification of reality was accepted as a kind of licensed misrepresentation. Staged tourism and the cosmetic improvement of the city were similar to the packaging and advertising of commercial goods. Zhang Jian was a skilled showman, whose manipulation of this commercial culture and exhibitory modernity was extremely effective. Neither Chinese nor foreign observers appreciated that the Nantong model was not just a fact but also an image constructed through an intense advertising and publicity campaign. To them, the packaging was the substance—the signifier of modernity and progress was misconceived as modernity and progress itself. Of course, Zhang Jian's showmanship and flair for publicity should not obscure the fact that he made a genuine effort to improve conditions in the community, which is also true of the creators of other models elsewhere.

This promotional culture was in no way limited to model construction either. Urban renewal in Chengdu, for instance, was accompanied by a campaign launched by the city administrators.[15] The image of West Lake, the centerpiece of Hangzhou's tourist attractions, resulted from targeted advertising.[16] This culture was intensified in the 1930s and 1940s. Carlton Benson has provided an interesting case where consumerism was exploited not only in business, but also in culture and politics during the New Life movement, when Shanghai merchants and the Nationalist government competed for the public acceptance of their different visions of modernity.[17] David Strand has described a mayor of Lanzhou as a "local booster," who made ambitious plans to gain that interior city a modern reputation.[18] These stories are rich in their implications, but they all indicate the emergence of a market for a political and cultural image that represented the modern and progressive. Consumerism thereby became an interactive force not only in commerce and culture but also in politics. The transformation from material to exhibitory modernity in Nantong, though its story is unique in many ways, exemplifies this emerging trend in early twentieth-century China. Accordingly, Zhang Jian, as innovative as he was, was a figure of his time, rather than a figure out of time.

By way of a postscript, at this writing (March 2003), some of the matters I have touched on have been resolved and others continue to unfold. The Nantong library and museum have finally purchased computers, and the Center for Zhang Jian Studies now has a telephone.[19] The cultural workers lost the battle to preserve the old city temple; in its place there is now a townspeople's square (*shimin guangchang*). They did, however, win the battle on the fire and clock tower. The municipal People's Congress decided that the tower was to stay for both its historical significance and its commercial value as a tourist attraction. Today, its arched gate is closed, and two roads have been opened on either side for traffic. The tower itself has undergone a significant refurbishment, which included restoring Zhang Jian's original couplet. The deputy mayor to whom the retired teacher Ji Xiufu wrote letters of protest was found guilty of corruption and given a life sentence. The fate of Temple Street is pending. The residents have twice launched petition drives and sent the results to the municipal and provincial governments, arguing for the preservation of their homes, but a developer from Beijing is pushing hard for demolition. The new mayor, a graduate of the Chinese department at Nanjing University, is said to be sympathetic with the townspeople.[20] On my next trip, I expect to return to both a familiar and a changing city, whose appearance will continue to tell me stories, just as it did when I first arrived there a decade ago.

Notes

For complete authors' names, titles, and publishing data for works cited in short form in the Notes, see the Bibliography. The following abbreviations are used in both places.

CCWS   *Congchuan wenshi* (Culture and history of Congchuan). Nantong, 1992–.

DSNJ   *Dasheng fangzhi gongsi nianjian* (Chronicle of the Dasheng Textile Company). Nanjing, 1998.

DXQS   *Dasheng xitong qiyeshi* (A History of the Dasheng System Enterprises). Nanjing, 1990.

NSWSZL   *Nantong shi wenshi ziliao* (Material on the culture and history of Nantong city). Nantong, 1981–.

NTJG   *Nantong jingu* (Nantong past and present). Nantong, 1987–.

NTSH   *Nantong shihua* (Historical talk about Nantong). Nantong, 1983–85.

NTYW   Nantong yiwen (Anecdotes about Nantong). Nantong, 1962.

NXWSZL   *Nantong xian wenshi ziliao* (Material on the culture and history of Nantong County). Nantong, 1987–92.

SJCF   *Nantong shiye jiaoyu cishan fengjing fu canguan zhinan* (Nantong industry, education, philanthropy, scenery with a tour guide appendix). Shanghai, 1920.

INTRODUCTION

1. A note on romanization: I use pinyin throughout the book but have retained the older transliterations used in English works that predate the adoption of the pinyin system.

2. Sites 1918: 587, 588.

3. *The Science* (Shanghai) 7.9 (1922): 987.

4. Sites 1918: 587.

5. Chu 1965; Bastid 1988; Walker 1999.

6. P. Huang 1990: 119; Finnane 1993: 125; Barkan 1983: 13, 40; Honig 1989: 254.

7. Hayashi 1981; Nakai 1983; Fujioka 1985; Nozawa 1993.

8. Song Xishang 1963; Liu Housheng 1965; Li Hongru 1986.

9. For various examples of similar attempts at city planning elsewhere, see Esherick 2000.

10. According to Michael North, the term "public relations" was first used in the West in 1922 (1999: 8). It is not clear when the Chinese equivalent, *gonggong guanxi*, or *gongguan* for short, first appeared. But it is certain that the practice and concept existed long before the term appeared.

11. Some examples of this growing body of scholarly literature: Yeh 1995 and Shao 1997 on space and time; Cheng 1996 on the theater; Judge 1996 on print; Morris 1997 on sports; Thiriez 1998 on photography; L. Wang 2000 on tourism.

12. Beacham 1999.

13. Schneer 1999: 98–99.

14. Tenorio-Trillo 1996: 12.

15. Rydell 1984; Bennett 1995: 209–10.

16. Conn 1998: 14; Schneer 1999: 108.

17. According to E. Bradford Burns, some of the modernization programs that Latin American elites imported from Europe and the United States and imposed in their countries were merely "cosmetic" changes that brought "a veneer of progress" (1980: 14, 132).

18. Not by coincidence, the "high-modernist ideology" and grand schemes to rapidly transform society described by James Scott (1998) were more prominent in third-world countries.

19. Yeh 1997; Cochran 1999.

20. Rankin 1997.

21. Esherick 2000.

22. H. Lu 1999: 14–15.

23. Scott 1998.

CHAPTER 1

1. Cuthbertson 1975.

2. The description of Nantong's past is drawn from Su Zilong et al. 1985: 2–3, 6–7, 26–29.

3. *Nantongxian tuzhi* 1964, 1: 14.

4. Ibid., 9–10.

5. See Honig 1989: 254 for the causes of Jiangbei's decline in the 19th century.

6. Chu 1965: 17; Lin Jubai 1984: 5–10; Zhang Kaiyuan 1986: 51; Bastid 1988: 29.

7. Lin Jubai 1984: 23.

8. Ibid., 5–7. According to Emily Honig, approximately 80–90 percent of the women in the Nantong region wove cloth at home (1989: 259).

9. Lin Jubai 1984: 5–8, 28–29.

10. Ibid., 9–10.

11. *Nantongxian tuzhi* 1964, 2: 2–4.

12. Honig 1989: 255–57.

13. Bastid 1988: 33.

14. Zhang Jian's life and career are detailed in many works, including two in English: Chu 1965; and Bastid 1988. For Chinese studies, see Song Xishang 1963; Liu Housheng 1965; Zhang Xiaoruo 1965; and Zhang Kaiyuan 1986, 2000.

15. Zhang Kaiyuan 2000: 43–44, 54–60. See also Chu 1965: 8–9 on Zhang Pengnian's role in Zhang Jian's education.

16. For details on Zhang Jian's early career and the Korean crisis, see Chu 1965: chap. 2; and Zhang Kaiyuan 2000: 13–24, 56, 70, 96–97.

17. Zhang Kaiyuan 2000: 67–68, 73–77, 112–13.

18. Ibid., 73–87.

19. *DXQS* 1990: 93–95.

20. Walker 1999: 116–17.

21. *Nantongxian tuzhi* 1964, 9: 1–2, 5, 7.

22. Esherick & Rankin 1990: 314.

23. Zhang Kaiyuan 1986: 44–45. During the period under consideration, one yuan, or Chinese silver dollar, was worth roughly 0.72 tael and U.S.$ 0.49. Of course, the exchange rate fluctuated, and it sometimes differed from region to region.

24. Shao 1994 : 111–12

25. Zou Qiang 1962: 419.

26. *Nantongxian tuzhi* 1964, 19: 16.

27. Gu Wenqian 1988: 146–47; Ling Junyu 1992: 114–18.

28. The merchant and scholarly communities were not entirely separate, of course. Liu Yishan, for instance, was a friend of one of Zhang Jian's scholarly supporters, Zhou Jialu (Song Jianren 1991: 35).

29. *Nantongxian tuzhi* 1964, 19: 5; Gu Wenqian 1989: 68.

30. Song Jianren 1991: 35.

31. Ren Zhong 1988: 18. The famous artist Fan Zeng, who went into exile in Paris in 1991, is from this Fan family; he later returned and now teaches at Nankai University (personal communication, April 2002).

32. *Nantongxian tuzhi* 1964, 19: 16–17; Li Benyi 1989: 30. See also Bastid 1988: 166.

33. *Nantongxian tuzhi* 1964, 6: 6–7.

34. Ibid., 9: 7.

35. Rankin 1986: 204–5.

36. Guan Jingcheng 1982a: 78–79.

37. *Osaka Asahi Shimbun*, 30 May, 4 June, 11 June 1903.

38. Zhang Jian 1965: 3445–3509.

39. Fukuzawa 1960: 133–35.

40. Zhang Jian 1965: 3485.

41. Ibid., 3453–54

42. Ibid., 3464.

43. Zhang Kaiyuan 2000: 128–34.

44. Ibid., 173–74.

45. Ibid., 174–75. For brief biographies of Tang Shouqian, Zhao Fengchang, and Zheng Xiaoxu, see Bastid 1988: 169, 171.

46. The rising tide of violent actions organized by the revolutionaries also contributed importantly to the Qing court's move toward reform (Spence 1990: 261–63).

47. Zhang Kaiyuan 2000: 188–89, 193–202.

48. Ibid., 176.

49. Ibid., 192, 195–96. See also Judge 1996: 187 on the close relationship between the Shanghai media and the constitutionalists.

50. For a discussions of Village-ism, see also Zhang Kaiyuan 2000: 204–9.

51. Hayford 1990: 104. See also Wen-hsin Yeh's description of a bank clerk's romantic dream of having his office in rural China in the 1930s (1995: 117–18).

52. Alitto 1986.

53. Zhang Jian 1994, 1: 599.

54. Gluck 1985: 192–93.

55. Waters 1983.

56. Gluck 1985: 195–97.

57. Zhang Jian 1994, 4: 490.

58. Min 1989: 89–91.

59. Kuhn 1975: 262–64; Min 1989: 91–97, 139.

60. Zhang Jian 1994, 4: 74.

61. Ibid., 490.

62. On Yuan Shikai's reforms in Tianjin, see Spence 1990: 247–48.

63. Shao 1994: 247–49; Zhang Kaiyuan 2000: 209.

64. The discussion of the proposal to experiment with local self-government is based on *Nantong difang zizhi shijiunian zhi chengji* 1915, zizhi: 19–21.

65. *Nantongxian tuzhi* 1964, 16: 2–4.

66. *Nantong difang zizhi shijiunian zhi chengji* 1915, zizhi: 1.

67. Ibid., 2, 19, 55; *Nangtongxian tuzhi* 1964, 2: 2, 3: 6.

68. *Nantong difang zizhi shijiunian zhi chengji* 1915, zizhi: 19.

69. Zou Qiang 1962: 422; *Nantongxian tuzhi* 1964, 3: 6; Fei Fanjiu 1981: 140–41.

70. For examples of the new elites, see Shao 1994: 90–107.

71. *Nantongxian tuzhi* 1964, 17: 7; Guan Jingcheng 1981: 65–73.

72. *Nantong difang zizhi shijiunian zhi chengji* 1915, zizhi: 9–11.

73. Huang Xingqiao n.d.: 14.

74. *DXQS* 1990: chaps. 2–3.

75. *Tongzhou zhili zhouzhi* 1970: preface.

76. See details on the towns and markets in Shao 1994: 53–55.

77. *Nantongxian tuzhi* 1964, 1: 11–14. Around 1920, Nantong county was divided into 21 districts, of which three were identified as urban districts (*shiqu*), ten as town districts (*zhenqu*), and eight as rural districts (*xiangqu*; Ibid., 3–9). What distinguished city and town from village districts was population. Those

with 40,000 or more people were classified as city and town districts, and those with fewer as village districts (Yan Jizhong 1988: 195–96). The administrative seat of each district was naturally a city or a town. Each district included several other towns, plus the surrounding rural areas with a great number of rural markets. There were more than 40 towns and cities in Nantong in the 1920s (*Nantongxian tuzhi* 1964, 1: 3–9).

78. Jiang Bohan et al. 1987: 1–5.

79. *Nantongxian tuzhi* 1964, 6: 3; *SJCF* 1920: 15, 20, 28.

80. *Nantongxian tuzhi* 1964, 2: 8–9; *SJCF* 1920: 102b–c, 103.

81. Feng Ping 1990: 25–26.

82. *Tongzhou zhili zhouzhi* 1970, 5: 70–82. There was also an official examination hall (*shiyuan*), built in 1724, which saved Tongzhou students a trip to Yangzhou for prefectural examinations (Ibid., 66–68).

83. Bastid 1988: 33.

84. *Nantongxian tuzhi* 1964, 9.

85. *DXQS* 1990: 97–98; Liu Daorong 1990: 17.

86. *Nantongxian tuzhi* 1964, 10; Zhang Jian 1994, 4: 108–9.

87. Zhang Jian 1994, 3: 387.

88. Chu 1965: 77–83.

89. Ibid., 86.

90. Bastid 1988: 100.

91. Hayford 1990: 87.

92. Zhang Jian 1994, 2: 233.

93. *Nantong difang zizhi shijiunian zhi chengji* 1915, zizhi: 30.

94. Zhang Jian 1994, 1: 243.

95. This paragraph and the next are based on Yang Liqiang et al. 1987: 60, 64; and Fei Fanjiu 1962: 30–31.

96. Yang Liqiang et al. 1987: 145–46.

97. Ibid., 146.

98. Zhang Jian 1994, 4: 426.

99. Ibid., 439.

100. Ibid., 1: 600.

101. Ibid., 4: 120.

102. *Nantongxian tuzhi* 1964, 2: 1; Yang Liqiang et al. 1987: 121.

103. *Jiangsu jiaoyu jinwunian jian gaikuang* 1916, 1: 1, 15–16.

104. Ibid., 2: 17–18.

105. Ibid., 18.

106. Zhang Jian 1994, 4: 126, 201.

107. Ibid., 119.

108. Ibid., 1: 324, 458.

109. *Jiangsu jiaoyu jinwunian jian gaikuang* 1916, 2: 17, 18.

110. Qian Gongpu 1916: 29–30.

111. Ibid., 29.

112. Zhang Jian 1994, 4: 138.

113. Ibid., 286.

114. *SJCF* 1920: 66.
115. Zhang Jian 1994, 4: 424.
116. Ibid., 1: 334, 336.
117. Ibid., 4: 457.
118. Yang Liqiang et al. 1987: 129–30.
119. Zhang Jian 1994, 4: 120.
120. Yang Liqiang et al. 1987: 132; Zhang Jian 1994, 1: 450, 458.
121. Hayford 1990: 143.
122. Ibid., 143–44.
123. Yang Liqiang et al. 1987: 491–92.
124. Zhang Jian 1994, 4: 146.
125. Examples of Shanghai press reports on doings in Nantong: *Shenbao*, 14 May 1920, 16 Feb. 1925.
126. *Millard's Review* (Shanghai) 9.10 (9 Aug. 1919): 400.
127. Zhang Jian 1994, 4: 436.
128. *Nantongxian zizhihui baogaoshu* 1921, wenjia: 18, 19; Zhang Jian 1994, 4: 432, 436.
129. Zhang Jian 1994, 4: 467–68.
130. *Tonghai xinbao* (Nantong), 21 April 1924.
131. Xu Dongchang et al. 1989: 4.
132. *SJCF* 1920: unpaginated ads.
133. Zhang Jian 1994, 4: 431.
134. Ibid., 149.
135. Ibid., 163, 431.
136. Yang Guzhong 1987: 60–63.
137. Ibid.
138. Sites 1918: 592.
139. Zhang Jian 1994, 4: 458.
140. Chesneaux 1969.
141. *Nantong zazhi*, 1.1 (1920): 1–7, 1.3 (1920): 1–6.
142. Zhang Jian 1994, 4: 459.
143. Ibid., 458.
144. Ibid., 459.
145. *DXQS* 1990: 102–3.
146. Ibid., 101–2.
147. Ibid., passim.
148. Ibid., 101–2; Zou Qiang 1962: 409–10.
149. Zhang Jian 1994, 2: 416.
150. Ibid., 4: 444.
151. Ibid., 2: 416.
152. Ibid., 4: 149.
153. *SJCF* 1920.
154. Zhang Jian 1994, 2: 417.
155. Ibid., 4: 431, 460.
156. Ibid., 3: 804.

157. Ibid., 4: 428–29.

158. For instance, Kwauk Ser-zung, a Cornell graduate and then a professor at the Nantong Agricultural College, acted as an interpreter during Sites's visit (Sites 1918: 589).

159. Zhang Jian 1994, 4: 426.

160. Qiu Yuenzhang & Yao Qian 1991: 60.

161. Zhang Jian 1994, 4: 432–34.

162. Ibid., 467–68.

163. Zhao He 1994: 8.

164. Zhang Jian 1994, 4: 155; see also 4: 147.

165. Zhang Kaiyuan 1986: 44.

166. Zhang Jian 1994, 4: 25.

167. Ibid., 111.

168. Ibid., 110, 3: 804.

169. Some scholars have taken Zhang Jian's words at face value, especially concerning the origins of Dasheng. Samuel Chu, for instance, has concluded that for Zhang Jian, "business served as a means to attain the end of education" (1965: 89). But Marianne Bastid, among others, has doubts. In her opinion, Zhang Jian's idea of developing education and industry simultaneously was "imposed on his action after the fact" (1988: 23). The question of when Zhang Jian started to give equal importance to industry and education has also been a matter of debate among historians of the People's Republic. Cao Congpo, for instance, argues that Zhang later made up the story about the connection between the mill and the normal school. In fact, Cao believes that many of the early projects started as separate undertakings, and that only later did Zhang Jian present them as parts of a large agenda (1962: 33).

170. According to Zhang Jian, when he started the Dasheng project, of every ten people, six attacked him, three pitied him, and one approved of him; he put the number who actually helped him at fewer than one (1994, 3: 117).

171. Guan Jingcheng 1985: 215; Zhang Jian 1994, 5b: 113.

172. Zhang Jian 1994, 2: 646.

173. Cuthbertson 1975: 2.

174. Ibid.

175. Sites 1918: 592.

176. Bastid 1988: 145.

CHAPTER 2

1. In her study of the French Revolution, Mona Ozouf illustrates how political arrangement involves orchestrating urban space to create specific power and images (1988: chap. 6). In his work on the "red city" of Limoges, John Merriman discusses how the city's appearance affected the views of visitors (1985: 80–81). Wen-hsin Yeh points out that the Bank of China's dormitory compounds were expected to contribute to "uniformity in thinking" (1995: 108).

2. Yao Qian 1995: 9–10.

3. *Nantongxian tuzhi* 1964, 2: 1; Yang Liqiang et al. 1987: 121.
4. Today the city of Nantong has ballooned to 8,000 sq. km.
5. Yao Qian 1995: 11.
6. Ji Xiufu 1991: 44–45.
7. Ji Xiufu 1987: 23, 36.
8. Sun Mo 1995: 60.
9. *SJCF* 1920: 66.
10. Dai Buzhou 1987: 10.
11. Yao Qian 1995: 10.
12. *SJCF* 1920: 54e.
13. Zhang Jian 1994, 4: 293–94.
14. Yao Qian 1995: 10.
15. Zhang Jian 1994, 4: 411, 413.
16. Yao Qian 1995: 15.
17. The description of the parks and their purposes is based on Zhang Jian 1994, 4: 410–13, 18; 5a: 176–77; and 5b: 212.
18. Yao Qian 1995: 16.
19. *The Science* (Shanghai), 7.9 (1922): 974.
20. Zhang Jian 1994, 6: 789, 798.
21. Yao Qian 1995: 12.
22. Youfei was part of the Dasheng enterprises, sponsored mainly by the Zhang brothers and other local elites. Taozhihua was built by one of Zhang Jian's relatives with capital he received as gift money from the Zhang brothers (*DXQS* 1990: 203, 209).
23. *SJCF* 1920: unpaginated ad.
24. Ibid.
25. Sun Mo 1995: 62–63.
26. Sun Zhixia & Sun Qu 1995a: 32–33.
27. Dong He 1992b: 47.
28. Miao Zizhong 1987: 197–200.
29. *SJCF* 1920: unpaginated ad.
30. Yao Qian 1995: 10.
31. *SJCF* 1920: unpaginated ads.
32. Ibid.: 102a; Yao Qian 1995: 12–14.
33. Sun Mo 1995: 54–62.
34. Yan Xuexi et al. 1996: 24.
35. Chen Zhuoru 1992: 45–46; Zhang Jian 1994, 4: 420.
36. Jiang Binghe 1986: 212–18.
37. Yao Zhenguo 1993: 8–9.
38. Jiang Ping 1988: 35. For a list of the textile school's graduates from 1912 to 1927, see *Nantong Fangzhi Gongxueyuan chuangjian qishiwu zhounian xiaoyouhui zonghui chengli jiniance* 1988: 71–80.
39. Yu Jitang 1997: 8.
40. Yao Qian 1995: 11.
41. Yu Lizi 1992: 52.

42. Yao Qian 1995: 12.
43. *DXQS* 1990: 66–67.
44. Yao Qian 1995: 9.
45. Yu Cheng 1993: 13–15.
46. *SJCF* 1920: 17.
47. Chun Cao 1991: 36–38.
48. Yu Jitang 1993: 20–21.
49. Sheng-yen 1991: 52–54; Yu Jitang 1993: 22, 24–25.
50. Yu Jitang 1992a: 24–25.
51. Sun Zhixia & Sun Qu 1995a: 32–33.
52. Zhang Jian 1994, 4: 567.
53. Fang Zhenghua 1990: 66.
54. Langshan was a traditional gathering point for beggar groups that made a living out of pilgrims' kindness (Sheng-yen 1991: 61).
55. Zhang Jian 1994, 4: 108.
56. Ibid., 108–9, 351.
57. *SJCF* 1920: 60–64; Fang Zhenghua 1990: 66.
58. For *Millard's Review*, the fact that "there [was] not a single beggar" in Nantong was one of Zhang Jian's achievements, 9.10 (9 Aug. 1919): 400.
59. Sheng-yen 1991: 54.
60. Zhang Jian 1994, 5a: 190.
61. Ibid., 4: 424.
62. Yu Fu 1992: 32–33; Zhang Jian 1994, 5a: 172, 177–78.
63. Zhang Jian 1994, 4: 421–23. The Guanyin temple in Langshan subsequently became known as a repository for precious Guanyin portraits. In the following years, other temples sent their portraits there for safekeeping (Ibid., 437–38, 470–71).
64. Ibid., 425.
65. Ibid., 424. See also Sheng-yen 1991: 59.
66. Yu Jitang 1992b: 140.
67. Sheng-yen 1991: 56–57. For more details on Langshan temples and monks and their relationships with Zhang Jian, see Ibid., 55–60. Master Sheng-yen of Temple Nongchan in Taibei is a Nantong native who began his Buddhist career in Langshan at fourteen years of age (ibid.: 2–3, 35–43).
68. Zhang Jian 1994, 1: 617–18.
69. Lang Cun 1997: 16–18.
70. Zhang Jian 1994, 4: 423–25.
71. Liu Shui 1987: 13.
72. Sun Zhixia & Sun Qu 1995b: 35.
73. Ibid., 35–36.
74. Sun Mo 1987: 41.
75. I thank Nathan Knobler for a reading on these three buildings.
76. Sites 1918: 592.
77. Nozawa 1993: 150, 153.
78. Chun Cao 1991: 37.

79. Chen Lanfang 1989: 74. See Shao 1986 for a study of the *minben* concept.
80. Chun Cao 1991: 36–38.
81. Zhang Jian 1965: 3267–77.
82. Chen Lanfang 1989: 74.
83. Zhang Jian 1994, 4: 270.
84. For a brief discussion of Wu Changshi in English, see Cotter 2001.
85. Ling Junyu 1995: 152–54.
86. Ibid., 154–55.
87. Zhang Jian 1994, 5a: 176–77.
88. Ling Junyu 1995: 154.
89. Ibid., 146–47.
90. Jin Chengyi 1995: 202.
91. Sheng-yen 1991: 59–60.
92. Ling Junyu 1995: 156–67.
93. *Nantong zazhi*, 1.1 (1920): 9.
94. Chun Cao 1992: 9–11 has a good collection of interesting couplets. See also Jin Chengyi 1995: 199–201.
95. Interview 5.
96. Chen Lanfang 1989; Jin Chengyi 1995. See also the debate between Ji Tang and Lang Cun on a couplet in *NTJG* 5 (1987): 17.
97. Bourdieu 1991: 23.
98. Sites 1918: 588–89.
99. *Millard's Review* (Shanghai), 9.10 (1919): 400.
100. All the material on Tsurumi's visit to Nantong is drawn from Nozawa 1993: 147–56.
101. Zhang Jian 1994, 4: 427–28.
102. Unless otherwise noted, the discussion of the 1922 Science Society convention is based on *The Science* (Shanghai) 7.9 (1922): 965–98.
103. Zhang Jian 1994, 4: 301.
104. For some unknown reason, despite the title, the various editions of the gazetteer in the Nantong Library had no maps at all.
105. Ozouf 1988: 159; Zerubavel 1985: 35.
106. Rosenthal 2000.
107. On traditional Chinese holidays and festivals, see Naquin 1994. For particulars on Nantong, see Xiao Feng 1992; and Bai Bing 1987.
108. On the symbolic meaning of the queue to the Chinese and the struggle surrounding it during the 1911 Revolution, see Harrison 2000: 20–21, 30–40.
109. Guan Jingcheng 1981: 4.
110. *Tonghai xinbao*, 10 Oct. 1912.
111. Ibid., 11, 13 May 1913.
112. Ibid., 14 Oct. 1918.
113. Landes 1983: 47–49.
114. Sun Mo 1991: 20–21.
115. Yeh 1995: 101.

116. *Dasheng shachang gongren shenghuo de diaocha* 1994: 26.
117. Ibid., 30–31, 38, 101.
118. Chen Bingsheng 1989: 73.
119. Thompson, as cited in T. Smith 1988: 200.
120. Bartky 2000: 19–21.
121. Merriman 1985: 81.
122. Sun Mo 1991: 20–22.
123. Bartky 2000: chap. 4.
124. Sun Mo 1991: 21.
125. Sun Mo 1987: 41.
126. Nowotny 1994: chap. 1. See also Bartky 2000: 33.
127. Feng Ping 1990: 25. On the development of the telegraph in China generally, see Baark 1997.
128. For examples of Zhang Jian's telegraph messages during the Qing-Republican transition, see Zhang Jian 1994, 5: 144–45, 162, 174, 177.
129. Ibid., 4: 322.
130. Huang Ran 1987: 68–69.
131. For discussions of the inequities created by modern communications, see Nowotny 1994: chap. 1.
132. I do not mean to suggest here that ancient Chinese placed no value on time. See Needham 1981: 107 on how the traditional Chinese concept of time represented an "organic naturalism which invariably accepted the reality and importance of time."
133. Sun Zhixia 1981: 83.
134. Ji Tianfu 1981: 85–89.
135. On such developments elsewhere in China, see Borthwick 1983: 130, 132; and Bailey 1990: 199.
136. Zhang Jian 1994, 6: 665–822.
137. Nantong dianshang gonghui 1928: 4–5.
138. Landes 1983: 59–60, 71.
139. Rosenthal 2000.
140. Sun Mo 1991: 29.
141. *SJCF* 1920: 67.
142. Zhu Jianzhang 1989: 220–21.
143. Nozawa 1993: 152.
144. *Jingju gaige de xianqu* 1982: 144–45.
145. Chang Shou 1987: 59.
146. Zhang Jian 1994, 4: 418.
147. Ibid., 340.
148. Ibid., 340–41.
149. Ibid., 462–63.
150. Ibid., 359.
151. Ibid., 24–25.
152. Cao Zhendong 1987: 38.
153. Yang Liqiang et al. 1987: 195–96.

154. Zhang Jian 1994, 4: 466–67.
155. Ibid., 411.
156. Nowotny 1994: 105.

CHAPTER 3

1. Eisenstein 1979: 684.
2. See Eisenstein 1979; Marker 1985; Chartier 1987; Habermas 1993; and especially Dudley 1991: chap. 5 on the relationship between a new print-based information network and the birth of the first modern nation-state in Europe.
3. Darnton & Roche 1989: xiii.
4. Cohn 1997: 8.
5. Zhou Yu 1993: 434.
6. About 120 Chinese newspapers were founded between 1895 and 1898, of which 80 percent were operated by the Chinese, mainly the reformers (Fang Hanqi 1986: 539).
7. Ibid., 559.
8. P. Clark 2000; Sang Bing 1995. See also Schoppa 1995: 23.
9. For a general account of the constitutionalists' and the revolutionaries' publishing activities between 1900 and 1911, see Fang Hanqi 1986: 669–754.
10. Zhou Yu 1993: 434. Even some commercial newspapers in overseas Chinese communities were gradually politicized with the penetration of reformers and revolutionaries from China (Fang Hanqi 1986: 668).
11. Fang Hanqi 1986: 392–93.
12. During the early 1910s, *Minbao*, the official voice of the Revolutionary Alliance (Tongmeng hui), often published its editorial pieces under the pen name Minyi—People's Will or Opinion (Ibid., 820). To reach the majority of the Chinese population, newspapers started publishing in the vernacular as early as 1876, and there were more than 200 such newspapers between 1876 and 1919. Some targeted readers with only two years of schooling (Ibid., 784).
13. Ibid., 527–28.
14. Yang Liqiang et al. 1987: 8.
15. Ibid., 8–10.
16. Ibid., 9–10. See also Reynolds 1993: 187.
17. Zhang Jian 1994, 1: 555.
18. Zhang Caifu 1991: 45.
19. For examples of Zhang Jian's writings in *Shenbao*, see Zhang Jian 1994, 1: 465–66, 509–10, 556.
20. Fang Hanqi 1986: 776.
21. Zhang Jian 1994, 1: 642–45.
22. Ibid., 4: 135.
23. Ibid., 1: 460–61, 468, 488–89, 532–35.
24. *Tongzhou xingban shiye zhangcheng* 1905, Hanmolin: 1.
25. *Nantongxian tuzhi* 1964, 6: 3. "Hanmo" literally means brush and ink and

is extended to refer to writing, painting, or calligraphy; "lin" means forest and can be extended to mean richness and productiveness.

26. *DXQS* 1990: 97–98.

27. Zhang Jian 1994, 3: 748–54. People could also put their own books on sale at Hanmolin bookstores (*Tonghai xinbo*, 20 March 1913).

28. Zhang Jian 1994, 3: 749; Liu Daorong 1990: 19.

29. Liu Daorong 1990: 18–19.

30. A complete record of Hanmolin publications is not available because the publishing house, from its printing machines to records of all its publications to date, was ruined during the Japanese occupation of Nantong in 1937 (ibid., 20).

31. For instance, the *Documents of Industrial Development in Tongzhou* was anonymously published in 1905, but it was later included in the *Nine Records of Zhang Jian*.

32. Guan Jingcheng 1962: 29.

33. Ibid.

34. Yang Liqiang et al. 1987: 64.

35. Fei Fanjiu 1962: 30.

36. The account of Zhang Jian's activities in connection with the *Achievements* is based on Yang Liqiang et al. 1987: 60, 64, 68–69, 79.

37. For instance, whereas the old people's home claimed four pages of text and three tables, the Nantong County Hospital was covered in a mere 12 lines and a blueprint (*Nantong difang zizhi shijiunian zhi chengji* 1915, cishan: 23–27, 35). Both Zhang Jian and Zhang Cha were aware of the uneven quality of the work (Yang Liqiang et al. 1987: 79).

38. Fei Fanjiu 1962: 31.

39. Zhang Jian 1994, 4: 197.

40. *Nantong difang zizhi shijiunian zhi chengji* 1915, cishan: 26.

41. Ibid., cishan. The pagination of the book is inconsistent, and maps and blueprints are not numbered. They are cited by their sections.

42. Ibid., cishan: 35.

43. Of the 17 documents listed under this section, 10 were about erosion. They included reports on erosion damage and proposals of erosion protection by various Chinese and foreign experts, tables of land lost to flood, and budgets for water control (ibid., zizhi).

44. For details on flood damage and state-local tension over erosion protection in Nantong, see Shao 1994: 202–8.

45. *Nantong difang zizhi shijiunian zhi chengji* 1915, zizhi: 97–104; Xu Jingchang 1991: 22–23.

46. Zhang Jian's 1920 report on erosion protection in Nantong contained some sharp criticism of the central and provincial governments for ignoring the damage of floods (1994, 4: 446).

47. Geertz 1980: 68–77; Perdue 1987: 171, 174.

48. The survey for the Tong-Hai Reclamation Company in 1901 was conducted by experts from outside of Nantong (Chu 1965: 117).

49. *Nantong difang zizhi shijiunian zhi chengji* 1915, zizhi: 20–26.
50. Ibid., 28.
51. Ibid., 55.
52. Ibid., 60–62.
53. Zhang Jian 1994, 4: 493.
54. Ibid., 2: 431.
55. Ibid., 5: 173–74.
56. Ibid., 170–71, 175.
57. *Nantongxian tuzhi* 1964, 2: 5–6.
58. Zhang Jian 1994, 4: 203.
59. According to a catalogue in the Nantong Library, the Hanmolin publications during this period included titles such as *A History of the Tong-Hai Land Reclamation Company in the Past Decade* (1911), *Nantong County's First Higher Primary School in the Past Fifteen Years* (1920), and *A General Account of the Nantong County Women's Normal School in the Past Decade* (1926).
60. The compilation of local gazetteers (*difangzhi*) was an officially sponsored, continuous undertaking in imperial China. About 7,500 of them have survived (Wilkinson 1973: 114).
61. Sha Jincheng 1990: 50
62. Liu Daorong 1991: 45; Yang Naiqi 1998: 11.
63. Yang Naiqi 1998: 11–12.
64. On Zhang Jian's subtle criticism of Fan Kai, see *Nantongxian tuzhi* 1964, 24: 1.
65. Liu Daorong 1991: 45.
66. For instance, *Nantongbao* published installments of the chapter on the biographies of women during February 1920.
67. In 1964, the Nantong Library reprinted the 1922 edition without any maps. The maps, more than 100 of them, were discovered in the 1980s and are now kept in the Nantong Library (Liu Daorong 1991: 45).
68. This shift away from personal biographies occurred in other historical works as well, representing a new trend in late 19th- and early 20th-century Chinese history writing (Wang Rongsheng 2002).
69. *Nantongxian zuzhi* 1964, 24: 3.
70. Ibid., 2: 1.
71. Ibid., 6: 1.
72. The book title is written in both Chinese and English. The English title does not include the phrase "with a tour guide appendix."
73. Interview 4.
74. *Xinyou suyihui ranxilu* 1922, 4: 97–98.
75. Porter 2000: 30.
76. *SJCF* 1920: 71.
77. Ibid.: preface.
78. Naquin 2000: 690–91. Naquin mentions that such books were published, for instance, by the Commercial Press in Shanghai, which also happened to be the publisher of the *SJCF*.

79. The Chinese title of the *SJCF* indicates it has a tour guide as an appendix, but that idea was apparently dropped at some point in favor of a separate publication. One of Hanmolin's advertisements for the book stated that a Nantong tour guide would be given as a bonus to those who purchased the book (*Nantongbao*, 1 Nov. 1926).

80. *SJCF* 1920: 7.

81. Ibid., 8a.

82. Ibid., 9.

83. Ibid., 15.

84. Ibid., 16–36.

85. Ibid., 58a.

86. Ibid., 58b.

87. Ibid., 68–76.

88. Ibid., 69, 72.

89. Ibid., 66. The reason the jail was included in this section was that the jobs assigned to criminals, such as knitting, weaving, and soap making, as the caption pointed out, were considered a way to educate them.

90. Ibid., 32a, 107.

91. On Nantong teahouses, see Shao 1998. See also Xu Haiping 1992: 35–36.

92. *SJCF* 1920: 37, 48.

93. Ibid., 15.

94. Ibid., 15, 66, 102a.

95. Ibid., 36. On China's exhibition at the fair, see Rydell 1984: 228–29.

96. *SJCF* 1920: 15, 37. The money unit used in the book was inconsistent. Taels, yuan, and dollars were all cited at various points.

97. Ibid., 5.

98. Ibid., 46a–c.

99. Zhao Zongpu 1990: 37–38.

100. *Nantong daxue chengli jinian kan* 1928: 23–24, 31–32, 36, 39; Yu Lizi 1995: 196.

101. *SJCF* 1920: unpaginated ads.

102. Scholars in Nantong have an established list of important publications that they consider to have best documented the Nantong of the day; it does not include the *SJCF* (Guan Jingcheng 1962: 29–30).

103. For an insightful discussion of the significance of the photograph in the European context, see North 1999: 107–19.

104. Ibid., 110–19; Borthwick 1983: 138. For information on the development of photography and on foreign photographers in China in the late 19th century, see Thiriez 1998.

105. *Tonghai xinbao*, 11 May 1913.

106. Zhang Jian 1994, 4: 540–41.

107. Ibid., 1: 445, 452–53, 565.

108. Ibid., 4: 538. In a 1914 letter to a foreigner, Zhang noted that his picture was enclosed (Yang Liqiang et al. 1987: 63).

109. Thiriez 1998: 120–21.

110. Mukerji 1983: x.

111. A copy of the *SJCF* in one of the American university libraries, for instance, was inscribed "J. W. Chang" to his "Dear Comrade."

112. Zhang Jian 1994, 1: 565, 566.

113. Guan Jingcheng 1983: 11–12.

114. Liu Daorong 1990: 19–20.

115. Guan Jingcheng 1983: 12–13.

116. Ibid., 13–14.

117. Ibid., 25, 27.

118. Guan Jingcheng 1983: 25–28; Zhang Caifu 1991: 46.

119. See *Nantong zazhi* 1920, 1: 1, 2, 3.

120. See, for example, *Nantongbao*, 1 Nov. 1926.

121. Guan Jingcheng 1983: 25–28. After Zhang Xiaoruo's death in 1935, *Nantongbao* became an organ of the county Educational Association (Guan Jingcheng 1983: 27).

122. Ibid., 18. See also *Nantongxian tuzhi* 1964, 2: 3.

123. Guan Jingcheng 1983: 18.

124. Ibid., 18–19, 22.

125. *Tonghai xinbao*, 18 March 1913.

126. Shao 1991: 37–40.

127. For a discussion of the May Thirtieth Incident, see Spence 1990: 340–41.

128. Guan Jingcheng 1983: 22–23.

129. Ibid., 18, 21, 23.

130. Ibid., 22.

131. At the time, Zhang Xiaoruo was being considered for the position of ambassador to Chile (*Tonghai xinbao*, 21 April 1924).

132. Guan Jingcheng 1983: 19.

133. All the information on the Nantong film companies comes from Zhang Ziqiang 1992: 110–13.

134. For instance, the company hired an American photographer. He alone cost $600 a month in salary, plus room and board.

135. *Nantong daxue chengli jinian kan* 1928.

136. Xu Dongchang et al. 1987: 4.

137. Xu Haiping 1981: 99.

138. Zhang Jian 1994, 1: 578.

139. *Xinyou suyihui ranxilu* 1922, 2: 40.

140. Zhang Jian 1994, 1: 563, 578.

141. *Tonghai xinbao*, 17 May 1913; *Nantongbao*, 1 Nov. 1926.

142. *Gongyuan ribao*, 1, 28 Jan. 1920.

143. Guan Jingcheng 1983: 18–19.

144. Borthwick 1983: 122–23.

145. Bailey 1990: 196, 205.

146. Interview 4.

147. *Tonghai xinbao,* 9 Nov. 1918, 13 Dec. 1919.
148. Eisenstein 1979: xiii.
149. Lin Jubai 1962: 28–29.
150. Grierson 1975: 3–4.
151. Ibid., 5.
152. Chartier 1994: viii.
153. For a concise discussion of the role of the author and his/her relationship with the text, see ibid.: chap. 2.

CHAPTER 4

1. Habermas 1993.
2. McClellan 1999: 8.
3. Ibid., 200.
4. Buckingham 1973 [1849]: 25.
5. Among the most notable of the 19th-century world fairs were the Great Exhibition of 1851, the Philadelphia Centennial Exposition of 1876, the Melbourne International Exhibition of 1888, and the Chicago World's Columbian Exhibition of 1893. Many left lasting monuments, like the Eiffel Tower, erected for the 1889 Paris International Exposition. For more information on these fairs, see Rydell 1984; and Bennett 1995.
6. Tenorio-Trillo 1996.
7. Dong He 1992a: 41; *Jiangsu jiaoyu jinwunian jian gaikuang* 1916, 1: 19–20.
8. *SJCF* 1920: 36; Rydell 1984: 30, 228–29.
9. Dong He 1992a: 41; *Jiangsu jiaoyu jinwunian jian gaikuang* 1916, 1: 19–20.
10. Dong He 1992a: 41.
11. Geertz 1983: 124.
12. Zhang Jian 1994, 6: 483, 508, 512.
13. Ibid., 4: 272–77.
14. See Bailey 1990: 204.
15. Unless otherwise indicated, the discussion of Zhang's proposal is based on Zhang Jian 1994, 4: 272–77.
16. McClellan 1999: 49, 50.
17. Bennett 1995: 213.
18. For a study of the impact of fin-de-siècle thought in China, see L. Sun 1996.
19. For discussions of the views of the European cultural reformers, see Bennett 1995: 21; and McClellan 1999: 8.
20. McClellan 1999: 9.
21. Zhang Jian 1994, 4: 275.
22. The museum was planned from the start as a separate institution from the Nantong Library. By the time the library was created, in 1912, the idea of a public library had gained currency throughout China, and most provincial capitals had public libraries by 1914 (Bailey 1990: 204). Converted from a declining

temple, the library occupied seven mu of land south of the Hao River near the museum. It was open daily except for Tuesdays. Borrowing privileges were granted to anyone who had a reference letter and paid a small fee (*SJCF* 1920: 55–57; Xu Hui 1993: 33).

23. Sun Qu 1982: 108–9.

24. Ibid., 109; Mu Xuan 1998a: 210.

25. The more formal observatory atop Junshan was not built till 1916 (*SJCF* 1920: 98–99).

26. Ibid., 68–76; Huang Ran 1995: 140–41.

27. Sun Qu 1982: 111–12.

28. Ibid., 109.

29. Zhang Jian 1994, 4: 278, 285.

30. Huang Ran 1995: 143.

31. For a discussion of the differences between ancient and modern museums, see Bennett 1995: 2–3.

32. Conn 1998: 21; Bennett 1995: 2.

33. According to Andrew McClellan, Alexandre Lenoir's catalogues for the Museum of French Monuments in the late 18th and early 19th centuries were the forerunner of the modern museum catalogue (1999: 192).

34. Sun Qu 1982: 114. A supplemental catalogue of the Nantong Museum was published in 1933 (ibid.).

35. Ibid., 107, 115.

36. *Nantong Bowuyuan wenxianji* 1985: 43.

37. Sun Qu 1982: 120–21.

38. *DXQS* 1990: 214; *Nantongxian tuzhi* 1964, 9: 7; *Jiangsu jiaoyu jinwunian jian gaikuang* 1916, 2: 17.

39. *Nantong Bowuyuan wenxianji* 1985: 36.

40. Zhang Jian 1994, 4: 284.

41. *Nantong Bowuyuan wenxianji* 1985: 36.

42. Ibid.

43. Sun Qu 1982: 119.

44. *Nantong Bowuyuan wenxianji* 1985: 37–38.

45. One exception was made for the normal school faculty in case they needed to take their classes to the museum for teaching purposes.

46. See Bailey 1990: 205.

47. Bennett 1995: 6–7, 48–58.

48. McClellan 1999: 9–10.

49. Bennett 1995: 8.

50. Sun Qu 1982: 121.

51. Bennett 1995: 7.

52. Sun Qu 1982: 112–13.

53. Ibid.

54. McClellan 1999: 191–92.

55. Zhang Jian 1994, 4: 283–84.

56. Ibid., 284.

57. See Helms 1993, especially chap. 7.

58. Sun Qu 1982: 114–15.

59. Saddened by the death of his sons, as well as that of Zhang Jian, and disillusioned by the fight between the GMD and the CCP, Kim Changkang committed suicide after the April Twelfth Incident of 1927 (Yu Lizi 1988: 25).

60. Sun Mo 1988: 23.

61. Ibid., 21–23.

62. Chen once wrote a satirical poem about one of Zhang Jian's villas (Guan Jingcheng 1985: 218).

63. Sun Mo 1988: 23.

64. Zhu Ronghua 1987: 52.

65. Ibid., 52–53.

66. Ibid., 53–54.

67. Zhang Jian 1994, 4: 120.

68. Mu Xuan 1985: 11.

69. Ibid., 8.

70. Sun Qu 1982: 114; Mu Xuan 1985: 12; Sun Mo 1988: 23; Huang Ran 1995: 142.

71. Kwok 1965: 3.

72. M. Smith 1983: 182. See also M. Smith 1993.

73. Sun Qu 1982: 111.

74. Uchiyama 1960: 65.

75. Sites 1918: 591–92.

76. See the *New York Times* story about how the Massachusetts Museum of Contemporary Art served as an economic catalyst for the declining mill town of North Adams in the 1990s (Kifner 2000: A14).

77. Mu Xuan 1998a: 210.

78. *Jiangsu jiaoyu jinwunian jian gaikuang* 1916, 2: 17.

79. Lü Jimin 1996: 885.

80. Zhang Jian 1994, 4: 275.

81. Conn 1998: 10.

82. For instance, after the completion of the No. 1 mill, Zhang Jian had an artist make a number of satirical drawings to expose six people who had opposed his effort to build the factory. Those paintings were prominently hung in the Dasheng general office (*DXQS* 1990: 17).

83. Bastid 1988: 266.

84. *Nantongxian tuzhi* 1964, 9: 5.

85. Zhang Jian 1994, 4: 147.

86. Zhang Weibin & Zhu Pei 1988: 40.

87. *Jiangsu jiaoyu jinwunian jian gaikuang* 1916, 2: 19–20.

88. Borthwick 1983: 135–36.

89. See Borthwick 1983; Bastid 1988; and Bailey 1990.

90. Borthwick 1983: 138.

91. Ibid., 139.

92. *Tonghai xinbao*, 5, 13, 21 Nov. 1918, 18 April 1924.

93. Ibid., 7 May 1913.

94. The Empress Dowager's birthday in 1907, for instance, was celebrated with a school sports event, which was reported under the headline "Progress Among the People" (Borthwick 1983: 138–39).

95. According to Sally Borthwick, in 1903, one of Zhang Zhidong's new schools in Wuchang held the first organized school sports day in China (1983: 138).

96. The 1921 soccer match between the Nantong middle schools and the Shanghai Railroad team was the first game in which an outside team was involved. Soccer or ball games of any kind were still quite new in Nantong. Though the Nantong team lost, the game stirred much excitement about the new ball games (Li Danren 1982: 148).

97. *Jiangsu jiaoyu jinwunian jian gaikuang* 1916, 1: 18.

98. *Nantong jiaoyu nianjian* 1926: 1.

99. Sun Mo 1993: 16.

100. *Nantong jiaoyu nianjian* 1926: 1–2.

101. Sun Mo 1993: 17. At the time it was not unique for officials and local elites to participate in school sports as a token of support (Borthwick 1983: 138).

102. Yang Liqiang et al. 1987: 195–96.

103. Zhang Jian 1994, 4: 148–49.

104. Ibid., 173.

105. Li Danren 1982: 147–48.

106. The figures on the participants in the 1919 meet are from *SJCF* 1920: 54e. I doubt that these numbers are accurate, since the book was published exclusively to boost Nantong's success. As noted in Chap. 3, it tended to exaggerate things.

107. Yin Weilun 1989: 209–10.

108. Bastid 1988: 78–79, 151.

109. Ibid., 149.

110. Ibid., 149–51.

111. Chang Shou 1989: 23.

112. Borthwick 1983: 136; Bailey 1990: 192.

113. *Tonghai xinbao*, 11 May 1913.

114. Zhang Jian 1994, 5b: 135–36, 166, 251, 268, 271, 297. Zhang Jian wrote other songs, and even drafted two national anthems; one, composed in 1913, was written at the invitation of the Ministry of Education (ibid., 135, 166, 211). On the conservatives' concern about singing and dancing as a school activity, see Borthwick 1983: 136.

115. Zhang Jian 1994, 5b: 136.

116. Ibid., 166.

117. Ibid., 6: 600, 869.

118. Sun Mo 1993: 16–17.

119. Yang Liqiang et al. 1987: 598–99.

120. Yin Weilun 1989: 209–10.

121. A few Nantong athletes participated in the Third National Games held in Wuchang in 1925 and in the Sixth and Seventh Far East games in 1923 and 1925 (Sun Mo 1993: 17–18).

122. Holt 1981.

123. Yang Liqiang et al. 1987: 598.

124. Known as a promoter of modern sports, Zhang Jian was appointed to be one of the two committee chairmen for the Fifth Far East Games held in Shanghai in 1921 (Sun Mo 1993: 16–17).

125. MacClancy 1996: 2.

126. Strand 1997: 21.

127. Harrison 2000: 9; Strand 1997.

128. Chow 1960: 191–93; Bailey 1990: 194–200.

129. *Jiangsu jiaoyu jinwunian jian gaikuang* 1916, 1: 11.

130. Ibid., 19.

131. *Nantongxian tuzhi* 1964, 9: 21, 24.

132. Chauncey 1992.

133. *Nantongxian tuzhi* 1964, 9: 21, 24.

134. Ibid., 23.

135. *Nantong jiaoyu nianjian* 1926: 4.

136. *Nantongxian tuzhi* 1964, 9: 23.

137. Ibid.

138. *Nantong jiaoyu nianjian* 1926: 4.

139. *Nantongxian tuzhi* 1964, 9: 5.

140. Ji Nengjin 1992: 20.

141. Lang Cun 1995: 224–26.

142. Ibid., 229–31.

143. Li Danren 1982: 149.

144. Bastid 1988: 64–65.

145. Zhang Jian 1994, 4: 114.

146. Li Danren 1982: 149.

147. Zhang Jian 1994, 4: 25.

148. Ibid., 24–29.

149. Ibid., 110.

150. Ibid., 108–9.

151. On Zhang Jian's detachment from the Qing before the 1911 Revolution, see Bastid 1988: 146–47.

152. Ibid., 140–43.

153. Zhang Jian 1994, 4: 147.

154. Edward T. Channing, as cited in G. Clark & Halloran 1993: 17.

155. Zhang Jian 1994, 4: 213.

156. Ibid., 187–190, 213–18.

157. Ibid., 212.

158. *Ershinianlai zhi Nantong* 1930: 49.

159. Dewey & Dewey 1920: 150. Referring to those returned students, Dewey said, "If and when China gets on its feet, the American university will have a fair share of the glory to its credit" (ibid.).

160. Chow 1960: 192–93.

161. Dewey 1964: 162.

162. According to Zhang Jian, the Nantong educational community (*jie*) invited Dewey to visit (1994, 4: 163).

163. Yu Lizi 1992: 52.

164. Zhang Jian 1994, 4: 163–64.

165. *Jingju gaige de xianqu* 1982: 162.

166. Yu Lizi 1992: 52.

167. Dewey 1964: 166.

168. For a brief intellectual biography of Huang Yanpei, see Bastid 1988: 264.

169. Lu Bosheng 1991: 12.

170. *Nantong zazhi*, 1.3 (1921): 1, 5.

171. *The Science* (Shanghai) 7.9 (1922): 986–89.

172. Bailey 1990: 186–90.

173. Zhang Jian 1994, 4: 289.

174. Ibid., 289–90, 292.

175. *Jingju gaige de xianqu* 1982: 65–67.

176. Ouyang 1984: 463–64.

177. Ibid., 463; Ouyang 1990, 6: 5.

178. For a long time, Ouyang did not let his family know his work. Some of his relatives, upon learning of Ouyang's career, thought that he was "finished." His wife was the only one in the family who understood Ouyang's interest in theater, but she still considered scholarly activities the priority (Ouyang 1990, 6: 32, 62).

179. Howard 1994: 48.

180. Ouyang 1990, 6: 49.

181. Barish 1981: 450.

182. *Jingju gaige de xianqu* 1982: 11–13.

183. Ibid., 11–14.

184. It is impossible to give "avant-garde," a historical term, an absolute definition. I use it here to refer to intellectuals and artists who are more advanced in such qualities as strong individual consciousness, pursuit of newness rather than tradition, and pursuit of aesthetics rather than commercialism. Avant-garde can also be politically and socially radical (see Pronko 1962: 1–4; and Calinescu 1987: 95–125).

185. *Jingju gaige de xianqu* 1982: 12.

186. Ouyang 1990, 6: 28–33.

187. *Jingju gaige de xianqu* 1982: 15, 19.

188. Ouyang 1990, 6: 28.

189. *Jingju gaige de xianqu* 1982: 14.

190. Ibid., 66–69.

191. Ibid.

192. Ibid., 90.
193. Ibid., 67–70.
194. Ibid., 141.
195. Ibid., 63.
196. Ibid., 30.
197. X. Chen 1995: 137–38.
198. *Jingju gaige de xianqu* 1982: 68.
199. Ibid., 34.
200. Ibid., 57.
201. Ibid., 101–3.
202. Ibid., 104–5.
203. Ibid., 105–6, 176.
204. Ibid., 143.
205. Mei Lanfang 1987: 304.
206. *Jingju gaige de xianqu* 1982: 106.
207. For details on the Gengsu's ticket prices, see Ibid., 134–35.
208. Ibid., 101, 109.
209. Tang Xuejiao 1988: 25. See also Zhao Dan 1980: 4–9. Zhao was one of the brightest screen stars of China, and first became interested in the theater while growing up in Nantong.
210. *Jingju gaige de xianqu* 1982: 96.
211. In a 1921 letter to Ouyang, Zhang Jian seemed to understand that the situation in Nantong was discouraging to Ouyang, but to Zhang, it was only because of "the year's flooding that slowed down everything," and he tried to persuade Ouyang to stay for the sake of "art" (Yang Liqing et al. 1987: 338–39).
212. Ouyang wrote the autobiography in 1929 after he became associated with some of the more radical dramatists and drama organizations. His view of Zhang Jian was colored by his newly developed "class consciousness," and he was especially disgusted by Zhang Jian's criticism of the workers and students during the May Thirtieth movement (*Jingju gaige de xianqu* 1982: 162–63).
213. Ibid., 70–71.
214. Ibid., 157–58.
215. For details on Ouyang's personal and professional conflicts, see Shao 1996: 53–54.
216. *Jingju gaige de xianqu* 1982: 110.
217. Ouyang 1990, 6: 181; Hung 1994: 19.
218. Ouyang 1990, 6: 33, 62.
219. Ouyang 1984: 194–95.
220. Ibid., 224.
221. Schwarcz 1986: 148; Ouyang 1990, 6: 230–31.
222. *Jingju gaige de xianqu* 1982: 145–46.
223. Ibid., 110, 147.
224. Interview 1.
225. *Jingju gaige de xianqu* 1982: 73. For a brief discussion of Kunqu and its popularity, see Naquin & Rawski 1987: 61.

226. *Jingju gaige de xianqu* 1982: 110–11. Some people in Nantong still vividly remembered Ouyang and the excitement of watching Chinese opera in the Gengsu Theater, even the prices of the tickets and the seats they took, but had no recollection whatsoever about spoken drama. They were surprised when I mentioned spoken drama. "No, never was there any *huaju* [spoken drama], only *jingju* [Beijing opera]," one man said (interview 2).

227. *Jingju gaige de xianqu* 1982: 51.

228. Ibid., 95.

229. Ibid., 96.

230. Ibid., 139.

231. Ibid., 106–7; Guan Jingcheng 1983: 33.

232. *Jingju gaige de xianqu* 1982: 117, 142.

233. Zhang Jian 1994, 4: 466–67.

234. *Zhang Jian yu Mei Lanfang* 1999: 34.

235. Zhang Jian 1994, 4: 288–92.

236. Ibid., 288.

237. *Zhang Jian yu Mei Lanfang* 1999: 121, 124.

238. Ibid., 98–99.

239. Li Kangqi 1991: 32.

240. Ibid., 33.

241. One item Mei received was an embroidery of plum flowers (*meihua*, a flower with Mei Lanfang's surname) designed by Shen Shou (*Jingju gaige de xianqu* 1982: 195–96).

242. Ibid., 207.

243. Ibid., 148.

244. See *Gongyuan ribao*, 30 May 1920.

245. Li Kangqi 1991: 33–34.

246. Ji Tang 1989: 29–30.

247. Mei Lanfang 1987: 7, 21.

248. *Tonghai xinbao*, 18 Nov. 1916, 16 Nov. 1917, 1 Jan. 1919.

249. Zhang Jian 1994, 4: 292.

250. *Jingju gaige de xianqu* 1982: 197.

251. *Nantongbao*, 27 May 1920.

252. *Gongyuan ribao*, 21 Jan. 1920.

253. *Jingju gaige de xianqu* 1982: 195–97.

254. *Gongyuan ribao*, 20 Jan. 1920.

255. Ibid., 28 May 1920.

256. Ibid., 12–22 Jan. 1920.

257. Ibid., 28 May 1920.

258. Ibid., 4–11 Jan. 1920.

259. Ibid., 18, 21 Jan., 28 May 1920; *Tonghai xinbao*, 23 Jan. 1920.

260. *Nantongbao*, 2 Feb. 1920.

261. *Tonghai xinbao*, 13 Jan. 1920.

262. *Gongyuan ribao*, 22 Jan. 1920.

263. *Jingju gaige de xianqu* 1982: 195.

264. *Gongyuan ribao,* 20 Jan., 23 Feb. 1920.
265. Ibid., 21 Jan. 1920.
266. Li Kangqi 1991: 34.
267. *Jingju gaige de xianqu* 1982: 97.
268. Yang Guzhong 1987: 62.
269. Ibid.
270. *Jingju gaige de xianqu* 1982: 160.
271. Bailey 1990: chap. 5; Hayford 1990: 10.
272. Drama reform was also being experimented with in Shanxi, Hunan, and elsewhere in China (Ouyang 1990: 32–33, 104).
273. Zhang Jian 1994, 4: 458.

CHAPTER 5

1. Zhang Jian 1994, 3: 806.
2. Samuel Chu 1965: 33.
3. *DSNJ* 1998: 149–53, 161.
4. Ibid., 157.
5. Zhang Jian 1994, 4: 354–55.
6. *DSNJ* 1998: 4.
7. Ibid., 154.
8. *DXQS* 1990: 142.
9. *DSNJ* 1998: 4.
10. For examples of such enterprises, see *DXQS* 1990: 200–201.
11. Ibid., 144–48.
12. Ibid., 148, 151.
13. Zhang Jian 1994, 4: 468.
14. Komai 1982: 154–55.
15. *DXQS* 1990: 220.
16. Ibid., 180–82.
17. Ibid., 186–88.
18. *DSNJ* 1998: 169. For more information on Zhang Jian's land and salt reclamation activities, see Chu 1965: chap. 6.
19. Dewey 1964: 163.
20. *DXQS* 1990: 221–22.
21. Zhang Jian 1994, 3: 806–7.
22. *DSNJ* 1998: 168.
23. *DXQS* 1990: 222.
24. Zhang Jian 4: 166, 176, 185.
25. Ibid., 3: 113, 813.
26. Ibid., 4: 166.
27. Ibid., 464. Unless otherwise noted, this page is the source of the material in this and the next two paragraphs.
28. Ibid., 470.
29. *Tonghai xinbao* 17 Jan., 8 Sept. 1921.

30. *Jingju gaige de xianqu* 1982: 162.
31. Zhang Jian 1994, 4: 352–53, 360.
32. Ibid., 354–55.
33. Ibid., 443–45.
34. During this period, the advertising pages of newspapers in Shanghai were filled with information of various stock exchanges. For instance, *Shenbao* 11 Oct. 1921: 3 contains ads for 18 exchanges.
35. *DXQS* 1990: 195.
36. Yang Tong 1987: 8.
37. *DXQS* 1990: 196.
38. Zhang Jian 1994, 3: 808–9.
39. *DXQS* 1990: 198.
40. Zhang Jian 1994, 3: 809.
41. *DXQS* 1990: 198–99.
42. Zhang Jian 1994, 3: 811–12.
43. Xu Gengqi 1982: 55.
44. *DXQS* 1990: 199.
45. Zhang Jian 1994, 3: 812.
46. Yang Tong 1987: 9; *DXQS* 1990: 199.
47. Zhang Jian 1994, 1: 44–45, 47, 89–91.
48. Ibid., 2: 169–71.
49. Komai 1982: 145.
50. Zhang Jian 1994, 1: 165–68.
51. Ibid., 238–40.
52. Ibid., 3: 820–27.
53. Ibid., 4: 677, 679.
54. Komai 1982: 145–46.
55. Guan Jingcheng 1982c: 131–36.
56. Komai 1982: 143, 155.
57. Ibid., 143, 150–51.
58. Ibid., 175.
59. Zhang Jian 1994, 3: 825–26.
60. Guan Jingcheng 1982c: 139.
61. Zhang Jian 1994, 3: 803.
62. Ibid., 824–27.
63. Ibid., 4: 205–6.
64. *DXQS* 1990: 224.
65. Ibid., 226.
66. Sources do not indicate who first invited Li Shengbo to Nantong, but it was most likely someone in his father's bank, if not his father himself, who was concerned with the bank's investment in the Dasheng factory and wanted to have an expert evaluation of the situation.
67. Jiang Ping 1997: 6–8.
68. Li Shengbo 1983: 106–9.
69. Ibid., 109–12.

70. *DXQS* 1990: 248–49. For a brief history of the No. 1 mill after 1925, see Shao 1994: 370–73.

71. As in other aspects of Chinese life, nepotism was prevalent in the industrial sector, a practice that John Dewey saw as a common and "impossible burden" on China (1964: 162).

72. A changing of the guard was also seen in the political domain, especially in municipal governance, where traditional bureaucrats were replaced by specially trained experts in modern city planning (Shi Mingzheng 1992: 11).

73. Speculation was rife about the causes of Xiaoruo's murder, from personal revenge to assassination by gangsters. It remains a mystery to this day (Chang Zonghu 2000: 182–89).

74. Ibid., 190–91.

75. Zhang Jian 1994, 6: 857; Chang Zonghu 2000: 115.

76. Chang Zonghu 2000: 125.

77. The other three "Princes of the Republic" were the sons of Sun Zhongshan, Zhang Zuolin, and Duan Qirui, all prominent political figures of the early Republic (Guo Shilong 1995: 55).

78. Zhang Jian 1994, 6: 887; Chang Zonghu 2000: 133–34.

79. *SJCF* 1920: 9.

80. *Nantong zazhi*, 1.1 (1920): 8–9.

81. *SJCF* 1920.

82. Miao Zizhong 1987: 200.

83. Xu Gengqi 1982: 52.

84. Miao Zizhong 1987: 200.

85. *Xinyou suyihui ranxilu* 1922, 1: 2–3, 7.

86. Ibid., 1–4.

87. Ibid., 1.

88. Ibid., 2: 1–5.

89. Ibid., 1.

90. Ibid., 3: 1.

91. Ibid., 1: 16–17.

92. Ibid., 2: 39–40.

93. Ibid., 4.

94. Ibid., 37–39.

95. Ibid., 1: 7, 2: 1, 3.

96. Zhang Jian 1994, 1: 470.

97. *Xinyou suyihui ranxilu* 1922, 1: 2.

98. Ibid., 6, 9, 20.

99. Ibid., 1–2, 7.

100. Ibid., 6–7.

101. Ibid., 30.

102. Ibid., 2–3.

103. Ibid., 4: 69.

104. Ibid., 1: 2–3.

105. Ibid., 4: 1–2.

106. Ibid., 1: 46–47; Guan Jingcheng 1983: 26.
107. *Jingju gaige de xianqu* 1982: 162.
108. Zhang Jian 1994, 1: 462.
109. *Xinyou suyihui ranxilu* 1922, 3: 8.
110. Ibid., 1: 2–3.
111. Ibid., 21.
112. Ibid., 2: 5.
113. Ibid., 1: 15, 21, 2: 7.
114. Ibid., 1: 11.
115. Ibid., 40.
116. Ibid., 26–29.
117. Ibid., 22–29.
118. Ibid., 4: 3–29
119. Ibid., 1: 49–50.
120. Ibid., 4: 2.
121. Ibid., 1: 10, 4: 1.
122. Ibid., 4: 1.
123. Ibid., 1–2.
124. Ibid., 96–101.
125. Ibid., 2: 38–39.
126. Chang Zonghu 2000: 120, 147, 151.
127. Zhang Jian 1994, 1: 525.
128. Chang Zonghu 2000: 148–51.
129. Zhang Jian 1994, 1: 484–85.
130. Ibid., 462, 556.
131. Ibid., 495, 513. On Zhang Jian's rejection of other positions, see ibid., 579, 600.
132. A prime example of the press's unfriendly attitude toward the Zhang family is *Controversy of the 1921 Jiangsu Provincial Assembly Meeting* (*Xinyou suyihui ranxilu*). Published only six months after the election, it is a collection of hundreds of reports and news items about the election from various newspapers in the Jiangsu region. The contents are overwhelmingly against Zhang Xiaoruo.
133. Zhang Jian 1994, 1: 563, 582, 641.
134. Ibid., 582.
135. Ibid., 495.
136. Shao 1994: 98, 194–95.
137. For details of the May Fourth movement and its causes, see Spence 1990: 310–13.
138. Li Danren 1982: 146–47.
139. Chu 1965: 98.
140. Guan Jingcheng 1982a: 85.
141. Guan Jingcheng 1982b: 161–64.
142. Zhang Jian 1994, 1: 617–23, 4: 188.
143. Ibid., 4: 152, 156–57.

144. Ibid., 152, 157, 213.
145. Ibid., 155.
146. Ibid., 188, 211, 216–17.
147. Ibid., 163, 171, 213.
148. Ibid., 152–55, 212.
149. Ibid., 436.
150. Ibid., 161–62.
151. Ibid., 219–22.
152. Ibid., 221.
153. Ibid., 162, 211–12, 214, 217.
154. Guan Jingcheng 1982a: 84.
155. Zhonggong Nantong shiwei dangshi gongzuo weiyuanhui 1991: 8.
156. Barkan 1983: 461.
157. Zhonggong Nantong shiwei dangshi gongzuo weiyuanhui 1991: 9–10.
158. Ibid., 8–9.
159. Cao Hanchen 1987: 85.
160. Li Danren 1982: 157–59; Fei Xuehua 1992: 13–14.
161. Dou Zhijing 1984: 64–66.
162. Zhongong Nantong shiwei dangshi gongzuo weiyuanhui 1991: 8–10. For a brief discussion of Nantong during the war, see Shao 1994: 378, 386–88.
163. Yan Jizhong 1988: 196–97.
164. Guan Jingcheng n.d.a.: 2, 4–6. Local tyrants were the early targets of the Northern Expedition. That changed after the open split between the GMD and the CCP and the anti-Communist purge of April 1927 (Wilbur 1984: 65–68, 99–112).
165. Yan Jizhong 1988: 196–97.
166. Guan Jingcheng n.d.a.: 7; Wang Shiming 1987: 12.
167. For more information on the situation with Sun Chuanfang, see Wilbur 1984: 156–57.
168. Guan Jingcheng n.d.b.: 4–5.
169. Chang Zonghu 2000: 276.
170. *Nantongshi xingzheng niankan* 1929: 2.
171. Scott 1998: 4–6

CHAPTER 6

1. Le Goff 1992: 60.
2. In recent years the topic of memory has gained a certain primacy across disciplines. Much effort has been made to define the topic in terms of its own evolving history; its relationship to the field of history, to knowledge, to social and cultural identity, and to political power; its manifestation in actions, objects, and ideas; its transmission in the oral tradition and in written texts; its forms as collective, social, or individual; and its value as an objective or subjective reflection of the past (ibid., 51–99; Fentress & Wickham 1992; Halbwachs 1992). Though most works are consistent in their own arguments, a

well-defined and agreed-upon concept of memory remains as elusive as the past itself. In a sense, the abundance of literature on the topic almost threatens the possibility of a coherent understanding of it. This difficulty also betrays the complex nature of the topic, especially in the modern era, when every person is a potential memory maker and the use and abuse of memory are common practice. Here I treat memory as an ongoing dialogue between the present and the past that routinely takes place at various levels of consciousness in individuals, families, communities, and nations to primarily serve the interests of the memory maker.

3. See Bakken 2000: 17–18 on how memory can serve as a binding force and a mechanism of social control in dealing with potential disorder caused by modernization in contemporary China.

4. Jiang Ping 1988: 35–36.

5. Tong Shifan 1982: 88.

6. *DXQS* 1990: 296–98.

7. For a brief history of the nationalization of industry, see Spence 1990: 546–47.

8. Xu Dongchang et al. 1987: 1. The PPCC was originated in 1946. In 1949, on the eve of the CCP takeover, Mao established a new PPCC that was supposed to be a "democratic coalition government." It included representatives from other political parties but was controlled by the CCP (Spence 1990: 488, 512, 515).

9. Ling Xiang 1991: 30.

10. Mu Xuan 1997: 1.

11. *Dasheng fangzhi gongsi nianjian* 1998, preface: 4.

12. The aim of the anti-rightist campaign was to purge and attack the intellectuals who criticized the CCP (Spence 1990: 572).

13. *Zhang Jian shoucang shuhua xuan* 1995: 3.

14. Mu Xuan 1998b: 10.

15. On Peng Dehuai and his ouster by Mao Zedong, see Spence 1990: 581–83.

16. Mu Xuan 1998b: 10.

17. Mu Xuan 1997: 1–2.

18. Mu Xuan 1962: 1–3.

19. Ibid., 3–6.

20. On the Great Leap Forward, see Spence 1990: 574–81.

21. Mu Xuan 1962.

22. IMu Xuan 1996: 403–4, 1997: 2–3.

23. Mu Xuan 1997: 2–3.

24. Mu Xuan 1998b: 10.

25. For the events that led to the Cultural Revolution, see Spence 1990: 590–617.

26. The Cultural Revolution started with the criticism of some intellectuals in Beijing. Prominent among them were Wu Han, Deng Tuo, and Liao Mosha, who wrote under the joint pseudonym Three-Family Village (Sanjia cun) and whose works were said to represent reactionary bourgeois ideology. The term

Three-Family Village was extended to include any intellectuals whose writings were considered subversive (Spence 1990: 600–601).

27. Mu Xuan 1997: 4–5.

28. Ibid.

29. Sun Mo 1990: 11.

30. Interview 6.

31. The "four olds"—old customs, old habits, old culture, and old thinking—were attacked by Red Guards during the Cultural Revolution (Spence 1990: 606).

32. Interview 6.

33. Mu Xuan 1997: 4–5, 1998b: 10–11.

34. Interview 6.

35. Watson 1994: 4. Political pressure is not the only force that shapes the way the past is remembered. See Yoneyama 1994: 99–129 on the reconstruction of Hiroshima; and O'Toole 2001 on the amnesia of the great Irish famine of 1845–52.

36. Mu Xuan 1997: 5.

37. Xu Dongchang et al. 1987: 1–3.

38. Ibid., 3.

39. Ibid., 3–4.

40. Mu Xuan 1997: 5.

41. Xu Dongchang et al. 1987.

42. Conversations with Nantong residents, 1992–99.

43. For information on Hua Guofeng and his failed political struggle with Deng Xiaoping, see Spence 1990: 652, 675–78.

44. *Zhang Jian yanjiu ziliao* 1980: 4.

45. Mu Xuan, personal communication, Jan. 1995.

46. Mu Xuan 1997: 5–6.

47. Mu Xuan 1996: 406–7.

48. *Shelian tongxun*, 1–2 (1985): 4.

49. "Zhang Jian yanjiu ziliao" 1980: 4.

50. Guan Jingcheng 1982c: 130.

51. Mu Xuan 1998b: 11.

52. *Zhang Jian yanjiu jianxun* 1997: 1.

53. The publication of the *Complete Works* obviously made some of these books less valuable.

54. Watson 1994.

55. The CCP has even gone so far as to celebrate the legendary Yellow Emperor and the birthday of Confucius (Bakken 2000: 18).

56. Li Mingxun et al. 1993.

57. *Zhang Jian yanjiu jianxun* 1999: 11.

58. Schwarcz 1994: 50.

59. *NTJG*, 5–6 (1993): 72, 73.

60. Yan Xuexi et al. 1996: 380–87.

61. Ibid., 388–89.

62. "Zhang Jian," *Zhonghua gongshang shibao*, 29 Aug. 1995; Yan Xuexi et al. 1996: 380–89.

63. *Nantong Bowuyuan* 1980 (unpaginated).

64. Yan Xuexi et al. 1996: 11, 18, 22, 24.

65. *Zhang Jian yanjiu jianxun* 1998: 6.

66. *Zhang Jian yanjiu jianxun* 1997: 4.

67. *Zhang Jian yanjiu jianxun* 1999: 11.

68. *Zhang Jian yanjiu jianxun* 1997: 1.

69. *Zhang Jian yanjiu jianxun* 1997: 3.

70. *Nantong ribao*, 9 Aug. 1985.

71. Boyarin 1994: 20.

72. *Nantong ribao*, 9 Aug. 1985.

73. *Nantong Bowuyuan* 1980 (unpaginated).

74. Ibid.

75. Liu Weidong 1987: 14.

76. Ibid., 15–16.

77. *Nantong fangzhi shi tulu* 1987: 35, 82.

78. Ibid., 41–80.

79. Ibid., 70.

80. Liu Weidong 1987: 16.

81. Interview 3.

82. Interview 6.

83. Mu Xuan 1993b: 1–2.

84. Mu Xuan 1993a: 1–2.

85. Yuan Ming et al. 1994.

86. Ibid.

87. Xu Hui 1993: 33–34.

88. Yuan Ming et al. 1994.

89. In some cases, spiritual civilization was indeed used to promote economic growth; see Zweig 1997: 11.

90. Interview 6.

91. Ibid.

92. *Nantong ribao*, 22 July 1994.

93. This paragraph and the next two are based on interview 4.

94. Ji Xiufu 1995.

95. Ding Hong 1995.

96. Zweig 1997: 10–11.

97. *NTJG* 1 (1991): 6; 4 (1993): 5.

98. Lu Bosheng 1995: 3–4.

99. Eight of the 59 papers presented at the first international symposium were by foreign scholars, of whom six were Japanese (Yan Xuexi et al. 1993); at the second symposium, there were 102 papers, but again, only eight were by foreign scholars (Yan Xuexi et al. 1996).

100. *Zhang Jian yanjiu jianxun* 1997: 1.

101. See *NTJG* 1 (1988): 34, and 2–3 (1990): 66.
102. Borthwick 1983: 119.
103. Zhang Jingli 1989: 26–30.
104. Chang Zonghu 2000: 201, 207–14, 217–19.
105. The All-China Federation of Industry and Commerce oversees mainly private entrepreneurs—an equivalent of the chambers of commerce before 1949. It exists at various levels of government. Zhang Xuwu headed the national headquarters.
106. Chang Zonghu 2000: 223, 225, 232–33.
107. *Nantong fangzhi shi tulu* 1987: 104.
108. *Zhang Jian yanjiu jianxun* 1997: 3.
109. Yan Xuexi et al. 1993: 4. In one of my interviews with Zhang Xuwu, when I asked for some information on his life, he immediately said that he did not want to talk about himself; instead, he wanted to be like his grandfather, to work hard on practical, useful things for the public. Indeed, like his grandfather, Xuwu seems to have assumed this unselfish, modest persona naturally.
110. Zou Qiang 1962: 422–24.
111. Mu Xuan 1997: 3, 5. My discussion of Zou's article is based on his original essay.
112. *DXQS* 1990: 1–2.
113. *Zhang Jian yanjiu jianxun* 1998: 6.
114. Mu Xuan 1996: 402.
115. Yan Xuexi et al. 1996.
116. *Zhang Jian yu Mei Lanfang* 1999: 171.
117. *Zhang Jian yanjiu jianxun* 1999: 11.
118. *Zhang Jian yanjiu jianxun* 1998: 6.
119. Chang Zonghu 2000: 256.
120. Mu Xuan & Yan Xuexi 1994.
121. Jiang Guohong 1996: 390–93.
122. Ibid., 394.
123. Ibid., 397, 400.
124. Zhang Xiyang 1996: 410–17.
125. Mu Xuan 1996: 406–7.
126. In 1925, Zhang Jian reported that he and his brother had spent 85,080 yuan of their private funds annually to support local projects (Zhang Jian 1994, 3: 111).
127. For the first extensive discussion in recent years of Zhang Xiaoruo's death, see Chang Zonghu 2000: 182–91.
128. *Zhang Jian yunjiu jianxun* 1998: 6.
129. Mu Xuan 1996: 406.
130. Interview 7.
131. Boym 2001.
132. Boyarin 1994: xiv.
133. Bakken 2000: 5.
134. Ibid., 9.

CONCLUSION

1. Foucault, as cited in Lipsitz 1990: 213.
2. Dewey 1964: 166.
3. Amin 1995: 118.
4. Ibid., 4.
5. On cultural reform in rural China, see Hayford 1990. Evidently, cultural reform started in Ding county long before James Yen arrived there (Ibid., 87).
6. Cochran 1999; Strand 2000: 104; Lee, 1999.
7. Bakken 2000.
8. Alitto 1986; Hayford 1990.
9. Spence 1990: 593–94.
10. Zweig 1997; Gilley 2001.
11. Hayford 1990: 63.
12. Ibid., 89, 91–92, 115, 119, 141, 143–45.
13. Alitto 1986: 137, 140, 147, 173, 176, 246.
14. Ibid., 238.
15. Stapleton 2000.
16. Liping Wang 2000: 117–18.
17. Benson 1999.
18. Strand 2000: 100.
19. Interview 6.
20. Ibid.

Chinese Names and Terms

Bao ta hui	保塔会s
Beidaihe	北戴河
Beifajun	北伐军
benwei zhuyi guandian	本位主义观点
bolanguan	博览馆
bowuyuan	博物苑
Cai Yuanpei	蔡元培
canguan	参观
canguan tuan	参观团
Cehui ju	测绘局
chenghuang miao	城隍庙
chenlie shi	陈列室
Chen Shizeng	陈师曾
chuncui zhi zizhi	纯粹之自治
Chunliushe	春柳社
cong mofanxian dao huayuan chengshi	从模范县到花园城市
cuixi	催戏
Cunluo zhuyi	村落主义
Dadao tuhao lieshen	打倒土豪劣绅
Dasheng fangzhi gongsi nianjian	大生纺织公司年鉴
Dasheng qiye xitong dang'an xuanbian	大生企业系统档案选编
Dasheng shachang gongren shenghuo de diaocha	大生纱厂工人生活的调查
Dasheng xitong qiye	大生系统企业
Dasheng xitong qiyeshi	大生系统企业史

Difang zizhi yanjiu suo	地方自治研究所
Dongfang zazhi	东方杂志
Dongshihui	董事会
Dongyou riji	东游日记
duoyue	踱月
Dushu shijian	读书时间
fan'an	翻案
Fazheng jiangxisuo	法政讲习所
fei zhiye xiju yundong	非职业戏剧运动
gaixian er gengzhang	改弦而更张
Gengsu	更俗
Gongshang ju	工商局
gongyi	公益
goutou yiyuan	狗头议员
Guangjiao	广教
guanliao zichan jieji	官僚资产阶级
Guanyinshan	观音山
guoyu	国语
Hanmolin shuju	翰墨林书局
Huang Yanpei	黄炎培
Huang Zunxian	黄遵宪
Jiaoyu jiuguo	教育救国
jiayan	家宴
jiazhang	甲长
Jinghai lou	静海楼
jingshi pao	静市炮
jinqian yiyuan	金钱议员
Jinqian Yizhang	金钱议长
Jinshi	进士
juben wenxue	剧本文学
jukuan	巨款
junguomin jiaoyu	军国民教育
junxian	郡县
junzi guo	君子国
jushen	巨绅
Kang Youwei	康有为
kaocha	考察
Kunqu	昆曲
Langshan	狼山
Liang Qichao	梁启超

Liang Shuming   梁漱溟
lianhe yundong hui   联合运动会
lishi wenhua mingcheng   历史文化名城

Mei Lanfang   梅兰芳
Mei-Ou ge   梅欧阁
Meng Sen   孟森
mianzi   面子
Minben   民本
mingliu   名流
mingren shenghui   名人盛会
minguo lifa   民国历法
minguo si gongzi   民国四公子
minzhu renshi   民主人士
minzu zichan jieji   民族资产阶级
Mofan Lu   模范路
Mofan Xian   模范县
mofan yundong hui   模范运动会
mousheng   谋生

Nanshe   南社
*Nantong difang zizhi shijiunian zhi
    chengji*   南通地方自治十九年之成绩
Nantong fangzhishi tulu   南通纺织史图录
Nantong mianye shaye zhengquan
    zaliang lianhe jiaoyisuo   南通棉业纱业证券杂粮联合交易所
*Nantong shiye jiaoyu cishan feng
    jing fu canguan zhinan*   南通实业教育慈善风景附参观指南
Nantongbao   南通报
Nantongxian tuzhi   南通县图志
Nanyang quanye hui   南洋劝业会
Nong hui   农会
Nüjiao   女教

Ouyang Yuqian   欧阳予倩

Paotaijie   炮台街

qianglong yabuguo ditoushe   强龙压不过地头蛇
Qianling guan   千龄馆
qianzhuang   钱庄

rixin yueyi   日新月异

shagui   纱鬼
Shenbao   申报

shengju	盛举
shenshi	绅士
Shen Shou	沈寿
shenyou	神游
shexue	社学
Shibao	时报
shifan xuexiao	师范学校
shihui	市徽
shijian	尸谏
Shiwubao	时务报
Shizeng Yimo	师曾遗墨
shuyuan	书院
Sushe	苏社
Tangzha	唐闸
Taowu	桃坞
Tao Xingzhi	陶行之
tian bupa di bupa	天不怕地不怕
tiandi zhi dade yue sheng	天地之大德曰生
Tianzhiren	天之人
Tongbao	通报
Tonghai kenmu gongsi	通海垦牧公司
Tonghai shiye gongsi	通海实业公司
Tonghai xinbao	通海新报
Tongmenghui	同盟会
Tong[zhou]-Chong[ming]-Hai[men] zong shanghui	通州崇明海门总商会
Tongzhou xingban shiye zhangcheng	通州兴办实业章程
Tuhuangdi	土皇帝
Wang Guangying	王光英
Wang Guowei	王国维
Weichihui	维持会
weimei zhuyi	唯美主义
wenhua gongzuozhe	文化工作者
wenmingxi	文明戏
woguo jinzheng zhi yaoduan	我国近政之要端
wumian zhi wang	无冕之王
xialiu piqi	下流脾气
Xiangdao	向导
xiangzhen qiye	乡镇企业
Xingbao	星报
xinggeng pao	醒更炮
Xizhuangxi	西装戏

Xuanjiang lianxi suo	宣讲练习所
Xuewu gongsuo	学务公所
yange zhuyi	严格主义
yanshuo	演说
Yi jing	易经
yinhun busan	阴魂不散
yishihui	议事会
yiyou	艺友
Youfei	有斐
Youqing	右倾
Youyi julebu	友益俱乐部
Yuan Shikai	袁世凯
Yubei lixian gonghui gongbao	预备立宪公会公报
yulun jie	舆论界
Yuzhong	与众
Zhang Cha	张詧
Zhang Jian	张謇
Zhang Jian quanji	张謇全集
Zhang Xiaoruo	张孝若
Zhang Xuwu	张绪武
Zhang Zhidong	张之洞
Zheren zhizhe	浙人治浙
Zizhihui	自治会

Bibliography

INTERVIEWS

1. Male, in his 60s. Retired businessman. Nantong, August 1996.
2. A group of three males, in their 80s. Retired workers. Nantong, August 1996.
3. Male, in his 40s. Cultural worker. Nantong, July 1999.
4. Male, in his 60s. Cultural worker. Nantong, July 1999.
5. Male, in his 60s. Scholar and Nantong native. Taibei, August 2000.
6. Male, in his 70s. Cultural worker. Nantong, July–August 1995, 1996, 1999, June 2001, June 2002 (the last two by telephone).
7. Male, in his 70s. Government official. June 2001 (by telephone).

PUBLISHED AND UNPUBLISHED WORKS

Alitto, Guy S. 1986. *The Last Confucian: Liang Shu-ming and the Chinese Dilemma of Modernity*. Berkeley: University of California Press.
Amin, Shahid. 1995. *Event, Metaphor, Memory: Chauri Chaura, 1922–1992*. Berkeley: University of California Press.
Baark, Erik. 1997. *Lightning Wires: The Telegraph and China's Technological Modernization, 1860–1890*. Westport, Conn.: Greenwood Press.
Bai Bing. 1987. "Miaohui" (Temple festivals). *NTJG* 4.
Bailey, Paul J. 1990. *Reform the People: Changing Attitudes Towards Popular Education in Early Twentieth-Century China*. Edinburgh: Edinburgh University Press.
Bakken, Børge. 2000. *The Exemplary Society: Human Improvement, Social Control, and the Dangers of Modernity in China*. New York: Oxford University Press.
Barish, Jonas. 1981. *The Antitheatrical Prejudice*. Berkeley: University of California Press.
Barkan, Lenore. 1983. "Nationalists, Communists, and Rural Leaders: Political

Dynamics in a Chinese County, 1927–1937." Ph.D. diss., University of Washington.

Bartky, Ian R. 2000. *Selling the True Time: Nineteenth-Century Timekeeping in America*. Stanford, Calif.: Stanford University Press.

Bastid, Marianne. 1988 [1968]. *Educational Reform in Early 20th-Century China*. Tr. Paul J. Bailey. Ann Arbor: University of Michigan.

Beacham, Richard C. 1999. *Spectacle Entertainments of Early Imperial Rome*. New Haven, Conn.: Yale University Press.

Bennett, Tony. 1995. *The Birth of the Museum: History, Theory, Politics*. New York: Routledge.

Benson, Carlton. 1999. "Consumers Are Also Soldiers: Subversive Songs from Nanjing Road During the New Life Movement." In Sherman Cochran, ed., *Inventing Nanjing Road: Commercial Culture in Shanghai, 1900–1945*. Ithaca, N.Y.: Cornell University Press.

Borthwick, Sally. 1983. *Education and Social Change in China: The Beginnings of the Modern Era*. Stanford, Calif.: Hoover Institution Press.

Bourdieu, Pierre. 1991. *Language and Symbolic Power*. Ed. John B. Thompson. Tr. Gina Raymond and Matthew Adamson. Cambridge, Mass.: Harvard University Press.

Boyarin, Jonathan, ed. 1994. *Remapping Memory: The Politics of TimeSpace*. Minneapolis: University of Minnesota Press.

Boym, Svetlana. 2001. *The Future of Nostalgia*. New York: Basic Books.

Buckingham, James Silk. 1973 [1849]. *National Evils and Practical Remedies with the Plan of a Model Town*. Clifton, N.J.: Augustus M. Kelley Publishers.

Burns, E. Bradford. 1980. *The Poverty of Progress: Latin America in the Nineteenth Century*. Berkeley: University of California Press.

Calinescu, Matei. 1987. *Five Faces of Modernity: Modernism, Avant-Garde, Decadence, Kitsch, Postmodernism*. Durham, N.C.: Duke University Press.

Cao Congpo. 1962. "Zhang Jian de beiju" (The tragedy of Zhang Jian). *Jianghai xuekan 7*.

Cao Hanchen. 1987. "Yu Chen shiji shulüe" (Things about Yu Chen). *NXWSZL* 1.

Cao Zhendong. 1987. "Nantong shifan—woguo zuizao xingjian de shifan xuexiao" (Nantong Normal School—the earliest normal school in China). *NTJG* 2.

CCWS, see *Congchuan wenshi*

Chang Shou. 1987. "Wu gongyuan he Yuelong qiao" (The five parks and the Yuelong Bridge). *NTJG* 4.

———. 1989. "Qishi nianqian de yici junxun: yingjiaolian" (A military drill seventy years earlier: battalion training). *NTJG* 2.

Chang Zonghu. 2000. *Modai zhuangyuan: Zhang Jian jiazu bainian ji* (Last Zhuangyuan: one hundred years of history of the Zhang Jian family). Beijing: Zhongguo shehui chubanshe.

Chartier, Roger. 1987. *The Cultural Use of Print in Early Modern France*. Tr. Lydia G. Cochrane. Princeton, N.J.: Princeton University Press.

———. 1994. *The Order of Books: Readers, Authors, and Libraries in Europe Between the Fourteenth and Eighteenth Centuries*. Tr. Lydia G. Cochrane. Stanford, Calif.: Stanford University Press.

Chauncey, Helen. 1992. *Schoolhouse Politicians: Locality and State During the Chinese Republic*. Honolulu: University of Hawaii Press.

Chen Bingsheng. 1989. "Nantong fangzhi nügong de xingming" (The names of female textile workers in Nantong). *NTJG* 3–4.

Chen Lanfang. 1989. "Modai zhuangyuan zhuan yinlian" (The antithetical couplets of the last Zhuangyuan). *NTJG* 3–4.

Chen, Xiaomei. 1995. *Occidentalism: A Theory of Counter-Discourse in Post-Mao China*. New York: Oxford University Press.

Chen Zhuoru. 1992. "de Reike dui Nantong chengshi jianshe gongxian jilüe" (de Reike's contribution to the city planning of Nantong). *NTJG* 1.

Cheng, Weikun. 1996. "The Challenge of the Actress: Female Performers and Cultural Alternatives in Early Twentieth Century Beijing and Tianjin." *Modern China* 22.2 (April).

Chesneaux, Jean. 1969. "The Federalist Movement in China, 1920–23." In Jack Gray, ed., *Modern China's Search for a Political Form*. London: Oxford University Press.

Chow, Tse-tsung. 1960. *The May 4th Movement: Intellectual Revolution in Modern China*. Cambridge, Mass.: Harvard University Press.

Chu, Samuel C. 1965. *Reformer in Modern China: Chang Chien, 1853–1926*. New York: Columbia University Press.

Chun Cao. 1991. "Gangzha jianxiang qutan" (Interesting talks about [the names of] ports, dikes, streets, and lanes). *NTJG* 3.

———. 1992. "Nantong chunlian duoqu" (Spring Festival couplets in Nantong). *NTJG* 6.

Clark, Gregory, and Michael Halloran, eds. 1993. *Oratorical Culture in Nineteenth-Century America: Transformations in the Theory and Practice of Rhetoric*. Carbondale: Southern Illinois University Press.

Clark, Peter. 2000. *British Clubs and Societies, c. 1580–1800: The Origins of an Associational World*. New York: Oxford University Press.

Clunas, Craig. 1991. *Superfluous Things: Material Culture and Social Status in Early Modern China*. Urbana: University of Illinois Press.

Cochran, Sherman, ed. 1999. *Inventing Nanjing Road: Commercial Culture in Shanghai, 1900–1945*. Ithaca, N.Y.: Cornell University Press.

Cohn, Bernard S. 1997. *Colonialism and Its Forms of Knowledge: The British in India*. Delhi: Oxford University Press.

Conn, Steven. 1998. *Museums and American Intellectual Life, 1876–1926*. Chicago: University of Chicago Press.

Cotter, Holland. 2001. "The World Invades, and Chinese Art Surrenders? Look Again." *New York Times*, 2 Feb.: E 35.

Cuthbertson, Gilbert Morris. 1975. *Political Myth and Epic*. East Lansing: Michigan State University Press.

Dai Buzhou. 1987. "1929 nian Nantongcheng de yici bingbian" (The 1929 military coup in Nantong city). *NTJG* 5.

Darnton, Robert, and Daniel Roche, eds. 1989. *Revolution in Print: The Press in France 1775–1800*. Berkeley: University of California Press.

Dasheng fangzhi gongsi nianjian: 1895–1947 (Chronicle of the Dasheng Textile Company: 1895–1947). 1998. Ed. Zhang Jizhi xiansheng shiye bianzhuan zu (Editing group of Mr. Zhang Jizhi's enterprises). Nanjing: Jiangsu renmin chubanshe.

Dasheng shachang gongren shenghuo de diaocha: 1899–1949 (Investigation of the life of workers in the Dasheng mills, 1899–1949). 1994. Ed. Mu Xuan and Yan Xuexi. Nanjing: Jiangsu renmin chubanshe.

Dasheng xitong qiyeshi (A History of the Dasheng System Enterprises). 1990. Ed. Dasheng xitong qi yeshi bianxiezu (Editing group of A History of the Dasheng System Enterprises). Nanjing: Jiangsu guji chubanshe.

Dewey, John. 1964. *John Dewey's Impressions of Soviet Russia and the Revolutionary World: Mexico-China-Turkey*. Ed. William W. Brickman. New York: Columbia University Press.

Dewey, John, and Alice Chipman Dewey. 1920. *Letters from China and Japan*. Ed. Evelyn Dewey. New York: Dutton.

Ding Hong. 1995. "Jianyi jiaqiang wenwu yishi" (Suggestion on strengthening the awareness of historical and cultural material). Unpublished manuscript.

Dong He. 1992a. "Nantong yu Nanyang quanyehui youhe guanxi" (How was Nantong related to the Nanyang Exhortation Fair?). *NTJG* 3.

———. 1992b. "Nantong chengqu kaishi fadian yu heshi" (When did Nantong city have electricity?). *NTJG* 3.

Dou Zhijing. 1984. "Nantong minzhu geming yundong de xianquzhe: Wu Zhenyi" (Pioneer in the democratic revolution of Nantong: Wu Zhenyi). *NTSH* 2.

DSNJ, see *Dasheng fangzhi gongsi nianjian*

Dudley, Leonard M. 1991. *The Word and the Sword: How Techniques of Information and Violence Have Shaped our World*. Oxford: Blackwell.

DXQS, see *Dasheng xitong qiyeshi*

Eisenstein, Elizabeth L. 1979. *The Printing Press as an Agent of Change: Communications and Cultural Transformations in Early-Modern Europe*. Vol. 1. Cambridge: Cambridge University Press.

Ershinianlai zhi Nantong (Nantong in the past two decades). 1930. Nantong.

Esherick, Joseph W., ed. 2000. *Remaking the Chinese City: Modernity and National Identity, 1900–1950*. Honolulu: University of Hawaii Press.

Esherick, Joseph W., and Mary B. Rankin, eds. 1990. *Chinese Local Elites and Patterns of Dominance*. Berkeley: University of California Press.

Fang Hanqi, ed. 1986. *Zhongguo xinwen shiye tongshi* (A general history of Chinese journalism). Beijing: Zhongguo renmin daxue chubanshe.

Fang Zhenghua. 1990. "Zhongguo zuizao de mangya xuexiao" (The earliest school for the blind and the deaf-mute in China). *NTJG* 2–3.

Fei Fanjiu. 1962. "Nantong Zhang Jian yinxing *difang zizhi shijiunian zhi chengji* zhi jingguo" (How Nantong Zhang Jian printed the *Achievements of Nantong Local Self-government in the Last Nineteen Years*). In NTYW.

————. 1981. "Xinhai geming qianhou shangnong jiaoyu gejie chuangli zuzhi" (The creation of business, agricultural, and educational organizations around the time of the 1911 Revolution). *NSWSZL* 1.

Fei Xuehua. 1992. "Sanci lixian jishi"(Recollection of three risks). *NXWSZL* 8.

Feng Ping. 1990. "Nantong youdian tongxin shilüe" (History of postal service and telegraph in Nantong). *NTJG* 2–3.

Fentress, James, and Chris Wickham. 1992. *Social Memory.* Oxford: Blackwell.

Finnane, Antonia. 1993. "Yangzhou: A Central Place in the Qing Empire." In Linda C. Johnson, ed., *Cities of Jiangnan in Late Imperial China.* Albany: State University of New York Press.

Fujioka Kikuo. 1985. *Cho Ken to shingai kakumei* (Zhang Jian and the 1911 revolution). Sapporo: Hokkaidō daigaku toshokankōkai.

Fukuzawa Yukichi. 1960. *The Autobiography of Yukichi Fukuzawa.* Tr. Eiichi Kiyooka. New York: Columbia University Press.

Geertz, Clifford. 1980. *Negara: The Theater State in Nineteenth-Century Bali.* Princeton, N.J.: Princeton University Press.

————. 1983. *Local Knowledge: Further Essays in Interpretive Anthropology.* New York: Basic Books.

Gilley, Bruce. 2001. *Model Rebels: The Rise and Fall of China's Richest Village.* Berkeley: University of California Press.

Gluck, Carol. 1985. *Japan's Modern Myths: Ideology in the Late Meiji Period.* Princeton, N.J.: Princeton University Press.

Grierson, Philip. 1975. *Numismatics.* London: Oxford University Press.

Gu Wenqian. 1988. "Liu Guangqian de waijiao shengya" (The diplomatic career of Liu Guangqian). *NXWSZL* 2.

————. 1989. "Zhou Jialu xiansheng zhuanlüe" (Biography of Mr. Zhou Jialu). *NXWSZL* 6.

Guan Jingcheng. 1962. "Zhang Jian zizhi huodong de wuge shiliao huiluben" (Five documents on Zhang Jian's local self-government activities). In NTYW.

————. 1981. "Xinhai Tongzhou guangfu shimoji" (Political change in Tongzhou during the 1911 Revolution). *NSWSZL* 1.

————. 1982a. "Tongzhou shifande chuangban he fazhan" (The creation and development of the Tongzhou Normal School). *NSWSZL* 2.

————. 1982b. "'Wusan' yundong zai Nantong" (The May Thirtieth movement in Nantong). *NSWSZL* 2.

————. 1982c. "Qianyan" (Introduction) to Komai Tokuzoo, "Zhang Jian guanxi shiye diaocha baogaoshu" (Report on the investigation of Zhang Jian's enterprises). *Jiangsu wenshi zhiliao* 10.

————. 1983. "Nantong baokan shiliao" (Historical materials about Nantong newspapers). *NSWSZL* 3.

————. 1985. *Nantong lishi zhaji* (Notes on the history of Nantong). Rudong: Rudong caiyinchang.

————. n.d.a "1927 nian dageming qijian Nantong shangceng shenshi de dongtai" (The movements of upper-level elites in Nantong during the 1927 revolution). Nantong Library.

————. n.d.b "1927 nian Nantong zhujun guojun qingkuang" (The military forces stationed in and around Nantong in 1927). Nantong Library.

Guo Shilong. 1995. Zhang Xueliang yu Nantong (Zhang Xueliang and Nantong). *NTJG* 1–2.

Habermas, Jürgen. 1993. *The Structural Transformation of the Public Sphere: An Inquiry into a Category of Bourgeois Society*. Tr. Thomas Burger with Frederick Lawrence. Cambridge, Mass.: MIT Press.

Halbwachs, Maurice. 1992. *On Collective Memory*. Ed. and tr. Lewis A. Coser. Chicago: University of Chicago Press.

Harrison, Henrietta. 2000. *The Making of the Republican Citizen: Political Ceremonies and Symbols in China, 1911–1929*. New York: Oxford University Press.

Hayashi Yoshimasa. 1981. "Cho Ken no jitsugyo kōsō" (Zhang Jian's industrial ideas). *Nagoya-gakuin daigaku ronshū*: Shakaikagaku-hen 17: 1.

Hayford, Charles W. 1990. *To the People: James Yen and Village China*. New York: Columbia University Press.

Helms, Mary W. 1993. *Craft and the Kingly Ideal: Art, Trade, and Power*. Austin: University of Texas Press.

Holt, Richard. 1981. *Sport and Society in Modern France*. Hamden, Conn.: Archon.

Honig, Emily. 1989. "The Politics of Prejudice: Subei People in Republican-Era Shanghai." *Modern China* 15.3 (July).

Howard, Jean E. 1994. *The Stage and Social Struggle in Early Modern England*. New York: Routledge.

Huang, Philip C. C. 1990. *The Peasant Family and Rural Development in the Yangzi Delta, 1350–1988*. Stanford, Calif.: Stanford University Press.

Huang Ran. 1987. "Junshan qixiangtai" (Junshan observatory). *NTJG* 3–4.

————. 1995. "Nantong Bowuyuan" (Nantong Museum). In Zu Dingyuan and Yao E, eds., *Mengyou meihualou: Nantong renwen jingguan* (Dream walk in the plum chamber: cultural landscape in Nantong). Tianjin: Baihua chubanshe.

Huang Xingqiao. n.d. "Huang Xingqiao xiansheng huiyi Zhang Jian" (Mr. Huang Xingqiao's recollection of Zhang Jian). Unpublished manuscript.

Hung, Chang-tai. 1994. *War and Popular Culture: Resistance in Modern China, 1937–1945*. Berkeley: University of California Press.

Ji Nengjin. 1992. "Nantong zhongxiaoxue waiyu jiaoxue huajiu" (Foreign language teaching in Nantong's middle and elementary schools in the past). *NTJG* 2.

Ji Tang. 1989. "Zhang Jian langwushan yishi" (Anecdotes about Zhang Jian and the five hills). *NTJG* 6.

Ji Tianfu. 1981. "Ji Tianfu riji youguan xinhai geming zai Nantong de bufen zhailu" (Excerpts of Ji Tianfu's diary on the 1911 Revolution in Nantong). *NSWSZL* 1.

Ji Xiufu. 1987. "Jiushi Nantongcheng de chunjie" (Chinese New Year in old Nantong city). *NTJG* 6.

————. 1991. "Fengjian shidai de Nantong" (Nantong in the premodern era). *NTJG* 1.

————. 1993. "Tongzhoucheng minju tan" (Houses of Tongzhou city). *NTJG* 1.

————. 1995. "Ge Pan Baocai fushizhang de yi fengxin" (Letter to deputy mayor Pan Baocai). Unpublished document, 5 Aug.

Jiang Binghe. 1986. "Nantong Tangzha zhen liangshi ye fazhan jianshi" (A brief history of the grain business in Tangzha). *NSWSZL* 6.

Jiang Bohan, Wu Fuchao, and Liu Qicheng. 1987. "Jinlindang, Dayoujin, San Yuzhen" (From Jinlindang to Sanyu Town). *NXWSZL* 1.

Jiang Guohong. 1996. "Zhang Jian zai ziyou pingdeng, funü jiefang, he zunkong dujing zhu wenti shang de renshi tanxi" (An analysis of Zhang Jian's ideas on freedom, equality, women's liberation, Confucian worship, and other issues). In Yan Xuexi et al., eds., *Jindai gaigejia Zhang Jian*, listed below.

Jiang Ping. 1988. "Nantong xueyuan fangzhike" (The Nantong College textile department). *NTJG* 1.

————. 1997. "Li Shengbo yu Zhang Jian Dasheng fangzhi qiye guanxi zai yanjiu" (Further investigation into the relationship between Li Shengbo and Zhang Jian's Dasheng textile enterprises). Unpublished manuscript.

Jiangsu jiaoyu jinwunian jian gaikuang (The general situation of education in Jiangsu province in the last five years). 1916. Ed. Jiangsusheng gongshu jiaoyu ke (Educational bureau of Jiangsu province). Shanghai: Shangwu yinshuguan.

Jin Chengyi. 1995. "Nantong diming lianyu congtan" (Names and couplets of places in Nantong). *CCWS* 2.

Jingju gaige de xianqu (Pioneers of Chinese opera reform). 1982. Ed. Nantong shi wenlian (The Literature Association of Nantong City). Nanjing: Jiangsu renmin chubanshe.

Judge, Joan. 1996. *Print and Politics: "Shibao" and the Culture of Reform in Late Qing China*. Stanford, Calif.: Stanford University Press.

Keenan, Barry. 1977. *The Dewey Experiment in China: Educational Reform and Political Power in the Early Republic*. Cambridge, Mass.: Harvard University Press.

Kifner, John. 2000. "Museum Brings Town Back to Life: Converted Factory Is Economic Catalyst for Massachusetts City." *New York Times*, 30 May: A14.

Komai Tokuzoo. 1982 [1924]. "Zhang Jian guanxi shiye diaocha baogaoshu" (Report on the investigation of Zhang Jian's enterprises). *Jiangsu wenshi ziliao* 10.

Kuhn, Philip A. 1975. "Local Self-government Under the Republic: Problems of Control, Autonomy, and Mobilization." In Frederic Wakeman, Jr., and Carolyn Grant, eds., *Conflict and Control in Late Imperial China*. Berkeley: University of California Press.

Kwok, D.W.Y. 1965. *Scientism in Chinese Thought: 1900–1950*. New Haven, Conn.: Yale University Press.

Landes, David S. 1983. *Revolution in Time: Clocks and the Making of the Modern World*. Cambridge, Mass.: Harvard University Press.

Lang Cun. 1995. "Jiang Xizeng xiansheng ziliao buju" (Additional material about Mr. Jiang Xizeng). *CCWS* 2.

————. 1997. "Hongyi fashi he Langshan" (Master Hongyi and Langshan). *NSWSZL* 16.

Le Goff, Jacques. 1992. *History and Memory*. Tr. Steven Rendall and Elizabeth Claman. New York: Columbia University Press.

Lee, Leo Ou-Fan. 1999. *Shanghai Modern: The Flowering of a New Urban Culture in China, 1930-1945*. Cambridge, Mass.: Harvard University Press.

Li Benyi. 1989. "Tongzhou mingshi Fan Dangshi" (Tongzhou celebrity Fan Dangshi). *NTJG* 2.

Li Danren. 1982. "Nantong wenhua jiaoyu jiuwen zayi" (Recollection of educational and cultural development in Nantong). *NSWSZL* 3.

Li Hongru, ed. 1986. *Nantong Zhang Jizhi xiansheng shishi liushi zhounian jinianji* (Souvenir book of the sixtieth anniversary of the death of Mr. Zhang Jizhi of Nantong). Taibei: Zhongxi yinzhi chang.

Li Kangqi. 1991. "Mei Lanfang zai Nantong" (Mei Lanfang in Nantong). *NTJG* 6.

Li Mingxun, Zhu Peiyan, and You Shiwei, eds. 1993. *Kaituo yu fazhan: Zhang Jian suochuang qishiye jinxi* (Pioneering and development: the today and yesterday of Zhang Jian's enterprises). Nanjing: Jiangsu renmin chubanshe.

Li Shengbo. 1983. "Wodui Shanghai yintuan weichi jingying Dasheng xitong de chouhua" (My proposal to the consortium of Shanghai banks on managing the Dasheng System). *NSWSZL* 3.

Lin Jubai. 1962. "Zhang Jian suoban qiye zai Nantong faxing de sanzhong zhibi" (The three kinds of paper money Zhang Jian's enterprises issued in Nantong). In NTYW.

———. 1984. *Jindai Nantong tubu shi* (History of the modern handwoven cloth industry in Nantong). Dafeng: Dazhong yinshua chang.

Ling Junyu. 1992. "*Xiandai Pinglun* bianji Liu Shuhe" (The editor of *Modern Review*, Liu Shuhe). *NXWSZL* 8.

———. 1995. "Nantong yuanlin shiliao manshu" (Informal discussion about material on Nantong gardens). *CCWS* 2.

Ling Xiang. 1991. "Seyuan" (Se Garden). *NTJG* 5.

Lipsitz, George. 1990. *Time Passages: Collective Memory and American Popular Culture*. Minneapolis: University of Minnesota Press.

Liu Daorong. 1990. "Nantong Hanmolin yinshuju" (Nantong Hanmolin Publishing House). *NTJG* 1.

———. 1991. "*Nantongxian tuzhi* jilüe" (About the *Illustrated Gazetteer of Nantong County*). *NTJG* 2.

Liu Housheng. 1965. *Zhang Jian zhuanji* (Biography of Zhang Jian). Hong Kong: Longmen shudian.

Liu Shui. 1987. "Yicheng sanzhen" (One city and three towns). *NTJG* 3-4.

Liu Weidong. 1987. "Nantong fangzhi bowuguan" (The Nantong Textile Museum). *NTJG* 6.

Lu Bosheng. 1991. "Huang Yanpei lai Nantong" (Huang Yanpei's Visit to Nantong). *NTJG* 1.

———. 1995. "Zongshuji yijia he Nantong" (The General Secretary's family and Nantong). *NTJG* 1-2.

Lu, Hanchao. 1999. *Beyond the Neon Lights: Everyday Shanghai in the Early Twentieth Century*. Berkeley: University of California Press.

Lü Jimin. 1996. "Zhang Jian, Zhuangyuan, bowuguan" (Zhang Jian, Zhuang-yuan, museums). In Yan Xuexi et al., eds., *Jindai gaigejia Zhang Jian*, listed below.

MacClancy, Jeremy, ed. 1996. *Sport, Identity and Ethnicity*. Oxford: Berg.

Marker, Gary. 1985. *Publishing, Printing, and the Origins of Intellectual Life in Russia, 1700–1800*. Princeton, N.J.: Princeton University Press.

Mason, Laura. 1989. "Songs: Mixing Media." In Robert Darnton and Daniel Roche, eds., *Revolution in Print: The Press in France, 1775–1800*. Berkeley: University of California Press.

McClellan, Andrew. 1999. *Inventing the Louvre: Art, Politics, and the Origins of the Modern Museum in Eighteenth-Century Paris*. Berkeley: University of California Press.

Mei Lanfang. 1987. *Wutai shengya sishinian* (Forty years on stage). Beijing: Zhongguo xiju chubanshe.

Merriman, John M. 1985. *The Red City: Limoges and the French Nineteenth Century*. New York: Oxford University Press.

Miao Zizhong. 1987. "Jiefang qian Nantong yinhang de gaikuang" (The general situation of banks in Nantong before 1949). *NSWSZL* 7.

Min, Tu-ki (Min Tu-gi). 1989. *National Polity and Local Power: The Transformation of Late Imperial China*. Cambridge, Mass.: Harvard University Press.

Morris, Andrew. 1997. "Mastery Without Enmity: Athletics, Modernity and the Nation in Early Republican China." *Republican China* 22.2 (April).

Mu Xuan. 1962. "Dangqian xueshujie guanyu Zhang Jian pingjia wenti de taolun" (Current scholarly opinions on Zhang Jian). Unpublished manuscript.

———. 1980. "Changyi jianli fangzhi bowuguan de zuotanhui yaoqing han" (Invitation letter for the workshop on the creation of the Nantong Textile Museum). Unpublished document.

———. 1985. "Zhang Jian yu Zhongguo bowuguan shiye de zhaoshi" (Zhang Jian and the inception of museums in China). Unpublished manuscript.

———. 1993a. "Cong mofanxian dao huayuan chengshi" (From model county to garden city). Unpublished manuscript.

———. 1993b. "Nantong yao zhengqu lishi mingcheng de rongyu" (Nantong should apply for the honor of "Famous City in History and Culture"). Unpublished manuscript.

———. 1996. "Hongyang Zhang Jian jingshen, jianshe dangdai Nantong" (Enhance the spirit of Zhang Jian to develop today's Nantong). In Yan Xuexi et al., eds., *Jindai gaigejia Zhang Jian*, listed below.

———. 1997. "Zhang Jian yanjiu lishi jiyao" (A brief history of studies on Zhang Jian). Unpublished manuscript.

———. 1998a. "Zhongguo zuizao de buwuguan: Nantong Bowuyuan" (The earliest Chinese museum: Nantong Museum). *NSWSZL* 17.

———. 1998b. "Cao Congpo yu Zhang Jian yanjiu" (Cao Congpo and studies on Zhang Jian). *NTJG* 4.

Mu Xuan and Yan Xuexi, eds. 1994. *Dasheng shachang gongren shenghuo de diaocha: 1899–1949* (Investigation of the life of workers in the Dasheng mill, 1899–1949). Nanjing: Jiangsu renmin chubanshe.

Mukerji, Chandra. 1983. *From Graven Images: Patterns of Modern Materialism.* New York: Columbia University Press.

Nakai Hideki. 1983. "Shinmatsu Chugoku niokeru 'seiryū' to kigyōsha katsudō—Cho Ken no shōgai to sono yakuwari" (The activities of the "pure party" industrialists in late imperial China—Zhang Jian's career and role). In Abe Hiroshi, ed., *Nicchu kankei to bunka-masatsu* (Cultural conflict in Sino-Japanese relationships). Tokyo: Gannan-dō shoten.

Nantong Bowuyuan (Nantong Museum). 1980. Ed. Nantong Bowuyuan. Nantong: Taofen yinshuchang.

Nantong Bowuyuan wenxianji (Collection of documents on the Nantong Museum). 1985. Ed. Nantong Bowuyuan. Nantong.

Nantong daxue chengli jinian kan (Souvenir book for the creation of Nantong College). 1928. Nantong: Hanmolin shuju.

Nantong dianshang gonghui (Nantong Pawnbrokers' Union). 1928. "Nantong xianshu dianshang cheng zhengfu wen" (A letter from the Nantong county pawnbrokers to the government). Nantong: Hanmolin shuju.

Nantong difang zizhi shijiunian zhi chengji (Achievements of Nantong local self-government in the last nineteen years). 1915. Nantong: Hanmolin shuju.

Nantong Fangzhi Gongxueyuan chuangjian qishiwu zhounian xiaoyouhui zonghui chengli jiniance: 1912–1987 (Souvenir book for the seventy-fifth anniversary of the Nantong Textile College and the creation of its General Alumni Association: 1912–1987). 1988. Nantong.

Nantong fangzhi shi tulu (Illustrated record of the textile industry in Nantong). 1987. Nanjing: Nanjing daxue chubanshe.

Nantong jiaoyu nianjian (The yearbook of Nantong education). 1926. Ed. Nantongxian jiaoyuju (Educational Bureau of Nantong county). Nantong: Hanmolin shuju.

Nantong jingu (Nantong Past and Present). Nantong, 1987–.

Nantong shi wenshi ziliao (Material on the culture and history of Nantong city). Nantong, 1981–.

Nantong shihua (Historical talk about Nantong). Nantong, 1983–85.

Nantong shiye jiaoyu cishan fengjing fu canguan zhinan (Nantong industry, education, philanthropy, scenery with a tour guide appendix). 1920. Ed. Nantong youyi julebu (Nantong Friendship Club). Shanghai: Shangwu yinshuguan.

Nantong xian wenshi ziliao (Material on the culture and history of Nantong county). Nantong, 1987–92.

"Nantong yiwen" (Anecdotes about Nantong). 1962. Nantong Library.

Nantongbao (Nantong Times). Nantong, 1919–37.

Nantongshi xingzheng niankan (The yearbook of the Nantong City Administration). 1929. Ed. Nantongshi xingzhengju (Bureau of the Nantong City Administration). Nantong: Hanmolin shuju.

Nantongxian tuzhi (Illustrated gazetteer of Nantong county). 1964 [1922]. Nantong: Hanmolin shuju.

Nantongxian zizhihui baogaoshu (Report of the Local Self-government Association of Nantong county). 1921. Ed. Nantongxian zizhihui (Local Self-government Association of Nantong county). Nantong: Hanmolin shuju.

Naquin, Susan. 1994. "The Annual Festival of Peking." In *Minjian xinyang yu Zhangguo wenhua guoji yantao hui lunwenji* (Proceedings of the International Conference on Popular Beliefs and Chinese Culture). Taibei: Center for Chinese Studies.

————. 2000. *Peking: Temples and City Life, 1400–1900*. Berkeley: University of California Press.

Naquin, Susan, and Evelyn S. Rawski, eds. 1987. *Chinese Society in the Eighteenth Century*. New Haven, Conn.: Yale University Press.

Needham, Joseph. 1981. *Science in Traditional China: A Comparative Perspective*. Hong Kong: Chinese University Press.

North, Michael. 1999. *Reading 1922: A Return to the Scene of the Modern*. New York: Oxford University Press.

Nowotny, Helga. 1994. *Time: The Modern and Postmodern Experience*. Tr. Neville Plaice. Cambridge, Eng.: Polity Press.

Nozawa Yutaka. 1993. "Riben wenxian zhongde Zhang Jian he Nantong" (Zhang Jian and Nantong in Japanese sources). In Yan Xuexi and Ni Youchun, eds., *Lun Zhang Jian: Zhang Jian guoji xueshu taolunhui lunweiji* (On Zhang Jian: papers from the international symposium on Zhang Jian). Nanjing: Jiangsu renmin chubanshe.

NSWSZL, see *Nantong shi wenshi ziliao*

NTJG, see *Nantong jingu*

NTSH, see *Nantong shihua*

NTYW, see "Nantong yiwen."

NXWSZL, see *Nantong xian wenshi ziliao*

O'Toole, Fintan. 2001. "Trying Not to Awake." *New Republic*, 15 Oct.

Ouyang Yuqian. 1984. *Ouyang Yuqian xiju lunwenji* (Collection of Ouyang Yuqian's essays on theater and drama). Shanghai: Shanghai wenyi chubanshe.

————. 1990. *Ouyang Yuqian quanji* (Complete works of Ouyang Yuqian). Ed. Zhongyang xiju xueyuan (The Central Drama College). Shanghai: Shanghai wenyi chubanshe.

Ozouf, Mona. 1988. *Festivals and the French Revolution*. Tr. Alan Sheridan. Cambridge, Mass.: Harvard University Press.

Perdue, Peter C. 1987. *Exhausting the Earth: State and Peasant in Hunan, 1500–1850*. Cambridge, Mass.: Harvard University Press.

Porter, Roy. 2000. "The Need for Buddies." *London Review of Books* 22.12 (22 June).

Pronko, Leonard Cabell. 1962. *Avant-Garde: The Experimental Theater in France*. Berkeley: University of California Press.

Qian Gongpu. 1916. "Nantong xian xuewu canguan ji" (Account of an inspection of educational affairs in Nantong). *Jiaoyu zazhi* 8.11 (Nov.).

Qiu Yuenzhang and Yao Qian. 1991. "Tonghai kenmu sishinian" (Forty years of land reclamation in Tonghai). *NSWSZL* 11.

Rankin, Mary B. 1986. *Elite Activism and Political Transformation in China: Zhejiang Province, 1865–1911*. Stanford, Calif.: Stanford University Press.

———. 1997. "State and Society in Early Republican Politics, 1912–18." *China Quarterly* 150 (June).

Ren Zhong. 1988. "Xiangxian yishi" (Anecdotes of prominent local figures). *NTJG* 1.

Reynolds, Douglas R. 1993. *China, 1898–1912: The Xinzheng Revolution and Japan*. Cambridge, Mass.: Harvard University Press.

Rosenthal, Elisabeth. 2000. "Defiant Chinese Muslims Keep Their Own Time." *New York Times*, 19 Nov.: A3.

Rydell, Robert W. 1984. *All the World's a Fair: Visions of Empire at American International Expositions, 1876–1916*. Chicago: University of Chicago Press.

Sang Bing. 1995. *Qingmo xin zhishijie de shetuan yu huodong* (The societies and activities of the new intellectuals of the late Qing). Beijing: Sanlian sudian.

Schneer, Jonathan. 1999. *London 1900: The Imperial Metropolis*. New Haven, Conn.: Yale University Press.

Schoppa, R. Keith. 1995. *Blood Road: The Mystery of Shen Dingyi in Revolutionary China*. Berkeley: University of California Press.

Schwarcz, Vera. 1986. *The Chinese Enlightenment: Intellectuals and the Legacy of the May Fourth Movement of 1919*. Berkeley: University of California Press.

———. 1994. "Strangers No More: Personal Memory in the Interstices of Public Commemoration." In Rubie S. Watson, ed., *Memory, History, and Opposition Under State Socialism*. Santa Fe, N.M.: School of American Research Press.

The Science. Shanghai monthly, 1915–49, 1957–60.

Scott, James C. 1998. *Seeing Like a State: How Certain Schemes to Improve the Human Condition Have Failed*. New Haven, Conn.: Yale University Press.

Sha Jincheng. 1990. "Zhang Jian yu difangzhi" (Zhang Jian and local gazetteers). *NTJG* 5–6.

Shao, Qin. 1986. "Xi 'Minben': dui xian Qin zhi xi Han 'Minben' sixiang de kaocha" ("Minben": an investigation of the concept from the pre-Qin to the Western Han period). *Lishi yanjiu* 6.

———. 1991. "Zhang Jian's Attitude Toward Educational Reform." *Chinese Historians* 4.2 (June).

———. 1994. "Making Political Culture—The Case of Nantong, 1894–1930." Ph.D. diss., Michigan State University.

———. 1996. "The Mismatch: Ouyang Yuqian and Theater Reform in Nantong, 1919–1922." *Chinoperl Papers* [Chinese Oral and Performing Literature papers] 19.

———. 1997. "Space, Time, and Politics in Early Twentieth Century Nantong." *Modern China* 23.1 (Jan.).

———. 1998. "Tempest over Teapots: The Vilification of Teahouse Culture in Early Republican China." *Journal of Asian Studies* 57.4 (Nov.).

Shelian tongxun (Newsletter of the Association of Social Sciences). 1985. Nantong.

Sheng-yen [Master]. 1991. *Guicheng* (Journey of return). Taibei: Dongchu chubanshe.

Shi, Mingzheng. 1992. "The Development of Municipal Institutions and Public Works in Early Twentieth-Century Beijing." *Chinese Historians* 5: 2 (Fall).

Sites, Frederick R. 1918. "Chang Chien—A Man Who Would Reform a Nation by Precept and Practice in a Model City." *Asia* 18 (July).

SJCF, see *Nantong shiye jiaoyu cishan fengjing fu canguan zhinan*

Smith, Michael L. 1983. "Selling the Moon: The U.S. Manned Space Program and the Triumph of Commodity Scientism." In Richard Wightman Fox and T. J. Jackson Lears, eds., *The Culture of Consumption: Critical Essays in American History: 1880–1980*. New York: Pantheon Books.

———. 1993. "Making Time: Representations of Technology at the 1964 World's Fair." In Richard Wightman Fox and T. J. Jackson Lears, eds., *The Power of Culture: Critical Essays in American History*. Chicago: University of Chicago Press.

Smith, Thomas C. 1988. *Native Sources of Japanese Industrialization, 1750–1920*. Berkeley: University of California Press.

Song Jianren. 1991. "Nantong de diyisuo xuexiao—Baihua xueshu" (The first modern school in Nantong—Baihua School). *NTJG* 2.

Song Xishang. 1963. *Zhang Jian de shengping* (Life of Zhang Jian). Taibei: Zhonghua congshu bianshen weiyuanhui.

Spence, Jonathan D. 1990. *The Search for Modern China*. New York: Norton.

Stapleton, Kristin. 2000. "Yang Sen in Chengdu: Urban Planning in the Interior." In Joseph W. Esherick, ed., *Remaking the Chinese City: Modernity and National Identity, 1900–1950*. Honolulu: University of Hawaii Press.

Strand, David. 1997. "'Getting Up and Giving a Speech Isn't Easy': Orators Meet Hecklers in Modern China." Unpublished manuscript.

———. 2000. "'A High Place Is No Better Than a Low Place': The City in the Making of Modern China." In Wen-hsin Yeh, ed., *Becoming Chinese: Passages to Modernity and Beyond*. Berkeley: University of California Press.

Su Zilong, Mu Xuan, Jia Taogen, and Yang Jianping. 1985. *Nantong de meili* (The attraction of Nantong). Beijing: Haiyang chubanshe.

Sun, Lung-kee. 1996. "The Presence of the Fin-de-Siècle in the May Fourth Era." In Gail Hershatter, Emily Honig, Jonathan N. Lipman, and Randall Stross, eds. *Remapping China: Fissures in Historical Terrain*. Stanford, Calif.: Stanford University Press.

Sun Mo. 1987. "Nantong jianzhushi Sun Zhixia" (Nantong architect Sun Zhixia). *NSWSZL* 7.

———. 1988. "Chen Shizeng he tazai Nantong de jiushi" (Chen Shizeng and his experience in Nantong). *NTJG* 1.

———. 1990. "Gangming biangeng jian shiqing" (Social change as seen in the change of street names). *NTJG* 4.

———. 1991. "Nantong baoshi xiaoshi" (A brief history of time services in Nantong). *NTJG* 6.

———. 1993. "Nantong tiyu jiuwen" (Sports in olden-day Nantong). *NTJG* 1.

———. 1995. "Yu Zhongguo jindai diyi chengshi guihua tongzai shice: woguo zuizao de jianzhushi Sun Zhixia he tade sheji" (Making history with the first urban planning in modern China: the earliest Chinese architect, Sun Zhixia, and his work). *CCWS* 2.

Sun Qu. 1982. "Huiyi Nantong bowuyuan jianwen" (Recollection of my experience with the Nantong Museum). *NSWSZL* 2.

Sun Zhixia. 1981. "Minyuan Nantongxian de minzheng fenfu" (Nantong county administration during the 1911 Revolution). *NSWSZL* 1.

Sun Zhixia and Sun Qu. 1995a. "Nantong wushi nian jianzhu dashi nianbiao: 1896–1947" (A chronology of major construction work in Nantong: 1896–1947). *CCWS* 2.

———. 1995b. "Nantong xingban shiye hou wushi yunian lai jianzhu de fazhan" (The growth of construction work in Nantong in the fifty years since industrial development). *CCWS* 2.

Sushe tekan (Special issue of the Jiangsu Society). 1922. Shanghai.

Tang Xuejiao. 1988. "Ouyang Yuqian zai Nantong" (Ouyang Yuqian in Nantong). *NTJG* 1.

Tenorio-Trillo, Mauricio. 1996. *Mexico at the World's Fairs: Crafting a Modern Nation*. Berkeley: University of California Press.

Thiriez, Régine. 1998. *Barbarian Lens: Western Photographers of the Qianlong Emperor's European Palaces*. Amsterdam: Gordon & Breach.

Tong Shifan (Nantong Normal School). 1982. "Tongzhou shifan shulüe" (A brief account of Tongzhou Normal School). *NSWSZL* 2.

Tongzhou xingban shiye zhangcheng (Documents of industrial development in Tongzhou). 1905. Nantong.

Tongzhou zhili zhouzhi (Gazetteer of Tong prefecture). 1970 [1875]. Taibei: Chengwen chubanshe

Uchiyama Kanzō. 1960. *Kakōroku* (Recollection of the past). Tokyo: Iwanamishoten.

Walker, Kathy L. 1999. *Chinese Modernity and the Peasant Path: Semicolonialism in the Northern Yangzi Delta*. Stanford, Calif.: Stanford University Press.

Wang, Liping. 2000. "Tourism and Spatial Change in Hangzhou, 1911–1927." In Joseph W. Esherick, ed., *Remaking the Chinese City: Modernity and National Identity, 1900–1950*. Honolulu: University of Hawaii Press.

Wang Rongsheng. 2002. "Paoqi 'zhengshi,' chuang xinticai" (Abolishing "formal history," creating a new system). *Wen Hui Bao*, 27 July.

Wang Shiming. 1987. "Nantong zuizao de Tongmenghui huiyuan zhiyi Si Shuzhi xiansheng" (One of the earliest members of the Alliance League in Nantong—Mr. Shi Shuzhi). *NTJG* 6.

Waters, Neil L. 1983. *Japan's Local Pragmatists: The Transition from Bakumatsu to Meiji in the Kawasaki Region*. Cambridge, Mass.: Harvard University Press.

Watson, Rubie S., ed. 1994. *Memory, History, and Opposition Under State Socialism*. Santa Fe, N.M.: School of American Research Press.

Wilbur, C. Martin. 1984. *The Nationalist Revolution in China, 1923–1928*. Cambridge: Cambridge University Press.

Wilkinson, Endymion. 1973. *The History of Imperial China: A Research Guide*. Cambridge, Mass.: Harvard University Press.

Wu Sansheng. 2000. "Mingpian de gushi" (Stories about name cards). *Xinmin wanbao* 25 (Nov.).

Xiao Feng. 1992. "Nantong sishi bajie duoyin" (Holidays and festivals in Nantong). *NTJG* 2.

Xinyou suyihui ranxilu (Controversy of the 1921 Jiangsu provincial assembly meeting). 1922. Ed. Feng Yin. Shanghai.

Xu Dongchang, Mu Xuan, and Yao E. 1987. "Zhang Jingli huiyi Mao Zedong Zhou Enlai tanlun Zhang Jian" (Zhang Jingli's recollection of Mao Zedong's and Zhou Enlai's discussion about Zhang Jian). *NSWSZL* 7.

Xu Gengqi. 1982. "Nantong jinrongye lishi ziliao" (Historical material about banking in Nantong). *NSWSZL* 2.

Xu Haiping. 1981. "Xinhai geming hou fengjian zhidu de gaige" (The change of the feudal system after the 1911 Revolution). *NSWSZL* 1.

———. 1992. "Nantong de shuchang" (Storytelling halls in Nantong). *NTJG* 5-6.

Xu Haiping and Wang Jieyu. 1982. "Langshan zhenshu zaowangu he mingpao" (Morning and evening drum-beating and gun-firing at the Langshan General Military Yamen). In Nantong xishu zailu (Records of Nantong culture and customs). Nantong Library.

Xu Hui. 1993. "Nantong tushuguan bashinian" (Eighty years of the Nantong Library). *NTJG* 1.

Xu Jingchang. 1991. "Jindai Nantong baota" (Erosion protection in modern Nantong). *NSWSZL* 11.

Yan Jizhong. 1988. "Nantong guangfuhou zhi kangri mingzhu zhengfu jianliqian xianji xingzheng jiguan he zhiguan biangeng qingkuang" (Changes of county administrations and officials in Nantong from 1911 to 1938). *NXWSZL* 2.

Yan Xuexi and Ni Youchun, eds. 1993. *Lun Zhang Jian: Zhang Jian guoji xueshu yantanhui lunwenji* (On Zhang Jian: papers from the international symposium on Zhang Jian). Nanjing: Jiangsu renmin chubanshe.

Yan Xuexi, Ni Youchun, and You Shiwei, eds. 1996. *Jindai gaigejia Zhang Jian: dierjie Zhang Jian guoji xueshu yantaohui lunwenji* (Modern reformer Zhang Jian: papers from the second international symposium on Zhang Jian). Nanjing: Jiangsu guji chubanshe.

Yang Guzhong. 1987. "Zhang Jian banxiju" (Zhang Jian's involvement in theater activities). *NSWSZL* 7.

Yang Liqiang, Shen Weibin, Xia Lin'gen, Guan Xiaqi, and Huang Zisong, eds. 1987. *Zhang Jian cungao* (Additional works of Zhang Jian). Shanghai: Shanghai renmin chubanshe.

Yang Naqi. 1998. "Fan Fengyi shi lidai Tongzhouzhi bianzhuanshi you zhenglun de renwu" (Fan Fengyi was a controversial figure in several Tongzhou gazetteers). Unpublished manuscript.

Yang Tong. 1987. "Tanhua yixia de Nantong jiaoyi suo" (The short-lived Nantong Stock Exhange). *NTJG* 2.

Yao Qian. 1995. "Zhang Jian yu chengshi jianshe" (Zhang Jian and urban planning). *CCWS* 2.

Yao Zhenguo. 1993. "Yunhe guzhen hua chunqiu: Tangzha zhen zoubi" (An old town along the canal: Tangzha). In Nantongshi zhengxie wenshi bianjibu (The Culture and History Editorial Department of the PPCC of Nantong), ed., *Nantong mingzhen fengqing lu* (A record of the beauty of famous towns in Nantong). Taibei: Jia'en chubanshe.

Yeh, Wen-hsin. 1995. "Corporate Space, Communal Time: Everyday Life in Shanghai's Bank of China." *American Historical Review* 100.1 (Feb.).

———. 1997. "Shanghai Modernity: Commerce and Culture in a Republican City." *China Quarterly* 150 (June).

Yin Weilun. 1989. "Ji Segong qing women guanguang yundonghui" (Mr. Se invited us to attend a sports game). *Haimen xian wenshi ziliao* 8.

Yoneyama, Lisa. 1994. "Taming the Memoryscape: Hiroshima's Urban Renewal." In Jonathan Boyarin, ed., *Remapping Memory: The Politics of Time-Space*. Minneapolis: University of Minnesota Press.

Yu Cheng. 1993. "Yishi yinhe luojiutian: Tiansheng gang jishi" (Like the galaxy falling to the ninth heaven: report on Port Tiansheng). In Nantongshi zhengxie wenshi bianjibu (The Culture and History Editorial Department of the PPCC of Nantong), ed., *Nantong mingzhen fengqing lu* (A record of the beauty of famous towns in Nantong). Taibei: Jia'en chubanshe.

Yu Fu. 1992. "Langshan Guanyin chanyuan" (The meditation room in the Guanyin temple on Langshan). *NTJG* 2.

Yu Jitang. 1992a. "Langwushan zaolinji" (Afforestation in the five hills of Langshan). *NTJG* 6.

———. 1992b. "Nantong de miaochan xingxue he sengban xuexiao" (Nantong schools built on temple property by Buddhists). *CCWS* 1.

———. 1993. "Jiangshan xiaozhen jinfengliu: Langshanzhen jishi" (A beautiful small town by the river and hill: Langshan). In Nantongshi zhengxie wenshi bianjibu (The Culture and History Editorial Department of the PPCC of Nantong), ed., *Nantong mingzhen fengqing lu* (A record of the beauty of famous towns in Nantong). Taibei: Jia'en chubanshe.

———. 1997. "Nantong jushilin chunqiu" (The gathering-points of lay Buddhists in Nantong). *NSWSZL* 16.

Yu Lizi. 1988. "Zhang Jian yu liuwang hanshi Kim Changkang" (Zhang Jian and the exiled Korean scholar Kim Changkang). *NTJG* 6.

———. 1992. "Dewey fangtong ji" (John Dewey's visit to Nantong). *NTJG* 3.

———. 1995. "Cong chaopiao shang de Huai Hai shiye yinhanglou jianzhu suoqi" (Comment on the picture of the Huai Hai Industrial Bank building printed on the paper money). *CCWS* 2.

Yuan Ming, Lu Xianzhu, Liu Gufeng, Feng Zhao, and Lu Feng. 1994. "Ge wenhuaju dangzu de yi fengxin" (Letter to the CCP branch of the Cultural Bureau). Unpublished document.. 26 Aug.

Zerubavel, Eviatar. 1985. *The Seven Day Circle: The History and Meaning of the Week*. New York: Free Press.

Zhang Caifu. 1991. "Zhang Jian he baoye" (Zhang Jian and the newspaper business). *NTJG* 4.

Zhang Jian. 1965. *Zhang Jizi jiulu* (The nine records of Zhang Jian). Ed. Zhang Xiaoruo. Taibei: Wenhai chubanshe.

———. 1994. *Zhang Jian quanji* (Complete works of Zhang Jian). Ed. Cao Cong-po et al. Nanjing: Jiangsu guji chubanshe.

"Zhang Jian." 1995. *Zhonghua gongshang shibao*, 29 Aug.

Zhang Jian shoucang shuhua xuan (Selected paintings and calligraphy from Zhang Jian's collection). 1995. Ed. Nantong Bowuyuan (Nantong Museum). Guangzhou: Youli yinwu youxian gongsi.

Zhang Jian yanjiu jianxun (Newsletter on Zhang Jian studies). 1997–. Nantong: Center for Zhang Jian Studies.

"Zhang Jian yanjiu ziliao" (Material on Zhang Jian studies). 1980–. Nantong Library.

Zhang Jian yu Mei Lanfang (Zhang Jian and Mei Lanfang). 1999. Ed. Zhang Xuwu and Mei Shaowu. Beijing: Zhongguo gongshang lianhe chubanshe.

Zhang Jingli. 1989. "Nantong Dasheng fangzhi gongside bianqian" (The change of the Nantong Dasheng Textile Company). *NSWSZL* 9.

Zhang Kaiyuan. 1986. *Kaituo zhede zuji—Zhang Jian zhuangao* (The footprint of a pioneer—biography of Zhang Jian). Beijing: Zhonghua shuju.

———. 2000. *Zhang Jian zhuan* (Biography of Zhang Jian). Beijing: Zhonghua gongshang lianhe chubanshe.

Zhang Weibin and Zhu Pei. 1988. "Nantong de diyici renti jiepo" (The first autopsy in Nantong). *NTJG* 2.

Zhang Xiaoruo. 1965. *Nantong Zhang Jizhi xiansheng zhuanji* (Biography of Mr. Zhang Jizhi of Nantong). Taibei: Wenhai chubanshe.

Zhang Xiyang. 1996. "Jianlun Zhang Jian zai jinda Zhongguo chengshihua jincheng zhongde gongxian: jianping Zhang Jian de difang zizhi sixiang" (On Zhang Jian's contribution to China's urbanization and his ideas on local self-government). In Yan Xuexi, Ni Youchun, and You Shiwei, eds. *Jindai gaigejia Zhang Jian: dierjie Zhang Jian guoji xueshu yantaohui lunwenji* (Modern reformer Zhang Jian: papers from the second international symposium on Zhang Jian). Nanjing: Jiangsu guji chubanshe.

Zhang Ziqiang. 1992. "Kai Jiangsu dianying zhi xianhe: Nantong dianying zhipianshi gaishu" (Pioneers in filmmaking in Jiangsu province: a brief account of the history of film in Nantong). *CCWS* 1.

Zhao Dan. 1980. *Diyu zimen* (Hell's gate). Shanghai: Shanghai wenyi chubanshe.

Zhao He. 1994. "Xiting Zhang Jian zuju wangshi shulüe" (Memories of Zhang Jian's ancestral house in Xiting). *Tongzhou wenshi* 11.

Zhao Zongpu. 1990. "Nantong yixue shishang zhide yiti de jiwei waiguo yisheng" (Prominent foreign doctors in the medical history of Nantong). *NTJG* 5–6.

Zhonggong Nantong shiwei dangshi gongzuo weiyuanhui (Nantong CCP Committee on Party History). 1991. "Jianku zhuojue gongbiao qingshi: Nantong diqu renmin geming douzheng sanshinian" (Arduous effort and historical success: thirty years of people's revolutionary struggle in the Nantong region). *NTJG* 3.

Zhou Yu. 1993. *Dagongbao* (Dagong Newspaper). Nanjing: Jiangsu guji chuban-she.

Zhu Jianzhang. 1989. "Zhang Jian xiansheng zaijiaxiang de yishi shiling" (A few anecdotes about Zhang Jian in his hometown). *Haimen xian wenshi ziliao* 8.

Zhu Ronghua. 1987. "Jindai cixiu yishujia Shen Shou: shenzheng" (The divine needle: modern embroidery artist Shen Shou). *NTJG* 3–4.

Zou Qiang. 1962. "Dasheng ziben jituan de jianlizhe—Zhang Jian" (The founder of the Dasheng capital group—Zhang Jian). Unpublished manu-script.

Zweig, David. 1997. "Institutional Constraints, Path Dependence, and Entre-preneurship: Comparing Nantong and Zhangjiagang, 1984–1996." In *Working Papers in the Social Sciences* 15. Division of Social Sciences, Hong Kong University of Science and Technology.